LANGUAGE
and
CULTURAL DIVERSITY
in
AMERICAN EDUCATION

LANGUAGE
and
CULTURAL DIVERSITY
in
AMERICAN EDUCATION

EDITED BY

Roger D. Abrahams and Rudolph C. Troike

University of Texas

PRENTICE-HALL, INC., *Englewood Cliffs, New Jersey*

Library of Congress Cataloging in Publication Data

Troike, Rudolph C.   comp.
    Language and cultural diversity in American education.

    Includes bibliographical references.
    1. Minorities—Education—U. S.   I. Abrahams,
Roger D., joint comp.   II. Title.
LC3701.T76   371.9'67   78–38716
ISBN 0–13–522896–4
ISBN 0–13–522888–3 (pbk.)

PRENTICE-HALL INTERNATIONAL, INC., London
PRENTICE-HALL OF AUSTRALIA, PTY. LTD., Sydney
PRENTICE-HALL OF CANADA, LTD., Toronto
PRENTICE-HALL OF INDIA PRIVATE LIMITED, New Delhi
PRENTICE-HALL OF JAPAN, INC., Tokyo

Contents

4 Sociolinguistics   141

5 Black English   209

6 Applications   295

Phonetic Symbols

The phonetic symbols given below are used in some of the articles in this book to represent regional and social differences in pronunciation. Because more than one system of notation is used, an attempt is made here to equate them. Symbols are placed between either square brackets or slant lines; the latter represent what is technically called a phonemic transcription, though the distinction is not significant for present purposes. Note, however, that /i/ is equivalent to [ɪ], not to [i].

[i], [i:], /iy/	as in b<u>ee</u>t
[ɪ], /i/	as in b<u>i</u>t
[e], /ey/	as in b<u>ai</u>t
[ɛ], /e/	as in b<u>e</u>t
[æ], /æ/	as in b<u>a</u>t
[ə], /ə/	as in b<u>u</u>t
[ɑ], [a], /ɑ/	as in p<u>o</u>t, f<u>a</u>ther
[u], /uw/	as in b<u>oo</u>t
[ʊ], /u/	as in p<u>u</u>t
[o], /o/, /ow/	as in b<u>oa</u>t
[ɔ], /ɔ/	as in b<u>ou</u>ght
[ɔə], /ɔh/	an [ɔ] followed by an [ə]-like glide
[ɔu], /ɔw/	an [ɔ] followed by a [w]-like glide
[:]	following a vowel indicates length
/h/	following a vowel, e.g., /eh/, indicates length or an [ə]-like glide
[ɑɪ], /ay/	as in b<u>i</u>te, b<u>uy</u>
[ɑʊ], /aw/	as in b<u>ou</u>t, b<u>ow</u>

Most consonant symbols have the same value as they do in ordinary spelling. However, the following special symbols are used.

[θ]	as in <u>th</u>in
[ð]	as in <u>th</u>en
[š], [ʃ]	as in <u>sh</u>in
[ž], [ʒ]	as in a<u>z</u>ure
[tš,] [tʃ], [č]	as in <u>ch</u>in
[dž], [dʒ], [ǰ]	as in <u>g</u>in
[φ]	a sound made by blowing through the lips placed closely together
[ʾ], [ʼ]	a glottal stop, as in the quick pause found in ah-ah or oh-oh, or in certain Northern pronunciations of bo<u>tt</u>le.
[ŋ]	as in si<u>ng</u>

Navajo: In the transcriptions given of Navajo, an accent mark over a vowel indicates a high tone, and a doubled vowel symbol, e.g. /ee/, indicates a vowel pronounced with length, i.e., held longer than a single vowel.

Introduction

This book is an anthology of essays about the effects of the diversity of languages and cultures in the United States on the educational system —especially as they pertain to so-called minorities. We, as anthropologists interested in different aspects of expressive culture (in one case, language, in the other, folklore and interactional and discourse systems), have been amazed and disconcerted by the amount of nonsense which has been purveyed in the area of "education for the disadvantaged." It is nonsense because it betrays an ethnocentric approach to the problems incurred in dealing with the linguistically and culturally different.

We are not alone in our discomfort, but we have been more fortunate than most because we have been provided with an opportunity over the last four years to try out some of our anthropological ideas on classroom teachers in school districts undergoing integration. In this way we have been able to see how teachers could handle and even capitalize upon diversity in the classroom to build a greater understanding of the greatness inherent in the cultural pluralism of the United States. We have given in-service courses throughout large parts of Texas, under the sponsorship of the Texas Education Agency, the Region XII and XI Service Centers, and the involved local school districts.[1] In this we were immeasurably aided by the third member of our team, Mary Galvan, who brought to our work not only a deep and schooled understanding of both language and culture but also a wealth of experience as a classroom teacher who has actually dealt with these problems on an hour-by-hour basis. Were it not for a

[1] These are reported on in "The East Texas Dialect Project," pp. 297–304.

state law prohibiting it, she would be a co-editor of this volume; her influence and understanding pervade the book, nonetheless.

This, then, is a reader concerned with analyzing and understanding the life-ways of Americans who are linguistically and culturally different from mainstream middle-class America, i.e., from those who formulate our educational policy and for the most part run our schools. We have made an attempt to include studies of a wide number of groups who so depart from this all-American norm. In this we have not been as successful as we had wished, and the reader will notice a heavy preponderance of studies of Black language and culture. This situation exists not just because our in-service experience has led us to deal primarily with those confronted with Black–white educational problems. There simply seems to have been much more research done in this area, certainly due to the threat posed by the Civil Rights and Soul Movements; more, but not nearly enough to meet even our immediate needs. In putting the volume together we constantly found areas—even of Afro-American culture— which we wanted to have described in an article but about which nothing had yet been written. We will try to indicate these areas briefly in our introductions to the various sections.

One group we have included here which is not usually recognized as culturally and linguistically distinct is that of lower socio-economic class whites (we are not here speaking just of those in Appalachia). Because of their ethnic and linguistic closeness to the middle-class majority, they have been so "transparent" to middle-class observers that they are truly an "invisible minority." But they have stable and well-organized cultural patterns which are quite distinct, and in many instances radically opposed to those of the middle class. Their speech patterns have traditionally been made the target of condemnation and repression in the schools, and their divergent value system has produced a major lack of fit with an educational system designed to enculturate them in middle-class ways. The result is usually viewed as failure on the part of the student, although it should be viewed as a failure on the part of the schools. Teachers who have been raised and trained with a negative stereotype of lower-class cultural and linguistic patterns will find this change in viewpoint difficult to accept, but it is one of the aims of this book to show that such a change is necessary if this and other groups in our midst are not to be denied access to the potential advantages of education.

Readers familiar with the recent literature on minority groups will note the absence here of most of the better known writers on the subject. The reason is that much of the research and writings on the education of the "disadvantaged" has been based on an ethnocentric definition of "disadvantaged," one which defines the condition in terms of *differences* from urban middle-class characteristics, either linguistically or culturally. The underlying assumption of such work is that to be *different* is to be *deprived*.

Most "education for the disadvantaged" therefore operates on what has been called a "deficit model," which sees the minority group (including the lower class) child as having no true culture of his own, but as simply being deficient in middle-class modes of speech, behavior, and cognition, which are tacitly taken as representing the only "real" culture. This failure to recognize the cultural integrity of minority groups vitiates the results of most of the very studies which form the foundation of educational programs for these groups.

Any method of cultural or social analysis, however sophisticated and replicable, which defines the other group in terms of what it does not do or does not have is simply a form of stereotyping, for it is not merely describing the other group in terms of differences—it is prejudging them as well. To stereotype is to define outsiders by traits which represent the inverse of one's own in-group value system. The essence of this prejudgment is that the other group possesses order only insofar as it approximates the observer's own culture. Until we are able to carry into the cross-cultural encounter the expectation of other equally valid forms of cultural organization, we will never be able to understand these others, let alone "help" them.

If we argue that the work of many social scientists and educators has been ethnocentric, we do not mean this is bigotry; on the contrary, these people are liberal in their sympathies, and have shown their willingness to call an unfortunate social situation when they see one, and then try to remedy it. But their research concerns are conditioned by this social problem approach, and we can now see that, laudable as their sympathies may be, their approach has actually served only to obscure the nature of the so-called "problem." Not until we are ready simply to understand can we determine what needs do in fact exist, and an offer of help based on ignorance is a hollow one indeed.

For example, among Negro groups in the United States there is a systematic culture that in many ways differs from that of mainstream Anglo-America, and if we are to understand the needs of Blacks we must first learn about this culture. Not to do so would be to continue our present approach, which assumes that Blacks are like whites only more impoverished, more ignorant, and less attuned to the technological and bureaucratic modern world. This missionary approach backfires specifically because it does not take into consideration the different perspectives of Blacks.

Though social scientists are here indicted, the fault is shared by numerous others who also should "know better." For instance, nowhere has the missionary spirit been maintained quite so strongly as in the educational system imposed by whites on Blacks, and nowhere has the resultant cultural friction had deeper and longer lasting effects. Educators are like other middle Americans only more so, because they are led to regard themselves as the guardians and the inculcators of values and ideals—which is certainly what they must be, to some extent. The problem with this approach is that it leads to the seldom examined assumption that the teacher's culture is the only proper model for students, and this includes not only values and ideals but also practices. Thus, the school is run in line with the sense of order inherited by the teacher, without any recognition of the fact that there may be alternative systems carried into the classroom by students.

The United States is a culturally plural society, a political aggregate with a wide variety of life-styles in its midst. In such a state of cultural pluralism, the result is the subordination by one group of all others, creating great ambivalence on the part of these others in regard to their own life-styles. This ambivalence on the part of minority group members occurs because they are constantly reminded of their subordinate status through the imposition of a negative stereotype image on them by the dominant group. This does not eliminate the culture of the subordinate groups, but it does provide socio-psychological complications.

For many years—indeed, throughout most of our history until the recent past—any group that did not speak some brand of standard American English was socially ostracized until its members learned how to conform linguistically. European groups commonly found themselves in sufficient agreement with the consensus values and progressive capitalistic orientation to learn very quickly the tricks of disguise leading to assimilation. They gave up, for the most part, their native language and developed a dialect of English sufficiently like the regional standard that they were able to "pass" within one native-born generation. This was especially true of the immigrant groups which came to the cities and were in contact with the mainstream all of the time.

But there are certain groups who had other stigmatizable features which were not so easily lost. These were peoples whose skin color is different—Negroes, Mexicans, Indians—and who were more rigidly excluded socially, politically, and economically, than any other group. Thus while the Europeans became acculturated to American ways and developed into American sub-cultures (that is, they kept only a few traits of their life-style and only a modicum of the feeling of groupness), these other groups remained culturally distinct. They continued to speak their accustomed language and to follow their different life-ways, though their cultural practices, attitudes, and values were inevitably affected by their being excluded and kept in a subordinate status.

Now new programs of education are being developed overnight in an attempt to do the job of assimilation that everyone else ostensibly went through years ago. But one of the problems with this approach is that these subordinate and stigmatized groups are suddenly saying "no" to such efforts. They are finding an integrity and an identity in their own culture, their own way.

Though our reaction to this rejection is often shock, it should be praise. If we expect to be able to teach students from such groups effectively, we must learn wherein their cultural differences lie and we must capitalize upon them as a resource, rather than doing what we have always done and disregarding the differences or placing the students in the category of "non-communicative," thereby denigrating both the differences and the students.

The lesson taught by cultural relativity is that one must develop a sensitivity to all behavioral differences. By this one may more easily capitalize upon what one encounters in one's students. This is crucial because the students themselves place such high value on these differences as a means, conscious or not, of defining themselves. Even if it is just the differences on the vocabulary level which occur because of the development of a slang, this is something which the teacher should be able to recognize and build upon—for it is those very terms which are the focus of energy and attitude for those who use them. This seems important not just because it serves our educational needs, but because a sensitivity to these matters is crucial to communications in everyday intercultural encounters.

It is these disparities of stylized actions and expectations which have resulted in a large number of misunderstandings and embarrassments between members of the different cultures. Furthermore, for years these embarrassments have been ignored by white middle-class mainstream culture. Any disruptive differences could be overlooked, the argument seemed to run, because the "others" have to learn to be Americans. But we realize now that this is a cultural luxury we can no longer afford. We are constantly told about different cultural perspectives by spokesmen of these other cultures, but we manage to misread the message consistently. The reason why we allow this to turn into embarrassment and failure of communication is that we will not permit ourselves to recognize not only that a viable perspective is given voice by these "others," but also that it is vocalized by someone who has a way of talking and arguing which is notably different from our own way.

It is important for all Americans to learn something about this difference, so that we may begin to carry into intercultural encounters some of the same expectations. But even more than this, the process of learning about cultural differences on this level of personal interaction will become a crucial element in our understanding of the varieties of oral language styles which are available to us in the culturally plural situation. Recognition of these different modes of speaking will also permit us to build a more meaningful education system for students from other cultures for it will disabuse us of the idea that they are necessarily non-verbal and have little or nothing to build upon in learning language arts.

The most important function of this book, then, is the attempt to clear the air of stereotypic misconceptions so that we can begin to put together an effective approach to educating students who happen to be different from the middle Americans for whom the education system was designed. To do this, we must first learn the basic concepts of cultural and linguistic analysis, as we have learned that this is the most reliable means of opening the eyes and ears of teachers to the life-order by which their students live. But it is equally important, in the meantime, to recognize that these analytic tools can and must be used on ourselves; the educational fault has been in ourselves, not the cultural others. That is, we must learn to investigate and understand what it is in our own public and shared attitudes that has made it difficult to teach these students effectively—especially, what it is about our own cultural mechanisms which, in the face of the threat posed by a person we do not understand, results in our resorting to the most overt and highly structured dimensions of our own ordering system—rules and regulations.

This anthology, then, is put together to serve the teacher of cultural and linguistic minorities in pluralistic America. It attempts to show how the analysis of language and culture will lead to a fuller understanding of the nature and uses of diversity. It will demonstrate in some dimensions what the characteristics of these alternative cultural systems—especially communications systems—are. But ultimately it attempts to do only one thing—to humanize students by opening the eyes and the ears of educators to the possible alternative systems which the young may bring into class. There seems to us to be no other way of educating these students than to provide them with a sense of dignity in the selves they bring with them into school, and to build on this by demonstrating the social and linguistic and cultural alternatives around them.

1

The Problem

The major aim of this book is to teach present or prospective teachers how to recognize the linguistic and cultural differences of their students. First, we shall examine some of the forces in our mainstream culture which, operating tangibly within our rigid school system, have actually increased our difficulties in making out these differences. This first section is devoted to articles which pinpoint some of the misleading preconceptions which have inhibited the development of effective teaching procedures within our schools. The focus is, of necessity, on ill-considered and often self-defeating techniques fostered by our systems of education and on the subsequent failures of insight and understanding on the part of thousands of individual teachers. We hope that these articles will lead teachers to a larger consideration of the cultural bases of education, and make them more aware of themselves and others as cultural creatures. Our lesson is a simple rephrasing of the concepts of linguistic and cultural relativity—emphasizing that differences in language or life-style does not mean better or worse.

There have been a number of recent autobiographical accounts of adept and sensitive beginning teachers and their confrontations with the simultaneous problems of teaching culturally different students and a non-responsive teaching and administrative system. These much celebrated books, like Jonathan Kozol's *Death at an Early Age* (Boston: Houghton-Mifflin Co., 1967), James Herndon's *The Way It Spozed to Be* (New York: Simon & Schuster, 1968), and Herbert Kohl's *Thirty-Six Children* (New York: New American Library, 1967), are useful "scare" books—that is, they dramatize the frustrations and the solutions which an imaginative teacher can improvise. But none of these writers recognize and work with the different cultural patterns, feeling (and rightly) that sympathy and patience with the students will bridge the communications gap. It would be unrealistic, however, to expect any large number of teachers to attempt such an approach on their own—especially since none of these authors suggests that they found any long-range solutions.

Since we are centering on the problem of linguistic and cultural differences in education, we begin with two articles which serve in part to define the problem and its implications. The first (Light) describes the failure of the language programs directed by mainstreamers toward subcultural groups. The second (Fantini) treats the debilitating effects of assuming that the fault of educational failure lies with the culturally different—an assumption fundamental to such concepts as "deprivation" and "deficiency." In the third article, Abrahams focuses on the pervasive and distorting influence of stereotyping in intercultural relations.

These articles do not, in any way, exhaust the inventory of the problems of educating the linguistically and culturally different. They only serve as examples of the range of problems the teacher will encounter in entering a school system. The central problem, however, to which this book addresses itself, is the need for Americans in the mainstream to recognize the integrity, usefulness, and national strength inherent in linguistic and cultural diversity, and to put this awareness to work in the classroom.

ON LANGUAGE ARTS AND
MINORITY GROUP CHILDREN
Richard L. Light

Millions of dollars are being spent each year on special programs aimed at improving the education of minority-group children in our schools, but most of these programs have been and will continue to be ineffective and the money wasted until their most crucial inadequacy has been recognized. Richard Light, formerly of the U. S. Office of Education, points out the shocking lack of understanding of cultural and linguistic differences which is responsible for the failure of many of these programs to achieve their intended effect. The inadequate preparation of teachers and administrators to understand and serve the needs of students from different cultural and linguistic backgrounds can only be termed appalling. Here, then, is the crux of the problem. Teacher training institutions and in-service programs must provide courses in linguistics, cultural anthropology, and methods of second language and second dialect teaching, if teachers are to acquire the necessary understanding for working effectively with students whose language and culture differ from their own.

An impressive array of educators agree on at least two points concerning the education of children from minority groups. They state that the schools in this country have failed to educate these children, and they single out instruction in the language arts as critically important in any educational program for them. While there is widespread agreement concerning the importance of language arts programs for minority children, present conditions in most schools preclude their effectiveness. This is a major factor contributing to the failure of the schools to educate them. Further, additional millions of dollars for "language arts instruction" made available directly to schools in which such conditions exist will continue to be ineffective. Although there are promising projects currently being conducted which aim at improving these conditions, stronger national leadership is necessary if significant changes are to be realized in education for minority children.

From *The Florida FL Reporter*, vol. 7, no. 2 (Fall 1969), pp. 5–7, 20; Alfred C. Aarons, ed. Reprinted by permission.

Regarding the failure of the schools (and our society's failure as well), Donald Smith has recorded what is probably a typical indictment of the educational process for children from minority groups. "Teachers have failed," he feels, "because, for the most part, they don't know anything about, care little about, and have not been trained to teach their Black and brown pupils." [1] Pinpointing failure in more specific terms, the report of a national conference on the education of the disadvantaged has noted that the schools refuse to accept the reality that thousands of American children cannot speak standard English when they are in kindergarten or first grade, that to ignore this reality is to doom these children to failure, and that "educational statistics prove this is exactly what we are doing." [2]

There also appears to be general agreement that a sound language arts program is particularly crucial to success in the education of children from different linguistic and cultural backgrounds. In 1966 the National Advisory Council on the Education of Disadvantaged Children stated that "the major weakness [that undermines the educational achievement of minority children] lies in the area of the language arts." [3] A year later the section concerning education for disadvantaged youth in the Kerner Report recommended intensive programs "to improve the verbal skills of people in low-income areas, with primary emphasis on language problems of minority groups." [4] The U.S. Commissioner of Education has stated that a major educational target for the 1970's will be to insure that "no one shall be leaving our schools without the skills necessary to read." [5] And the head of the bureau in the U.S. Office of Education responsible for federally supported teacher training programs has noted that education in this country needs to move from a single culture, white, western, with a primarily Protestant view of past and present, to a multi-cultural view of education, and that "this won't be done until we get administrators and teachers and support personnel in our schools who themselves have a multi-cultural point of view." [6]

[1] Donald H. Smith, "Imperative Issues in Urban Education," *Teacher Education: Issues and Innovations* (Washington, D.C.: American Association of Colleges for Teacher Education, 1968), p. 50.

[2] *Report of the Proceedings of the National Conference on the Education of the Disadvantaged* (Washington, D.C.: U.S. Government Printing Office, 1966), p. 11.

[3] *Annual Report of the National Advisory Council on the Education of Disadvantaged Children* (Washington, D.C.: U.S. Government Printing Office, 1966), p. 7.

[4] *Report of the National Advisory Commission on Civil Disorders* (New York: New York Times Company, 1968), p. 449.

[5] James E. Allen, Jr., "The Right to Read—Target for the 70's," paper delivered before the National Association of State Boards of Education, September 23, 1969, (Washington, D.C.: U.S. Office of Education), p. 4.

[6] Statement by Don Davies, Associate Commissioner for Educational Personnel Development, U.S. Office of Education, reported in NCTE *Council-Grams*, XXX (4 May, 1969), p. 5.

Results of studies which examine both the formal preparation and the established attitudes of educators working with minority children reveal an incredible gap between the conditions necessary to achieve these ideals proclaimed by the nation's top educational advisors, and actual conditions existing in the schools. They raise grave doubts concerning the effectiveness of the millions of dollars in federal funds being made available directly to local schools for use in "language arts for the disadvantaged." [7]

One study which raises such doubts is concerned with the preparation of teachers of English as a second language, that is, those who are entrusted with the teaching of English to Mexican-American, Puerto Rican, American Indian, and other minority group children in our nation.[8] It reveals that such teachers are almost totally unprepared for their work, indicating that of the elementary and secondary school teachers sampled:

> 91% had no practice teaching in ESL. [English as a Second Language]
>
> 85% had no formal study in methods of teaching ESL.
>
> 80% had no formal training in English syntax.
>
> 65% had no training in general linquistics.

As part of a larger survey of speech in Detroit, Roger Shuy made a revealing study of teacher attitudes toward the language of Black students in their classes.[9] The results indicated an extraordinary lack of understanding on the part of the teachers sampled, concerning the nature of the language of their black students. They came up with such views as:

> "they have only about one hundred words in their vocabulary."
>
> "they are non-verbal, or speak in single words, not sentences."
>
> "they don't communicate with their families."

Teachers with such views concerning the linguistic characteristics of their Black students are also likely to harbor misconceptions regarding their capacities and abilities in other areas. But in spite of the information coming from carefully conducted studies of social dialects by linguists at the Center for Applied Linguistics and elsewhere, we still find large educational projects, supported by government grants and purporting to educate Black

[7] Under one federal program alone, fiscal year 1967 expenditures for language arts instruction for disadvantaged children amounted to $350 million, and involved over 4.5 million pupils. From *Statistical Report, Fiscal Year 1967, Title I, Year II* (Washington, D.C.: Office of Education, 1968), pp. 4, 24. Using reading scores as measures of achievement, the Office of Education's TEMPO study found children had made "little, if any" improvement after the first year of such expenditures.

[8] Harold B. Allen, *The Survey of the Teaching of English to Non-English Speakers in the United States* (Champaign, Illinois: National Council of Teachers of English, 1966), pp. 29–30.

[9] Roger Shuy, Walter Wolfram, and William Riley, *Linguistic Correlates of Social Stratification in Detroit Speech*, Cooperative Research Project No. 6-1347, Part IV (East Lansing, Michigan: Michigan State University, 1967), pp. 2–5.

children, concerned with such questionable or impossible tasks as "replacing poor speech habits" (instead of *adding* a second dialect) and "cataloguing specific speech deficiencies" (instead of specifying speech *differences*).

Another recent report which reveals more damaging inadequacies concerns the education of Mexican-American children in the San Antonio schools. Completed by the Civil Rights Commission, it indicates that inadequate understanding, on the part of many educators, of the language and culture of Mexican-American children has resulted in drastic shortcomings in their education and disruption of their lives.[10] Specifically, the report reveals among other things, that Mexican-American children are sometimes *assigned to classes for the mentally retarded merely because their language happens to be different from that of the majority culture.* How often this kind of atrocity is inflicted upon other minority group children in other areas of this country can only be surmised.[11]

Studies have shown that teacher attitudes toward their students have very powerful impacts upon educational achievement,[12] and the changing of teacher attitudes and expectations regarding minority children has been called "the number one imperative in urban education." [13] Yet influential educators continue to perpetuate unsubstantiated views concerning the nature of the language of minority children which can be expected to adversely influence the attitudes of teachers toward their students. It has been reported, for example, that the speech of poor children "seems to consist not of distinct words, as does the speech of middle class children of the same ages, [but rather of] phrases or sentences that function like giant words [and that such children] at four years of age hardly speak at all." [14] This continues in spite of the fact that such views have been carefully refuted by scholars studying social dialects.[15]

[10] *Staff Report, A Study of Equality of Educational Opportunity for Mexican Americans in Nine School Districts of the San Antonio Area* (Washington, D.C.: U.S. Commission on Civil Rights, 1969), pp. 34–35.

[11] One indication of the extent of this practice is revealed in a report that the California State Board of Education recently had to be required by court action to begin giving intelligence tests in the language of the children being tested. Evidence cited the action included an estimate that 22,000 Mexican-American children were in classes for the mentally retarded in California schools, evidently because educators there were making the judgment that ability to read a foreign language was somehow an accurate measure of intelligence. Reported in *The New York Times*, Feb. 8, 1970.

[12] This has been demonstrated in "Self-Fulfilling Prophecies in the Classroom: Teacher's Expectations as Unintended Determinates of Pupils' Intellectual Competence," a paper by Robert Rosenthal and Lenore Jacobson, delivered at the American Psychological Association Meeting, Washington, D.C., Sept., 1967, reprinted in *Scientific American*, 218, 4 (April, 1968), pp. 20–25.

[13] Donald H. Smith, *op. cit.*, p. 51.

[14] Carl Bereiter and Sigfried Engelmann, *Teaching Disadvantaged Children in the Pre-School* (Englewood Cliffs, N.J.: Prentice-Hall, 1966), pp. 31–34.

[15] Most notably, William Labov in *The Study of Non-Standard English* (Washington, D.C.: The Center for Applied Linguistics, 1969), pp. 47–51.

Research studies may also suffer when careful attention is not given to the linguistic and cultural characteristics of minority children. A recent report on minority education in New York state, for example, noted that weaknesses in intervention research derived in large measure from "incredible ignorance about the culture from which 'culturally deprived' children come." [16] Programs for minority children based upon such research are not likely to be effective.

Teachers, administrators and researchers with such misconceptions about minority children cannot be expected to design and implement effective programs for them in any subject area, let alone the language arts. Yet the attitudes of educators will not change without an understanding of the backgrounds of these children, and such understanding cannot take place without study of other languages, other dialects, and other cultures.

Read together, these statements and studies constitute a convincing argument for the view that the schools have failed minority group children, that a major cause of this has been a failure to understand the linguistic and cultural backgrounds of such children, and that there must be increased attention given to training educational personnel to bring about this understanding, if education for minority children is to improve. In the past, a small number of such persons have been trained for work in bilingual education projects, in English as a second language, social dialectology, reading, and other areas of the language arts. Some training has been done through institutes and fellowship programs supported by the U. S. Office of Education, but the number of participants in these programs has not been significant in relation to what is needed. During the period 1964–1968, for example, some 1650 ESL teachers were trained under the NDEA, and during 1969–1970, the first year of the Education Professions Development Act (EPDA), some 800 are being trained, although there are over 100,000 English teachers in the schools today.

Despite these needs, and despite the good intentions of both the Commissioner of Education ("no one shall be leaving the schools without the skills necessary to read") and the Associate Commissioner in charge of teacher education ("we must move . . . to a multi-cultural view of education"), substantial resources needed to achieve these goals do not appear to be forthcoming. For example, the response of the Associate Commissioner in charge of teacher education to this (his own) challenge has been to inform colleges and universities throughout the nation that support would no longer be available to train educational personnel in such subjects as foreign languages, linguistics, English, history, and others crucial to an understanding of the language and culture of minority group children. Those colleges and universities which do have the expertise available to help train educators in these critical areas are, with few exceptions, cut off from resources to do the job.

[16] The University of the State of New York, *Racial and Social Class Isolation in the School* (Albany, New York: The State Education Department, 1969), p. 418.

This is particularly unfortunate since the present state of affairs in the schools can be attributed in large measure to teacher preparation institutions which lack realistic curriculums for language arts teachers who will work with minority children, and which have failed to produce educators sensitive to the cultural and linguistic characteristics of such children. How many such institutions, for example, offer courses in linguistics, social dialects, English structure, cultural anthropology, and others—most crucial if educators are to have that multi-cultural view of education which the Associate Commissioner has called for? It is likely that a survey would reveal few, if any, teacher preparation institutions requiring such courses.

The outlook is not entirely bleak of course. There are projects continuing to be funded by the U. S. Office of Education which are attempting to train educators in these areas, to bring about changes in the institutions which produce teachers, and to provide realistic language arts programs for children whose first language or dialect is other than standard English. Perhaps the most promising programs currently being conducted are those supported under the Bilingual Education Act. Providing for instruction through the child's first language as well as instruction in English as a second language, these projects attempt to protect the non-English speaking child from the absurdity of expecting him to learn subjects solely through English, even though he may not be able to speak or understand it. (This has been standard practice, even in schools with majority concentrations of non-English speaking children.) In addition to providing instruction through a language which the child understands, the projects are designed to furnish him (as well as participating Anglo children) with the valuable asset of fluency and literacy in two languages, and to provide status for the minority child's first language and culture.

The success of all such projects as they relate to language arts depends in large measure upon the validity of the assumption that there is information concerning language learning, language in general, social dialects, other cultures, and other languages, which is not currently available to educators, and which if made available to them, would improve the education of children from minority backgrounds. We clearly have not reached the millennium with regard to knowledge in any of these areas; yet it is fair to assume that there is a great deal known of these topics which has not been given sufficient attention by those running the schools and the teacher preparation institutions.

It would seem that those who work with or train others to work with children whose first dialect or language is other than standard English should have at the minimum:

• information concerning what we know of the nature of language and how it is learned, including an understanding that by the time they enter school all normal children regardless of cultural backgrounds control the phonology and grammar of at least one language, and if this happens to be a language or dialect other than standard English it is not an indication of some mental or physical aberration on the part of the child.

• an understanding that language variations arise through social and cultural forces, through interactions with people who use these forms and not through such things as "lazy tongues" or "stupidity." It is particularly important that this understanding be communicated to the teachers who themselves have arisen from working- or lower-class backgrounds and who are too often the most rigid and intolerant toward non-standard English, or even toward teaching through a language other than English in bilingual education programs.

• a realization that a first language or dialect other than standard English interferes seriously with performance in applications of such language skills as reading and writing—and with ultimate performance in subject matter areas.

• an awareness that any new mode of speech should be taught as a supplementary mode rather than as a replacive one. The child is ultimately the one to decide which mode to use on what occasion.

• an understanding that language features which are systematic are to be emphasized in any language arts program rather than those which are incidental items, that attention should be directed to those systematic features of a non-standard dialect that are diagnostic socially, and that each non-English group has, in addition, its own systematic problems.

• an understanding that situational factors strongly influence and may inhibit speech, and that the so-called "non-verbal" child has yet to be discovered, given adequate control for situational variables.

• finally, educators should have an awareness of the resources and studies concerning social dialects, reading, second language teaching and learning, and other aspects of the language arts that are available through such organizations as NCTE and the Center for Applied Linguistics.

Until educators know about and act upon this kind of information and much more concerning the linguistic and cultural backgrounds of minority group children, it is likely that education for them will continue to be inadequate. Strong leadership at the national level is necessary to insure improvement of educational programs for such children, to guarantee that the millions of dollars continuing to go directly to the schools do not merely support what has proven damaging in the past, and to assure that those running the schools, training the teachers and teaching in the classrooms have the information necessary to more effectively educate minority group children in all subjects, and particularly in the crucial set of courses known as the language arts.

BEYOND CULTURAL DEPRIVATION AND COMPENSATORY EDUCATION

Mario D. Fantini

Nothing illustrates the arrogant ethnocentricity of our past approaches to educating the culturally different quite so fully as the cultural force-feeding or "compensation" subsumed under the term "early intervention programs." In this article Dr. Mario Fantini caustically surveys the assumptions lying behind the concept of compensatory education, suggesting alternative strategies for teaching minority and lower-class students.

When Gerald Weinstein and I wrote *The Disadvantaged* we began the book with the question, "Who are the disadvantaged?" and immediately answered, "Most of us." We wanted to establish at the outset that the book would not repeat the basic assumptions of earlier works on the same education problem. To most writers the educational problem was with individuals and groups of learners classified as "culturally deprived." They were "disadvantaged" because of this "cultural deprivation." To Weinstein and me, "disadvantaged" referred to all learners who are blocked in any way from fulfilling their human potential. To us the schools lacked the capability for maximizing the potential of most who attend—middle class included. The problem to us was not the learner but the institutions, whose outdatedness made us all disadvantaged. Writers who diagnose the problem as cultural deprivation invariably prescribe compensatory education as the remedy.

The use of such terms as "culturally deprived" in referring to largely minority populations reflects a kind of colonial stance. This is especially true if those rendering the "professional diagnosis" are white. Moreover, the use of such terms carries with it the further implication that the problem is really with the learner—with his environmental and cultural deficiencies—not with the school and its educational process.

Looking beyond compensatory education will require a reorientation

From *Psychiatry and Social Science Review*, vol. 3, no. 6 (June 1969), pp. 6–13. Reprinted by permission of *Psychiatry and Social Science Review* and the author.

from our present "student-fault" to a stronger "system-fault" position. Ironically, most analysts continue to emphasize the learner *per se*. For example, two of the most highly emphasized studies in the past decade added impetus to the learner-fault disposition. Benjamin Bloom at the University of Chicago reviewed over 1000 studies which dealt with changes in intelligence over time. In a book entitled *Stability and Change in Human Characteristics* outlining his findings, Professor Bloom reported that IQ is 50 percent developed by age four and 80 percent developed by age eight. The implication was that the time the child spends in schools contributes little to his further intelligence development. James Coleman conducted an extensive study of 645,000 pupils throughout the country for the U. S. Office of Education. Among other findings of this report—*Equal Educational Opportunity*—was that student social class was a stronger determinant of achievement than the school program.

Both studies seem to indicate that schooling makes little difference. However, what these studies also reveal is that *standard* school programs make little difference. This is not to say that if school programs *were altered—reformed*—the same conclusions would be warranted. Stated somewhat differently, the standard, conventional educational process makes little difference in intelligence and achievement and is, therefore, in need of reform.

The question for education is: How can an educational process be developed that can deal effectively with diversity? It is clear that the present educational mold cannot deal with individual and group differences and is, therefore, dysfunctional to both and also to the needs of modern society.

Compensatory education is currently the most prevalent form of intervention. It is based on the assumption that the education of the poor can be improved by utilizing remedial measures to deal with such problems as underachievement and lack of motivation. (Such measures include, for example, lower class size, added reading teachers, extra counsellors, more materials, etc.)

In essence, compensatory education programs attempt to get the child "ready" for the regular school program. The rationale is simple and direct: The disadvantaged child's deficiencies are diagnosed, and programs of concentrated remediation are planned to correct the deficits. For example, Project Head Start, the Office of Economic Opportunity's pre-school program, attempts to prepare the disadvantaged child for school by starting him at an earlier age. Similarly, Upward Bound, another OEO Project, is planned to help prepare the disadvantaged high-school student for college without requiring the colleges to change their conventional admissions standards. The assumption in each case is that, once compensatory efforts are accomplished, the student is rehabilitated and can join the normal or regular learners in the standard educational process.

Advocates of one school of thought believe that there would be less need for compensatory education programs geared to pupils in the middle and upper grades if children were reached during the preschool period. This current preschool movement (not to be confused with the nursery-school movement of the 1930's and 1940's) has been stimulated by Project Head Start. Child-development research, important to this movement, contends that there are optimal periods of development and learning in the human organism. But the establishment of a "Follow Through" Program in the early grades to back up the gains achieved under Head Start gives further evidence of the need to deal with both the learner and the school's process on a continuous basis.

This preschool movement, as well as the other forms of compensatory education, are additive to the conventional process, and most of them function as appendages of the established educational system. In other words, they do not attempt to alter the fundamental process, but merely add new layers to the old. Clearly, rehabilitating the learner to fit the standard process is less threatening to those who are involved with the existing process than are attempts to change the educational process to fit individual learners, since the former approach does not focus upon them and the program with which they are identified. The children, they maintain, are not responding simply because of certain inadequacies in their own backgrounds.

When "disadvantaged" learners are given a more concentrated dosage of what they have not been able to swallow the first time, many proceed to drop out again, while the program that originally frustrated them remains virtually unchanged.

Yet books such as *Compensatory Education for Cultural Deprivation* tend to reinforce these remedial programs that seek to change the product. Its authors maintain:

> What is needed to solve our current as well as future crises in education is a system of compensatory education which can prevent or overcome earlier deficiences in the development of each individual. . . . Compensatory education as we understand it is not the reduction of all education to a least common denominator. It is a type of education which should help socially disadvantaged students without reducing the quality of education for those who are progressing satisfactorily under existing conditions.[1]

The major failure of this and similar books—and the entire compensatory movement—was pointed out by Harry Passow, Professor of Education at Teachers College, Columbia University: "The disappointment of the book is that none of its proposed major revisions would drastically modify conventional school patterns." [2]

[1] B. Bloom, A. Davis, and R. Hess, *Compensatory Education for Cultural Deprivation.* New York: Holt, Rinehart & Winston, 1965, p. 6.

[2] A. H. Passow, "Diagnosis and Prescription," review of Bloom, et al. (see above), *Saturday Review* (May 15, 1965), p. 82.

Attempts to change the learner before he reaches the conventional process have been somewhat more successful, but as children proceed through the early grades of the conventional process, the good results of these programs tend to disappear.[3] Certainly early childhood education is extremely important, and an extension of public education to include these early years is a valuable innovation, but it cannot be considered a substitute for changing the conventional process.

The danger is that compensatory education may become an end in itself. The current impetus in federal legislation has made compensatory education so widespread that it may actually become part of the same unwieldy educational process that must be reformed.

Yet, despite its failure to solve these problems at their roots, compensatory education has served usefully; it has brought needed attention to the problem of the disadvantaged, and it has shown us that the present generation is not prepared to sacrifice people while we search for more adequate solutions. It has also made contact with the problem and the people. Undoubtedly, too, it has helped many children who might otherwise have been totally forsaken. Consequently, compensatory education must not be considered a mistake, but rather, as a first step in a series aimed at structural overhaul of the entire educational process.

STEREOTYPING AND BEYOND

Roger D. Abrahams

> *There is no feature of culture which affects behavior towards others more deeply than the way in which these others are "typed"—that is, put into a category and interacted with on the basis of the expectations carried with that category. These categories, when they extend to those of other cultures, are generally imposed because of a combination of defensiveness on the part of the stereotyper and some external sign or group of signs (like skin color, clothing, walking style, etc.) which activates the already-learned stereotype.*

[3] M. Wolff, *Six Months Later: A Comparison of Children who had Head Start, Summer 1965, with their Classmates in Kindergarten: A Case Study of the Kindergartens in the Public Elementary Schools in New York City*, sponsored by the Graduate School of Education, Yeshiva University.

As this Abrahams article shows, the category of "other" and the associated cluster of traits (such as laziness, lack of proper eating habits, dirtiness, peculiar family structure) are held independently by many peoples throughout the world and are probably knee-jerk responses to the threat inherent in simply coming into contact with the culturally different or socially distinct. In the case of some other behavior traits, there may be an accurate recognition of real cultural differences, but a misreading of what the behavior signifies. For example, silence on the part of Apache Indians has more often than not been interpreted as hostility by Anglo-Americans. But repeated contact by trained observers has shown that although silence is observed by the Apache where Anglo-Americans expect discussion, hostility is not at the bottom of it. Silence is simply regarded by the Apache as appropriate in situations where the unexpected might occur. Thus silence is the appropriate or "natural" behavior within the Apache culture, but it stimulates in the non-Indian a stereotypic response which leads to further misunderstanding.

This article argues that stereotyping might provide the major obstacle in educating across cultures, but also that when we become conscious of our own tendency to stereotype others it can become an extremely useful technique for the understanding of these others and their cultural differences.

Repeatedly the discussions in the social sciences' literature of stereotyping emphasize that the procedure illustrates a *failure of rationality*. Just why any process of culture should be assumed to be rational in the sense of the logical is a major unexplored question. Furthermore, if rationality is (as we generally use the term) an operation of the ordering capacities of the mind, then stereotyping is emphatically rational. By rationality we seem to mean things ordered as perceived and tested inductively, but we must acknowledge that the deductive process is equally ordered, and that there are numerous such classifications which are made (by ourselves) in groups which are never questioned as irrational. We must recognize that stereotyping is simply a process of ordering which is regarded by those who so designate it as illegitimate because it is misleading. Such a designation could only be made in groups in which there is a set of competing norms and orders.

This is simply saying that stereotyping is one widely observable way in a cultural pluralism of establishing not just stratification but a *social structure*. "Social structure" as I employ it here is the system by which each individual is classified by others in his group in terms of class or caste, or sex or age, or other similar criteria. Most interpersonal relationships are determined in some way by this classification. Such groupings are part of the shared system of values and manners of the community.

The distinctions on which descriptions of social structure depend are a dimension of the ordering process by which we "type" other people as we observe, meet, and interact with them. This typing is implicitly recognized and acted upon by ourselves. We attempt to "manage our own identities" (by which we really mean our own *image*). We want to choose our repertoire of roles in order to control how others react to us. We dramatize ourselves by dressing in certain ways, walking and standing in certain patterns, and any number of other such expressive techniques. This is an operation of our common-sense (and often unconscious) understanding that we are being typed by others, just as we do typing ourselves, and that such typing carries with it certain traditional attitudes and ways of treating each other.

This typifying procedure is one of our major means of organizing life, of making it predictable and comfortable. However, there is a wide range of modes of typing, depending upon how personal or impersonal we are willing to be with individuals as we encounter them. As Peter Berger and Thomas Luckmann discuss the subject:

> The social reality of everyday life is . . . apprehended in a continuum of typifications which are progressively anonymous as they are removed from the "here and now" of the face-to-face situation. At one pole of the continuum are those others with whom I frequently and intensely interact. . . . At the other pole are highly anonymous abstractions, which by their very nature can never be available in face-to-face interaction. Social structure is the sum total of these typifications and of the recurrent patterns of interaction established by means of them.[1]

There is one segment of this continuum, however, which operates differently. A number of social types are removed from most interactions not because they are "unavailable" but because they carry with them symbols demanding social distance. On the one hand these symbols may signal social superiority; on the other, they imply inferiority. It is these latter which we usually rationalize with stereotypical attributions. But as I shall argue in the final section, these "distanced" individuals share one assigned feature—they are attributed great power and energy.

Our lives are affected by the typing done of us by others all along this continuum. When we say we can "be ourselves" only when in the company of those we know well and who understand and share our values, we are simply saying that "ourselves" refers to that part of our identities which functions under fewest insecurities and anxieties and that this kind of

---

[1] Berger and Luckmann, *The Social Construction of Reality* (New York: Doubleday, 1967), pp. 32–33.

experience can only occur with people or types with whom we are so familiar that we can predict the operation of their "idiosyncrasies." But the amount of time we spend in such company is of necessity limited, and so we place ourselves in the position of greater constraint or anonymity. And the greater the anonymity, the more restrictive and categorical the typing will become. The less we know and are known by those with whom we are in contact, the more we are subject to being involved in what has often been referred to as a stereotyping situation between us, judged by certain criteria over which we have no control, since the interaction is determined by the role assigned to us and the expectations associated with this role. That this does not aways result in stereotyping is clear, however, since being assigned a role in a group of strangers may, if the role is prestigious, lead to a high level of communication. Though we don't commonly call this stereotyping, the limitations arising from this categorization are strongly felt by the person so typed, and this constraint inevitably causes the kinds of tensions which are most fully recognized in a stereotyping situation.

Stereotyping is the fixed dimension of a system of social typology by which we may quickly define other individuals and both formulate a strategy for the conduct of relationships with them and provide a rationale for this conduct. This typing process is useful and unavoidable, since it provides us under normal circumstances with a constant means of orientation, a technique for establishing conventional and therefore comfortable social distance. We are dealing here with cultural senses of decorum, manners, the habits and conventions of interpersonal relations, or what Goffman appropriately calls "interaction ritual."

However, when the typing becomes exaggeratedly defensive, decorum is then over-extended and rigidified and the process becomes self-defeating in terms of communication. What is used in normal circumstances as a means of establishing preliminary relationships with people may become a justification for not permitting oneself such relationships. Under such circumstances, typing may become, instead of a technique of socialization, a mode of disaffiliation, subordination, or rejection.

Often we are thus affected in the development of our self-image by a typing imposed on us by others. There is, in every real-life character conventionalization, the possibility of over-categorization and therefore the possibility of breakdown in the relationship. This is as true of in-group social types as it is of out-group stereotypes: for instance, stigma-typing, in which the traits used to categorize are abnormal appearances (leper, blindman, cripple, "queer"), and negative character-typing in which the traits arise from signals implying condemned activities ("slicker," "bounder," "brute"). Furthermore, as members of out-groups, we feel and understand exclusion in terms of how we don't conform to in-group specifications, and in the ways we are purported to be different. We react to this by accepting or rejecting the in-group's image of us. In either case, negative typing is just as *real*, though not necessarily as *valid* or true, as any social types that we may propose to ourselves and our friends. What role we play is determined not only by adopting approved masks, but also by the ways in which we react to masks we are imputed to wear. This latter consideration becomes more important the more one is placed in a negative out-group type, being most suitable in understanding the roles assumed by the stigmatized or the deviant.

From such a perspective, stereotyping is a procedure by which a person is typed because of features of appearance or life-style over which he has no control. But this does not differ in nature or degree from other negative typing.

This brings us to the definition of stereotype by Gordon Allport in his classic study of prejudice.[2] This definition begins with the concept of stereotyping residing in the *exaggeration* of belief associated with a category, not with the belief or the categorization itself. Allport's definition, which at first glance seems to be value-free, is really indicating that stereotyping is an operation of a value system, for who is it that registers that this image is an exaggeration, or on whom is it registered and therefore observable? Stereotyping occurs when exaggeration becomes part of the typing process, but is not exaggeration a necessary condition for the typing process to begin with? If this is so, why then insist upon the distinction between social- and stereo-typing?

The answer is that at some point in the typing operation, some seem to feel that there has been an inhibition of communication between groups at the very point where such communication is needed. Therefore, they develop a separate term for a typing operation which is found inconvenient and illegitimate because it does not conform to at least one aspect of our social ideal—that of operating in relation to others with equality. What we do, when we insist on the distinction between stereotyping and other typing procedures, is to indicate that there exists within our understanding of *our own* social structure a conflict of perspectives and norms.

The awareness that there is stereotyping going on, as I see it, arises in groups in which there is the beginning of a reaction against the dominant-subservient relationships between groups in a situation of cultural pluralism. It does not seem possible that a dimension of social typing would be conceived of as wrong—even stigma-typing—until there is a recognition, by at least some segment of the dominant community, that attributing traits to a subordinate group violates some aspect of the dominant value system (equality). This leads to an understanding on the part of this segment that in a culturally pluralistic situation there is what

[2] Gordon Allport, *The Nature of Prejudice*, Cambridge, Mass.: Addison-Wesley, 1954.

S. F. Nadel has termed a "plurality of norms": "diverse, but equally legitimate 'value patterns,' ideologies or schools of thought."

All of this discussion of stereotyping leads to the conclusion that by the time one can designate certain attitudes and activities as stereotypical, one is well on the way to being able to control these reactions. Stereotyping, along with social typing, may be inevitable, but with an understanding of the process we can begin to recognize the tendency toward over-categorization, and in this recognition we can learn to control it rather than having it control us.

There is a further question that the process of stereotyping poses: what causes certain traits to be selected by the in-group in stigmatizing the out-group? There is a subsidiary question here, of course: how far do these traits depart from observable reality? It is very tempting to say in regard to the latter question that they are figments of the cultural imagination, but this would be misleading. There are in fact two kinds of stereotype traits: those which are negations of values held by the in-group, and those which are observable cultural differences centered upon simply because they are differences. Thus, one must distinguish between traits used to stereotype the Negro such as the shuffling of his feet and the rolling of his eyes (which *are* or used to be observable in situations of deference) and imputed attributes such as laziness, childishness, and dishonesty, which are neither culture-specific nor inductively reasonable. The distinction between these two kinds of traits is important if one wants to effectively describe the true differences in culture between two groups. The problem is that whenever the culture-specific trait is used, even if it has a dimension of truth to it, it will invoke in the minds of the stigmatizers the entire range of the stereotype. One trait, in other words, suggests virtually all of the others.

However, the more deeply based and distancing of the traits are those which one might term "deep" attributes of the stereotype—deep because they are used by many groups when stereotyping out-groups. In an article in the *American Anthropologist* the following was reported of what the Walbiri of Central Australia say about their distant neighbors, the Lungga:

> They [the Lungga] are generally thought to be cannibals and drinkers of human blood. Although the few Walbiri who meet them on droving trips to Wyndham admit that this reputation may be somewhat exaggerated, others who do not know them have given me remarkably circumstantial accounts of Lungga cannibalism, which they have obtained second-hand from the Waringari and Walmadjari. One such story ended with a bloody description of a European massacre of a party of Lungga men, women, and children who were supposed to have eaten a native stockman. When I commented on the magnitude of the slaughter, I was silenced by the remark that the victims were after all, only Lungga cannibals who deserved to be shot.

The Lungga also have a shocking reputation for lechery, and they are be-
lieved to ignore their own marriage rules and incest taboos in their attempts to
copulate with women normally forbidden to them. Walbiri men speak with
manifest disgust of the huge genital organs that Lungga men are reputed to
possess. . . . It is of interest that this constellation of beliefs and attitudes . . . is
found among other aboriginal tribes.

It is important for us to understand the meaning of this attribution
of cannibalism, and the strange notion concerning the size of the male
genitalia and the misuses to which they are put, for these notions stand
at the very center of an understanding of the ways in which stereotypes
work. Stereotypes inevitably focus on the ways in which peoples other than
oneself exhibit themselves as immoral, without restraint, without a knowledge of manners or rules of laws. In short, *stereotypes focus on the lack of
culture of the members of another (often threatening) group*. This lack
of culture is exhibited by childish or animalistic attributes and behavior
patterns, that is, actions done by creatures who cannot be held responsible
because of their physical make-up and their related lack of understanding
of social rules, social constraints.

The "deep" traits found cross-culturally focus then on the social
orders of greatest importance to the maintenance of the community.
Though the content of the categorical belief changes from one intercultural situation to the next, the domains remain constant. Thus one
constantly encounters stereotyping directed, among other things, at:
strange eating habits (cooking being one of the major means of distinguishing man from animals); the ignoring of sexual and other familistic
rules; a lack of cleanliness; and an inability to engage in a peaceable mode
of communication.

Such attributions arise, in part, out of fear of the other group, especially among aboriginals. But they also serve a number of functions that
relate directly to the sense of groupness which the group imposing the
stereotype derives from being able to feel superior in cultural practices to
others. Social cohesion is achieved by picking out a group within which one
can imagine occurring all manner of violations of the ideals of behavior. It
is not difficult to discover how widespread the technique is, and how often
it has been used to rationalize behavior toward other, culturally different
groups. For instance, here is a description of the early European travel
literature concerning Subsaharan Africa:

The classical concensus . . . is that these peoples in the hidden interior and on
the farthest shores of Africa not only lack civilization but any worthy ethic of
social organization or conduct as well. Anarchic, promiscuous, and cruel, they live
the life of beasts rather than that of men. The most remote, in addition, are often
denied possession of a truly human form. The dominant attitude in these accounts
conceived of civilization—Graeco-Roman civilization in particular—as an essential

discipline imposed upon the irregularities of nature: as nature—blind nature—
without restraint and guidance, runs to monstrosities, so [peoples] without civilization run to disorder and excess. There was established thus early the pattern of
thought which for many future centuries formed a basis for approach to the primi-
tives of Africa, and which defined them primarily not in terms of what they were
and what they had, but in terms of what they presumably were not and had not—
in terms, that is, of their inhumanity, their wildness, and their lack of proper law.[3]

These kinds of stereotype conceptions continue to focus on the same
features relating to a lack of civilising traits; indeed, the attribution of the
very same characteristics by Graeco-Romans upon Africa and Africans are
still being voiced by a large majority of people in the United States, and
this in spite of all the work of anthropologists who have shown that there
have been high civilizations in West Africa, and that even African aboriginal groups have extremely complex and logical cultures. But this is
hardly surprising when one considers that these same traits are attributed
to the Irish by the English, to the Gypsies by most Europeans, and to
Lapps by Scandinavians.

The important aspect of stereotyping for our present purposes is
that the stigmatized groups are described primarily in terms not of what
behavior its members exhibit, but what they lack. Stereotyping, in other
words, uses the cultural norms of the group doing the typing as a basis for
comparison and finds the other group deficient in these central properties
(culture) and practices (manners).

One thing which must have hit the reader in the discussion of the
Walbiri attitudes toward the Lungga, and the European attitudes toward
Africans almost before they had been encountered, is that the traits imposed upon these other people are remarkably similar to those often
attributed here to Afro-Americans, and to a somewhat lesser extent to
Mexican-Americans. But there is a great difference between stigmatizing
peoples who live at some distance and doing so to ones who live in one's
midst. The operation of the typing procedure among the Walbiri has little
or no effect upon the Lungga; rather, trait attributions serve to underline
the sense of group unity of the Walbiri in terms of their highest values
(which show them to have culture, be mannered). To be sure, the stereotyping of the Lungga establishes a social distance between the two groups,
but this is of little importance in the lives of either peoples, since the
social distance is accompanied by a geographical separation which means
that they seldom come into contact anyway. This is patently not true
of Blacks and whites in the United States.

Here the stereotyping procedures arise in a culturally pluralistic situation—where groups with different life-styles are living side-by-side. In such

[3] Katherine George, "The Civilized West Looks at Primitive Africa: 1400–1800,
A Study in Ethnocentrism," *Isis*, vol. 49 (1958), pp. 63–64.

a case, once again the stereotype is used to establish social distance and to erect social boundaries, but now the distinctions are used to maintain the subordination of the stigmatized group and the dominance of the ones imposing the stereotype. In this case, the operation of the stereotype becomes much more complicated and generates many more social problems. But its very complexities result in the possibility of arriving at an understanding and a control of such subordinating practice.

The process by which stereotyping is used by the in-group has been described by Robin M. Williams in his study of the way in which stereotyping works in one community in upstate New York. As in primitive groups, he notes that there is an intimate relation between ideals and stereotype traits:

> Negative stereotypes used by majority-group members . . . to stigmatize outgroups usually are the reversed images of dominant positive traits. The epithet of laziness reflects the value (and the burden) of industriousness. Ignorance contrasts with the virtues of competence, education, self-improvement. Dishonesty is the opposite of upright, moral, fair dealings.[4]

But the difference is that here the negative rendering of these ideals arises not just for purposes of maintaining social boundaries, but also for rationalizing political and social domination.

The stream of culture runs very deep, and with it the tendency to regard any activities of other groups as evidence of a deficiency, or as wrong, bad, debased, or evidence of group pathology. One would have thought that social scientists, above all, would be highly sensitive to the operation of stereotyping. But it is clear from their long history of studying Afro-Americans in the United States that very few of them have made any attempt to frame their studies in such a way as to recognize differences without weighing them, in value terms, against our middle-class norms and ideals. Consequently, reports of social investigations, and especially the interpretation of the data, have been suffused with the assumption of a social and cultural deficiency or pathology among a majority of lower-class Blacks. Once this is assumed, it is not difficult to make one's observations of differences conform to this deficiency image. Thus, even in these purportedly "objective" investigations by ones who profess to be friends to such Blacks, the stereotyping process has persisted. There emerges continuously published and widely publicized studies which confirm in so many ways the image of Afro-American communities as dysfunctional, as the locus for little but immoral activities on the part of individuals who have no sense of personality organization, due to "broken" or "fatherless" homes and the emotional and cognitive deficits that are endemic to such

---

[4] Robin M. Williams, et al., *Strangers Next Door* (Englewood Cliffs, N.J.: Prentice-Hall, Inc., 1964), p. 40.

settings. That this image is just as stereotypical, misleading and false as the racists' view of Blacks I hope is self-evident. That we cannot build a meaningful educational process for Afro-Americans until we rid ourselves of such attitudes and modes of operation is the burden of the argument.

I hope that it has become clear that social typing as a process is a part of the social equipment of every group that calls itself a group. Furthermore, there is a very dim line between social typing and stereotyping, for both seek to categorize others so that we may better handle at least the initial encounters with others whom we have not known in the past.

It seems ironic that few Euro-Americans have ever considered whether Blacks (or any other minority) have stereotypes of whites. When asked whether they imagine that such exist, whites generally reply, "Well, I guess so." The reason for this oversight is obvious enough—the stereotype of whites has done very little to manage the identities of the Euro-American and therefore affects his life very little. To be sure, it affects inter-ethnic communications just as much as the white stereotyping of others, but from their superordinate position there is little need felt to communicate except as a superior. Furthermore, to think about stereotypes by others is both unpleasant and would bestow on the stereotypers a trait of culture, of humanity.

Blacks not only have a consciousness of the stereotype of them (and have used the traits for aggressive purposes in their traditional stories) but they do indeed stereotype whites in return. In fact, for nearly every trait that whites impute to Blacks, Blacks have an answering trait which they attribute to whites. To the charge that Blacks have no sense of how to set up a family, Blacks say "What kind of people would bring someone who is no kin and who they don't even know and let them raise their kids." To the attribution of hypersexuality, they respond "Well, we know about whites and sex, 'cause we see them sneaking around over on our side of town often enough." The imputation of irrationality and over-emotionalism of Blacks is responded to by attributions of coldness on the part of whites; and on the subject of smells, Blacks aver that whites often smell like dogs (or goats) just come in from the rain. But the one trait of whites emphasized most by Blacks of whites is hatred: "They don't like me and I don't like them."

To acknowledge this counter-stereotype is simply to accept the existence of a Black sense of ethnicity, and to recognize that Blacks in groups act like human beings—and are capable of being just as over-categorical and prejudiced as whites. But it must be remembered that there is a major operational difference between the two sets of attributed traits, for with Blacks their identity is being managed for them. With both groups, however, the type inhibits communication between members of these ethnic groups and is therefore equally troubling to those who are concerned with the problems of inter-ethnic rub. Perhaps because we are so concerned with a guarantee of freedom, we have become especially conscious of doing this sort of typing, and for this reason we have invented a pejorative word for it—*stereotyping*. Just the invention of the term is the first step toward eliminating it, for we can't diagnose a social ill until we have a name for it and understand its symptoms.

This does not mean that we are automatically going to control our stereotyping reactions. But it does mean that we can learn where in our experience cultural "rub" occurs most often; and we can learn how to control our actions in regard to others who come from a different cultural system and whom we therefore cannot expect to understand and get along with immediately. Going into any truly intercultural situation is the most intensely unsettling experience anyone can go through, as any inveterate and adventurous traveler will tell you, and as the many anthropological autobiographies attest. But one can, and does, learn from experience. But in order to learn from experience in the community or the classroom it is necessary to learn how to control the stereotypical judgments that arise, especially in situations of embarrassment. These embarrassments often arise because those involved in the encounter are operating in regard to different systems of communications, different cultures. It is only by being willing to recognize and accept these systematic differences that we can get beyond stereotyping.

2

Cultures in Education

Culture has been the key concept-term in anthropology. Like any such term, it has developed a wide variety of meanings—definitions generally dependent upon the range of problems which the investigator has wanted to solve. A whole book, in fact, has been usefully devoted to definitions and discussions of culture, *Culture: A Critical Review of Concepts and Definitions*, Clyde Kluckhohn and A. L. Kroeber (New York: Random House, 1963), as well as numerous articles. It does not seem useful here, however, to replay these controversies. Rather, we simply introduce the term and some of the ways in which the concept has been usefully related to education.

As the term has often and generally been used, the culture of a people includes all of the systems, techniques, and tools which make up their way of life. Material culture includes all of the physical artifacts produced by the society: money, houses, cars, canoes, bows and arrows, clothing. Non-material or expressive and institutional culture includes all of the systems for the regulation of man to man, of man to the super-natural, and of man to the environment, and all of the bodies of custom, belief, and values regarding these. This dimension of culture deals with the "manners" of the group, their life-style, and their more abstract systems of family, religion, government, and so on.

Members of different cultures cannot live in the same objective world; the whole organization of knowledge, perception, and behavior is strongly determined by one's culture. Nor can concepts ever be assumed to have correspondences across cultural boundaries: the notions designated in English by such terms as *snow*, *blue*, *walk*, *family*, or *good*, can probably never be equated exactly with categories in other cultures. There is nothing "natural" in human experience, for all experience is culturally conditioned, and no two cultures are ever alike.

Elements of material culture, being visible, are readily transmitted across cultural boundaries, often with relatively little influence on the way of life of the borrowing group. Features of expressive and institutional culture are less readily borrowed, in part because they are less observable, but more importantly because they belong to a complex of interlocking systems in the donor culture, and cannot be taken over without producing dislocations in the borrowing culture. The American educational system itself is a cultural invention which serves primarily to prepare middle-class children to participate in their own cultural system, and which trains teachers to meet the educational needs of only this group of students. Teachers working with students from other cultural groups, including lower-class ethnic groups, must learn to see the schools and themselves in this perspective, and learn to respect and at the same time deal with the culturally different background which their students bring into the classroom encounter.

To do this, it is necessary to recognize the varieties of ways in which cultural differences may assert themselves in the classroom. The most obvious way, of course, is in language differences, for language has been used as a means of demarcating distinct groups both by the group members and by outsiders. The importance of the linguistic dimension of culture cannot be overstressed to teachers, as the individuals in each culture will feel themselves under attack should their language be regarded as a stigmatizing feature. This is an especially important feature of the Mexican-American movement which defensively has focused on the rejection of Spanish as the major threat to their integrity.

There are numerous other dimensions of culture, however, which must be better recognized as being culturally relative, which are not so obviously different as languages are. A knowledge of systems of family organization and distribution of power, resources, and responsibilities is crucial in an understanding of the student and the ways in which his culture has taught him to give order to the social and natural world around him. Equally important are matters of decorum—how people communicate with each other by observing rules of interaction. We know from repeated disruptions of our own sense of manners that people from different cultures speak louder or softer than do we, or that they stand closer or farther away.

The articles in this section deal with some of these dimensions of shared cultural order. The selections have been made on the basis of their usefulness to the teacher, not on their importance in anthropological theory. A wide range of subjects is covered here, from a multi-cultural and usually cross-cultural point of view, but no attempt has been made to cover the entire range of the features of culture with which anthropologists have been concerned.

To return to definitions for the moment, one group of anthropologists has recently been looking at "culture" as those things which a person has to know in order to live successfully on a day-by-day basis within the group. It is this kind of intimate interactional detail that we feel is important for teachers to learn to recognize among students, so that teachers may better learn to live with students day-by-day, as students must learn to live with the teacher.

CULTURE

Robert W. Young

Language is both a part of culture and a means for encoding and transmitting cultural information. Young here discusses a number of differences between Navajo and English, which illustrate how differently languages may organize experience. The teacher of students from other cultural groups must recognize her role as a cross-cultural interpreter, and realize the need to make aspects of the dominant culture meaningful to her students in such a way that these become a meaningful part of their experience without displacing or conflicting with the corresponding parts of their native cultures.

In everyday parlance we use the term *culture* in a wide variety of contexts and meanings ranging from "proper" social deportment to the acquisition of "refined" tastes in music, literature, and the arts. In addition, the term forms part of the specialized vocabulary of several disciplines, including agriculture, bacteriology and anthropology. In the latter, and in this essay, *culture* refers to the varied systems developed by human societies as media for adaptation to the environment in which their members live; in its totality, a cultural system constitutes the means through which the group to which it pertains achieves survival as an organized society. Such systems range from simple to the complex and sophisticated, and among themselves they exhibit a wide variety of differences in form and content.

When we speak of the culture of a society or community, we have reference to the entire gamut of tools, institutions, social values, customs, traditions, techniques, concepts and other traits that characterize the way of life of the group. The specific items that make up a cultural system, or *elements* as they are called, fall into two broad categories: material and non-material. In the first are included such features as tools (axes, hammers, jacks), vehicles (wagons, cars, airplanes), clothing (shirts, dresses, shoes), and shelter (houses, tents, hogans); and among the non-material

From *English as a Second Language for Navajos*, Robert W. Young (Albuquerque Area Office—Navajo Area Office Division of Education, 1968). Reprinted by permission of the Bureau of Indian Affairs.

elements of culture are such institutions as social organization, kinship systems, marriage, government, religion, and language.

The content of a given cultural system is determined by a wide range of factors, including the physical environment, inventiveness, influence of surrounding communities, trade, opportunities for borrowing, and many others. For obvious reasons the material content of traditional Eskimo culture contained elements of a type not found in the cultures of the peoples living in the tropical rain forests or of those living in the hot deserts. The physical environment, in each instance, imposed different requirements for survival, and a different framework for cultural development.

Borrowing and trade have had a tremendous influence on cultural content, in modern as well as in ancient times, and a cursory glance at the present day Eskimo, the Navajo or, for that matter, virtually any community of people anywhere on earth, is sufficient to reflect the importance of these avenues for cultural change and growth. Guns, steel axes, knives, metal fishhooks, motor boats, rubber boots, stoves, tobacco, liquor, and a host of items have been borrowed and incorporated into Eskimo culture in the course of contact with outside cultural communities; horses, sheep, goats, iron tools, wagons, automobiles, radio, television, and many other elements have been borrowed by, and have become part of the cultural systems of such people as the Navajo since their first contact with Europeans. And in another part of the world Western European and American influences have changed the way of life of a large community—Japan—in less than a century.

In Alaska, in the American Southwest, and elsewhere, the pace of cultural change has quickened with each generation as aboriginal peoples respond to changing conditions of life. To no small degree, the dominant Anglo-American system, with its emphasis on molding the environment itself to human need, has established new conditions for life and survival; new conditions so complex in nature that the institution of the school has come to occupy a position of primary importance providing, as it does, the training necessary for successful living.

Formal education, in modern American society, is designed to facilitate the successful adaptation and survival of its members within an environment and under conditions that the society itself, to a large extent, has created. The educational system is not only one that cultural minorities have borrowed, but one which the Anglo-American cultural community has imposed upon them. With reference to such culturally divergent minorities, formal education is the instrument used by the dominant society to generate and accelerate cultural change through the medium of induced "acculturation"—that is, the process through which such communities as the Navajo are induced and trained to participate in the dominant national cultural system. It is, in a broad sense, a form of cultural borrowing, differing however from the more usual process of voluntarily picking and choosing, on the part of the borrower, in that some of the stimuli for change are imposed and the initiative is taken by, the "lending" system itself. Unfortunately, the process of induced or—as it often turns out, compelled—acculturation is not without its problems for the "lender" as well as for the "borrower." The need for change is not always as apparent to the latter as it is to the former, and in the absence of recognition of compelling necessity, the borrower is sometimes reluctant to accept what is held out to him. It may not appear, from his viewpoint, to fit his requirements, or its acceptance may threaten existing institutions and practices upon which he places value.

Consequently, compulsory education, when first imposed upon Indian communities by the Federal Government just before the turn of the century, met with strenuous resistance. From the hopeful point of view of the would-be "lender," schooling offered improved tools for survival in a changing environment; but from that of the "borrower" the educational process threatened cultural extinction. It removed the child from the home where he received his traditional training in the language, values, religion, and other institutions of his own culture and promised to leave him ill-prepared for life in the only world his parents knew. They resisted and the "lenders" applied force. A long tug-of-war followed.

A comparable situation developed when, in the 1930's, the compelling need to conserve natural resources in the Navajo country, led to livestock reduction and the introduction of a wage economy as a new economic base for the Navajo people. From the point of view of the lending society, this was a new and superior device for survival; but from the Navajo viewpoint it threatened cultural extinction. Coupled with the process of formal education, the new economic system constituted a threat to the traditional social organization of the Tribe, as well as to the religious life of the people, not to mention the economic pursuits, residence patterns and associated values that were basic to the traditional Navajo way of life. Like compulsory education in the days of Black Horse [in the 1890's], the new economic urgings so necessary from the viewpoint of the "lender" met with violent resistance by the prospective "borrowers."

Time, among other factors, is usually an important ingredient in cultural change whether it takes place through a process of voluntary borrowing or through one of induced acculturation. *In the latter case, the degree of success and the quantity of time required hinge, to no small degree, on the depth of understanding attained by the "lender," and on the effectiveness of applied techniques.*

The fact is that a culture is more than a system of material and non-material elements that can be listed, catalogued and classified. A culture constitutes a complex set of habits of doing, thinking and reacting to stimuli—habits which one acquires in early childhood and which, for the most part, he continues to share, throughout his life, with fellow members of his cultural community. In its totality, a cultural system is a frame of reference that shapes and governs one's picture of the world around him. Within this framework and, as Whorf pointed out nearly a generation ago, within the frame of reference imposed by the structure of the language he speaks, one is conditioned to look upon the world about him in a manner that may differ substantially from that characterizing another and distinct cultural system.

As a consequence, from the point of view of his own system one man, looking at a vast expanse of trees through his cultural window, may choose the expansiveness of the forest as the salient feature of the landscape, without reference to the species that compose it, and so describe the scene by applying appropriate terms in his language; another man, viewing the same scene from the vantage point of another cultural window might see and describe it quite differently as large numbers of specific types of trees—oaks, elms, maples. From the point of view of his own system one man, looking at the past age of time within the limits imposed by his cultural perspective, may conceive of it, measure and describe it *only* in terms of the rising and setting of the sun, the recurring phases of the moon, or the sequence of seasons; another man may add mechanical and mathematical or astronomical measurements including hours, minutes, seconds, days, months, years, decades, centuries, millennia, and light years —one system may place maximum importance on the element of time and its exact measurement, while another may attach little or no importance to the same phenomenon. Similarly, one may look at an object and describe its color as *green* in contradistinction to *blue;* but another may apply a term meaning both green and blue (Navajo dootł'izh, for example), and if the distinction is of paramount importance the Navajo may make it by comparison with something possessing the proper shade (tatł'id naxalingo dootł'izh = blue/green like water-scum = green).

The manner in which the members of one cultural community conceive of the world around them, and their relationship with it, may differ substantially from the manner in which the members of another such community look upon and react to it—this is true even where the cultural groups concerned occupy similar physical environments, and in situations where the concepts are not conditioned by geographical factors.

Likewise, what is "logical" and "reasonable" to one system may be quite the contrary to another. There are few, if any, cultural absolutes but many "relatives," in this regard. To a Navajo or Pueblo Indian, whose culture has developed an elaborate system through which Man strives for the maintenance of harmony with nature, the Anglo-American concept of actively controlling natural forces in the interest of Man's survival, and the media through which to accomplish this, may not always appear reasonable. A little more than a decade ago, the Navajo Tribal Council, after long debate and against the better judgment of most of the Navajo community, authorized the use of a small amount ($10,000) of Tribal funds to employ a technician to seed the clouds with silver iodide in an effort to break a period of severe drought. The experiment met with very limited success, especially in view of the paucity of appropriate clouds—and there were those who complained that the propellers of the airplane blew away such rainclouds as appeared over the horizon—so in subsequent Council action, which met with the enthusiastic support of most tribal leaders and members, the unused residue of the appropriation was diverted to defray the cost of reconstructing and carrying on a ceremony that had fallen into disuse, and which had formerly been relied upon to produce rain. The ceremonial procedure was "logical" to traditionally oriented members of the Tribe because it was consonant with the position that Man must maintain himself in harmony with nature; at the same time, the cloud-seeding process was "logical" to non-Navajos who are culturally conditioned to a scientific approach in attaining control over nature for Man's benefit. The two processes reflect fundamentally different points of view regarding natural phenomena and Man's relationship to them; they pertain to different cultural frames of reference—and, to the delight of the proponents of the ceremonial approach, it did, in fact, rain!

Borrowed elements of material culture generally find ready acceptance if they represent an obvious improvement or otherwise meet an immediate need in the estimation of the borrower. Replacement of a stone ax by one made of steel does not require radical complementary cultural changes; both instruments have the same function. Such patently practical improvements are capable of smooth incorporation into a system, with few if any repercussions. Even the horse, whose introduction revolutionized the way of life of peoples such as the Navajo and the Indians of the Great Plains, was readily accommodated within their several cultures, apparently without seriously shaking the foundations on which those systems rested. Wagons, automobiles, trucks, radios, televisions, Pendleton blankets, and a host of other objects have since entered the Navajo scene, and have become part of the system without creating insuperable problems or generating a high level of resistance. The cultural system merely flowed around such innovations, after the fashion of amoeba around its prey, and made them part of itself without seriously modifying its own basic structure. History seems to reflect the fact that people literally threw away their stone axes and knives when steel tools became available; and the production of pottery for utilitarian purposes has all but disappeared since the advent of more durable utensils for the Indian housewife.

Not so, however, with the non-material elements of culture—the institutions pertaining to religion, social organization, kinship, language, marriage or social values. The Navajo and the Pueblo did not junk his own religion for Christianity, discard his own language for Spanish or English, or drop his clan, kinship, or other social system in favor of a borrowed replacement. Such non-material elements as these are among the mainstays in the cultural framework and, as such, they undergo change at a much slower rate than do those relating to the tangible material culture. The successful incorporation of such Anglo-American institutions as formal education, representative democratic government, the father-centered family, a system of justice based on coercive laws, and modern medical practices into Navajo culture has been slow and painful because they are or were elements that did not fit the accustomed cultural framework; their incorporation would necessitate a host of radical adjustments in the complex of fundamental cultural habits of the people before they could be accommodated—in fact, incorporation of the entire range of such alien institutions had profound implications for the very survival of the borrowing system itself.

The immediate value of these institutions as improved tools for survival, intangible and complex as they are, was not as readily apparent to the potential borrower as it was in the case of the steel ax, the horse, or the gun. Material elements from non-Indian culture continued to be accepted and incorporated wholesale into that of the Navajo and other Indian Tribes, but incorporation of the values, customs, concepts, language, associated habits, and institutions of the outside community enter slowly and painfully, often only as the result of heavy pressure.

The concept of coercion, in the sense of imposing one's will on another person or animate being without physical contact or force, is part of the Anglo-American cultural heritage, and the English language is replete with terms expressing various aspects of the concept—cause, force, oblige, make, compel, order, command, constrain, must, have to, ought to, shall, come quickly to mind. They are part of the heritage of a culture with a long history of kings, emperors, dictators, deities, governments, and family patriarchs whose authority to impose their will on others has been long accepted as part of the worldview of the communities participating in the system. So deeply engrained is this area of habitual acceptance of the compelling, coercive need to do certain things that we are astonished and annoyed by the lack of concern in the same area on the part of people like the Navajo, as reflected by the paucity of terms in the language of the latter corresponding to those listed above. How does one say *ought to, must, duty, responsibility* in Navajo? Such circumlocutions, from the English point of view, as "ákǫ́ǫ́ deesháałgo t'éiyá yá'át'ééh, it is only good that I shall go there," seems to lack the force of compelling necessity implicit in "I *must* go there, I *have to* go there." Likewise, when "I *make* the horse run," the action of the horse is implicitly the result of the imposition of my will over his. "Łį́į́' shá yilghoł, the horse is running *for* me," implies an action, on the part of the horse, that is essentially voluntary. Again, the Navajo expression appears to be weak and lacking in the important overtone of coercive authority—of yielding to the will of a master—to the English speaking person. And when we find that not even the deities of the Navajo pantheon or the political leaders of the Tribe are wont to issue mandates to be obeyed by men, we are likely to be as perplexed as the Navajo who finds the reverse to be true in Anglo-American society.

Navajo culture does not have a heritage of coercive religions, political or patriarchal family figures and in the Navajo scheme of things one does not usually impose his will on another animate being to the same extent, and in the same ways as one does from the English point of view. "I *made* my wife sing" becomes, in Navajo, simply "even though my wife did not want to do so, she sang when I told her to sing (she'esdzáán doo íinízin da ndi xótaal bidishníigo xóótáál)." From the Navajo point of view, one can compel his children to go to school in the sense that he drives him (bíníshchééh) or them (bínishkad) there; or he can *place* them in school (nininil), but none of these terms reflect the imposition of one's will independently of physical force—the children do not comply with a mandate. They are animate "objects" with wills of their own.

On the other hand, with references to inanimate objects, lacking a will of their own, appropriate causative verb forms exist. "Yibąs," in Navajo, means "it (a wheel-like object) is rolling along," while a causative form "yoołbąs" conveys the meaning "he is *making* it roll along; he is rolling it along" (by physical contact). "Naaghá" means "he is walking around," and a causative form "nabiishłá" can be translated "I am making him walk around"—but only in the sense "I am walking him around" (as a baby or a drunk person, for example, by holding him up and physically moving him about). The causative action expressed by "yoołbąs" and "nabiishłá" has, in both instances the same connotation; both actions are produced as a result of physical contact, and not by the imposition of the agent's will with acquiescence by the actor. To express the concept of obliging a person to walk against his will, by mandate, one is likely to take the same approach as that described with reference to "making" one's wife sing, even though she does not wish to do so. One can, of course, order or command another persn (yíł'aad) but the term carries the connotation of send him to perform an action; and it does not follow that he complies. In the Navajo cultural-linguistic framework, animate objects are more frequently and commonly viewed as acting voluntarily than as the result of imposition of another animate object's will.

The Navajo parent is likely to ask a child if it *wants* to go to school, rather than issue a mandate to the effect that it must go. By the same token, coercive laws are distasteful from the Navajo point of view, and the Tribal leadership has long preferred persuasion to force, even in applying "compulsory" education laws on the Reservation.

Nor is the concept of impersonal punishment through the imposition of a fine or jail sentence, in lieu of payment to the victim of a crime or act of violence, "reasonable" from the traditional Navajo viewpoint. Many types of disputes, both civil and criminal, were customarily resolved in local community meetings in the very recent past, and the procedure probably continues to the present day. In some instances, such solutions involved payment of money or goods by one party to another.

In the *Final Report, Indian Research Study,* conducted during the period 1957–1960 by the College of Education, University of New Mexico, under the able direction of Dr. Miles V. Zintz, an excellent analysis of conflicting cultural values relating to Southwestern Indians and Spanish American communities is provided. The authors of this report contrast a variety of conflicting cultural situations, including Harmony with Nature vs. Mastery over Nature; Future Time Orientation vs. Present Time Orientation; Saving vs. Sharing; Acceptance of Change vs. Resistance to Change; Adherence to Close Time Schedules vs. Lack of Concern for Time Schedules; Scientific Explanations vs. Non-Scientific; Aggressive Competition vs. a Non-Competitive Role; and Individuality vs. Group Anonymity. To these we might add the differences that may obtain between cultural communities—and, for that matter, between strata within such a community as our own—with reference to the nature of knowledge, and the purpose and methods of education, whether the latter process be a traditional Indian or a modern Anglo-American procedure. Traditionally, in Navajo society, the acquisition of knowledge involved rote learning and practical experience. The process of rote learning was predicated on the premise that the answers to all philosophical questions are already contained in the body of folk literature (mythology, as it is often termed) and one has only to seek it out; while adequate methods relating to such practices as animal husbandry and agriculture had already been developed in Navajo culture, and therefore had only to be learned by experience. The learner was not expected to question the body of facts or the traditional methodology. To no small degree rote learning is a factor in our own Anglo-American education system, but generally we have accepted the fact that we do not possess all knowledge, in an absolute sense, and we encourage our children to question and test theories and hypotheses and to themselves strive to make a contribution to the fund of human knowledge. This approach to the acquisition of knowledge reflects Anglo-American acceptance of change in the interest of "progress," and the requirement in the latter society that opinions and practices be supported by a strong rationale. Rote learning is defensible on the premise that it provides the tools required to support initiative thinking, but it is not universally accepted in Anglo-American society, as an ideal end in itself.

Many of the foregoing conflicts cannot be readily resolved within the framework of traditional Indian cultures. They constitute divergent habits, habitual attitudes and systems, which are part of the main fabric of the societies to which they belong, and change in one carries the need for change in others. Such situations sometimes resemble houses of cards: the removal of one card in a key location threatens to tumble the entire structure.

CROSS-CULTURAL COMMUNICATION

Cross-cultural interpretation involving, as it does, the explanation of concepts which lie outside the experience of the cultural-linguistic system of the receiver, requires special training and highly developed communicational skills on the part of the interpreter. Just any bilingual person, chosen at random, is not sufficient. In fact, the effectiveness of cross-cultural communication can be greatly enhanced if the English speaking technician, for whom an interpreter acts as intermediary, himself has some modicum of understanding of the cultural and linguistic factors that limit ready understanding on the part of the receivers—i.e. if he himself has a degree of insight into the culture and language—the worldview—of the people to whom he addresses himself. To draw an analogy, the nuclear physicist is more likely to succeed in explaining nuclear fission to the layman if he knows something of the educational background and previous experience in the sciences on the part of the person or audience to whom he addresses himself. If he uses the somewhat esoteric language of physics and proceeds with a mathematical explanation, he may find that his listener has received little or no insight into the subject. If, on the other hand, having informed himself previously regarding the educational and experiential characteristics of his audience, he couches his explanatory remarks in terms that lie within the scope of their experience and understanding, the effectiveness with which he communicates is likely to be greatly increased.

Cross-cultural interpretation is not exclusively a process of trans-linguistic, trans-cultural explanation involving two languages in such formal situations as Tribal Council sessions or doctor-patient relationships. The school-teacher is also a cross-cultural interpreter whenever she functions in situations involving the education of children from cultural-linguistic minorities—or, for that matter, even children from highly divergent sub-cultures related to that of the teacher herself. It is the role of such a teacher to introduce and explain a broad spectrum of new concepts to children who come to her with a different set of cultural habits and experiences. She must make such concepts meaningful to her pupils to such a degree that they become a functional part of their experience and, at the same time the teacher in cross-cultural, cross-linguistic situations must develop in her pupils the skills they require to communicate with regard to the new concepts in the language of the culture to which the new ideas relate. She is at once their interpreter and their mentor.

As in the case of most physicians, attorneys, and other technicians, the conventional training of teachers does not provide them with the special skills they require to function effectively in situations requiring cross-cultural communication. Few have taken courses in linguistics or anthropology, and those who ultimately acquire necessary skill often do so on a trial and error basis. Conventional training prepares teachers to meet the educational needs of children of their own culture—children from middle-class American society; as we pointed out previously, formal schooling essentially is an institution of Anglo-American culture designed to prepare Anglo-American children to participate in their own cultural system, with an acceptable level of economic standards and social values. The same conventional training is woefully inadequate in a classroom filled with bewildered little children with whom the teacher cannot so much as communicate.

The average cross-cultural teacher cannot be expected to attain competency in the speech system, or deeply intimate first-hand knowledge of the cultural system, of such highly divergent communities as the Navajo. The teacher cannot be expected to achieve bi-culturalism and bi-lingualism as a condition of employment, desirable as it might be. However, the average cross-cultural teacher *can* learn something *about* the characteristics of the language and way of life of the children she teaches. She *can*, in fact, achieve a professional skill level as a teacher of English as a second language, and as an interpreter of Anglo-American culture, providing she receives necessary technical training to prepare her for the highly specialized work involved.

The preparation of teachers whose interest lies in the field of cross-cultural education, highly specialized as this facet of the profession should be, must perforce include at least an introduction to anthropology and linguistic science. The average citizen may be able to afford the luxury of assuming that all people share his culture and worldview or that, if they do not, they are inferior; but this is a luxury that the cross-cultural teacher cannot afford. She must develop a clear understanding of the fact that different cultural communities differ within a wide range of variation on the basis of their way of life, their mode of communication, and the manner in which they conceive of the world in which they live; that these distinguishing characteristics are essentially a complex system of habits; and that the relative "superiority" of one cultural system over another is debatable, assuming that both have enabled the communities involved to survive.

Like other habits, culture and language are not easily modified; in fact existing habits commonly interfere with our efforts to acquire new skills and new understandings.

Confronted with a problem, we attempt to explain the unfamiliar in terms of the familiar, whether the problem relates to the features of another culture generally, or to those of another language in particular. We try to identify a new speech sound by relating it to some phoneme with which we are familiar in our own language; and we are so tightly bound by the peculiar set of habits attaching to our own culture and language that we even allow ourselves the extravagance of assuming that, because certain features are part of our experience and therefore logical to us, they *must* be part of the experience of other peoples as well. This fallacy leads us to look for tense forms in languages that are not time oriented in the expression of verbal concepts; it leads us to search for authoritative political figures in societies that are not organized around a coercive system of governmental control; and it leads us to a fruitless search for corresponding principles and figures in the religious systems of societies whose religions do not share the characteristics of our own. As cross-cultural teachers, we cannot afford the luxury of such comfortable fictions; it is essential that we broaden the background of experience and knowledge against which we develop our understanding of other peoples, other societies and other languages if we are to succeed in the area of cross-cultural interpretation and, by extension, cross-cultural education. To illustrate, both English and Spanish use a phoneme of the type represented graphically by the letter *r*. It is represented in the English word *run*, and in the Spanish word *ron* (rum), but the written symbol does not, in fact, represent the same sound in the two languages. In Spanish, the phoneme is articulated by flapping the tongue tip against the alveolar ridge; in most dialects of American English the sound is produced as something of a glide, raising the tongue but without contact with the alveolar ridge. The English speaker and the speaker of Spanish each produce the phoneme in reference, in accordance with his own set of speech habits, and when the speaker of one of the two languages attempts to learn the other, he draws on his past experience and transfers the phoneme with which he is familiar from his native speech to the language he is learning. The Spaniard produces the initial phoneme of English *run* like that of Spanish *ron*; and the English speaker does the reverse. The native speaker of either language immediately detects the departure from accepted norms, and a large number of such transfers from one language to another results in the "accent" that so commonly characterizes the speech of non-native speakers. So characteristic are such transfer patterns—reflecting an original set of speech habits, that we can even identify the national origin of the speaker as Spanish, German, Italian, and the like. Habits of speech, like other customary ways of doing things, are powerful forces, and if we are to learn another language we cannot allow ourselves the luxury of permanent satisfaction with the first analogies we draw between its forms and what we assume to be corresponding features of our own familiar speech system. We cannot use the Navajo language as an effective communicational tool if we remain satisfied with analogies drawn on the basis of initial experience, equating the Navajo phoneme *dl* with English *gl*; Navajo *ł* with *lth*; *gh* with *g*; and ignoring the distinctive features of vowel length and tone. Nor can we substitute English patterns such as "my son is now five" and make ourselves intelligible to the Spanish speaking person by saying "mi hijo es ahora cinco," to convey the concept of age. Only the bilingual or highly imaginative listener would get our message, because the Spanish pattern requires "my son now has five years" (mi hijo ahora tiene cinco años).

In a comparable manner, we are prone to misinterpret cultural phenomena by attempting to relate what we observe to something that is familiar in terms of our own experience; or we mistakenly assume that cultural features that are familiar parts of our own system must have their counterparts in the components of other societies. The latter fallacy is illustrated by the observations of J. H. Beadle [1] who visited the Navajo Country in 1871. Mr. Beadle apparently assumed that the Navajos, like himself, must believe in a Supreme Being representing good, and a Satanic Being representing evil. Through his interpreters (a process involving English → Spanish → Navajo/Navajo → Spanish → English because no English-speaking person of the time spoke Navajo) he elicited the term *Chinda* (ch'įįdįį) as the name applied to the Devil, and for Supreme Being he lists a name *Whaillahay*, with the comment that "Chinda, the Devil, is a more important personage in all their daily affairs than Whaillahay, the God." Apparently, he had posed his questions against the background of his own culture, in the delusion that the features and figures of Christianity had their counterparts in Navajo religion. Mr. Beadle would no doubt be deeply chagrined today if he knew that the Navajo term he ascribed to the Supreme Being—the one he spelled Whaillahay—was very probably xólahéi! meaning "Damned if I know!"

It is part of the Anglo-American cultural system to distinguish between such separate categories as *kinfolk* and *friends* in describing interpersonal relationships. We normally have a close relationship with both classes, but the first, in conjunction with the associated terminology (father, mother, brother, sister, etc.), is usually applied only to persons to whom we are related by blood, marriage or adoption; the second class, with its associated terms (buddy, pal, sweetheart, etc.) is generally applied to persons to whom we are unrelated. As Anglo-Americans, this dichotomy appears so fundamental that we are inclined to assume that it must be universal. It is frustrating, from our viewpoint, to find that kinship terms are used, in Navajo, for both categories. "My friend" may equate with "my brother" (sik'is),[2] "my sister" (shilah),[2] or with a number of other kinship terms (sitsilí, my younger brother; shínaaí, my older brother; shideezhí, my younger sister; shádí, my older sister; shichai, my maternal grandfather; shaadaaní, my son-in-law, etc.).

The fact is that, in the Navajo frame of reference, the concept of friendship is associated with kinship. The noun stem—"k'éí" translates "relative, kinsman," and a cognate form "k'é" occurs as a verbal prefix relating to friendship and, by extension, to *peace*. Thus "shik'éí," my

<hr/>

[1] J. H. Beadle, *Five Years in the Territories.*

[2] That is, my sibling of the same sex as myself. "Sik'is," used by a male to a male translates "my brother"; but used by a female to a female it translates "my sister."

relatives, including clan relatives; "k'é ghósh'ní," I am friendly with him, on good terms with him; "k'énáxásdlii," peace was restored, friendly relations returned, the war ended (lit. k'é-, friendship, peace; -náxásdlįį', things became back, things returned to a state of durative being). Thus, in the Navajo worldview, the concepts of friendship, peace, and kinship are all aspects of the same idea; while from the Anglo-American point of view they are separate and distinct from one another.

It is interesting to note that, under Anglo-American influences, the term *shibádí* has come into use by some of the Navajo school children—it is a "Navajo-ized" form of the English term *my buddy*. Likewise, one hears today such terms as "she'et'ééd," my girl, and "she'ashkii," my boy (-friend), describing a relationship that was not part of traditional Navajo society.

A broad foundation in the nature of human culture and language provides us with a much improved background against which to understand and cope with cross-cultural problems, and specific knowledge of the culture and language of specific groups with which we work permits us to *predict* probable areas of cultural conflict and linguistic interference in the process of acculturation and language learning.

THE WORKING CLASS, LOWER CLASS AND MIDDLE CLASS

Herbert Gans

> To this point, the arguments in this work have been directed towards observing and capitalizing on cultural differences. But even the casual observer knows that there are social class factors which affect behaviors no matter what ethnic community the individuals may presently live in. There is some question whether these class-based attitudes and behaviors are to be considered an element of the culture of an ethnic community or not, a conceptual problem only partially handled by Milton Gordon's term, ethclass.
> Though it is true that there is a correlation between a rise in in-

From *The Urban Villages* (New York: The Free Press, 1962), pp. 244–49, 252–56, 267. Reprinted by permission of the publisher.

come and a change in life-style toward the middle class model, it
would be a mistake to assume that all lower- and working-class
ethnic cultural features are class-derived. If this were so then all
lower-class people would operate according to the same interactional
patterns and institutional systems. Casual observation shows this to
be far from the truth, and any discussion among a Euro-American
lower class group about Afro-Americans would give voice to
numerous differences.

   Yet there are some important cultural features in the urban environment that can be noted across ethnic lines. Herbert Gans, in
this excerpt from his classic study in ethnic behaviors The Urban
Villagers, provides a useful inventory of some of these shared
features with useful references to class attitudes toward schools and
education.

   Perhaps the most important—or at least the most visible—difference
between the classes is one of family structure. *The working-class subculture*
is distinguished by the dominant role of the family circle, and considers
everything outside it as either a means to its maintenance or to its de-
struction. But while the outside world is to be used for the benefit of this
circle, it is faced with detachment and even hostility in most other respects.
Whenever feasible, then, work is sought within establishments connected
to the family circle. When this is not possible—and it rarely is—work is
primarily a means of obtaining income to maintain life amidst a considerable degree of poverty, and thereafter, a means of maximizing the pleasures
of life within the family circle. The work itself may be skilled or unskilled;
it can take place in the factory or in the office—the type of collar is not
important. What does matter is that identification with work, work success,
and job advancement—while not absolutely rejected—are of secondary
priority to the life that goes on within the family circle. The purpose of
education is to learn techniques necessary to obtain the most lucrative type
of work. Thus the central theme of American, and all Western, education—
that the student is an individual who should use his schooling to detach
himself from ascribed relationships like the family circle in order to maximize his personal development and achievement in work, play, and other
spheres of life—is ignored or openly rejected.

   The specific characteristics of the family circle may differ widely—from
the collateral peer group form of the West Enders [the inhabitants of the
neighborhood under study], to the hierarchical type of the Irish, or to the
classic three-generation extended family. Friends may also be included in
the circle, as in the West Enders' peer group society. What matters most—
and distinguishes this subculture from others—is that there be a family
circle which is wider than the nuclear family, and that all of the oppor-

tunities, temptations, and pressures of the larger society be evaluated in terms of how they affect the ongoing way of life that has been built around this circle.

The *lower-class subculture* is distinguished by the female-based family and the marginal male. Although a family circle may also exist, it includes only female relatives. The male, whether husband or lover, is physically present only part of the time, and is recognized neither as a stable nor dominant member of the household. He is a sexual partner, and he is asked to provide economic support. But he participates only minimally in the exchange of affection and emotional support, and has little to do with the rearing of children. Should he serve as a model for the male children, he does so largely in a negative sense. That is, the women use him as an example of what a man should not be.

The female-based family must be distinguished, however, from one in which the woman is dominant, for example, the English working-class family. Although this family may indeed revolve around the "Mum," she does not reject the husband. Not only is he a member of the family, but he is also a participant—and a positive model—in child-rearing.

In the lower class, the segregation of the sexes—only partial in the working class—is complete. The woman tries to develop a stable routine in the midst of poverty and deprivation; the action-seeking man upsets it. In order to have any male relationships, however, the woman must participate to some extent in his episodic life style. On rare occasions, she may even pursue it herself. Even then, however, she will try to encourage her children to seek a routine way of life. Thus the woman is much closer to working-class culture, at least in her aspirations, although she is not often successful in achieving them.

For lower-class men, life is almost totally unpredictable. If they have sought stability at all, it has slipped from their grasp so quickly, often, and consistently that they no longer pursue it. From childhood on, their only real gratifications come from action-seeking, but even these are few and short-lived. Relationships with women are of brief duration, and some men remain single all their lives. Work, like all other relationships with the outside world, is transitory. Indeed, there can be no identification with work at all. Usually, the lower-class individual gravitates from one job to another, with little hope or interest of keeping a job for any length of time. His hostility to the outside world therefore is quite intense, and its attempts to interfere with the episodic quality of his life are fought. Education is rejected by the male, for all of its aims are diametrically opposed to action-seeking.

The *middle-class subculture* is built around the nuclear family and its desire to make its way in the larger society. Although the family circle may exist, it plays only a secondary role in middle-class life. Contact with close relatives is maintained, but even they participate in a subordinate role.

Individuals derive most of their social and emotional gratifications from the nuclear family itself. One of the most important of these is child-rearing. Consequently, the middle-class family is much more child-centered than the working-class one and spends more of its spare time together. Outside social life takes place with friends who share similar interests. The nuclear family depends on its friends—as well as on some caretaking institutions—for help and support. Relatives may also help, especially in emergencies.

The middle class does not make the distinction between the family and the outside world. In fact, it does not even see an outside world, but only a larger society, which it believes to support its aims, and in which the family participates. The nuclear family makes its way in the larger society mainly through the career of its breadwinner. Thus work is not merely a job that maximizes income, but a series of related jobs or job advances which provide the breadwinner with higher income, greater responsibility, and, if possible, greater job satisfaction. In turn his career enhances the way of life of the rest of the family, through increases in status and in the standard of living.

Education is viewed, and used, as an important method for achieving these goals. The purpose of education is to provide the skills needed for the man's career and for the woman's role as a mother. In and out of school, it is also used to develop the skills necessary to the maintenance and increase of status, the proper use of leisure time, and the occasional participation in community activities. Thus, much of the central theme of education is accepted. But the idea that education is an end in itself, and should be used to maximize individual development of the person, receives only lip service.

The subculture I have described here is a basic middle-class one; a more detailed analysis would distinguish between what is currently called the middle-middle class and the lower-middle class. The upper-middle class subculture is also a variant of the basic middle-class culture. There are at least two such subcultures, the managerial and the professional, [the latter of which] is of primary interest here.

The *professional upper-middle-class culture* is also organized around the nuclear family, but places greater emphasis on the independent functioning of its individual members. Whereas the middle-class family is a companionship unit in which individuals exist most intensely in their relationships with each other, the upper-middle-class family is a companionship unit in which individuals seeking to maximize their own development as persons come together on the basis of common interests. For this subculture, life is, to a considerable extent, a striving for individual development and self-expression, and these strivings pervade many of its relationships with the larger society.

Therefore, work is not simply a means for achieving the well-being of the nuclear family, but also an opportunity for individual achievement and social service. Although the career, income, status, and job responsibility are important, job satisfaction is even more important, although it is not always found. Indeed, professional work satisfaction is a focal concern not only for the breadwinner, but often for the woman as well. If she is not interested in a profession, she develops an alternative but equally intense interest in motherhood, or in community activity. Child-rearing, moreover, gives the woman an opportunity not only to maximize her own individual achievements as a mother, but to develop in her children the same striving for self-development. As a result, the professional upper-middle-class family is not child-centered, but adult-directed. As education is the primary tool for a life of individual achievement, the professional upper-middle-class person not only goes to school longer than anyone else in society, but he also accepts its central theme more fully than do the rest of the middle class.

This concern with individual achievement and education further enables and encourages the members of this subculture to be deliberate and self-conscious about their choices. They are a little more understanding of the actions of others than the members of less educated strata. Their ability to participate in the larger society, plus their high social and economic status, also gives them somewhat greater control over their fate than other people, and makes the environment more predictable. This in turn facilitates the practice of self-consciousness, empathy, and abstraction or generalization.

The possession of these skills distinguishes the upper-middle class from the rest of the middle class, and even more so from the working and lower class. For the latter not only live in a less predictable environment, but they are also detached from the outside world, which increases their feeling that it, and, indeed, all of life, is unpredictable. In turn this feeling encourages a pervasive fatalism that pre-empts the optimism or pessimism of which the other classes are capable. The fatalism of the working and lower classes, as well as their lack of of education and interest in personal development and object goals, minimizes introspection, self-consciousness, and empathy for the behavior of others. . . .

The movement from one class to another is a cultural change that requires not only access to the prerequisite opportunities, but the willingness and ability to accept them. This is especially true of the move from working class to middle class, and may be illustrated by a description of the mobility process among the West Enders.

So far, West Enders have had relatively few of the opportunities necessary for entry into the middle-class subculture, and even those few are of recent vintage. On the other hand they have not demanded access to these opportunities. For example, a number of college scholarships offered by one of the area settlement houses had frequently gone begging ever since the Jewish exodus from the West End . . . the West Enders are not yet eager to move into the middle class. While they now have many of the comforts and artifacts that once only the middle class could buy, they have not thereby become middle class. Their culture is still that of the working class.

This applies not only to the routine-seekers, but even to some of the action-seekers as well. Aside from the never married, only the married action-seekers who have effectively detached themselves from their families, and made them female-based, can be considered lower class. The remaining action-seekers have at least one foot in the working-class culture, and participate sufficiently in the family to maintain a viable role. Thus their children are likely to grow up without the characteristics found in children from female-based families.

One of the distinguishing marks of a working-class group is its detachment from the larger society. This is found also among some ethnic groups, but it is not an ethnic phenomenon per se. While it is true, for example, that the West Enders' detachment from the larger society has been supported by ethnic differences between themselves and the outside world, it is also true that the detachment has not been caused by these differences. Indeed, the review of other working-class studies has indicated that this detachment from the outside world can be found among all working-class populations even when they are not ethnic minorities. Conversely, the high degree of Jewish mobility would suggest that ethnic status is no significant hindrance in entering either the larger society or the middle class.

Because working-class culture is different from middle-class culture, the move from one to the other is a difficult one, requiring behavior and attitude changes of considerable social and emotional magnitude. The most important changes are cutting the attachment to the family circle and the peer group society, and a concurrent shift from person- to object-orientation.

Thus, in order for a West Ender to begin the move into the middle class, he must first break—or have broken for him—his dependence on family and peers. His striving must shift moreover from peer group goals toward object goals, such as a career, prestige, wealth, or individual development. And these goals must be pursued alone, or with people of like mind.

Since these goals conflict with family and peer group relationships, the peer group society naturally discourages such striving. The opposition to mobility which I described in the previous chapter is specifically directed against object-orientation. Indeed, what West Enders dislike most about the outside world and the middle-class culture is their stress on object-goals that interfere with person-oriented relationships. This is clearly illustrated by the West Enders' belief that suburbanites are lonely people and that the middle-class career requires inhuman exploitation of others. It is also exemplified by their complaints that adults today are striving for individual goals, and children for things, rather than for the emotional satisfactions of a cohesive family circle, as in the past. . . . the peer group society's opposition to mobility is such that movement into the middle class must therefore be an individual venture.

This venture, a process which seems to begin in childhood or adolescence, requires that the young person be isolated from his family and peer group by a combination of pressures which push him out of these groups, and incentives which pull him into the outside world. Many events can produce the requisite isolation, but among the most frequent are the possession of special talents, personal crises, and late arrival into the peer group.

Every population—even a low-income one—produces a number of young people with special gifts or talents, be these intellectual or artistic. Among the West Enders, however, young people with such talents are generally ostracized by their peers. And, unless their gifts are athletic or forensic and are useful to the group, these young people are often forced to choose between their talents and their peers. Parents are more tolerant of their talents, but since they are detached from the children's activities, they can offer little overt support. In fact, they may even discourage the child should his talent be identified with the opposite sex. On the other hand, representatives from the outside world, such as teachers and settlement house workers, do offer incentives. They encourage the young person to develop his talent, and provide opportunities for proper training. At the same time, these caretakers also make special efforts to draw gifted West Enders out of the peer group society. This in turn helps to isolate the youngster even further from his peers.

When the individual's talents are moderate, and his motivation to develop them weak, he is likely to suppress them in order to stay with the group. Should he be especially talented and strongly motivated, however, the peer group ostracism and the incentives from outside world representatives can combine and take him out of the peer group society, and into the training grounds of the middle class. Even so, he is likely to be ambivalent about this break. One West End youngster, for example, who wanted to be a singer of semiclassical music practiced on the sly, because his friends made fun of him. Another West Ender, an extremely creative adult, has never reconciled the conflict between his desire to use his talents and his wish to be a part of a peer group that shows little interest in and even some hostility toward them. Still ambivalent as to these gifts, he envies creative people who are encouraged by their families and friends. Needless to say, in a low-income group, hurdles are also placed in the way of the talented person by economic considerations and the immense social distance between the low-income person and the upper-middle- and upper-class world of the arts.

A second impetus to mobility seems to come from crises or traumatic experiences that are accompanied by unexpected isolation from the peer group society. This hypothesis is based on the experiences of two West

Enders. One, a young man who had contracted tuberculosis in adolescence, developed a new set of goals while spending a year in a hospital bed. After recovery, he went to college and, later, into a profession. Another young man, who comes from a respected West End family, had been failing in school and participating in delinquent acts. Finally, when his life had reached an absolute nadir, he spent an entire night sitting up with his father, reviewing his past and his prospects for the future. He explained that as a result of these experiences, he developed a new set of goals. Subsequently, he too entered the professions. Such instances as these suggest that, for some, the move into middle-class culture requires a personal crisis, which is followed by a transformation that bears some resemblance to a religious conversion.

A third factor that encourages mobility is delayed entrance into the peer group society, which thus isolates the individual from the group during his formative years. This possibility was suggested by the fact that two of the most mobile individuals whom I encountered in the West End had both been born in Italy and had come to America just before their teens. Only marginally attached to peer groups as adolescents, both have departed considerably, although not entirely, from the ways of the peer group society in adulthood.

Another factor that acts on the individual is parental or familial encouragement to become upwardly mobile, but . . . this is largely absent among the West Enders, although it seems to be important among Jews.

These factors function as pressures on the individual. In addition, almost all young West Enders are exposed to some pulls from the outside world—albeit in varying degrees of intensity—which offer them incentives for leaving the group. These come from the mass media, as well as from the schools and the other caretakers. But as only a few individuals respond to them, it must be assumed that the incentives themselves are not sufficient. Isolating pressures which push the individual out of the group are also necessary, and seemingly even more important. . . .

My limited observations suggest that, on the whole, the advantages of working-class subculture do outweigh the disadvantages. The latter are real, and ought to be removed, but they are not overwhelming. Thus, given our present knowledge, there is no justification for planning and caretaking programs which try to do away with the working-class subculture. John Seeley has suggested why it should not be done away with in his description of a Polish working-class group with whom he once lived:

> . . . no society I have lived in before or since seemed to me to present so many of its members . . . so many possibilities and actualities of fulfillment of a number at least of basic human demands: for an outlet for aggressiveness, for adventure, for a sense of effectiveness, for deep feelings of belonging without undue sacrifice of uniqueness or identity, for sex satisfaction, for strong if not fierce loyalties, for a sense of independence from the pervasive omnicompetent, omni-

scient authority-in-general which at that time still overwhelmed to a greater degree the middle-class child. . . . These things had their prices, of course—not all values can be simultaneously maximized. But few of the inhabitants whom I reciprocally took "slumming" into middle-class life understood it or, where they did, were at all envious of it. And, be it asserted, this was not a matter of "ignorance" or incapacity to "appreciate finer things," but an inability to see one moderately coherent and sense-making satisfaction-system which they didn't know as preferable to the quite coherent and sense-making satisfaction-system they did know.

THE INVISIBLE MINORITY

Though this article sketches in a few features of Mexican-American culture and history, its primary focus is on strategies for engineering changes in schooling for Chicanos. The emphasis upon the degrading effects of imposed compensatory teaching from an Anglo-American point of view parallel the experiences of other ethnic minorities.

While a majority of the Spanish-speaking people in the Southwest were born in this country and are citizens of the United States, they tend to be regarded both by themselves and others as Mexicans. The term Mexican-American would be more nearly accurate. More important than technicalities, however, is how they feel . . . how they regard themselves.

Me

To begin with, I am a Mexican. That sentence has a scent of bitterness as it is written. I feel that if it weren't for my nationality I would accomplish more. My being a Mexican has brought about my lack of initiative. No matter what I attempt to do, my dark skin always makes me feel that I will fail.

Another thing that "gripes" me is that I am such a coward. I absolutely will not fight for something even if I know I'm right. I do not have the vocabulary that it would take to express myself strongly enough.

Many people, including most of my teachers, have tried to tell me I'm a leader. Well, I know better! Just because I may get better grades than most of my fellow

Report of the NEA-Tucson Survey on the Teaching of Spanish to the Spanish Speaking; Department of Rural Education, National Education Association, Washington, D.C., 1966. Reprinted by permission of National Education Association.

Mexicans doesn't mean a thing. I could no more get an original idea in my head than be President of the United States. I don't know how to think for myself.

I want to go to college, sure, but what do I want to be? Even worse, where do I want to go? These questions are only a few that trouble me. I'd like to prove to my parents that I can do something. Just because I don't have the gumption to go out and get a job doesn't mean that I can't become something they'll be proud of. But if I find that I can't bring myself to go to college, I'll get married and they'll still get rid of me.

After reading this, you'll probably be surprised. This is the way I feel about myself, and nobody can change me. Believe me, many have tried and failed. If God wants me to reach all my goals, I will. No parents, teachers, or priest will change the course that my life is to follow. Don't try.

This was a paper turned in by a 13-year-old girl for an English assignment in the eighth grade of a school in one of the Southwestern states. The assignment was to write about "Me." The melancholy tone of the essay would suggest that the youngster was a "loner"—obscure, unattractive, not very popular. But no. She was attractive, articulate, an honor student, member of the band, outstanding in girls' athletics, popular among her fellow students, admired by her teachers. "She never *seemed* to be a child with a problem," remarked one of the teachers, in some puzzlement, after reading "Me."

The problem can be stated plainly and simply: The young girl who wrote that essay was Mexican-American. If she, with all her advantages, felt that her lot inevitably would be failure, how must thousands of other Mexican-American children—many of them less endowed physically and intellectually—view their own prospects?

357 Years of History

To understand the problem fully, we must understand how it came about. The first white people to migrate into what is now the American Southwest were Spanish-speaking. They came by way of Mexico during the period of Spain's colonial expansion and settled portions of the Southwest even before the founding of the Plymouth Colony. Plymouth was established in 1620, but the first Spaniards settled at Santa Fe, New Mexico, a full 11 years before that—in 1609. By 1680 there were some 2,500 Spanish-speaking settlers in what we now call New Mexico. By 1790 there were an estimated 23,000 Spanish-speaking people in the five Southwestern states covered by this study area. Indeed, the white population of the Southwest—what there was of it—was practically all Spanish. New Mexico had the largest concentration.

But soon after the 13 colonies gained their independence from England, the migration of English-speaking Americans into the Southwest began. Mexico, its own independence newly-won from Spain, encouraged such migration. This vast Southwestern area, stretching from the western border of Louisiana to the Pacific, belonged to Mexico. She was anxious to see it settled and developed, and few Mexican colonists were moving there. So the government of Mexico granted large blocks of land to contractors who would bring in colonists. The response was large and prompt. By 1835 there were 25,000 to 35,000 American farmers, planters and traders in Texas, and more were on the way.

The deluge dismayed Mexico, and she tried to check it. Land grants were cancelled. The Texans became irked, and in 1836 they revolted against Mexican over-lordship and won their independence. Shortly afterward Texas was admitted to the Union. A dispute broke out between the U.S. and Mexico over the southwestern boundary of Texas. The result was the Mexican War and the loss by Mexico of nearly all that remained of her Northernmost empire. To the U.S. were ceded much of New Mexico, most of Arizona, the future states of California, Nevada and Utah, and parts of Colorado and Wyoming. Five years later the Gadsden Purchase added a strip of land between the Gila River and the present southern boundary of Arizona and New Mexico, completing the American acquisition of what is now the Southwest.

Alien and Alienated

Thus, by one of history's ironies, the majority became a minority. Spanish-speaking people who had been the first whites to settle the Southwest became, if not an alien group, an alienated group. They were Americans, yes, but with a language and culture different from the language and culture of the region in which they found themselves. On both sides feelings had been exacerbated by the way.

Nationalistic passions have long since cooled. Mexico and the United States live side by side in peace. But in the Southwest a cultural and linguistic gulf still exists between Mexican-Americans—the "invisible minority," as they have been called—and Anglo-Americans. "Unlike the immigrant from Europe," says John M. Sharp, Professor of Modern Languages at Texas Western College, El Paso, "(the Mexican-American) is by no means willing to abandon his ancient cultural and linguistic heritage, in which he takes—however inarticulately—traditional pride, to accept the cultural pattern common to native speakers of English in our nation. His position may, perhaps, be compared to that of the Greeks in Sicily, who, though citizens of a Latin-speaking area, have maintained their language and mores for some 23 centuries." Thus the strong assimilationist impulses of other immigrant groups—Jewish, Irish, Italian, etc.—are not so conspicuous among the Mexican-Americans. Nor are all Mexican-Americans possessed of the strong materialistic drive—the "individual success psychology," as one authority has put it—of so many Anglo-Americans.

The Legacy of Poverty

There is another factor which makes the gulf difficult to bridge—which to a considerable extent keeps the Mexican-American an "outsider" in his own land. It is the fact that so many immigrants from Mexico were well down on the economic scale when they came to this country. They were, in the main, unskilled and semi-skilled laborers, dissatisfied with conditions in Mexico, hoping that in the North they would be able to improve their lot. And, as is so often the case, first-generation immigrants tended to bequeath their poverty to the generations that come after them.

Thus we find poverty far more prevalent among Mexican-Americans than among Anglo-Americans. In all five Southwestern states, the average income of white people with Spanish surnames is well below that of the general population, as the following table illustrates:

TABLE I • *Frequency of Low and High Family Incomes in the Southwest (Census of 1960)*

	Families with Incomes under $1000		Families with Incomes under $3000		Families with Incomes of $10,000 or more	
	General Population	White-Spanish Surname Population	General Population	White-Spanish Surname Population	General Population	White-Spanish Surname Population
Arizona	5.9%	7.2%	21.3%	30.8%	14.4%	4.6%
California	3.3	4.5	14.1	19.1	21.8	10.8
Colorado	3.5	6.4	18.3	35.0	14.6	4.8
New Mexico	6.9	11.3	24.4	41.5	14.3	4.5
Texas	7.6	13.6	32.5	51.6	11.8	2.7
Southwest	4.9	8.8	21.0	34.8	17.6	6.6

Low Achievers . . . Dropouts

An almost inevitable concomitant of poverty is low educational achievement. Herschel T. Manuel, in his definitive book, *Spanish-Speaking Children of the Southwest: Their Education and the Public Welfare* (University of Texas Press, Austin, Texas), reports that one-sixth of the school-age population of the five Southwestern states is Spanish-speaking. Yet, he notes, the proportion of school dropouts among the Spanish-speaking is far higher than one-sixth. California made a study of the educational disparity between the Mexican-American and his fellow citizens as of 1960. It found that the level of education reached by that part of the population bearing Spanish surnames was well below the level of the total population and even below that of the non-white population. More than half of the males and nearly half of the females 14 years old and over had not gone beyond the eighth grade. By contrast, only 27.9 percent of the males and 25 percent of the females over 14 in the total population had not gone beyond the eighth grade. A little over 72 percent of the males in the total population and 75 percent of the females had completed one or more years of high school, but only 48.5 percent of the males and 52 percent of the females of Spanish surnames had done so. In the total population, 23.4 percent of the males and 19.4 percent of the females had completed one or more years of college. But no more than 8.8 percent of the Spanish-surnamed males and 6.2 percent of the females had reached that educational eminence.

Why does the Mexican-American youngster drop out of school in such large numbers? For an answer, we need to look at his performance while he is still in school. Again California supplies us with some vital clues. An analysis of achievement tests was made in the Lindsay Unified School District of Lindsay, California, a city of 5,500 located about midway between Fresno and Bakersfield. It is an agricultural community with a high proportion of Mexican-Americans. The analysis showed that in all the educational fundamentals—reading, arithmetic and language—Mexican-American children lagged far behind the Anglo-Americans, as measured by the California Achievement Tests. In reading, 63.9 percent of the Mexican-American children were below grade level compared to 27.3 percent of the Anglo-Americans. In arithmetic, 38.7 percent of the Mexican-Americans were below grade level, compared to 20.8 percent of the Anglo-Americans. In language, the comparative percentages were 55.5 and 30.6 Total battery: 53.4 percent of the Mexican-Americans below grade level; 28.1 percent of the others.

Said the Lindsay report: ". . . These children (Mexican-Americans) start school with a decided handicap, fall behind their classmates in the first grade, and each passing year finds them farther behind. They are conditioned to failure in the early years of their schooling and each passing year only serves to reinforce their feelings of failure and frustration. Is it any wonder that as soon as they are 16 or can pass for 16, they begin dropping out of school?"

That question having been asked, we need then to ask another and more significant question: Is there something inherent in our system of public schooling that impedes the education of the Mexican-American child —that, indeed, drives him to drop out? And the answer, unhappily, must be yes. ". . . The greatest barrier to the Mexican-American child's scholastic achievement . . . is that the schools, reflecting the dominant view of the dominant culture, want that child to grow up as another Anglo. This he cannot do except by denying himself and his family and his forebears." Dr. Manuel puts it another way: "Ironically the child who enters school with a language deficiency and the cultural deprivation of long-continued poverty is often made unbearably aware of his disadvantages. School is supposed to help him solve these problems; instead it convinces him that they are beyond solution."

The Spanish-Speaking Home

Let us see what happens to the average Mexican-American child when he starts school. He comes to school speaking Spanish. He knows some English but has used it infrequently. The language of his home, the language of his childhood, his first years, is Spanish. His environment, his experiences, his very personality have been shaped by it.

To understand how totally Spanish the background of such a child may be, consider the results of a study made in 1965 in San Antonio, Texas, and reported to the El Paso conference of foreign language teachers. Six hundred Mexican-American adults were interviewed in San Antonio, and it was found that 71 percent of husbands and wives spoke only Spanish to each other. Among the grandparents, 94 percent spoke only Spanish to their children and 89 percent spoke only Spanish to their grandchildren.

Understandably, therefore, the child from this Spanish-saturated environment, once embarked on his school career, finds himself in a strange and even threatening situation. The language of instruction is English. Yet English, as John M. Sharp expressed it at the El Paso conference, may be "no less a foreign language to him that it would be to a child from Argentina or Colombia. He suddenly finds himself not only with the pressing need to master a (to him) alien tongue, but, also at the same time, to make immediate use of it in order to function as a pupil. His parents, to whom he has always looked for protection and aid, can be of no help at all to him in his perplexity. Moreover, as a result of cultural and economic differences between the English-speaking and Spanish-speaking segments of his community, many of the objects, social relationships and cultural attitudes presented to him in his lessons, though perfectly familiar to an Anglo youngster, lie without the Latin American's home experience. Accordingly, the problem of learning English is, for him, enormously increased by his unfamiliarity with what objects and situations the no less unfamiliar words and phrases stand for."

Barriers and Bastions

Even in schools with an almost totally Spanish-American enrollment —schools which are for all practical purposes *de facto* segregated—textbooks and curricula used are often the same as in schools with a large Anglo-American majority. As Professor Sharp tells us: "The three R's are taught in English from the first grade up, and *no classes specifically with*

English as a foreign language are offered. Operating under such unrealistic conditions (which appear to have been devised by people who seemed to believe that if they paid no attention to the problem it would go away), conscientious teachers and administrators have done the best they could for their students. Subject matter is watered down and used as a means to teach English. During the two or three years of primary school while the pupil is acquiring a minimal knowledge of English, he falls seriously behind his English-speaking contemporaries in other phases of the curriculum. This loss in subject-knowledge is seldom made up by the time he enters high school, where he finds himself unable to compete scholastically with his Anglo-American schoolmates."

The Mexican-American child encounters not only linguistic barriers but psychological barriers. One of the working committee reports developed at the El Paso conference described them in these words: ". . . A sudden immersion in English at six years of age, especially in an environment which lacks the plasticity and warmth of human relationships found in the home, occurring at the same time that new demands of work and discipline are made, may create psychological barriers almost instantaneously which will not disappear in a lifetime. The teacher may sense the presence of these barriers and may react by putting up barriers of his own, unconsciously attempting to compensate thereby for his sense of inadequacy in dealing with the child. The result may be that the Spanish language becomes a refuge into which the child retreats at every opportunity, and the Spanish-speaking community a bastion of defense against the outside world."

The Laws of the Anglos

In most states, the schools are actually mandated by law to make English the language of instruction. An appropriate comment on this type of law was forthcoming recently from Charles Olstad, Assistant Professor of Romance Languages at the University of Arizona: "I had always thought such a law archaic, a carry-over from early days of benighted ethnocentrism, a distorted form of super-patriotism which saw anything non-English as a threat to the nation." In some schools the speaking of Spanish is forbidden both in classrooms and on the playground, except, of course, in classes where Spanish is taught. Not infrequently students have been punished for lapsing into Spanish. This has even extended to corporal punishment. A member of our Survey team tells of one school at which such punishment was dealt out to children who lapsed into Spanish despite the fact that 99 percent of the school's enrollment was Mexican-American! The obvious theory is that a child will learn English if he is required to speak English and nothing but English, at least during those hours of the day when he is in school. "If you want to be American, speak American," he is admonished over and over again.

Fitting the Stereotype

Nor is it only a different language that the newly-arrived Mexican-American child encounters. He also encounters a strange and different set of cultural patterns, an accelerated tempo of living and, more often than not, teachers who, though sympathetic and sincere, have little understanding of the Spanish-speaking people, their customs, beliefs and sensitivities. He is given an intelligence test in which language and cultural and socio-economic background are depressing factors. He may have fully as much intellectual potential as his Anglo-American classmates, but he shows up on the test as a "low achiever." He tends thus to become stereotyped in the eyes of the adults whose lives impinge on his. All of them—teachers, administrators, even parents—expect little of him, and he usually measures up (or down) to their expectations.

If he knows little or no English, he may be placed in a special class with other non-English-speaking children for a year and then "promoted" to the first grade the following year. But that means he must go through school a year behind other children of his age, and this embarrasses him.

Even if he speaks both English and Spanish, he may be only nominally bilingual—not truly so. He may have, as he often does, a low level of literacy in both languages. He watches television at home, as do his Anglo-American schoolmates. He listens to the radio. Soon he is speaking a language which is neither Spanish nor English but a mixture of the two—a kind of linguistic hybrid. He doesn't speak English correctly and he doesn't speak Spanish correctly.

There is something sadly paradoxical about the schools' well-meaning effort to make the Mexican-American child "talk American"—to eradicate his Spanish. For they are at the same time working strenuously to teach Spanish to the Anglo-American student, acclaiming the advantages of being able to communicate fluently in a language other than one's own. The National Defense Education Act is providing funds to schools to strengthen the teaching of modern foreign languages as well as mathematics, science, and other subjects. And so, while they strive to make the monolingual student bilingual, they are making—or trying to make the bilingual student monolingual.

Compulsion Breeds Withdrawal

The prohibition against speaking Spanish leads to some curious situations. For one thing, the school cannot enforce it. Or, rather it cannot accomplish what the rule is intended to accomplish, which is the universal speaking of English. "Obviously," says James Burton, who teaches English and speech to Mexican-American students at Jefferson High School in El Paso, Texas, "it is impossible to make a person speak a language. Any teacher in control of his classroom can prevent his students from speaking Spanish, but the result is likely to be a thundering silence; it is certainly no guarantee that fluent, idiomatic English will gush forth like the water from the biblical rock. Arrogance or even thoughtlessness in enforcing such a regulation is easily self-defeating. If the student is somehow left with the feeling that the person doing the enforcing is belittling him in an alien language for his normal use of his own language, bitter resentment is sure to ensue. Punitive measures in this case are only too likely to prove ineffectual under most circumstances. After all, few students speak Spanish as a deliberate act of defiance."

John M. Sharp of Texas Western remarks, too, on the absurdity of a dictum that says a teacher facing a class of Spanish-speaking youngsters may never use an occasional word of Spanish to clarify a point. Yet it may be perfectly clear, he observes, "that the point being made is not 'getting across' in English." And he adds, "It should be noted here, to the credit of teachers, that conscientious instructors frequently violate this prohibition."

The Damaged Self-Image

The harm done the Mexican-American child linguistically is paralleled—perhaps even exceeded—by the harm done to him as a person. In telling him that he must not speak his native language, we are saying to him by implication that Spanish and the culture which it represents are of no worth. Therefore (it follows) the people who speak Spanish are of no worth. Therefore (it follows again) this particular child is of no worth. It should come as no surprise to us, then, that he develops a negative self-concept—an inferiority complex. If he is no good, how can he succeed? And if he can't succeed, why try? Suddenly the full import of the essay about "Me"—the poignant outcry of the Mexican-American girl who "never *seemed* to be a child with a problem"—becomes crystal clear.

"Somewhere along the way," says Marcos de León, School-Community Coordinator of the Los Angeles Public Schools and member of the board of the Latin-American Civic Association and the board of the Council for Mexican Affairs of Los Angeles, "the Mexican-American must make a stand and recognize the fact that if there is to be progress against those barriers which prevent and obstruct a more functional citizenship, he must above all things retrieve his dignity and worth as a person with a specific ethnic heritage, possessing a positive contribution to civilization. No man can find a true expression for living, or much less think right, who is ashamed of himself or his people."

At a Mexican-American seminar held in Phoenix in 1963, Daniel Schreiber, then Director of the NEA's Project Dropout, spoke of the need of young people to "achieve confident self-identity." "The youngster," he said, "whose school experience begins and ends in failure—and those of minority children too often do—having discovered that he is good *at* nothing, stands a strong chance of becoming good *for* nothing. And far too many young lives, with all the potentials and real talents and capabilities they embody, are being wasted and crushed. The challenge is to redeem them, through inventiveness and energy and dedication."

This is the challenge that the public schools face in the education of tens of thousands of Mexican-American children in the five Southwestern states. It is a challenge which, with an appropriate approach and sound techniques, can be fully and triumphantly met. We believe these techniques are at hand.

WHAT IS BEING DONE: SOME SPECIFICS

Encouraging and exciting programs directed specifically to a more appropriate educational accommodation of children in bicultural communities have been developed in some places. The following reports are illustrative of the wide variety of innovative practice the NEA-Tucson Survey Committee observed in the schools selected for visitation.

Laredo, Texas

Laredo is a Texas border community of some 65,000 population, located on the Rio Grande, just opposite its Mexican counterpart, Nuevo Laredo. Its economic sustenance derives in good part from the pursuits of agriculture and a busy Air Force base.

Two school districts serve the metropolitan area of Laredo. The larger of the two in population is the Laredo Independent School District, serving the city of Laredo proper. Far larger in area is the United Consolidated Independent School District. It is larger, in fact, than Rhode Island, taking in no less than 2440 square miles and entirely surrounding the Laredo Independent School District on three sides, with the Rio Grande constituting the fourth side. Located within the far-flung boundaries of the United Consolidated Independent School District are the suburban homes of some of Laredo's Air Force families and ranches and farms where many Mexican-American families live.

The district operates three elementary schools and a unique high school, much of which has been built underground. This school was built underground to provide fallout protection in case of a nuclear attack on Laredo Air Force Base, to shut out the disrupting screams of jet planes, and for economy's sake. An underground school uses less land, is more economical to air condition, requires no shades or blinds or window cleaning and offers no tempting midnight target for vandals with air rifles.

The educational program of United Consolidated Independent School District has one strong common denominator: bilingualism. Students, Anglo-American as well as Mexican-American, are encouraged to become truly bilingual—speaking, reading and writing fluently in both English and Spanish. English instruction and Spanish instruction go side by side.

One Year At a Time

Federal funds had not yet become available for the Laredo "biliteracy" program (as they were subsequently to become available under the Elementary-Secondary Education Act of 1965). The United Consolidated Independent School District had to finance the program itself. And so it started the first year with only the first grade. The next year it expanded to the second grade. It was bilingualism not merely for the Mexican-American child but for both Mexican-American and Anglo-American—for all children.

Eventually bilingualism will extend through all the grades, including high school. Yet even now the high school reflects the beneficial effects of the bilingual-bicultural revolution taking place. Picturesquely displayed at the high school's main entrance, on equal terms, are the proud symbols of the two neighbor nations—the American eagle and the Mexican eagle. They are vividly colored, stylized cutouts made by students and suspended from wire supports. Student art work is displayed all through the school, and there is stress throughout on the worthiness of each of the two cultures. An unmistakable *esprit de corps* prevails among the students. They walk proudly. They dress neatly—all of them.

Bilingualism: A Valid Objective

The Laredo program and other similar programs that we observed in our Survey—plus our own experiences and independent studies—have persuaded us beyond any doubt of the validity of bilingualism. Unhappily a large majority of Southwestern school districts have no bilingual programs. In a few instances, such programs exist but they are conducted inadequately. Most school districts have yet to discover that bilingualism can be a tool. It can be a tool—indeed the most important tool—with which to educate and motivate the Mexican-American child. It can be the means by which he achieves an affirmative self-concept—by which he comes to know who and what he is, takes pride in his heritage and culture, and develops a sense of his own worth. It can be an invaluable asset to him as an adult, economically, intellectually and socially.

One of the proofs of the validity of this approach, it seems to us, is the fact that children born and receiving their early schooling in Mexico or some other Spanish-speaking country generally do better in our schools than Mexican-Americans born here.

Recommendations for Desirable Programs

This, then, might be the time to make some recommendations that the NEA-Tucson Survey Committee believes to be basic in the education of native speakers of Spanish:

1. Instruction in pre-school and throughout the early grades should be in both Spanish and English.
2. English should be taught as a second language.
3. Contemporaneously there should be emphasis on the reading, writing and speaking of good Spanish, since Mexican-American children are so often illiterate in it.
4. A well-articulated program of instruction in the mother tongue should be continued from pre-school through the high school years.
5. All possible measures should be taken to help Mexican-American children gain a pride in their ancestral culture and language.
6. Schools should recruit Spanish-speaking teachers and teachers' aides. Beyond that, a special effort should be made to encourage promising young Mexican-Americans in high school and college to consider education as a career.
7. Schools, colleges and universities should conduct research in bilingual education, train or retrain bilingual teachers, create appropriate materials and, in general, establish a strong tradition of bilingual education. (For this suggestion we are indebted to Theodore Andersson of the University of Texas who incorporated it into a memorandum directed to the Office of Economic Opportunity in Washington, D.C.)
8. School districts desiring to develop good bilingual programs but lacking funds should look to the possibility of financing them under new federal programs and in some cases state compensatory education programs.
9. State laws which specify English as the language of instruction and thus, by implication at least, outlaw the speaking of Spanish except in Spanish classes should be repealed.

We might set forth a tenth recommendation—that no two programs of Spanish for the Spanish-speaking need to be, nor are they likely to be, alike. Each school district has its own special problems. Each requires its own unique solution.

BLACK CULTURE IN THE CLASSROOM

Geneva Gay and Roger D. Abrahams

There has been little problem in advancing the idea that Indians and Latin-Americans live by different cultures; Blacks have commonly been regarded as essentially mainstream Americans who have never quite learned the system. However, as a number of recent works have begun to demonstrate—most notably Ulf Hannerz's Soulside (New York: Columbia University Press, 1969)—there is a distinct cultural grouping among rural and ghettoized Blacks. Differences from Anglo-American middle-class culture run the gamut from different patterns of interaction, movement, socializing and growing up, to a distinct and highly flexible family and household system, religious perspective and practice, and so on. This article brings out some of this evidence, trying to dramatize the deleterious effects upon education arising because of the failure to recognize these cultural differences.

One of the most ludicrous features of the crisis in the classrooms is that certain unpleasant and embarrassing scenes are being played and replayed between teachers and students, scenes which could be avoided if teachers would recognize the systematic basis of Black culture. The stereotype of Blacks as immoral and impulsive continues to control our responses to Afro-American children, leading us to assume that culturally they are Americans first, Blacks second. These cultural differences are recognized in the use of another vocabulary, but these words are only one surface manifestation of some deep disparities in life-style and patterns of expectation.

So many of the lessons can be learned from the students themselves, from listening and recognizing when a confrontation has occurred because of a failure of understanding, of cultural synchronization. For instance, it is important to learn of the important distinction which is made by Blacks, at least in Texas, between *to speak* and *to talk*. *Speaking* in some contexts means engaging in a person-to-person discussion. *Talking*, on the other hand, generally means being involved in an exchange in a larger group, and often the one who is the center of the discussion is the only one judged to be *talking*. This distinction has led to recurrent conflicts which are only now being recognized as communications failures.

The conflict occurs in this manner: a student raises his hand and, when recognized, says "Teacher, can I speak?" This at the outset may threaten the teacher, who feels that the student is accusing her of not permitting discussion. Her reply, "Of course you can speak," then further disorients her when the student leaves the room to speak with someone in the hall, or worse, goes over to someone in the room to hold private conversation. The proper response in terms of the teacher's needs would have been, "Who would you like to speak with?"

The other recurring scenario is even more upsetting because it so often leads to in-class arguments between the teacher and one of her students. During a hubbub in class, the teacher picks out one of the students obviously involved and says, "Johnny, stop talking!" He replies, "But teacher, I wasn't talking." She, feeling that he is both lying and challenging her authority, replies, "Sit down. I saw you talking." He self-righteously replies, "But I wasn't talking." And so it goes. What Johnny was trying to convey was that in the Black system of language socialization, talking means something done by someone who is able to get the others in the group to listen and to respond. Johnny may have been making sounds with his voice, but in response to something someone else had initiated. This kind of communications failure is repeated daily in every classroom in every Black school across the nation.

Whether because of their African heritage, the experience of enslavement, or the social exclusion which they have endured since emancipation, the great majority of lower-class Blacks in the United States have developed and maintain a cultural system very different from that of middle-class mainstream Americans. The two groups operate within different systems of expectation and interaction. However, those who control our educational policy refuse to consider the systematic basis for these conflicts and, in response, to adjust the educational strategies for teaching Black children. There is, to be sure, a feeling that *something* is wrong, but in our ethnocentric way we assume that this can be remedied by providing Blacks with heroes from among their own ranks and by putting pictures of a few children with coffee-colored complexion in the textbooks. But this is nothing more than a tranquilizer for the vocal middle-class Negroes who have loudly called for change, but who have accepted the white model of what those changes ought to be. This is why it seems so crucial to us, at this point, to demonstrate that we have known for some time that there is a different cultural system operating among working class Blacks, and that it is simply a matter of getting beyond our stereotypic reactions to these differences, so that we may begin to utilize these cultural perceptions in developing meaningful strategies for educating Blacks.

It would be pleasant and reassuring to be able to say that these misjudgments and oversights exist because teachers operate according to the "loving" principle of education—that everyone is the same beneath the skin and that if we just go to these "disadvantaged" others with love, we will be answered in kind. But this would be overlooking the fact that Black children seldom enter a ghetto classroom with love, but only with fear and a sense of insufficiency for the task. Furthermore, there are few educators in such a milieu who don't readily admit that their students *are* different, and they probably view this difference with some misgiving. To give voice to this publicly, however, as the educator has long since learned, is to be branded a racist, so she very often remains quiet and leaves this difference unexamined. In the past, attributions of cultural difference have commonly been associated with racist arguments, for in this line of ethnocentric argument, *difference* equals *inferiority*—or to use the most recent euphemisms, "deficiency," "disadvantage," or "social pathology."

But there *are* cultural differences which are observable, and they are ones which bear directly on whether or not the Black child receives an education. These differences often appear as small units of behavior, and those embarrassments and frustrations arising between teacher and student which are not discerned are therefore not avoided. Their reenactment simply adds to the avalanche of indignities to which both Black children and middle-class teachers are subjected. But the teachers are in a better position to do something about these differences.

The great majority of culture conflict in the schools arises because of differences in the communications or interaction system. Lower-class Blacks in the United States do not communicate the same way other Americans do, and that troubles us a good deal. It especially irritates those of us who have operated most of our lives on the assimilationist ideal—the melting pot set of expectations—and this must include a great majority of teachers in this country. Repeatedly, we are frustrated in our expectations, and this frustration is more often than not leveled not at our assumptions (for they remain unexamined, for the most part) but at our students. We have many problems which we share with Martin Joos' legendary schoolmarm, Miss Fidditch, not least of which is our astonishment that in the face of the obvious educational, economic, social, and political advantages to be garnered by speaking Standard English, this strange way of Negro talking, Black English, has not only persisted but has intensified and proliferated.

But we haven't tried to discern why the stigmatized traits of speech have persisted, other than to assume some kind of physical, mental, or social pathology. If Blacks can't learn to speak and act correctly, we seem to argue, there must be something genetically or socially wrong with them. The racists among us say, "Well, what else can we expect from people like that?" The liberals, on the other hand, say, "It's not their fault, for we've created the degrading social conditions and the economic deprivation which makes them incapable of capitalizing upon the advantages of our way of life." Though the latter is obviously more well-intentioned, both define lower-class Blacks by using the norms of white middle-class behavior and therefore implicitly assume that our way of life is superior, more civilized. All of these approaches would deny, denigrate, or simply overlook the fact that the language and the culture of Blacks in America is just as successful and just as systematic as our own, but (like all other languages and cultures) must be understood in its own terms. In fact, if we judge a culture in terms of its ability to endure in the face of threatening environmental forces, we would have to own to the superiority of Black culture.

Any study of Black culture should begin with the recognition that its surface similarities to mainstream American ways are often the major obstacles to its acceptance as a distinct system of culture. It would be ridiculous to pretend that traits found among Blacks cannot also be found among both lower-class and middle-class whites. But the essential differences between Black culture and any other reside in the way in which each group goes about setting up orders and patterns of behavior and expectation— that is, each culture differs in regard to its configuration of traits and behaviors and values. Furthermore, even when traits are shared, the priorities or rank-ordering of values and norms will differ from group to group. What may be an exceptional (but acceptable) behavior in mainstream society may be the rule in, say, Black street life.[1] In presenting some of these ideas in the past, we have so often encountered the argument, "But isn't the culture you're describing characteristic of all lower-class peoples?" The answer, of course, is both yes and no—yes in the sense that some of the traits are observable in other types of lower-class enclavements, but no in that the total pattern of culture differs considerably.

If Black culture were predominantly made up of shared lower-class behaviors and attitudes, then this commonality would surely be felt by other lower-class groups. To the contrary, other such ethnic enclavements recognize and are threatened by existing cultural differences. For instance, in a recent study of a multi-ethnic Chicago area, *The Social Order of the Slum*, Gerald Suttles notes that one set of behaviors revolving around the concept of "jiving" serves to differentiate the ethnic groups in this neighborhood:

> For the most part, syntactic and phonological differences divide the white and Negro residents in the area. An interesting departure is the use of "jive." This special vocabulary . . . is restricted according to both age and ethnicity, but its usage overlaps the Negro-white distinction. Negro boys are most expert at this sort of discourse, but the English-speaking Mexican and Puerto Rican boys are also

[1] "Street culture" and "Black culture" are used interchangeably to refer to the life styles prevalent among Blacks in this country, especially those living in ghetto areas. Occasionally "Black" will be used to refer only to working- or lower-class Black, but generally this class marker will be given.

> somewhat conversant. . . . The Italians seldom use any of this vocabulary even to the point of understanding it. In the case of "jive," however, the Italians do not regard language differences so much as an attempt to talk behind someone's back, "show off" one's knowledge of urban ways, or display one's emancipation from the homely virtues of family, ethnic group, or neighbors. To the Italians, the use of "jive" often indicates a person who has scuttled the surest signs of human feeling and concern for the bonds that secure personal relations within the neighborhood. To the Negroes, and less so among the Mexicans and Puerto Ricans, a familiarity with this youthful jargon is only a sign of a willingness to expand the magic circle of trust beyond that of family, ethnic group, and territorial compatriots.[2]

Suttles indicates an awareness of the larger framework of language behavior here, and notes accurately that the problem is often not a matter of conflicting ideal values but lies rather in what he calls *notational devices*, self-conscious units of behavior "that each group relies upon to express and encode their adherence to [their] basic social rules."[3] Misunderstanding between members of different ethnic communities as often as not arises because of a misunderstanding of externals rather than from a disparity between the values which lie behind the behaviors. But these externals and the resultant failures in understanding are just as real and important to an understanding of the intergroup behavior within such a community.

> Quite possibly, there is . . . a correspondence between the meanings attached to the gesture of Italians and Negroes. Yet, so long as each group does not know how to translate this correspondence they go on misunderstanding each other, and incorrectly interpreting each other's behavior . . . Language differences between each ethnic group are often exacerbated by nonverbal acts which accompany or supplant speech. . . Negro boys . . . have a "cool" way of walking ("pimp's walk") in which the upper trunk and pelvis rock fore and aft while the head remains stable with the eyes looking straight ahead. The "pimp's walk" is quite slow, and the Negroes take it as a way of "strutting" or "showing off." The whites usually interpret it as a pointed lack of concern for those adjacent to the walker.[4]

Almost certainly in a multi-ethnic situation such as the one Suttles describes, the Blacks who walk in this manner are made to know how the others regard this style of propulsion. One can predict with a reasonable degree of certainty, however, that if this affects their behavior at all it will be toward stylizing the walk even more, for it is characteristic of this type

[2] Gerald Suttles, *The Social Order of the Slum* (Chicago, Ill.: University of Chicago Press, 1968), p. 65.

[3] *Ibid.*, p. 62.

[4] *Ibid.*, pp. 62, 65.

of young Black performer to seize upon any presentational device which produces a high affect and response and to capitalize upon it, even when the affect may be negative, as in this case.

It is crucial, then, in developing an educational system for lower-class Blacks, to understand that these alternative behaviors exist and may be subject to misunderstanding. On the other hand, we would be falling into the stereotyping trap if we expected this kind of behavior from every Black student. There are important variables within the Black social system which any teacher will have taken note of (though most will have found it difficult to capitalize upon in the classroom because of their inability to see the range and system of behavior and the functions which lie behind these communicative performances).

Unfortunately, an attempt to outline the most important features of Black culture is limited by the dearth of valid information given us by trained observers of life-styles. To be sure, we have an abundance of sociological analyses of Black communities, but most of these have been carried out by people living outside the target community—social scientists who venture into a community or neighborhood to administer their questionnaires and then beat it out of there before things get too hot for them.

The importance of close observational studies as far as developing educational strategies is concerned is demonstrated by Virginia Heyer Young in her recent study of the child-rearing practices of one small Black Georgia community, "Family and Childhood in a Southern Georgia Community" (in the *American Anthropologist*, vol. 72, 1970, pp. 269–288). This article presents to us the systematic basis for certain oft-misunderstood Black behaviors, and demands that we recognize that much of our attitude toward the Black family system is the product of our stereotypical way of thinking.

Young's study provides some valuable insights into the socialization processes of Black children which lead us to question the popular belief in a lack of close interpersonal relations between Black family members. Her work reveals two interesting phenomena. The first is the Black family's emphasis on personal involvement during the first few years of the child's life. The baby is handled almost constantly by the parents and other family members. He is seldom allowed to be alone, even when eating and sleeping. He is held and talked to while eating and he sleeps with the mother. His explorations of inanimate objects are highly restricted. Rather, the animate is substituted for the inanimate, and the child's experiences are arranged to focus on personal involvement with other people.

A second phenomenon is the early attention given to developing the child's manipulative abilities. The mother encourages and tempts the child to be assertive and to challenge her authority. She frequently comments to others, and compliments the child himself, on his strength, his aggressiveness, and his defiance of authority. The result is an active interplay between mother and child, regulation and permissiveness which takes place in a setting of interpersonal involvement. This close contact begins at birth and continues throughout the knee-baby stage of development.

Young shows further that at about the age of three, when the knee-baby stage ends, control of the child's socialization processes shifts from the mother to the peer group. There is "an almost complete cessation of the close relationship with the mother and father and a shift in orientation to the children's gang." [5]

One of the important features of this changeover is in the kind of speaking which now goes on. "Often speech becomes an indistinct children's patois in contrast to the clear enunciation used by the knee-baby with his parents. Children speak less to adults, and get along adequately with 'Yes'm' and 'No'm'." [6]

The child is still encouraged to develop his manipulative abilities in relation to personal involvement, but the motivating force now comes from older siblings. Even the play world still revolves largely around people instead of inanimate objects. He becomes the center of attention—the "toy" —of the older members of the children's gang, and they teach him how to adapt to different circumstances. By the time another child comes along to replace him, he is well-versed in the socialization techniques, so that he may become somewhat of a teacher himself.

The Young study, to be sure, is of only one Black community; but her findings complement other, less rigorously carried out observations in other Black communities. If the patterns she outlines are more generally applicable, there are a great many implications here for the education of Black children. Studies like this highlight the need for other, similar research activities and begin to reveal the systematic basis of Black cultural differences. This leads us to elaborate a hypothetical growth—and socialization—pattern which may have some utility in developing different attitudes and strategies in the teaching of Blacks.

The most important variables to note in Black socialization are the same as those in other groups: age and sex. But the developmental sequence in which these variables figure is quite different from those of the American middle class. At the risk of being overschematic, the following diagram of lower class Black socialization gives a glimpse of how differently these variables operate:

> *Stage One:* "Lap Baby"—Infancy; the child given a great deal of attention by his mother (or mother-surrogate); he is seldom out of someone's arms except while asleep. The first motor activities and first language learning are carried on in adult-infant interactions.

[5] Virginia H. Young, "Family and Childhood in a Southern Georgia Community," *American Anthropologist*, vol. 72 (1970), p. 282.
[6] *Ibid.*

Stage Two: "Knee Baby"—When the child learns to walk, he or she is gradually placed in the charge of older children. Peer-grouping extends to the toddler stage. The older child takes over most interactional and educational roles, and communication becomes very restricted between adults and children at this point. Peer language, with many stigmatized features, is the variety of language which is learned and used. Concepts of work, responsibility, and household cooperation are learned from older children. Girls tend to be entrusted with more responsibilities than boys, though both learn a wide range of procedures (running errands, tending other children, washing, ironing, food preparation).

Stage Three: Older childhood—the child is entrusted with great responsibility within the home, especially if he is the oldest child. He teaches others how to live on the streets, how to socialize successfully, how to cooperate, etc. (This is the time when absence from school often occurs because of the need to care for younger children.)

Stage Four: Early adolescence—around age nine or ten for boys, later for girls, there begins to be an expectation that the child is no longer capable of acting responsibly within the household system. He enters the free time of life, with its attendant very strong peer-group orientation. Playful competition aimed at group entertainment becomes the primary mode of interaction, especially with the boys, but the play is extremely formulaic, repetitive, and imitative of the older adolescents and the young adult swingers. Sexual contacts begin; girls are just as aggressive as boys in these encounters.

Stage Five: Later adolescence and young adulthood—here being "hip" takes over; style is emphasized for the purpose of managing one's image, reputation. High value is placed on performance invention, improvisation, as a means of establishing one's style, but not just in talk and music but in clothing, walk, athletics, etc. Hip talk and jive walk become the marks of peer-group exclusiveness, exclusion being aimed at all of the "square" world, the young, the old, the white, etc. Sexual contacts produce children, but do not lead to the establishment of a household.

Stage Six: Adulthood—a limited range of alternative life-styles now come into play, and the individual is generally called upon to make a choice between setting up a household or continuing the peer-group oriented street life. Women, with the birth of a number of children, gravitate toward establishing households earlier than men. Two types of such households occur, those which approximate the middle-class model, with a resident male (generally father to most or all the children and husband to the female household head) and those with no continuing man present. This is the period, then, in which there develops a very strong male-female split, with household values associated with women.

There are, of course, different stages and styles of adult life. But these are the stages which have the greatest effect upon the socialization of the Black student and which therefore may affect his school behavior. Some of these features, such as the cooperative, peer-oriented early childhood pattern, are probably found among other lower-class groups in the United States, but other characteristics are uniquely Black. What is of greatest importance is the fact that the pattern departs in so many ways from that of mainstream America, and that these departures are not taken into consideration by teachers. Most teachers, who are by definition middle-class, assume that all children must adapt to school culture in essentially the same, middle-class way. The frustration of the students who bring a different kind of home experience, value system, and pattern of communication is visible in the response of Black children to school, and in the very large drop-out rate which occurs at those ages where the developmental system of the Black student departs most from middle class norms.

There are many ways in which these frustrations build, but there are some repeated failures of understanding that are so profound and long-lasting in their implications that they may be pointed out here as illustrations. It has almost become a cliché in educational circles that it is not fair to greet a child from this background with the message (delivered in so many subtle ways) that he comes from an unfortunate background and that he speaks badly because of it. Much more egregious, however, is the failure to understand that there is a perceptible life-pattern shared by these children, and it is one which has already bestowed a high level of responsibility upon most of them by the time they reach school age. The teacher, going on her middle-class assumptions, treats the Black child as she would the white, as if the pre-school period had been one of idyllic freedom in which only a minimal amount of responsibility had been taught. Imagine the frustration encountered in this situation by one who has been caring for younger children for years. This frustration, furthermore, is compounded, for just at the time when the Black child is entering upon a time of freedom at home, at school he is told that he is finally being expected to shoulder some social responsibilities. Also of crucial importance is the conflict between the peer-based cooperation which lies behind his socialization system and the definition of such learning cooperation as cheating within the classroom.

These are instances of regular and recurring ways in which our educational system either disregards or denigrates Black life-ways and the students who bring them into the school environment. There are many more. The area of Black culture which differs most radically from its middle-class counterpart is the system of communication and performance—that is, language in the largest sense. Most of the failures of Black education arise because the teacher does not understand the manner by which her students are communicating. Here, as in other areas of culture, we are restricted by the paucity of data, but there have been some recent studies carried out which permit some tentative remarks.

First and most important, a teacher should *never* assume that her lower-class Black students communicate in any way in the same manner as she does. For instance, even a technique as basic as question-and-answer elicitation may be wrongly interpreted as hostile by some Black children. Preliminary research indicates that a direct question from an adult (and parent-surrogate) may be misunderstood because in some Black children's experience such direct queries occur most commonly when an adult is mad at the child.

There is also some question as to whether a teacher in these early grades should take on the motherly role, since there seems to be such limited communication of the teaching-learning sort which goes on between parents and children at the pre-school level. Learning occurs, but between peers.

Another preliminary observation has been made of Black peer-group communications at all levels: the Black model of discussion is *not* our first-you-speak-and-I'll-be-quiet, then-I'll-speak-and-you-be-quiet sort. Rather, the voice is used as an expression of self and if one wants to be listened to he will not hesitate (at least among one's peers) to speak on top of other voices and to repeat the same sentiments either until he is responded to by someone in the group or until someone else catches his attention. Corollary to this, when someone speaks well he expects the overlap of other voices because that generally means that the others are listening and reacting to what he is saying. This is quite a contrast to our usual middle-class attitude toward noise and conversation.

The question-and-answer and voice overlap patterns are only two of many dimensions of speaking that need more investigation at many age-levels and in different social situations. (We will discuss other more overt and manipulative speaking techniques later.) They are mentioned here because speaking traits of this sort contribute to the total confusion encountered by people unprepared to deal with those of another culture in their own classroom.

The conviction of traditional public schools that education requires a highly regimented, formalized setting is in direct opposition to the learning experience of the Black child. Socialization in his culture takes place in an informal social setting, in the yard or street, with his peers. Once the student walks into the classroom he is expected to conform to rules, largely inflexible and alien to him. Both teacher and student experience culture shock and confusion. The teacher tends to react by saying that her Black charges seem incapable of learning even the simplest school rules. The confrontation between the two cultures causes teachers to conclude that these students lack a basic sense of order. They fall back on the stereotypical explanation that because they do not ordinarily have any order in their homes, Black children do not know how to adjust when they are exposed to it in school. They react to the situation by making specific rules and letting the students know what will and will not be tolerated early in the course of the school year. They justify this procedure with the belief that, "these students *want* to be disciplined and have some order in their lives for a change." No thought is given to the possibility that there may already exist in order in the lives of the students, but one which they do not understand. There are several aspects of this "lack of order" which need to be explored in relation to what teachers see in the behavior of these young carriers of street culture.

To support their convictions that Black students have no sense of order, teachers frequently refer to their lack of self-discipline, and this in turn is illustrated by their inability to remain with a given task for extended periods of time. They say that Black students are difficult to teach because they have such short attention spans or because they do not listen at all. But, is the attention span of Black children as short as their teachers claim, or is it that these teachers do not really understand when the child is listening and when he is not? This is an issue which needs extensive investigation. Teachers, in the main, seem to feel that a person is not listening unless he shows the outward signs of attention of our communications system, such as being silent and directing his gaze toward the speaker. According to our middle-class norms, the more interesting the presentation is the more attentive the audience will be. Therefore, the quality of a presentation is judged by the receptivity of the audience, and the audience involvement is indicated by the depth and longevity of its attention or silence. Anything less than complete silence is considered to be restlessness and a sign of inattentiveness. Black culture operates on a pattern almost directly the opposite. A Black child may be listening intently, yet to a white person he gives the appearance of distraction, often because of a different habit of directing his gaze. If the presentation is stimulating the audience will take an active part, becoming vocally and physically involved in the interchange, if only by murmuring and moving about in their seats. *Complete silence is a sure sign of boredom.* It may be more realistic for teachers to be concerned about how effectively they are communicating and how stimulating their presentations are when the classroom lapses into complete silence. When that happens the message radiating from the student is that, "you're not making any contacts at all."

When the child enters school he cannot divorce himself from the experiences he has been exposed to, nor should he. And he has had few experiences which demand prolonged silence and immobility. He is accustomed to a great degree of movement, and the mere presence of rigidly organized classrooms is not enough to cause him to do otherwise. When he associates mental activity and intellectual involvement with physical movement and acts accordingly, the teacher accuses him of restlessness and disorderly conduct. Conversely, the child equates the rigidly organized and systematized classroom with inactivity, since it does not allow for movement. Classroom activities automatically become dull, boring, dead! He cannot conceive of anything being exciting, interesting, and stimulating unless there is room for physical involvement. This orientation becomes more and more acute the older the child becomes, to the point that the young adolescent actively searches for "where the action is," rejecting immobilizing forces as being "cold" or "square." This inclination toward movement suggests a mutually supportive and deeply interdependent relationship between mental and physical activity. Understanding and accepting the fact that Black students derive the quality of an event from the nature, extent, and variety of the accompanying activities should cause teachers to provide for more flexibility in the classroom. Regardless of how frequently subject matter and teacher methodology are changed, if the classroom organization remains essentially the same and denies the student the opportunity for an active verbal and physical involvement, it is probable that he will perceive little change at all.

The teacher's background has usually taught her to conform to pre-set, externally fabricated rules and regulations, while the tendency in street culture is to derive order out of the situation as it happens. This difference in orientation causes teachers to constantly wonder why students will not obey rules. Very often the violation of a petty rule becomes a major infringement and the teacher will resort to punishment to force obedience at the expense of stifling learning. For instance, a teacher, being thoroughly convinced that everyone cannot talk at once, in order to maximize classroom orderliness, will establish "styles or procedures" of classroom behavior that students are expected to obey. One of these procedures is that a student must raise his hand and be recognized before he is allowed to speak. This parliamentary procedure stifles spontaneity and cools the enthusiasm of the student by forcing him to function according to a rigidly organized decorum not his own. If the student violates the rules, his comments are ignored, or worse yet, he is punished, even though his comments may have been exteremely pertinent to the discussion. The teacher feels her refusal to accept his contribution will force him to conform to the rules. She may even go as far as to say, "I will not accept your answer because you didn't raise your hand," or "If you keep blurting out, I am going to . . ." What he hears is, "I am not going to accept your answer," and he interprets the teacher's reaction as total rejection of *him* as well as his contribution. If this happens often enough, as it usually does, the child stops making any effort to be a part of the class and withdraws within himself or becomes overtly discontent with whatever the teacher does.

The middle-class conception of who is the "teacher" and who is the "student" serves to further lessen the effectiveness of the learning processes of Black students. Children in street culture frequently teach each other techniques of survival in street life. Black children and youths think of learning as a give-and-take relationship between one who knows and one who has yet to learn. A learner is one situation may be the teacher in another. In school the student must forget this active interplay between learner and teacher and adjust to a style of conveying knowledge which places the student in the position of passive recipient. But in Black communities, learning is an active event and is commonly carried on with one's peers rather than between adult and child. Further, when adults do teach children, it is generally by example rather than verbally, with stress placed on a strongly stated correction if the learner doesn't do the job correctly.

For the early school ages especially, there is an already well-established pattern of learning in which there are certain especially capable older children (usually girls) who have been given responsibilities because of their ability to lead and to teach. Often called "little mamas" or "nurse mamas," these children teach by word and example games, certain chores, and the more basic lessons of toilet training and how to anticipate and contend with the threats of street life. These capable young teachers are, of course, the ones most affected by teachers who make the assumption that students enter school without any sense of responsibility or order. This involves a double loss, for not only are these children turned off by schooling with such an approach, but a fund of teaching talent is not utilized. Group work, a common enough technique in the less impacted schools, is all too seldom encountered in primarily Black institutions of lower learning.

Teachers feel they must function as substitute parents while the child is in their care. They also feel that since they are older and more experienced they are better equipped to decide what is best for the student. In reality they are completely ignorant of how Black families relate to their children. Reacting to the middle-class emphasis on extended adolescence, they treat even high-school students as if they were still children, incapable of making independent decisions for themselves. Constantly fearing disorder, they expect students to ask permission for everything they do, even though by the time the average Black student reaches the upper elementary grades he has already had experience caring for younger brothers and sisters, teaching them the skills of personal hygiene and safety, and taking care of the home. And he is very much in command of disciplining himself.

Teachers overlook the potentials of group work as a technique to be used with Black students. They seem to be convinced that these students cannot work together because they do not operate by the same middle-class rules of group action and cooperation—if they are given the opportunity they spend most of their time socializing and talking. Since the teacher is also convinced that socializing and work cannot be combined, group activities are deemphasized. Yet, when such activity is observed closely, one finds that the student does indeed work *while* he is socializing. If confronted with this fact, teachers counter with, "True, he may be putting something down on paper, but he doesn't really understand what he is doing because he is not concentrating on it." As if working alone and complete silence were guarantees of concentration and understanding! It is conceivable that the child is getting more out of this kind of experience simply because it is not in competition with his normal way of approaching a learning situation. If this is the case, it would suggest that classroom organization and instructional methodology be revised to accommodate more student self-directed group activities.

Despite all that has been written about the early rates of maturity of Black youth, middle-class teachers seem completely oblivious to the fact. Black students are given little opportunity to practice their maturity in the classroom. Teachers underestimate the depth of their knowledge and experiences acquired through daily activities. The tendency of schools to try to shield students from the stark realities of life serve only to make school experiences appear like unreal fantasies to Black youth. The result is that the student perceives the teacher as engaged in a perpetual game of make-believe! For the most part he may be quite tolerant, but at some point he becomes impatient with this nonsense. He strikes out against it by overtly dismissing all the teacher says as unreal and will probably do something else to amuse himself. The teacher, greatly threatened, interprets this behavior as disrespect. She may resort to typical punitive actions such as expelling the student from class until he "learns how to behave," or by reporting his behavior to his parents.

This latter maneuver, a frequently used disciplinary action, is virtually useless with Black students. It is ineffective because it overlooks two basic facts about Black culture. First, the Black youth learns, at a very early age, to handle his own problems. Second, one's maturity is questionable, if he cannot take care of himself alone. The student reacts to the teacher calling his parents much the same way he would react to a classmate who, when challenged to defend his honor, runs to the protection of his parents. He questions the "maturity" of the teacher since she seems incapable of handling her own problems, and he loses respect for her. She thereafter becomes a challenge to see how often she can be made to call out for help. Eventually the student may be expelled or punished in some other way and the teacher considers herself the victor. The student thinks otherwise because she was unable to deal with the situation herself. In his estimation she is not much of a woman.

Because so much of the transmission of knowledge and the customs of street culture takes place within peer groups, this may explain why the Black student is prone to seek the aid and assistance of his classmates at least as frequently as he does the teacher's. He inherits a tendency toward cooperativeness in work tasks while his play activities are extremely competitive. His school experiences are just the opposite. Cooperation is reserved for sports and games while classroom and academic activities are primarily competitive. In his culture the Black student is accustomed to sharing information on an equal basis with adults rather than expecting them to teach him. He learns from his peers, and after he has reached a certain degree of mastery he interacts with other adults. It is extremely difficult for him to accept the teacher as one who is there to help him acquire knowledge. Little wonder that he will express his confusion and misunderstandings to his fellow classmates; but when invited to share them with the teacher he says nothing. This behavior is frustrating to the teacher because she is accustomed to someone saying, "I don't understand," when the information is not clear. She faces a perplexing dilemma because she is never quite sure whether her students clearly understand the information that is being presented. If the peer group could be incorporated into teaching techniques, thus duplicating his cultural concepts of learning, it is conceivable that the change would positively affect the Black student's academic performance.

As the impact of Black nationalism and cultural awareness increases we can expect the sources of irritation and tension between Black students and white middle-class teachers to increase unless teachers begin to understand the implications of their students' behavior. White teachers are quite right that their Black students are "hostile," "resent the authority they represent," "quick to anger," and "have chips on their shoulders." The question here is why are these attitudes so prevalent, and how can teachers go about understanding them?

To begin with, teachers need to recognize the fact that these attitudes are prevalent among all kinds of Black students, those who are receiving good grades as well as those who are about to drop out of school. Admittedly, it can be said that all students, regardless of racial or ethnic identity, are questioning teacher authority, but if we dismiss the relationship between Black students and white teachers as merely that, we are belittling the point if not avoiding it altogether. There is an additional factor that must be considered which compounds the Black student's reactions to suggestions of authority and discipline from white teachers. This factor is the Black experience with racism. White teachers are symbols of the racism that these students have known throughout their entire lives. The student, therefore, reacts to the teacher not so much as a person but as a member of a group which is defined primarily by skin tone and other physical attributes—just as they are used to being reacted to.

Second, when the white teacher becomes very assertive as a disciplinarian, especially if these actions are regarded as arbitrary and autocratic, the Black student's reaction is that a white man is *still* trying to tell him what to do, and current events have done a lot to convince him that he no longer needs to be submissive and docile. Merely saying that, "I understand why he should feel this way," means nothing. Understanding the complexities of life for a Black person in this country does not come that easy. It does not stop the teacher from becoming frustrated—even frightened—nor will it stop the student from being resentful. If we revamp our educational philosophies and activities toward changing the student's attitudes we will be wasting our time. That has been tried before and it was a miserable failure. Black students will continue to carry their own culture into the classroom, and they will continue to misunderstand their middle-class teacher as profoundly as she misunderstands them. It is the teacher who can be taught to expect and deal with cultural differences before she enters the classroom, and it is the teacher who should and will have to do the changing. These changes must begin with the teacher's acceptance of the fact that despite the desire, she may never be accepted as a person by her Black students. Resorting to traditional measures to remove the hostile students from class serves no purpose whatsoever; they only delay the inevitable confrontation between student and teacher and heighten the hostilities.

A few years ago Black people in general and particularly students were interested in doing whatever they could to remain in the good graces of the white folks. If the student were to do anything to anger the teacher, he was told to apologize, to avoid an all-out confrontation. This is no longer the case. Black people are too sensitive about always having to be the ones to "give" in interracial relations to be receptive to this approach any longer. Now, when a white teacher tells her Black student that she does not like his attitude, he is likely to answer in word and/or action, "that's tough, I don't like yours either, but you've got to live with it." Especially bewildered are teachers who were accustomed to the previous reaction, now trying to cope with this new attitude.

A third reason why Black students resent white teachers is that they are convinced of their racism and prejudice. The students' perceptions are very important in determining the direction of their relationship with the teachers. Regardless of how often the teacher professes her liberalism and unbiased attitudes, if the student perceives her differently all her testimony proves to no avail. This conviction may result from a certain movement, the way the teacher places herself in the classroom, the recurrent use of a certain word or phrase, or other idiosyncrasies which connote to the student an air of superiority. These speculations are areas which must be explored more deeply if teachers are to come to understand why Black students act and react as they do.

The Black youth's unconcern for the future and conspicuously absent aspirations for upward mobility have been interpreted as a basic lack of motivation and desire for economic and social betterment. Much attention has been given to school programs which would increase the motivation of Black students and get them to develop an appreciation for education. Unfortunately, these attempts have overlooked two essential factors— the cultural heritage which emphasizes immediacy, and the preference of pragmatism over abstraction in street culture. Traditional educational philosophy holds that a person has to have a theoretical frame of reference before he can engage in productive activity. For example, one must know the structural organization of the political system before he can truly comprehend its actual functioning. As a result, the greatest emphasis in school has been toward theoretical abstractions and preparing the student for some role he is to perform in the distant future. All of this is in contradiction to the heritage Black youth bring to the classroom. Circumstances are such that planning for and dreams of the distant future are idealistic fantasies. There are too many pressures and demands for survival for members of street culture to afford the luxury of planning for a future that may not be plausible at all. Existence is too marginal for this to be a worthy engagement. The future therefore becomes the present. Surviving from one day to the next is what occupies the energies of ghetto residents. This is not simply satisfying physiological needs. Emotional and psychological needs are just as important and demand as much time, if not more. The youth may have illusions about "getting ahead" but his real concerns are "getting by."

This concern for survival and immediacy permeates all aspects of ghetto life, and it is reflected in the student's attitude toward academic activities. He is content to complete an exam or a course with barely a passing grade. It is not important how well he can do but the fact that he does get by. This orientation explains why teachers' appeals to Black ghetto students ("You could do so much better if you tried harder") do not produce any noticeable changes in behavior.

What then is the answer to how teachers might successfully challenge their students to do more? Of primary importance is that activities be approached as if they were complete entities within themselves, as opposed to falling into a sequence of events which will eventually lead to some kind of distant reward. More emphasis should be placed on providing challenging problems and stimulating processes for the pupils to work with. The Black student is inclined to devalue abstractions, such as test scores, as proof of the successful completion of a task. This attitude can be very irritating to middle-class teachers. Consider this example: The teacher spends hours grading a theme or an exam and writing comments about how well the student did. When he receives the paper the student looks at the grade briefly and crumples the paper in the presence of the teacher. She is hurt that he was so unappreciative and considers this behavior a personal affront to her and her subject. Conversely, the student sees nothing wrong with what he did. The grade fulfilled a purpose, he is no longer personally involved and the activity is terminated. What good is a *used* test paper! He thus reacts according to his cultural training.

The Black student's perceptions about how one acquires status and success reflect his cultural experiences as well as affecting his performance in school. Status and success in street culture depend largely on one's ability to manipulate people and his surroundings. Performance, personal versatility, and adeptness are especially important in the process of acquiring status. Financial gain is secondary because the likelihood of most ghetto residents becoming wealthy is rather dubious. Therefore, leadership and power are directly related to how one "carries himself" instead of to the quantity of his material possessions. Whether a person becomes a leader or a follower in street culture is dependent upon his ability to exert influence and control over others. Although the same criteria are used in mainstream culture, the two cultures differ in their sources of power. Middle-class norms equate financial means and social awareness with potentials of leadership. Students are encouraged to work hard, to study diligently, to plan ahead, and after years of preparation, exposure, and making oneself accessible to others, one may emerge as a leader. In street culture it is not the hard-working person who is likely to be idolized and imitated. Rather it is the one who can control others and make his way by using his head with skill and subtlety. His most effective tool is language. The Black student who is very adept in the use of words is more likely to become a leader among his peers than one who makes good grades. His friends know that if he is to survive on the street or relate to school personnel with any finesse he *must* be an effective talker.

Middle-class teachers are thoroughly confused when confronted with this pattern. They cannot understand why others are quick to gather around a student who is "failing," cannot read, and is always getting into trouble. Why can't they imitate Johnny Black who is an honor student? They are likely to try to diminish the influence of this student by explaining to others that if the relationship is pursued it will only corrupt them as well. He is labeled as a troublemaker because he seems to have a natural talent to mislead others, and he is always in the forefront when trouble erupts in the classroom. The fact that the teacher is overlooking is that the "talker" is not misleading, but leading. If she were to find out what it is about him that causes others to follow his example she might be able to get a better understanding of what it means to succeed in Black street culture. This information could provide some valuable insights for the teacher who wants to help Black students develop more positive self-concepts by providing them with models to emulate. Her choices of "heroes" would be much more reliable and realistic.

EDUCATION AS AN INTERFACE INSTITUTION IN RURAL MEXICO AND THE AMERICAN INNER CITY

Robert Hunt and Eva Hunt

In the past decade and a half, a number of anthropologists have done research on education in culture in the United States and elsewhere. The result of this kind of cross-cultural perspective is that we understand much more fully not only how our concept of education serves and reflects our culture, but also what our alternatives might be. Furthermore, studying other educational systems permits us to see weaknesses within our own. This comparative perspective provides the theme for this article by the Hunts.

THE MULTIPLE SOCIETY: MEXICO

The educational institutions of rural Mexico share many of the problems which beset education in the American inner cities. Comparison of the two systems will, hopefully, provide some insight for thinking about the American public schools.[1]

Southern Mexico, a multiple society with plural cultures, is composed of two social segments, the closed corporate Indian villages, and Mestizos, who represent the national culture. Each of these segments, with its own culture, social structure, value system, and life-style, regards the other as immoral, and they try to avoid each other as much as possible. But the two segments still must interact in order to survive. This interaction is handled largely by interface institutions which include the impersonal market, the school system, government departments, and political parties,

From *Midway*, vol. 8, no. 2 (May 1967), pp. 99–109. Reprinted by permission of *Midway* and the author.

[1] The field work upon which this paper in part rests took place in Mexico during 1963–64 and was generously supported by the National Science Foundation, grant GS 87, which we gratefully acknowledge. We are heavily indebted to the comparative literature, and the specialist will note our great reliance upon the work of Eric Wolf and Morris Siegel.

among others. The people working in these institutions, such as merchants, political bosses, bureaucrats, and teachers, are brokers who tend to monopolize most of the interaction between the two segments.

The Indian can best be described as a subsistence peasant who cultivates food crops to feed his family. While he may occasionally hire some labor for help, this is rare. The Indians do not, by and large, produce cash crops, although they may earn cash by selling small amounts of surplus food products. Their major mechanism for obtaining cash is by selling their labor to Mestizos, who grow cash crops for the national and international markets. The value system of the Indian can be described as one fostering an economic homogeneity. The Indian surplus is not invested in ways which will increase productivity but instead is funneled into consumption activities for the whole village, which both raises the moral prestige of those individuals who can afford the expenditure and impoverishes them. Wealth differences thus tend to be leveled down to a subsistence level.

The Mestizos tend to be what an American would call authoritarian; the Indians are for most purposes and in most contexts highly democratic. The Indian subordinates his own desires and profits to those of the community; for the Mestizo every office is regarded as a profit-making opportunity for personal exploitation.

Each segment considers the other to be alien and rejects participation in the activities of the other. Moreover, each benefits emotionally from the perception of the differences. A Mestizo is decent, clean, civilized, and Christian, according to a Mestizo, while the Indians are dirty, drunken, brutal, ignorant savage pagans. To the Indian, however, the Mestizo is dictatorial, exploits others, is arbitrary and selfish, while he sees himself as morally responsible, hard-working, and civic-minded. Notwithstanding these ethnocentric attitudes, each is largely ignorant of the nature and workings of the other segment.

In addition to the many basic differences, membership in each segment is publicly proclaimed by highly visible markers. For example, Indians speak an Indian language and dress in clothing distinctive of their village. Mestizos speak (and may read) only Spanish, and dress in ordinary western tailored clothing.

INTERFACE INSTITUTIONS

Despite [some] mobility between the segments, the system remains stably differentiated. This is due not only to the desire on both sides for a cultural status quo but to the conservative role behavior of the brokers who conduct the interaction between the two segments.

There are two types of brokers serving the interface institutions. One type resides in the Mestizo-dominated towns. The Indians either come to them for services (such as governmental officials in the *cabecera* or county seat) or they travel at infrequent intervals to the Indian communities. In the latter category may be included government inspectors and traveling merchants. These brokers can be very significant in the lives of Indians, but, typically, their role and the Indian response to it are highly impersonal.

Much more interesting is the second type of broker: those who are resident in the Indian town. This includes the *cacique* (political boss), the town secretary, on occasion some merchants, and the grammar school teachers. These are the individuals who are face to face with both Indians and Mestizos on a continual and continuing basis, who face or produce the most pressure for acculturation, and who often attempt to manipulate the economy and polity for their own benefit.

Eric Wolf has pointed out that the broker must operate competently with both segments; to be successful, he must satisfy to some degree the members of his own segment and the significant members of the other segment. In order to do this, he must know a considerable amount about the demand schedules of both segments.

The teacher is an excellent example of this. He is an employee of a large, urban-centered bureaucracy with a distinctive style of life, a representative of Mestizo culture to himself, to other Mestizos, and to the Indians, and he has to somehow get along with the Indian population whose co-operation is necessary if his career is to advance.

It is immediately apparent, of course, that the goals of the national political elite are directly opposed to the goals of the local populace, or at least a powerful portion of it, among both Indians and Mestizos. In the typical Indian society, the period from the beginning of latency to the beginning of puberty is the time in which the child learns from his parents the skills required of competent adults in his community. Learning is gradual and occurs by the slow increase of task responsibilities given to the child. The process is an informal one and adjusted to the individual child's speed of learning. At the same time, in the typical Indian view, this is the period in which the most play and socially useless behavior are permissible in the life cycle. The contradiction with the school program becomes evident. Learning, attention span, and increased responsibility are imposed by the demands of a bureaucratic schedule and a crowded school and are not adjusted to the individual child's needs. As the formal school becomes more and more demanding, the child is also subject to heavier work demands from the home, for he is becoming an economic asset. Children respond first to the demands of the agricultural cycle and family, and, secondly, if at all, to the demands of the school year.

The information that is presented in school, while highly relevant from the point of view of the nation and the national culture, are supremely irrelevant when they are not boring to the Indian. Arithmetic, Spanish grammar, Aztec myths and dances, the meaning of national holidays, and all the other bits of information which every civilized Mexican knows, have no place in Indian culture, which has its own items of received knowledge regarding history, religion, technology, etc.

Because of the justifiable lack of interest of the pupils, the teachers typically regard the Indians as stupid and incapable of learning not only the national culture but anything. Slighting (even if unconscious) remarks about the lack of civilization and intelligence of the Indians, of their dirty habits, their self-imposed poverty, their outrageous language, all combine to both openly and more subtly communicate the basic attitude of the teacher to the Indians: rejection.

In many ways the teachers are often worse in these attitudes than many other brokers. Many teachers in these rural Indian towns are either newcomers to the Mestizo lower-middle class or upwardly mobile Indians whose objective in becoming teachers is to raise themselves in ethnic terms. The danger of slipping [back] into the cultural state of the Indian is personally threatening; they are the most vigorous in rejecting it.

Under the circumstances, the teachers are most closely allied with the local conservative Mestizos whose culture they consciously adopt as their own. If they were to be successful in carrying out the demands (realistically put as suggestions) of the national bureaucracy concerning acculturating the Indians, they would be violating the demands of the local Mestizos and their own outlook. In this conflict between an urban, progressive education bureaucracy and the local, conservative populace, it is the demands of the village that are met first.

Given all the above reasons, the teacher rarely serves as a significant source of identity formation for the children. On the contrary, his behavior creates social distance. He serves the needs of the Mestizo world. His presence in the community pacifies members of the national segment who think that the Indian should be civilized, or at least offered the benefits of civilization. He is also extremely useful to the local society (whether Indian or Mestizo) since a minimum knowledge of Spanish acquired in school allows some Indians to become hired laborers in the Mestizo market or to act as interpreters for the monolinguals in the community.

The role is useful to the teacher himself, as well. If he has little ambition, then he has a fairly comfortable formal position which clearly marks him as an important local figure. If he has ambition, however, the teacher post is a popular job in which to learn the skills to eventually become a political boss, or *cacique*. The *cacique*, like the teacher, must live and work with both cultures if he is to prosper. He has to have an intimate knowledge of the opposite segment which the teacher role allows him to acquire. The apprenticeship is usually quite long, taking upward of ten to fifteen years, but is a stepping stone to a political role.

Education which is supposed to be fomenting significant culture change is in fact organized (consciously or unconsciously) to accomplish the exact opposite. Thus Indian children "prefer" to remain Indians and later contacts in life reinforce their preference. The school as an interface institution, and the teacher as its broker, are successful in preserving social and cultural distance.

AMERICAN INNER-CITY SCHOOLS AS INTERFACE INSTITUTIONS

A comparison of American inner-city school systems and the Mexican system turns up some interesting similarities. In the schools, the children are exposed (and expected to learn) the technical skills, the psychological skills, and the information about society as a whole which are part and parcel of successful adult life in the United States.

The public schools have also been given another job: to prepare the immigrants to this country for life as Americans. According to the melting-pot theory, it is in the schools that children of foreigners learn to be Americans, through exposure to the American adult models who staff the schools, through American peers, and through the information which is transmitted in the schools in books and lectures. Here is an institution conceived and staffed by middle-class Americans, which has been given the job of converting the young into viable members of our industrial society. For the middle-class youngsters, the school is an extension of the home and the later job and is largely consistent with them. For the cultural immigrants (foreign or rural), at least some of them, it represents an effective route for cultural migration. It is in the latter case where our schools are interface institutions.

Recently, attention has been focused on the inability of the inner-city school to effectively cope with its pupils. Like the Mexican school, it maintains social distance rather than reduces it. The problem which this poses for the society as a whole is enormous and very serious, and it appears to be organized as a vicious circle. There is a large-scale alienation in the inner city from industrial middle-class society. The inner-city schools should play a crucial role for the population they serve and bear very importantly upon our most serious, and potentially most explosive, social problems. But overwhelming evidence points out that these schools are not achieving their social goals.

We can then ask two questions: why are the inner-city schools not doing their job, and what can be done to help them?

There has been considerable general discussion of the differences between the culture of the inner-city residents and middle-class America. Differences in values, motivations, behavior patterns, and expectations have all been claimed. There has been lamentably little solid empirical work on these cultural differences. It appears that what we have is a case of structural ignorance, just as in the Mexican example. The superordinate segment of the culture remains largely ignorant of the other segment, and what it perceives (or projects) it despises. The two populations therefore remain opaque to, and reject, each other. Our statements about the cultural differences of the two segments in what follows is therefore general and tentative.

The Northern inner-city child shares with his Indian counterpart a language which is significantly different from that of the dominant segment. Although in the Mexican situation the Indian speech is a distinct language, the Negro inner-city child is told that he speaks a corrupt and deficient version of English. There is mounting evidence that the inability to perform middle-class tasks, such as abstraction, in canonical English, does not reflect an impoverished mind but merely the inability to perform in what is almost certainly a foreign language. The culture of the subordinate segment is rich and sophisticated, and not merely an "impoverished" version of the dominant one.

It has been said that the inner-city pupil does not perform well in school in part because the home environment does not support the school objectives. The Mexican Indian knows that he can use the school to move into the Mestizo world if he desires. The change of markers is sufficient, since racially the populations are indistinguishable. The Negro child is confronted with the fact that learning the markers of the superordinate segment is not sufficient for mobility, since the major marker, skin color, cannot be changed. If the Indian learns the proper skills, he can be integrated into the Mestizo world. For the Negro, this is much more problematic. It is not surprising therefore to find that the Negro home does not support the objectives of the middle-class public school. It could hardly be expected to support an experience which is painful and, sorrowfully, irrelevant to adult Negro life. The same sense of alienation from the school situation and the curriculum that exists between the Indian and the Mestizo also exists between the recent Negro migrant from rural areas and the middle-class white urbanite.

One can question the genuineness of the local superordinate segment's desire to integrate Negroes into the middle-class culture even though the national policies may point (at least in the North) in that direction. But as the relative and absolute number of Negro migrants to the middle class increases, the attractiveness of the move will increase as well, for both segments.

Finally, we can suggest that the role of teacher in the Mexican Indian town and in the American inner-city is very similar. That is, an understanding of the functions of the school in the inner city cannot be gained without understanding the nature of the confrontation of members of two different social segments, middle-class teachers (usually white) and lower-class pupils (frequently not white). It is important of course to understand the culture that the child brings to the school, but an understanding of the school cannot be had without an understanding of the kinds of communications that take place between teacher and pupil, as representatives of two different cultural segments, both in school and out. In this case, the segmentary opposition is even more definite than that between Mestizo and Indian in Mexico. Our schools are staffed by middle-class personnel. They have been through college, which proves that they can meet the demands of the middle-class bureaucratized world. If only recently arrived in the middle class, they tend to hold rather rigidly to the values and behavior patterns of the middle class. Like the teacher in Mexico, if there is some danger of the teacher being identified with his pupils (especially if the teacher is a Negro himself), he will reject the pupils and what they stand for to the degree that he has recently migrated from their culture. The teachers who were raised in a middle-class environment feel justified in making middle-class demands of the pupils. Those who were not are forced to do so to avoid threats to their own change of identity. These demands include a taboo on physical aggression, giving overt signs of paying attention and respect, and meeting middle-class standards of language, cleanliness, and obedience.

3

Language

This section presents some basic facts regarding the nature of language which the teacher needs to know if she is to develop an adequate linguistic orientation in the classroom. There is probably no other area of the curriculum in which so little information and so many misconceptions exist as in language arts—English (the same deplorable situation extends to college courses as well). The schools have been incredibly resistant to efforts to replace prescientific beliefs and attitudes about language with the available knowledge provided by linguistic science. Yet perhaps with the sole exception of culture, of which language is of course a part, nothing so pervasively influences a teacher's entire teaching behavior as her ideas about language. In addition, it is in the classroom that students learn many of the attitudes and concepts about language—their own and others' —that they will carry through life. It is vital, therefore, if the present unsatisfactory educational situation is to be reformed, that teachers be equipped with a new set of facts and understandings about language.

The central understanding which arises from a knowledge of the nature of language is that of *linguistic relativity*—the realization that all languages and all varieties of a language are equally valid systems of communication, and that they are therefore equally deserving of respect. There is no basis whatsoever for regarding any language or any variety of a language as inherently better than any other. It is unlikely that a teacher who accepts this as a premise will alienate her students by rejecting their speech (which is so intimately a part of them as to be part of their very identity) on the grounds that it is wrong, bad, or otherwise inferior to her own. Instead, she will view their linguistic ability for what it is—a truly remarkable achievement—and use it as a foundation to build upon. Further, a knowledge of how language is learned will show how wrong are the traditional techniques of shaming a student ("What did you say?") or using various forms of punishment (grades, detention) to lead him to adopt the dominant language or a "standard" variety of the language. Here again, the spectacular failure of traditional methods shows the need for new, more soundly-based linguistic approaches, and adequately-prepared teachers to apply them.

The selections in this section can only begin to introduce the reader to some of the key understandings and facts that must form the basis for successful classroom practice. It is hoped that the reader will be sufficiently interested in this subject to pursue it further.

AN INITIAL LOOK AT LANGUAGE

Ronald W. Langacker

> In the first essay, Langacker shows that all normal children of
> whatever background naturally learn the language (and the variety
> of the language) which they hear spoken around them, largely
> without any direct instruction. How they do this is still not fully
> known, but studies in various languages have shown that by the
> time the child is five, he has learned most of the basic grammatical
> patterns of his language. Langacker also summarizes some of the
> basic tenets of linguistics, i.e., (1) that all human groups have
> language, (2) that there is no inherent relation between language
> and race, (3) that no language is any better or more complex than
> any other, no matter how simple or complex the cultures of the
> respective speakers, (4) that all languages are constantly changing,
> and (5) that change in language is neither good nor bad, since it
> leads neither to improvement nor to decay.

LANGUAGE ACQUISITION

Children display an amazing ability to become fluent speakers of
any language consistently spoken around them. Every normal human child
who is not reared in virtual isolation from language use soon comes to
speak one or more languages natively.

The child's acquisition of his native language is not dependent on
special tutoring. Parents may spend many hours "reinforcing" every rec-
ognizable bit of their child's verbal activity with a smile or some other
reward, or trying by means of "baby talk" to bridge the gap between their
mature linguistic competence and the child's incipient one. But there is
no particular reason to believe that such activity has any bearing on the
child's ultimate success in becoming a native speaker of his parents' language. Children can pick up a language by playing with other children
who happen to speak it just as well as they can through the concentrated

From *Language and Its Structure, Some Fundamental Linguistic Concepts*, Ronald
W. Langacker (New York: Harcourt Brace Jovanovich, 1968). Reprinted by permission of Harcourt Brace Jovanovich.

efforts of doting parents. All they seem to need is sufficient explosure to the
language in question.

This capacity for acquiring language is remarkable for a number of
reasons. It is remarkable first because of its uniformity throughout the
human race. There simply are no cases of normal human children who,
given the chance, fail to acquire a native language. By way of comparison,
it is not at all unusual for a child to fail to master arithmetic, reading,
swimming, or gymnastics despite a considerable amount of instruction.
Language acquisition, in other words, is species uniform. It is also species
specific. Every normal person learns a human language, but no other
animal, not even the most intelligent ape, has been shown to be capable
of making the slightest progress in this direction, although some animals
can learn to solve problems, use tools, and so on. Language acquisition thus
appears to be different in kind from acquisition of the other skills mentioned.

The process is further remarkable for its comparative speed and per-
fection. When we actually attempt to take a language apart to see how
it works, we find that it is extraordinarily complex and that it involves
highly abstract organizational principles. Yet, within the first few years of
his life, every human child has succeeded in mastering at least one such
system. Furthermore, the linguistic system that the child masters is for all
practical purposes identical to the one employed by the people around
him. The differences are slight indeed when measured against the magnitude of the accomplishment. If the child is regularly exposed to two
languages, he will very probably learn both; moreover, he will by and
large succeed in keeping the two linguistic systems separate, which is a
considerable achievement in itself.

It has often been observed that adults are not capable of learning a
language in the natural, spontaneous way that children are. For the adult,
learning a foreign language usually involves great effort and seldom results
in perfect mastery of the new idiom. An American child of six who moves
to Japan with his parents will be at home in Japanese in no time; his
parents, however, may have to depend on the child as an interpreter. The
differences between language learning in the child and in the adult may
have been exaggerated, but the onset of adolescence does seem to constitute
some sort of dividing line in the ability to master a new linguistic system.
For example, a person past adolescence is not likely to learn to speak a
foreign language without a noticeable accent, however slight.

The observation that every normal human child learns one or more
languages unless he is reared in isolation from the regular use of language
raises some interesting questions. What constitutes normality in this context? What happens when a child is not exposed to language during his
early years?

With regard to language acquisition, normality can be interpreted very broadly. In fact, language learning is possible despite severe physical or psychological deficiencies. Neither the inability to hear nor the inability to vocalize will necessarily prevent a child from mastering a linguistic system. In the case of deaf children, some special training is of course required, since the deaf obviously cannot learn a language by hearing it. Nevertheless, deaf children can acquire a very good grasp of a language through various visual devices. Language learning is even possible when deafness is accompanied by blindness, as shown by the accomplishments of Helen Keller. It is chiefly in the domain of vocal articulation that deaf children have the greatest difficulty, as would be expected. But language is like an iceberg: its overt manifestation is only a small part of the whole. The ability of the child to master all but this one small part, despite total deafness, is remarkable indeed. Moreover, even deaf children can make significant progress toward learning to speak normally, particularly when deafness sets in some time after birth.

Children who are unable to use their vocal organs to produce speech sounds nevertheless learn a language with no particular difficulty. They are able to understand language perfectly and can learn to communicate through writing as well as anyone else can. The acquisition of language is thus in no crucial way dependent on verbalization.

Native language acquisition is much less likely to be affected by mental retardation than is the acquisition of other intellectual skills. A child who is mentally deficient to the extent that he cannot be taught arithmetic can still acquire language. Only in the most severe cases, in the lower range of idiocy, is language completely absent. Here is another indication that language learning is different in kind, in some essential way, from the attainment of other intellectual abilities.

Children can be quite inventive in regard to language. Secret languages like pig latin provide good illustrations of their linguistic flexibility and creativeness. According to specific principles of transposition, the speaker of pig latin transforms ordinary English utterances into sound sequences that prove quite baffling to the uninitiated observer: *Is-thay entence-say, or-fay example-ay, is-ay itten-wray in-ay ig-pay atin-lay.* Such languages, usually based on a standard language in a straightforward way, are not at all uncommon. Children can easily become fluent in such a language, and, since adults are usually slower in these matters, can use it as a secret code to prevent adults from monitoring their conversations.

However, a child cannot invent a language from scratch. There are a number of cases on record of children who grew up in the wilderness in isolation from human society, in some instances raised by wolves as extra cubs. None of them had invented any kind of language when found. Similarly, there are cases of children raised in human society but in isolation from language use (for instance, raised by a deaf-mute or shut off from the world except for feeding). Under such conditions, language apparently does not develop, even when two children are raised together. Exposure to language is thus a minimum requirement for language acquisition. Once brought into normal society, where language is regularly used, children who have grown up in the wilderness or in linguistic isolation can usually make some progress toward learning to use a language. If the child is found at an early enough age and is not deficient in hearing or intelligence, the effects of isolation may be largely or totally overcome. It is difficult to say anything more conclusive because of the paucity of such cases and the difficulty of interpreting them.

As we noted in Chapter One, the business of linguistics is to arrive at an understanding of language. Central to this concern is an understanding of the capacity for language acquisition, which we have seen to be note-worthy for a number of reasons. An adequate account of language acquisi-tion is still very far from our grasp, but this goal provides a great deal of motivation for investigating the structure of languages. One reason why linguistics is worth doing, in other words, is that it can ultimately be expected to shed some light on the nature of this rather remarkable aspect of the psychological development of the human child.

ON ORIGIN AND SPECIES

We observed in the preceding section that language acquisition is species uniform and species specific. All human beings learn a language, but no other animals, not even the most intelligent ones, attain to anything comparable. These remarks deserve some amplification, since misconcep-tions related to this point are quite common.

People have sometimes supposed that racial differences are responsible for linguistic differences, but there is absolutely no evidence to support such a contention. Language acquisition is species uniform—any human child is capable of becoming a native speaker of any human language. Which language a child learns depends entirely on his models, those from whom he learns to talk. Consider the American Negro population, for instance. Imported originally from Africa, this population now has English for its native tongue. Thus both Negroes and whites speak English, and both English and African languages (which are unrelated to English) are spoken by Negroes; this observation is perhaps sufficient to establish that language and race are independent. We may also cite the children of American immigrants of all races and nationalities, who grow up speaking perfect American English.

American Negro speech is in general noticeably distinct from the speech of white Americans, and it might be supposed that the differences stem from racial characteristics. Differences in pronunciation might be attributed to anatomical details, such as the size of the lips, to take one conceivable hypothesis. In fact, however, the speech of many Negroes is indistinguishable from that of the white population, which rules out the possibility that race is the determining factor. No more significance is to be attached to the special character of Negro speech than, say, to the special character of New England speech. These race-correlated dialect differences are perpetuated because Negro children usually learn to talk from other Negroes.

Just as there is no inherent relation between language and race, there is none between language and culture. The Athabaskan family of American Indian languages embraces speakers of several distinct cultures. Conversely, languages of two unrelated families, Keresan and Tanoan, are represented in the Rio Grande Pueblo culture. Such examples demonstrate that neither language nor culture dictates the form the other will assume. Nevertheless, language and culture are tightly intertwined. The most obvious instance is literature, oral and written; principles of literary style, prosody, and so on that are developed in terms of one language cannot always find satisfactory equivalents in a second. Words designating concepts specific to a given culture are likely to present a serious translation problem. The adoption of a new language is often accompanied by the gradual adoption of a new culture. Language and culture are closely associated in practice, therefore, but they are basically independent from one another.

It has sometimes been maintained that primitive peoples speak primitive languages. In fact, however, there is no correlation between degree of cultural advancement and complexity of linguistic structure. The languages of primitive peoples can be every bit as complex and rich in expressive power as any European language. Anything that can be said in one language can be said in any other, though perhaps more clumsily. Claims that "primitive" languages have very small vocabularies, that they have no grammar, that most of their words are onomatopoetic, that they cannot express abstract ideas, and so on are just plain false. The Eskimos have words for specific varieties of snow but no generic, more abstract term (like our *snow*) that embraces all varieties of it. This does not mean that they are incapable of abstract thought or that their language is impoverished; it simply means that snow is more important to them than to us, so that their linguistic categorization in this area of experience is more detailed than ours.

Just as there are no primitive languages, there are no "corrupt" languages. Languages change, but they do not decay. On no rational basis is it correct to lament that language X, at some distant point in the past, was a pure and perfect vehicle to express our thoughts but that it has declined steadily to its present state of decadence. This is so much puristic nonsense. The English of today and the English of a thousand years ago are very different; by the same token, however, the English of a thousand years ago was radically different from its antecedent of a still earlier period. At any stage, a language is fully adequate to its purpose. It is the product of change and, if it continues to be spoken, will continue to undergo changes. The idea of a "pure" language is illusory.

The question of how language arose in the human species has intrigued scholars for centuries, but we really know nothing about the origin of language. As far back as we can trace any language historically, it looks like the same kind of entity as any contemporary language. The languages of two or three thousand years ago do not seem to be any simpler or any more primitive than the languages of today, or any different in kind. There must have been a time in the history of mankind when language was not fully developed, when men used some primitive forerunner of the complex linguistic systems used today. From all indications, however, this time must be so far in the past that we cannot hope to find any record of these earlier stages. With respect to the origin of human language, it is quite possible that we will always be limited to speculation.

Many theories concerning the origin of language have been advanced, but none worth taking seriously. Some people have speculated that language stems from primitive man's imitation of animal cries. Others have suggested that instinctive cries of pain or the grunts that accompany great physical exertion were the original sources of speech. Neither idea has any evidence in its favor. Moreover, such vocalizations are so untypical of human language that it is hard to see why they should be postulated as the source of all language. Beyond this, no one has ever demonstrated how, in accordance with reasonable psychological principles, language in all its present complexity and abstractness could ever develop from such modest beginnings. Future alleviation of our ignorance concerning the origin of language, if it ever comes, will have to be the by-product of a great increase in our understanding of psychological structure and the principles of neural evolution. It is almost certain that man acquired language as the result of evolutionary changes in the structure of his mind. It was not a matter of someone "getting the idea" and others "catching on," which is almost equivalent to the notion that a group of primitive men sat down around a conference table and decided to invent language.

We learn nothing about the origin of language by examining the various ways in which animals communicate. Some animal communication takes place via fixed systems of signals, but there the resemblance between animal communication and human languages ends.

LANGUAGE IN CULTURE

Robert W. Young

> One of the major objectives of a course in language and culture
> in education must be to get the teacher to learn to listen to her
> students for speaking differences. But the question will always arise
> of what to do with these differences once they are recognized.
> Simply stated, these distinct features may provide the crucial insights
> into the deepest held values and significant orders of the group.
>
> A case in point is the term in Black slang, dig. As it is used by
> Afro-Americans (and now by white hipsters and the youth culture)
> the term is untranslatable into a single word in Standard English, for
> dig means both to feel with (empathize) and to understand. The
> high—albeit conversational—incidence of use of this term indicates
> that the concept is important to its users. This is significant because
> it allows us to understand a whole segment of Black values which
> insists that reason and emotion, understanding and feeling must
> always go hand in hand, and that to insist on one without the other
> is either being cold or heating things up too much.
>
> In this present essay, Young explains in greater detail the im-
> portance of some seemingly insignificant concept words among the
> Navajo. In so doing, he shows the uses of these insights in devising
> more meaningful strategies for educating Navajo children.

A great many concepts are widely dispersed among human societies
across the globe, shared in one form or another by the people of widely
separated communities. Some are inherent in the very nature of things—
all people share the concepts denoted by *walk, run, eat, talk, see, sleep,
hear,* for example. Although different speech communities may conceive
and express these ideas in a variety of forms and patterns, the basic concepts are the common property of all cultures.

Thus, both English and Navajo include terms with which to express
the concept *walk.* However, they do not express it within the same frame

From *English As a Second Language for Navajos,* Robert W. Young (Albuquerque:
Area Office, Division of Education, 1968). Reprinted by permission of the Bureau of
Indian Affairs.

of reference. Among the distinctions with which both languages are concerned is the *number* of actors: English *he walks* (singular) and *they walk* (plural); Navajo: *yigááł,* he is walking along; *yi'ash,* they two are walking along; and *yikah,* they (more than two) are walking along. Both languages express the concept *walk,* and both concern themselves with the number of actors, but here the similarity begins to diverge between the two speech forms. Unlike English, Navajo is here concerned with distinguishing number in three categories as *one, two,* or *more than two* actors. Furthermore, if more than two actors are involved, their action of walking may be conceived as one which is performed en masse—collectively: *yikah,* they (a group of more than two actors) are walking along; or it may be viewed as an action performed by each individual composing the group in reference: *deíkááh,* they (each of a group of more than two actors) are walking along.

Both languages can express the simple command Come in!—but the English form does not concern itself even with the number of actors. *Come in!* may refer to one person or to a plurality of persons. In Navajo, the feature of number remains important: *Yah'aninááh,* come in (one person)! *Yah 'oh'aash,* come in (two persons); *Yah 'ohkááh,* come in (more than two persons)! In addition, the action as it involves a plurality of more than two persons may be conceived, from the Navajo viewpoint, as one in which the actors respond en masse, or as one in which they respond one after the other—*collective* in contrast with *segmental* action. *Yah 'ohkááh* directs a group of more than two persons to come in en masse; if the group is too large to permit the action to be performed simultaneously by all of the actors, the form *yah 'axohkááh* is more appropriate since it has the force of directing each member of the group to perform the action, *one after another*—segmentally.

As we will find in discussing the characteristics of the Navajo verb, many concepts which are viewed as aspects of the same verbal action, are described in English, by separate and distinct terms. As expressed in Navajo, the concepts *go, come, walk, start, arrive, enter, join, meet, divorce, separate, find,* and many others share the same set of verb stems, differing only in the adverbial and other derivativial prefixes which modify a basic stem meaning *to move on foot at a walk.* Thus, each of the verbs that follow share the same (perfective mode, singular number) verb stem—*yá,* moved at a walk, went, came; *níyá,* I came, went, arrived; *dah diiyá,* I started off; *yah'íiyá,* I went in, entered; *bik'íníyá,* I found it, came upon it; *bíiyá,* I joined it. The Navajo approach is comparable to such English formations as I walked *off,* I walked *in,* I went *into* (joined), I came *upon.*

Although Navajo and English share the concepts involved, the pattern governing their expression in the two languages is highly divergent. The two speech communities differ from each other in this aspect of their worldview. They look at the concept of *movement at a walk* in different ways. Consequently, there is not a single corresponding term in Navajo that exactly corresponds to a given English term with reference to this concept—we do not have two superimposed rings representing equivalent areas of meaning with reference, say, to the English form *Come in!* and its Navajo correspondents. We do *not* have:

but rather we have (using English as the starting point):

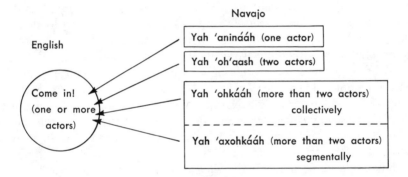

The basic concept expressed by the English term *Come in!* and its Navajo correspondents, is no doubt held in common by all people, irrespective of cultural-linguistic differences, but the pattern governing the manner in which the action is conceived and expressed differs radically between the two languages. However, given that all the essential elements requiring expression with regard to the idea are known (number of actors, manner of performance of the action) to the translator, there is no difficulty involved in conveying it from the English to the Navajo language. It is merely a matter of selecting an appropriate Navajo form to fit the situation as it is conceived from a Navajo viewpoint. And the same idea, as variously expressed in Navajo, can readily be conveyed in English by simply ignoring the several connotations that require expression in Navajo, but which are customarily left to the imagination of the listener in English. Neither is there any essential difficulty involved in expressing, in Navajo, concepts relating to *come, go, walk, arrive, meet, join,* etc., providing certain essential elements such as number of actors, identity of verb subject, mode and other features attaching to the action are known to the translator.

This relative ease of translation attenuates and finally disappears as the range of concepts held in common gives way to conceptual areas that are *not* shared by the two contrasting cultural-linguistic systems. At this point *translation* becomes impossible for the obvious reason that a language does not include terms for the expression of concepts that lie entirely outside the culture to which it belongs. At this point *interpretation* enters as the medium for cross-cultural communication. *Sleep, walk, eat, axe, needle, hat, good, high, sharp* are common to both Navajo and English; *atom, rhetoric, navigate, one-fourth, two-sixths, acre-foot,* and the like represent concepts that are not shared by Navajo culture and for which, consequently, there are no convenient labels in the Navajo language. The latter terms represent ideas that lie outside the Navajo world. As a result, they can be communicated from English to Navajo only by a descriptive, explanatory process to which we are here applying the term *interpretation* —in contradistinction to *translation,* which we are reserving to describe the process of trans-cultural, trans-linguistic communication by applying approximately corresponding word labels available in both languages.

And, of course, the process of interpretation across cultures goes in both directions. There are concepts in Navajo culture that are absent in Anglo-American society. The Navajo term *ńdíítį́į́h* attaches to an object that is not used by Anglo-Americans—consequently, there is no convenient corresponding English label with which to describe or identify it. It must be described in terms of its physical characteristics and its functions, as "a broom-like thing made of the wing feathers of the eagle, tied together at the quill end, and used ceremonially to brush away evil from a sick or moribund person." This description is sufficient to convey as much of the concept involved to the English speaking listener as was conveyed to the Navajo listener by simple definition of the term *acre-foot.* Actually, in both cases, full understanding can take place only with description of the alien concept in much greater depth and detail.

WHAT IS GRAMMAR?

Paul Roberts

In this essay, Roberts presents the modern linguistic recognition that the grammar of a language consists in the knowledge required to produce and understand sentences of that language, and that the locus of the grammar is in the head of the speaker. This realization has revolutionary consequences for the teacher, for it means the abandonment of the traditional notion that the student does not know grammar until he learns it in school. It also means that the teacher must realize that even the speaker of a non-standard variety of the language knows the grammar of that variety, and that it has cost him just as much effort to internalize it as for a speaker of a standard variety to internalize his grammar.

There are many ways of thinking about grammar, many senses in which the term is used. One way is this: grammar is something that produces the sentences of a language. This is what we shall mean by *grammar* in this book.

We may then ask, what do we mean by "something"? What sort of something? Well, the grammar might be a book or a series of books containing the rules for making the sentences of a language. An English grammar would be a set of rules for making English sentences. Or we might think of the "something" as a machine with the rules built into it. It is possible to conceive—it might even be possible to build—an electronic machine that, by following its rules, would come out with an English sentence every time it went through its operation and that never would produce a non-English sentence.

But there is another, and a more interesting, meaning that we can give to the "something" that produces English sentences. We can mean simply a speaker of English. If you speak English natively, you have built into you the rules of English grammar. In a sense, you *are* an English grammar. You possess, as an essential part of your being, a very complicated apparatus which enables you to produce infinitely many sentences, all

Abridged from *English Sentences* by Paul Roberts (New York: Harcourt Brace Jovanovich, 1962). Reprinted by permission of Harcourt Brace Jovanovich.

English ones, including many that you have never specifically learned. Furthermore, by applying your rules, you can easily tell whether a sentence that you hear is a grammatical English sentence or not.

This may strike you as absurd. You may protest that you have never studied English grammar or that you have studied it without profit or understanding—in any case, that you know nothing about it. But it is perfectly easy to demonstrate that, if you speak English natively, you know virtually all about English grammar, all its essential rules. For example, which of the following are grammatical English sentences and which are not?

1. Henry bought his mother some flowers.
2. Henry some flowers bought his mother.
3. He isn't very nice to me.
4. He are not to me very nice.
5. Those things don't trouble me at all.
6. Those thing to me are not of a troublesome.

Obviously, 1, 3, and 5 are grammatical English sentences, and 2, 4, and 6 are not.

Now, how do you know? You don't know because somebody told you. Nobody ever gave you the words "Those thing to me are not of a troublesome" and informed you that it was not an English sentence. You don't know by intuition. If it were intuition, it would presumably work just as well on Chinese as on English, but in fact whatever is working for you works only on English.

GRAMMATICALITY

What is working is your grammar. You reject sentences 2, 4, and 6 because they do not conform to the rules of English grammar as you know them. You know that *those* modifies plural nouns, not singulars, that an adjective like *troublesome* does not occur after *of a*, that such a prepositional phrase as *to me* comes more commonly after the verb than before it. What you may not know is how to talk about such matters. You may have a foggy understanding or none at all of such terms as *plural, adjective, prepositional phrase*, so that if someone asked you why sentence 6 is ungrammatical, you might not be able to explain very well. Nevertheless, you readily reject 6 as wrong, because it doesn't accord with the rules of English. You know the rules, whether you can describe them or not.

Knowing them is what makes you a speaker of English. Now what about this sentence?

> Horses that think for themselves smoke filter cigarettes.

Is that grammatical or not? Of course it is grammatical. It is also non-sensical: horses don't smoke cigarettes, filter-tipped or otherwise, and don't think for themselves either. But it is grammatical, conforming perfectly to the rules of English sentence structure. We see then that by *grammatical* we don't necessarily mean "meaningful" or "true." We can talk nonsense grammatically or lie grammatically and often do. Though the following are all nonsensical or untrue, they are all grammatical English sentences:

> Dick Tracy is the President of the United States.
> All Boy Scouts can swim six miles under water.
> Nobody seems to have chorkled these crambons.
> The earth is oblong.

Yet the following, though much more sensible, are ungrammatical:

> Dick Tracy very brave character of comic strip.
> Every Boy Scouts easy hike six miles.
> Nobody seem this plants to have watering.
> The earth almost round is.

THE STUDY OF GRAMMAR

We have said that all of us who speak English know English grammar, and you may ask, if that is so, why you are required to study it. What we are after now, of course, is not the knowledge that permits us to distinguish grammatical sentences from ungrammatical ones, but rather a conscious understanding of the system and the way it operates. Such an understanding has certain practical uses in the study of writing and other forms of communication. . . . However, the author of this book would not wish to recommend the study of grammar on practical grounds alone. Grammar is the heart of language, and language is the foremost of the features that make human beings human. We said earlier that every speaker of English *is* an English grammar. When you study English grammar, you inquire most intimately into yourself and the way you work.

COMPETENCE AND PERFORMANCE IN LANGUAGE

Owen Thomas

In this essay, Owen Thomas explains two terms which have become central in discussions of linguistic and cultural behavior, competence and performance. This distinction is one which will carry through in later sections, so that an adequate understanding of it will be important for understanding much of what follows. Thomas also points out that the study of the grammar of a language involves an attempt to construct a model of the knowledge possessed by the speaker.

The two terms in the title of this paper have great relevance and importance for teachers of the English language arts in the elementary schools. I would like to lead up to a definition of these terms gradually.

Consider, first, four six-year-old boys from different parts of the country and from different social backgrounds. It is an amazing and awesome fact that, if these four boys should meet, they could communicate with each other. Moreover, we can communicate with them. And to compound the amazement, each one of these boys, like any native speaker of English from the age of three—or thereabouts—onward, has the ability to produce and to understand an infinite number of sentences.

The only way to explain this almost incredible situation is to say that these four boys—as well as you and I—speak the same language; that is, for all practical purposes, we all use the same grammar (with minor dialectal and educational differences) in speaking and in understanding the language. If this were not true, the children could not understand each other, and we could not understand them.

WHAT LANGUAGE IS: A DEFINITION

What, then, is language, and how do people learn languages?

The first of these questions is the easier of the two, but even in trying

From *New Directions in Elementary English*, ed. Alexander Frazier (Champaign, Illinois: National Council of Teachers of English, 1967). Reprinted by permission of the publisher and Owen Thomas.

to formulate an answer to it we need to make a digression. Specifically, we need to look at "symbolic logic," which is, of course, that branch of philosophy that has had the greatest impact on academic research in the twentieth century.

Symbolic logic enables us to discuss the various systems that exist in the world. The so-called "new math," for example, is the product of applying logic to the teaching of mathematics. As all teachers in elementary schools know, the notion of "set theory" is important in the new math. We can say that a set is simply a collection of anything. The number of letters in the alphabet constitutes a set. Moreover, a set may contain only one thing, like the set of Mt. Rushmores in the world, or it may contain an infinite number of things, like the set of all the possible positive integers in arithmetic.

In discussing language, we are concerned with three kinds of sets: a set of elements, a set of operations, and a set of laws that govern the operations. The set of elements, of course, includes the sounds of the language, the standard prefixes and suffixes, the complete list of words in an unabridged dictionary, and so on. The number of such elements is finite; that is, we can count all the sounds necessary to speak English, all the words in a dictionary, and so on.

The set of operations is a bit more difficult to discuss. Let's take a simple sentence as a source of examples: "The boy ate the hamburger." Suppose, now, that I ask you to perform the following operations on this simple sentence: (1) change it into a question which can be answered by a "yes" or a "no," (2) make the sentence—which is now positive— negative, and (3) change the sentence from the active to the passive voice. You would probably produce the following three sentences:

1. Did the boy eat the hamburger?
2. The boy didn't eat the hamburger.
3. The hamburger was eaten by the boy.

The fact that all native speakers of English would produce the same three sentences—or would at least recognize the three which I produced as acceptable—can be explained only if we assume that there are certain basic operations which take place in the language and which everyone learns very early. Moreover, the operations must also explain such things as the occurrence of "did" in the first and second sentences. (There is no "did" in the original sentence.)

In short, every language has a set of operations which permit us to combine the elements of the language in various acceptable ways. Furthermore, this set of operations must be finite, or it would be impossible for speakers to learn the set.

But there are also laws that restrict the kinds of operations possible in a language. Consider the following three words: *brick, blick, bnick.* The first one is obviously an English word; the second could become an English word (it might be the name of a new detergent); but the third could never be an English word. All native speakers recognize these facts: they are part of the laws of the English language, or more specifically, of the sound system of the English language.

Now returning to our earlier question "What is a language?" we can place our definition within the context of symbolic logic. In particular, I would like to offer a definition that is adapted from one originally formulated by Noam Chomsky:

> A language consists of a set of sentences, formulated from a set of elements, according to a set of operations, that obey a set of laws.

The number of sentences is infinite. The set of elements, the set of operations, and the set of laws are all finite.

THE CONCEPT OF LANGUAGE COMPETENCE

Now we can define a grammar. Specifically, a grammar consists of the sets of elements, operations, and laws that a speaker uses in producing and understanding sentences. When we learn to speak a language, we must, in some fashion, learn the grammar of that language. . . .

Technically, this internalized knowledge which every native speaker has, this awesome ability which enables even children to speak and to understand grammatical sentences, is called "competence."

But even though we can give a name to this ability, we can not define it precisely. There is no way to open up the head of a child and to point to his competence. We cannot define it with absolute precision. We cannot dissect it.

What, then, can we do? For the moment, at least, we can turn back to the notion of system. More specifically, we can construct a "grammatical model" that duplicates the effect of an individual's competence; that is, we can use the model to produce sentences.

All grammars . . . are models of the reality of language. And as you might suspect, some models are "better"—more accurate, more useful, more complete—than others. Traditional grammar is a model and a useful one. It contains many accurate explanations of linguistic reality. Structural linguistics is also a model, and as such, it tells us many interesting and important things about language. But only one grammar, the transformational, specifically attempts to define all the elements, all the operations, and all the laws of a language. In other words, a transformational grammar is a model of an ideal speaker's competence, the closest thing we have to an actual definition of competence itself.

The notion of competence is an extremely useful one. Professor Kellogg Hunt, of Florida State University, has used the notion to establish the fact that children in various grades generally "know" most of the same operations. The primary difference between younger and older children consists of the fact that older children can perform *more* operations in a given sentence. Young children, for example, can construct negative sentences, or interrogative sentences, or sentences in the passive voice, but only rarely can they construct a negative-interrogative-passive ("Wasn't the hamburger eaten by the boy?"). In other words, young children have a far greater competence than we've generally given them credit for having. But they obviously need more practice in using this competence.

PERFORMANCE: WHAT ONE DOES
WITH HIS COMPETENCE

What, then, is performance? By now, the definition should be obvious. Performance is what an individual does with his competence in a particular situation. And performance can be affected by a number of totally nonlinguistic factors; for example, if a person is tired, or embarrassed, or in a hurry, his linguistic performance might well be affected although his linguistic competence would remain unchanged. I am sure we have all had the experience of someone saying to us, "Oh, you're an English teacher. I'll have to watch my grammar." Such persons are embarrassed and, for this reason alone, will occasionally make mistakes in performance, mistakes which they might not make under other circumstances. . . . In short, the distinction between competence and performance is an important one. Our competence is our grammar. Our performance is our use of the grammar.

All this is not to say that we should ignore the discussion of language in the schools. Far from it. It seems probable that we can increase the size of a child's performance significantly, and we can certainly give him greater facility in the use of this competence. This is precisely the point. In teaching the English language arts in the elementary school, we should first attempt to show a child how much he already knows about language —we should make him aware of his competence. Then, and only then, are we ready to go on to improve his performance.

LANGUAGE DIFFERENCES AND PRESCRIPTIVISM

Paul Postal

Postal contrasts the view of a grammatical description preferred by Thomas with the type of grammatical presentation traditionally used in school, which he labels "prescriptive grammar" because it tries to prescribe the grammar of one variety of the language for students to learn as though it were the only valid form. He also shows that the viewpoints underlying traditional grammar instruction implicitly deny all of the facts about language presented by Langacker. To those facts Postal also adds the important one that language is basically spoken, and that writing is a secondary, derived system for recording linguistic messages in a visible, preservable form. The traditional view has totally misconceived the relation between speech and writing, leading, among other things, to an unfortunate depreciation of the importance and significance of speech, and a curricular overemphasis on the skills of literacy.

We have used the term *English grammar* to refer to an over-all system which fully describes our knowledge of the phonetic, semantic, and syntactic properties of all English sentences. This term seems to assume that *English* is a monolithic whole, a uniform language spoken by millions. But it is well known that there are vast differences in the languages of those we refer to as "speakers of English." In fact, it is almost certain that no two people really have completely identical languages. The most obvious difference in individual languages is lexicon: It is inconceivable that two people would know exactly identical sets of lexical items. Differences in phonology are also common and familiar to all of us. Nor are distinctions in syntax lacking.

These differences are not purely individual. Speakers of English, and other languages as well, fall into groups defined by associations of similarities and differences. These groups are called *dialects*. Dialects exist as a

From *English Transformational Grammar*, Roderick Jacobs and Peter Rosenbaum, eds. (Boston, Massachusetts: Blaisdell Publishing Company, 1968). Reprinted by permission of the publisher.

function of all forms of linguistic isolation and separation—in space, time, social class, occupation, age, etc. But the existence of dialects does not preclude the sensible use of the term *English grammar*, because it is obvious that both dialects and individual variations of our language do share a large number of underlying similarities. This is especially true of English syntax, and it may be even more true of semantics, although at present we have hardly any means to investigate the latter. By studying the deeper underlying principles of syntax, we are in a better position to appreciate how minor the differences among variants of the same language really are. Studies of phonetic differences have already revealed that dialectic variations in phonology may in fact be the function of an overlay of superficial rules on an extensive body of common phonological principles.

This aspect of the study of grammar brings us to another important difference between grammar as it has been presented here and the grammar we are familiar with from our previous schooling. School instruction in grammar is usually dominated by two considerations which are foreign to our subject matter and aims: One is the teaching of writing and composition, a subject we will return to shortly; the other is the attempt to teach a more or less standardized dialect of English to students who often speak another dialect. A substantial portion of what is called "grammar" in schools is concerned with the minor features which distinguish different dialects. Long hours are spent rehearsing the differences between expressions such as those in (1) and (2):

(1) a. It is me
    b. It is I
(2) a. I am not going.
    b. I ain't going.

But much less attention is given to the vast body of sentence formation principles common to *all* dialects of English—principles which for all speakers of English distinguish between the sequences in (3) and the sequence in (4):

(3) a. *I up to in come will should off so
    b. *I saw the boy you like him
    c. *I book John give
(4) a. I should come in
    b. I saw the boy that you like
    c. I gave John a book.

* An asterisk before a sentence indicates that it represents an ungrammatical (i.e., impossible) sequence in the language.

In short, much of school grammar is concerned with teaching the forms of the prestigious "standard" language to speakers of the less "standard" (often labeled "substandard") dialects of English. But the so-called "standard" language is itself a dialect or variant of English, specifically the one which is linked to literacy and to the literary traditions. This is really a kind of social engineering in which certain speakers are asked to alter certain details of their language to fit those of the more prestigious speakers. This kind of instruction is perhaps a socially defensible goal, defined more precisely and achieved more efficiently in a number of other countries. One difficulty in the United States is that the standard which is taught is not very standard and may vary considerably from place to place.

But whatever value we attach to this linguistic "engineering," it has no real linguistic interest or importance, and most of the "linguistic" justifications for it are either imaginary or completely silly. It is often claimed, for example, that various non-standard forms of speech not only involve linguistic "decay" but also prevent effective communication. This particular argument is as pompous and indefensible as it is empirically without basis.

Another aspect of school grammar, which we refer to here as *prescriptive* grammar, is its insistence that old, even now archaic, forms must continue in use and that many new formations must be excluded. A good example of this is the endless struggle to prevent the use of "like" in those places where older forms of English would have used "as." Prescriptive grammar, virtually by definition, involves resistance to the never-ending process of linguistic change. The baseless assumption behind this resistance is that we are headed for a "breakdown in communication" unless linguistic change is opposed by the guardians of the language. And this assumption, groundless though it may be, dominates much popular discussion of grammar and usage both within the schools and without, and even the most obvious evidence to the contrary does not seem to shake this false view. Does anyone wish to maintain seriously that modern French is a less adequate vehicle for communication than the Latin from which, in a certain sense, it developed, by just those processes of change which prescriptive grammar seeks to resist? Similarly, many hundred of languages are maintained despite ongoing linguistic change without any tradition of grammatical prescriptivism, without any literary tradition, without any writing system. Prescriptive grammar tends to assume implicitly that human language is a fragile cultural invention, only with difficulty maintained in good working order. It fails to recognize that language is an innate attribute of human nature.

Prescriptive grammar is thus not very much concerned with the nature of language as such, nor with the nature of English in particular. It is interested instead in "correct English," that is, in enforcing the use of one particular dialect (that of the particular prescriptive grammarian, or at least that which he thinks is his). A final aspect of prescriptive approaches is a tendency to oppose colloquial styles of speech in favor of more formal ones (*is not* is better than *isn't*, etc.). This is linked to many things perhaps but probably most closely to a concern with the usages of the writing system which is more closely related to formal styles of speaking. There is a groundless tendency here to assume that writing has some sort of primacy over speech and to view colloquial styles as a "decay" from formal speaking, which is already taken to be a deviation from the "true language" given by writing.

Prescriptive grammar is closely linked to the curious assumption that it is necessary to teach "grammar" in schools—that is, to the assumption that the child comes to school with no knowledge of grammar. This assumption is obviously based on a very different conception of grammar from that discussed above. A five-year-old child already has a substantial grasp of most of the principles of sentence formation and interpretation. The truth of the assumption made by prescriptive grammar depends on interpreting the phrase "knowing grammar" to include the ability to discuss one's implicit linguistic knowledge, hence the teaching of concepts like the parts of speech; this interpretation of "knowing grammar" also involves knowledge of the writing system and its adequate use, and knowledge of the details of the prestigious or standard dialect.

It is important, therefore, that we do not confuse our concerns with those of prescriptive grammar. When it has been said that an expression like (5) is a "well-formed English sentence" but an expression like (6) is not, it is not meant that the expression is well formed in some ideal, "standard" language:

(5) Harry wants to go

(6) *Harry wants going.

The expression in (5) is a well-formed sentence in the particular dialect being described, which is actually that of the author. However, examples have generally been chosen which will almost certainly be valid for just about any dialect. The interest here is in the vast body of structural and syntactic principles which are common to *all* varieties of English rather than in the minor details which differentiate them. These details are what have occasioned so much argument and emotion within the framework of prescriptive grammar.

WRITING

We mentioned above that prescriptive grammar tends to view writing as the primary aspect of language, and speech, or the vocal aspect of language, as a kind of unstable deviation from writing. But this view is completely erroneous. Writing systems are without exception parasitic on language; they are attempts (often rather bad attempts) to represent certain aspects of linguistic structure, usually phonological aspects. Furthermore, writing systems are relatively new inventions, dating back only a few thousand years, compared to the much more enormous span of time which must be assumed for language. Most of the languages on earth still have no writing systems associated with them, and they exist perfectly well without writing.

It is important not to misinterpret what was just said. We have not said that *speech* is primary; we do assert, however, that *language* is primary. Speech, after all, is behavior or performance. As we have seen, language is the system of knowledge which underlies this behavior. There are, however, many ways in which speech is more naturally related to language than any form of writing activity. The vocal-auditory medium is built right into the human organism, and all normal humans can use the medium of speech for performing sentences. But millions of humans cannot use any writing system. Although speech is the "natural" medium for performing language, and writing is a derived or secondary technique, this fact tends to be obscured for us by the great value of writing and by the role which it plays in more complex forms of highly developed social life.

It is therefore neither by mistake nor by accident we have considered language as if, in effect, writing systems did not exist. This approach recognizes that language, together with its "natural" performance medium of articulate speech, is a natural consequence of the human organism. Writing, on the other hand, is a special technique for performing the elements of language, and as such it is a clever invention rather like the telephone or algebra.

SNOBS, SLOBS, AND THE
ENGLISH LANGUAGE

Donald J. Lloyd

In an entertaining discussion, Donald J. Lloyd reviews some of the facts about language generally agreed on by linguists, and demonstrates that those who view themselves as "guardians of linguistic purity" (which includes many teachers) are simply uninformed purveyors of an elitest myth.

There is at large among us today an unholy number of people who make it their business to correct the speech and writing of others. When Winston Churchill says, "It's me" in a radio address, their lips purse and murmur firmly, "It is I," and they sit down and write bitter letters to the New York *Times* about What is Happening to the English Language. Reading "I only had five dollars," they circle *only* and move it to the right of *had*, producing "I had only five dollars" with a sense of virtue that is beyond the measure of man. They are implacable enemies of "different than," of "loan" and "contract" used as verbs, and of dozens of other common expressions. They put triumphant exclamation marks in the margins of library books. They are ready to tangle the thread of any discussion by pouncing on a point of grammar.

If these people were all retired teachers of high-school English, their weight in the community would be negligible; but unfortunately they are not. They are authors, scholars, businessmen, librarians—indeed, they are to be found wherever educated people read and write English. And they are moved by a genuine concern for the language. They have brought us, it is true, to a state in which almost anybody, no matter what his education or the clarity of his expression, is likely to find himself attacked for some locution which he has used. Yet their intentions are of the best. It is only that their earnest minds are in the grip of two curious misconceptions. One is that there is a "correct" standard English which is uniform and definite and has been reduced to rule. The other is that this "correct" standard

From *The American Scholar*, vol. 20, no. 3 (Summer, 1951), pp. 279–88. Reprinted by permission of the author.

can only be maintained by the vigilant attention of everybody concerned with language—indeed, by the whole body of educated men and women.

The enemy these self-appointed linguistic sentries see lurking in every expression which stirs the correcter's instinct in them is something they call illiteracy—which is not a simple state of being unlettered, but something more. This illiteracy is a willful and obstinate disregard for the standards of civilized expression. It stirs anger in them when they think they see it, because it seems to them a voluntary ignorance, compounded out of carelessness and sloth. When they think they find it in men who hold responsible positions in the community, they feel it to be a summation of all the decline of the graces of culture, the last reaches of a great wave of vulgarity which is eroding the educated and literate classes. It seems to them to be a surge of crude populism; they hear in each solecism the faint, far-off cries of the rising mob. It is really a sort of ringing in their ears.

In view of the general agreement among the literate that a "correct" standard English exists, and in view of the vituperation directed at anyone suspected of corrupting it, one would expect some kind of agreement about what is correct. There is little to be found; the easy utterance of one educated man is the bane of another. "For all the fussiness about *which* and *that*," remarks Jacques Barzun in the *Nation*, "the combined editorial brass of the country have feebly allowed the word 'disinterested' to be absolutely lost in its original sense. One finds as careful a writer as Aldous Huxley using it to mean uninterested, so that by now a 'disinterested judge' is one that goes to sleep on the bench." And on the subject of what surely is a harmless word, *whom*, Kyle Crichton [formerly] editor of *Collier's* is quoted in *Harper's*: "The most loathsome word (to me at least) in the English language is 'whom.' You can always tell a half-educated buffoon by the care he takes in working the word in. When he starts it I know I am faced with a pompous illiterate who is not going to have me long as company."

Probably only a cynic would conclude from the abundance of such comments that those who demand correct English do not know it when they meet it; but some students of language must have been led to wonder, for they have made up lists of disputed locutions and polled the literate on them. So far, the only agreement they have reached has to be expressed in statistical terms.

The latest of these surveys, a questionnaire containing nineteen disputed expressions, was reported by Norman Lewis in *Harper's* Magazine for March, 1949. Lewis sent his list to 750 members of certain groups chosen mainly for their professional interest in the English language: lexicographers, high-school and college teachers of English, authors, editors, journalists, radio commentators, and "a random sampling of *Harper's* subscribers."

If we count out two groups on the basis of extremely special knowledge and interest—the college professors of English and the lexicographers—we find all the others accepting about half the expressions. The authors and editors (book and magazine) were highest with about 56 per cent, and the editors of women's magazines lowest with about 45. (The expression which was least favored was *less* in the sense of *fewer*—"I encountered *less* difficulties than I had expected"—but even that received an affirmative vote of 23 per cent.) The distinguished electors seem individually to have played hop, skip and jump down the column, each finding among the nineteen expressions about ten he could approve of. If any two fell on the same ten, it was merely a coincidence.

A person innocent in the ways of this controversy, but reasonably well-informed about the English language, noticing that the disputants ignore the massive conformity of most writers in most of their language practices, in order to quibble about fringe matters, might assume that they would welcome the cold light of linguistic science. This is a naïve assumption. In response to an attempt of mine to correct some of the misapprehensions I found in Mr. Barzun's article—among them his curious notion that "detached" and not "uninterested" was the original meaning of "disinterested"—he replied by letter that I represented a misplaced and breezy scientism, and that what I said struck him as "the raw material of 'populism' and willful resistance to Mind. . . . All dictionaries to the contrary notwithstanding, the word disinterested is now prevailingly used in the meaning I deprecated. . . . The fact that an illiterate mistake may become the correct form . . . is no reason for not combating it in its beginnings. . . ." This rejection both of the professional student of language and of the dictionary, when they disagree with the opinions of the writer, has the effect of making each man his own uninhibited authority on language and usage—an effect which I do not believe was exactly what Mr. Barzun had in mind.

What he did have in mind he stated clearly in one distinguished paragraph:

> A living culture in one nation (not to speak of one world) must insist on a standard of usage. And usage, as I need not tell you, has important social implications apart from elegance and expressiveness in literature. The work of communication in law, politics and diplomacy, in medicine, technology, and moral speculation depends on the maintenance of a medium of exchange whose values must be kept fixed, as far as possible, like those of any other reliable currency. To prevent debasement and fraud requires vigilance, and it implies the right to blame. It is not snobbery that is involved but literacy on its highest plane, and that literacy has to be protected from ignorance and sloth.

It is a pity that these sentiments, so deserving of approval, should receive it from almost all educated people except those who really know something about how language works. One feels like an uncultivated slob when he dissents—one of the low, inelegant, illiterate, unthinking mob. Yet as a statement about the English language, or about standard English, it is not merely partly true and partly false, but by the consensus of most professional students of language, totally false. It is one of those monstrous errors which gain their original currency by being especially plausible at a suitable time, and maintain themselves long after the circumstances which give rise to them have vanished. Mr. Barzun's remarks are an echo from the eighteenth century; they reek with an odor mustier than the lavender of Grandmother's sachet. They have little relevance to the use of the English language in America in our day.

In actual fact, the standard English used by literate Americans is no pale flower being overgrown by the weeds of vulgar usage: it is a strong, flourishing growth. Nor is it a simple, easily describable entity. Indeed, it can scarcely be called an entity at all, except in the loose sense in which we call the whole vast sum of all the dialects of English spoken and written throughout the world a single language. In this sense, standard American English is the sum of the language habits of the millions of educated people in this country. It is rooted in the intellectual life of this great and varied people. Its forms express what its users wish to express; its words mean what its users think they mean; it is correctly written when it is written by those who write it, and correctly spoken by those who speak it. No prim and self-conscious hoarding of the dead fashions of a superior class gives it its power, but its negligent use by minds intent on stubborn and important problems. There is no point in a tiresome carping about usage; the best thing to do is relax and enjoy it.

There are five simple facts about language in general which we must grasp before we can understand a specific language or pass judgment on a particular usage. It is a pity that they are not more widely known in place of the nonsense which now circulates, for they would relieve the native-born speaker of English of his present uncertainty, and give him a proper authority and confidence in his spontaneous employment of his mother tongue. They arise from a common-sense analysis of the nature of language and the conditions of its use.

In the first place, language is basically speech. Speech comes first in the life of the individual and of the race. It begins in infancy and continues throughout our lives; we produce and attend to a spoken wordage much greater than the written. Even the mass of writing which floods in upon us today is only the froth on an ocean of speech. In history, also, speech comes first. English has been written for only about fifteen hundred years; before this, it is of incalculable antiquity. In speech its grammar was developed; from changes in the sounds of speech, changes in its grammar come. The educated are inclined to feel that the most important aspect of language is the written form of it, and that the spoken language must and should take its standards from this. Actually, the great flow of influence is from speech to writing. Writing does influence speech somewhat, but its influence is like the interest a bank pays on the principal entrusted to it. No principal, no interest.

In the second place, language is personal. It is an experience and a pattern of habits of a very intimate kind. In the home, the family, the school and the neighborhood we learn the speechways of our community, learning to talk as those close to us talk in the give and take of daily life. We are at one with our nation in our easy command of the pitch, tune and phrase of our own home town. Language is personal, also, in that our grasp of it is no greater than our individual experience with it. The English we know is not that vast agglomeration of verbal signs which fills and yet escapes the largest lexicons and grammars, but what we have personally heard and spoken, read and written. The best-read man knows of his native language only a limited number of forms in a limited number of combinations. Outside of these, the wealth which a copious tongue has as its potential is out of his world, and out of everybody's, for no dictionary is so complete or grammar so compendious as to capture it.

The third fact about language is that it changes. It changes in its sounds, its meanings and its syntax. The transmission of sounds, words and meanings from generation to generation is always in some respects imprecise. Minute differences add up in time to perceptible changes, and changes to noticeable drifts. Difference in changes and in rates of change make local speech sounds, pitches, tones and vocabularies draw subtly and persistently away from one another. And all it takes to produce an identifiable dialect is sufficient segregation over a sufficient length of time.

The fourth great fact about language, then, is that its users are, in one way or another, isolated. Each has with only a few others the sort of familiar relationships which join them in one language community. Yet there are upward of two hundred million native speakers of English in the world. Obviously they cannot all be in close touch with one another. They congeal in nuclei—some stable, some transitory—which by a kind of double-action draw them together and enforce isolation of many more-or-less shifting kinds: the isolation of distance, of education, of economic levels, of occupation, age and sex, of hobbies and political boundaries. Any one of these will be reflected in language habits; any two or three will bring about, in one community, speech differences as great as those caused by oceans and mountain ranges.

The fifth great fact about language is that it is a historical growth of a specific kind. The nature of English is one of the absolutes of our world, like air, water and gravity. Its patterns are not subject to judgment; they simply are. Yet they have not always been what they are; like the physical world, they have changed with time, but always in terms of what they have been. *Boy loves girl* means something different from *girl loves boy*. It is futile for us to prefer another way of conveying these meanings: that is the

English way, and we must live with it. Yet students of the language see in this simple pattern the result of a cataclysmic change, great and slow like the geologic upheavals that have brought old salt beds to the very tops of mountain ranges, and as simple. Each is what it is because of what it has been before.

Language as a social instrument reflects all the tides which sweep society, reacting in a local or surface way easily and quickly—as a beach changes its contours to suit the waves—but it offers everywhere a stubborn rock core that only time and massive pressures can move. The whim of a girl can change its vocabulary, but no will of man can touch its essential structure; this is work for the long attrition of generations of human use. Ever lagging a little behind human needs, it offers a multitude of terms for the things men no longer care about, but keeps them improvising to say what has not been said before.

Spoken English is, then, by its own nature and the nature of man, a welter of divergences. The divergences of class and place are sharpest in Britain, where the same dialects have been spoken in the same shires and villages for more than a thousand years. Although these can be heard in America by any traveler, no matter how dull his ear, they are relatively slight, for our language is essentially and repeatedly a colonial speech. Each of the American colonies drew settlers from various parts of Britain; each worked out a common speech based mainly on the dialect of its most influential group of immigrants (which differed from colony to colony); each remained in relative isolation from the others for about a hundred years. Then many colonists began to move to the interior: wave after wave of settlers traveled along rather distinct lines of advance until the continent was covered. Everywhere there was a mingling of dialects, with a composite speech arising, based mainly on the speech of the dominant local group. And so we have a Northern speech fanning out from the Northeastern states, a Midland speech fanning out from the Mid-Atlantic states, and a Southern speech in the land of cotton-raisers, all crossing and merging as the pioneers moved west. Local differences are greatest along the Atlantic coast.

Wherever our people settled, they worked out local ways of talking about the things of common experience, and found their own verbal symbols of class distinctions. Here and there are areas where foreign-speaking groups clung together and developed special exotically-flavored dialects, but otherwise most speech patterns in America can be traced back to the dialects of Britain. Everywhere there is a common speech used by the multitude which works with its hands, and a slightly different dialect spoken by the professional and leisure classes.

The standard English written by Americans is not, however, the written form of educated speech, which shows great local variation. Its spellings have only a rough equivalence to the sounds we make; its grammatical system, which has nationwide and even worldwide currency, had its origin in the educated speech of the Northeastern states, and before that in the dialect of London, England. The concentration of schools, colleges, publishing houses and print shops in early New England and New York had the same effect in this country as the concentration in England, for centuries, of political power, commercial activity and intellectual life in London: it established a written standard, native only to those who grew up near the Hudson River or east of it. Elsewhere in America this written standard has been a learned class dialect—learned in the schools as the property and distinguishing mark of an educated class. Like many of its spellings, it is itself a relic of the past, an heirloom handed down from the days when the whole nation looked to the schoolmasters of New England for its book-learning.

The present controversy about usage is simply a sign that times have changed. The several vast and populous regions of this country have grown self-sufficient and self-conscious, and have taken the education of their youth into their own hands. Where the young once had to travel to the East for a respectable education, they receive it now in local public systems of rapid growth and great size. From local schools they may go to local universities of fifteen to fifty thousand students, where they can proceed to the highest degrees. Yale University is overcrowded with some six thousand students; in the community colleges alone of California more than 150,000 are enrolled. Most of these young people take their diplomas and go to work among their own people. They form a literate class greater in numbers and in proportion to the total population than the world has ever seen before. Speaking the speech of their region, they mingle naturally and easily with its people. When they write, they write the language they know, and they print it, for the most part, in presses close at hand. Everywhere they speak a standard literate English—but with differences: a regional speech derived from the usages of the early settlers.

Standard written English is, after all, an abstraction—a group of forms rather arbitrarily selected from the multitude offered by the language as a whole—an abstraction which serves the peculiar needs of the intellect. It achieves its wide currency because the interests of its users are the common interests of the educated, which transcend frontiers and negate distances— law, literature, science, industry and commerce. . . . And it is not static. As the needs of the intellect change, standard English changes. Change is its life, as anyone can see who picks up a book written only a little time ago, or examines almost any old newspaper.

The common speech of the uneducated, on the other hand, is comparatively static. Though it varies greatly from place to place, it is everywhere conservative; far from corrupting the standard language, it follows slowly after, preserving old forms long ago given up by literate speakers. "Them things" was once standard, and so were "he don't," "giv," and "clumb" and "riz." Its patterns are archaic, its forms homely and local. Only its vocabulary is rich and daring in metaphor (but the best of this is quickly swiped by writers of standard English). Seldom written because its speakers seldom write, it is yet capable of great literary beauties, uncomplicated force, compact suggestion, and moving sentiment. . . .

I have often wondered at the fear of common English and its speakers which the cultural aristocracy display, at their curious definition of illiteracy, and at the intemperance of their terms, which verges on the pathological. A Freudian should have a picnic with them. They use such epithets as *illiteracies, crudities, barbarisms, ignorance, carelessness* and *sloth.* But who is not negligent in language, as in the mechanics of driving a car? They mutter darkly about "inchoate mob feelings." They confess themselves snobs by denying that their attitudes are snobbish. The stridency of their self-assurance puzzles the mind.

We might better adjust our minds to the divergences of usage in standard written English, for time, space and normal drift of culture have put them there. We need not raise our eyebrows at a different twist of phrase, but enjoy it as an echo of a way of life somewhat different from our own, but just as good. We could do more than enjoy these things; we could recognize that the fixed forms of the language which do not come to our attention were developed in the past. We have come too late for the show. It is the changing forms that evidence the life in our language and in our society; we could learn much about our people and their ways by simply and objectively observing them.

If there is one thing which is of the essence of language, it is its drive to adapt. In an expanding culture like ours, which is invading whole new realms of thought and experience, the inherited language is not wholly suited to what we have to say. We need more exact and expressive modes of utterance than we have; we are working toward finer tolerances. The fabric of our language is flexible, and it can meet our needs. Indeed, we cannot stop it from doing so. Therefore it would be well and wholesome for us to see, in the locutions of the educated which bring us up sharply as we read, not evidences of a rising tide of illiteracy (which they are not), but marks of a grand shift in modes of expression, a self-reliant regionalism, and a persistent groping toward finer distinctions and a more precise utterance.

THE LINGUISTIC ATLASES:
OUR NEW RESOURCE

Harold B. Allen

In this essay Harold B. Allen presents information about regional variation in American English and provides some cogent examples to show why an awareness and acceptance of this variation is necessary if the teacher is to intelligently evaluate instructional materials and avoid serious mistakes in the classroom. Professor Allen is himself the director of the Linguistic Atlas of the Upper Midwest.

A few years ago a teacher in South Carolina was pushing her less than enthusiastic pupils through a grammar drill book, painfully but relentlessly. The class struggled on to an exercise intended to teach the correct use of the negative of *ought*. Here the students found sentences with the approved construction *ought not*. But they found also some sentences with a construction they were supposed to cross out, *hadn't ought*. This the pupils had never seen or heard before, and they were delighted with it. True, the book said it was wrong, and the teacher, as always, agreed with the book. But there it was—in the book—as plain as anything could be; and somehow it seemed marvelously sensible. *He hadn't intended to do it; he hadn't ought to do it. I hadn't wanted to go; I hadn't ought to go.* Why not? So within a week or two the puzzled teacher began to find more and more of her pupils using *hadn't ought*, pupils who up until then had used *ought not* with unconscious ease.

Such an incident cannot happen in the future if teachers and textbook writers know and use the new data now becoming accessible to them. This is the body of facts about American English coming from the great research projects collectively designated the Linguistic Atlas of the United States and Canada.

. . .

From *The English Journal*, vol. 45 (April, 1956), pp. 188–94. Reprinted by permission of *The English Journal*.

DATA ON PRONUNCIATION

What is the Linguistic Atlas of the United States? It is not a single project; it is a number of regional research projects using similar procedures and collecting the same kinds of evidence, hence producing results that can be added together and compared.

. . .

At present, organizations to gather this evidence have been effected in eight different areas: New England, Middle Atlantic States, South Atlantic States, North Central States, Upper Midwest, Rocky Mountain States, Pacific Coast, and Louisiana. The New England Atlas has been completed and published. From it and the unpublished materials of the other eastern surveys has come the evidence presented by Hans Kurath in 1949 in his *World Geography of the Eastern United States,* by E. B. Atwood in 1953 in his *Verb Forms of the Eastern United States* [and by Kurath & McDavid in 1960 in *The Pronunciation of English in the Atlantic States*]. Derivative articles by Raven I. McDavid, Jr., Atwood, Alva Davis, Walter Avis, Thomas Pearce, David Reed, Marjorie Kimmerle, and others have made public additional usage evidence in *American Speech, College English* and *The English Journal, Orbis, Language,* and *Language Learning.* . . .

For significant matters of pronunciation I would suggest reference to McDavid's excellent article, "Some Social Differences in Pronunciation," in *Language Learning* in 1953.[1] McDavid's thesis here is that, although certain pronunciations may lack recognition or distribution nationally, they can enjoy high prestige in a given region through the influence of such a focal center as Boston, New York, Philadelphia, Richmond, or Charleston. Differences in pronunciation, in other words, are not merely a matter of social and educational background; they may also be related to geographical differences.

For example, despite the tendency of the schools toward spelling-pronunciation, the unaspirated forms /wɪp/ "whip," /wilbæro/ "wheelbarrow," and /wɔrf/ "wharf" are in common cultured use in the Midland area and, as a matter of fact, occur sporadically elsewhere among cultured speakers. A few years ago a teacher in Utica, N.Y., yielding to the probably normal impulse to consider one's own speech or that of a textbook as the proper one, wrote to *College English* that she had never observed a person of true culture who lacked the /hw/ cluster in such words. Yet, as McDavid has observed, this teacher would have had to go only a few miles south to central Pennsylvania to observe thousands of cultivated speakers who say

---

[1] Vol. IV, pp. 102–16.

/wɪp/ and /wɪlbæro/; indeed, even in her own community the Atlas's cultivated informant is recorded as having /w/ and not /hw/ in these words. In the function words, of course, the customary lack of stress has resulted in the loss of aspiration everywhere, not just in certain areas; yet in my own state of Minnesota the new guide for instruction in the language arts enjoins the teacher to insist upon distinguishing /wɪč/ "witch" and /hwɪč/ "which" and /wjɛðər/ "weather" and /hwɛðer/ "whether."
. . .

The sounds represented by the letter *o* in *orange, horrid,* and *forest* also vary according to region. In much of New York state and in eastern Pennsylvania, for example, an unround /ɑ/ appears instead of the more common /ɔ/. Not long ago a teacher came to Minnesota from New York state and promptly began insisting that her pupils say only /ɑrɪnj/ and /fɑrɪst/; and recently a textbook came out with the same injunction, that the only correct form is /ɑrɪnj./

The diphthong /ɪu/, mistakenly called "long *u,*" offers another case in point. In the South, as in British English, a strongly consonantal /y/ beginning is heard in this diphthong in post-alveolar contexts, as in *newspaper, tube,* and *due* or *dew.* But in the North this beginning is quite weak, often almost imperceptible, and it is gone completely in northeastern New England and in Midland. Yet many teachers in the Middle West diligently drill their pupils in the pronunciation /nyuz/ instead of their normal /nuz/. More than half of my own students each year report that this was their high-school experience, although on only a few of them did the attempted inoculation "take." (To prevent misunderstanding, it should be clear that there can of course be no objection to the form /nyuz/ where it is the normal prestige form. What is objectionable is well-meaning but unenlightened tampering with acceptable speech.)

The same kind of thing, but with a much more complicated geographical picture, occurs with the pronunciation of a group of words spelled with *oo.* I should be surprised if many of the readers of this article . . . would have for all of these words the same pronunciation which I, a native of southern Michigan, have: /ruf, rut, huf, hup, hupɪŋ kɔf, kup, rum, brum, fud, spuk/ (with /ʊ/ as in *put* and /u/ as in *moon*). But I should also be surprised if you have not sometime been in a situation—on either the giving or the receiving end—where someone was being instructed to pronounce *root* and *roof,* perhaps even *soot,* with /u/ rather than /ʊ/. The Atlas files reveal a complicated distribution of these forms, each word having its own distinctive regional pattern; and nothing in this information supports the familiar injunctions.

Another vowel dilemma with historical roots in Middle English is that offered by *creek.* Many Northern teachers, probably swayed by the double *ee* spelling, for years have insisted upon their pupils' learning the Southern standard pronunciation /krik/ despite the fact, which should be obvious to an objective listener in a Northern community and which is fully attested by the Atlas records, that the basic Northern form is /krɪk/. Even in Battle Creek, Michigan, I am informed, there is this attempt to lift at least the school population to the cultural heaven, Southern division, where /krɪk/ is the shibboleth. . . .

DATA ON GRAMMAR AND IDIOM

Then the category of grammar and idiom is another in which Atlas materials contribute to our knowledge about usage. As with pronunciation we quite humanly yield to the notion that what is standard or customary for us either is, or ought to be, standard for others. A recent rhetoric textbook for the college freshman course was written by two authors of southern background. They say, "*Bucket* is more likely to be the ordinary word, *pail* . . . a little more old-fashioned and endowed with more 'poetic' suggestions." Any freshman speaking Northern English who finds this statement on page 372 must find it rather puzzling, for to him *bucket* refers to some unfamiliar wooden vessel in a well and is a word invariably preceded by *old oaken*. The Atlas files provide evidence for a much more objective statement about the relationship between *bucket* and *pail*.

Again, more than one textbook writer has condemned *sick to one's stomach* in favor of *sick at one's stomach*, but the Atlas findings reveal *sick to* as the usual Northern locution and *sick at* as a Midland variant, along with *sick from* and *sick with* and *sick in*.
. . .

APPLICATION OF THE DATA

For teachers of English, clearly the immediate application of this new source of information about our language is in the revision of previous statements about usage. In the simple interest of accuracy this revision is demanded. Those of us who have anything to do with the training of future teachers have the responsibility of using such revision in attention paid to usage items in our language and methods classes. The class room teacher has the special responsibility of using the new information in class drills, in class discussion, and in the evaluation of student oral and written language. As the experience of the South Carolina teacher with *hadn't ought* indicates, the teaching of standard forms must be done in full awareness of frequency and distribution of the contrasting non-standard forms.

But the teacher's application ordinarily must result from revision of usage statements in books of reference and in textbooks. Those who prepare texts, workbooks, drill exercises, and the like cannot in all conscience ignore the findings of the Atlases. Such revision is normal, of course, in the editing procedure of the main dictionaries, which constantly note the new evidence in published research. Full use of Atlas evidence was made, for example, by the editors of Webster's *Third*.

But we may look forward to a second kind of application of Atlas materials in the classroom. It is high time to recognize the validity of some regional speech in the scope of standard American English. There *are* standard forms which are regional and not national. The label *dial*, in a dictionary does not necessarily consign a linguistic form to either the linguistic slums or the linguistic backwoods. . . .

Recognizing the validity of our own regional speech as standard means also that we recognize the validity of the standard speech of other regions. The time is surely long past when we need to take seriously such an unenlightened statement as this which appeared in a speech textbook several years ago: "There is perhaps no deviation from standard English that sounds as provincial and uncultivated as [the retroflex or inverted r-sound]. . . . Inverted sounds are not used in standard English pronunciation. They will do more to make one's speech sound uncultivated than any other one thing."

Students can be helped toward recognition of this regional validity through various kinds of inductive exercises, especially in the vocabulary. Through such an exercise students for the first time approach objectively the language of their family, their neighbors, the community leaders, and speakers of other areas whom they hear. This particular investigative activity, it may be observed, fits naturally also into a language arts program that seeks to draw upon community resources.

Then, finally, a further utilization of the Atlas data, possible in both college and secondary school, would be for the aim of developing awareness that language is a complex, changing, and always relative structure, not a set of absolutes. The use of regional language information can help our students attain a desirable degree of objectivity in their observation of language matters, can help them see that language is essentially a system of habits related at every point to non-language habits of behavior. And this kind of awareness, this kind of objectivity, is at the heart of a disciplined and informed ability to use language effectively for the communication of meaning.

THE MAIN DIALECT AREAS OF THE U.S.A.

Jean Malmstrom and Annabel Ashley

The National Council of Teachers of English has long been active in educating teachers to an understanding of the nature of dialects and a respect for them as equally valid historical products. The following essay, drawn from an NCTE publication, summarizes the principal results from a number of Linguistic Atlas projects, and provides information on some of the distinguishing characteristics of the major regional dialects of the United States. In this picture, the prescientific concept of a supposed "General American" dialect disappears, and we find four major dialect areas, called by Kurath the Northern, North Midland, South Midland, and Southern, each with a number of distinctive sub-regional dialects (such as Eastern New England and New York City within the Northern area). From this data we can see that the homophonous pronunciation of pin and pen, or of cot and caught, or horse and hoarse are simply matters of regional difference, and that none of them should be considered nonstandard, or made the object of correction.

THE NORTHERN DIALECT AREA

On the Atlantic Seaboard, the Northern dialect area includes New England, the Hudson Valley, upstate New York, the northernmost strip of Pennsylvania, and Greater New York City. Moving westward into the area covered by the Atlas of the North Central States, we find the inland Northern area which includes Michigan, Wisconsin, the northern countries of Ohio, Indiana, Illinois, and Iowa. Still farther west, in the Upper Midwest Atlas area, the Northern dialect appears in Minnesota, North Dakota, the northern third of Iowa, and the northeastern half of South Dakota. In this area, there is some mingling of dialect forms so that the lines of separation between Northern and Midland are harder to draw. Apparently, in the

From *Dialects, U.S.A.*, by Jean Malmstrom and Annabel Ashley (Champaign, Illinois: National Council of Teachers of English, 1963). Reprinted by permission of the publisher and the authors.

Upper Midwest, the Northern dialect is contracting and the Midland is expanding. Farther west, in the Rocky Mountain States, only Colorado has been thoroughly studied. Here Denver and Gunnison are "islands" of Northern dialect. There is other evidence, too, of Northern forms in Colorado. However, overlapping of Northern and Midland dialects is the rule in this state. Utah generally shows a preference for Northern terms although the southern part of that state shows some Midland usage. Western Montana shows a Northern-Midland mixture. In the Pacific Northwest, Washington and northern and eastern Idaho are predominantly Northern in dialect. Preliminary editing of the California material shows that many words from Northern dialect areas in the East and Great Lakes region occur in California.

> Typical Northern pronunciation items are:
> Contrast between /o/ and /ɔ/ in the pairs: [1]
> *mourning* and *morning*   I, II, III.
> *hoarse* and *horse*   I, II, III.
> *fourteen* and *forty*   I, II, III.
> /ɨ/   in the unstressed syllable of *haunted* and *careless*   I, II, III.
> /ð/   regularly in *with*   I, II, III.
> /s/   in *grease* (verb) and *greasy* (adjective)   I, II, III.
> /bɨkəz/   *because*   I, II, III.

> Typical Northern vocabulary items are:
> *pail*   (Midland and Southern *bucket*)   I, II, III.
> *clapboards* 'finished siding' (Midland and Southern *weather-boards* and *weatherboarding*)   I, II, III.
> *brook*   'small stream'   I, II, III.
> *cherry pit*   'cherry seed'   I, II, III.
> *angleworm*   'earthworm'   I, II, III.
> *johnnycake*   'cornbread'   I, II, III.
> *eaves trough*   'gutter on roof'   I, II, [III].
> *spider*   'frying pan'   I, II.

> Typical Northern grammar items are:
> *dove* as past tense of *dive*   I, II, III.
> *sick to the stomach*   I, II, [III].
> *he isn't to home*   'he isn't at home'   I, II.
> *hadn't ought*   'oughtn't'   I, II.
> *clim* as past tense of *climb*   I, II.

[1] The Roman numerals after each item state the type of informants who characteristically use the term:
I. Old fashioned, rustic speakers of eighth-grade education.
II. Younger, more modern speakers of high-school education.
III. Cultured speakers of college education.
When these Roman numerals are enclosed in brackets, less currency in that group is indicated.

be as a finite verb   (*How be you?* for '*How are you?*')   I.
scairt '*scared*'   I, II.

THE MIDLAND DIALECT AREA

On the Atlantic Seaboard, the Midland dialect area includes central and southern Pennsylvania, northern Delaware, and the areas of Pennsylvania settlement on the Delaware, Susquehanna, and upper Ohio Rivers. It extends south into the Shenandoah Valley, the southern Appalachians, and the upper Piedmont of North and South Carolina. Moving westward to the North-Central States area, we find North Midland forms (and Midland forms) in central Ohio, central and northern Indiana, and central Illinois. South Midland forms (and Midland forms) occur in Kentucky and the areas settled by Kentuckians in southern Ohio, southern Indiana, and southern Illinois. Furthermore, because of migrations north on the Mississippi River, South Midland forms are found also in the mining regions of northwestern Illinois, southwestern Wisconsin, and southern Iowa.

The Upper Midwest also shares in this expansion north of the Midland dialect. Midland forms are found in all the states of the Upper Midwest Atlas area and South Midland forms in all except North Dakota. Farther west, in Colorado, we find competition between the Midland and the Northern dialects. Probably, however, Midland is Colorado's basic usage. Upon this early and continuing base, apparently, certain Northern features have been superimposed. In the Pacific Northwest, Oregon and western and southern Idaho show a preference for Midland forms, though there is a great and confusing overlapping which has not yet been completely analyzed. In California, Midland terms are as frequent and as widely distributed as Northern forms are.

In Texas the vocabulary is predominantly Midland and Southern, with purely Southern terms in a minority. Apparently Texas pronunciation, as far as it has been studied, shows definitely South Midland characteristics in the northern and western parts of the state.

In the Inland South, Midland and South Midland vocabulary items seem to form a distribution pattern which vaguely resembles a T. The top of the T goes along the northern borders of Tennessee, Arkansas, and Oklahoma, and expands southward into these states and into northern Mississippi and northwestern Georgia. The stem of the T goes south through Alabama to the Gulf of Mexico, bounded by the Chattahoochie River on the east and the Tombigbee River on the west. On the other hand, certain features of pronunciation suggest that the basic Midland-Southern dialect boundary across Alabama may lie just north of Montgomery. Until field interviews are conducted and furnish more evidence on the dialect situation in the Inland South, these two types of evidence are both of great interest to the student of dialect geography.

Typical Midland prounciation items are:

/r/   kept after vowels   I, II, III.

/ɔ/   in on;   /ɔh/   in *wash* and *wasp*;   /ɔw/   in *hog, frog,* and *fog*   I, II, III.

[ɛ]   in *Mary* and *dairy*   I, II, III.

/ə/   in the unstressed syllable of *haunted* and *careless*   I, II, III.

/θ/   regularly in *with*   I, II, III.

/r/   frequently intruding in *wash* and *Washington*   I, II.

Typical Midland vocabulary items are:

a little piece   'a short distance'   I, II, III.

blinds   'window shades'   I, II, III.

skillet   'frying pan'   I, II, III.

snake feeder   'dragon fly'   I, II, [III].

poke   'paper sack'   I, II, [III].

green beans   'string beans'   I, II, III.

to hull beans   'to shell beans'   I, II, [III].

spouts, spouting   'eaves troughs'   I, II, [III].

Typical Midland grammar items are:

all the further   'as far as'   I, II.

I'll wait on you   'I'll wait for you'   I, II, [III].

I want off   'I want to get off'   I, II, [III].

quarter till eleven   I, II, III.

THE SOUTHERN DIALECT AREA

On the Atlantic Seaboard, the Southern dialect area includes Delmarvia (the Eastern Shore of Maryland and Virginia, and southern Delaware). It extends southward into the Virginia Piedmont, northeastern North Carolina, eastern South Carolina, Georgia, and Florida. Along the Gulf Coast, Southern forms appear in central and southern Mississippi and throughout Louisiana and Texas. In *The Regional Vocabulary of Texas*, Professor Atwood says, "I have no hesitation in classing virtually all of Texas and an indeterminate portion of the surrounding states as a major branch of General Southern, which I will label *Southwestern.*" It contains Southern, Midland, and Southwestern words. In the North Central States, only Kentucky shows Southern forms—especially western Kentucky—since that state has always been somewhat dependent culturally on Tidewater and Piedmont Virginia. Southern forms are relatively rare in California and practically absent in the Pacific Northwest as well as in other Northern dialect areas.

Typical Southern pronunciation items are:
  /r/ lost except before vowels I, II, III.
  /ey/ in Mary I, II, III.
  /i/ in unstressed syllables of *haunted* and *careless* I, II, III.
  /il/ in *towel* and *funnel;* /in/ in *mountain* I, II, [III].
  /z/ in *Mrs.* [I], II, III.

Typical Southern vocabulary items are:
  low 'moo' I, II, III.
  carry 'escort, take' I, II, [III].
  snap beans, snaps 'string beans' I, II, III.
  harp, mouth harp 'harmonica' I, II, III.
  turn of wood 'armload of wood' I, II, [III].
  fritters I, II, III.

Typical Southern grammar items are:
  it wan't me I, II, [III].
  he belongs to be careful I, II.
  he fell outn the bed I.
  all two, all both 'both' I, [II].
  on account of 'because' I, [II].

SUMMARY

Although much more work has to be done to finish mapping the dialects of the United States, enough is now known so that we can make certain broad generalizations about our country's speech. The most important of these generalizations is that three different dialect bands extend from east to west across the U. S. A. These dialects are named Northern, Midland, and Southern. They are defined by means of differences in pronunciation, vocabulary, and grammar. On the Atlantic Seaboard, they reflect the patterns of original settlement. Farther inland, they reflect later migrations of people. The more recently settled the area, the less clearly defined are its patterns of dialect distribution.

These important conclusions wipe out earlier notions that something called "General American" speech exists. This supposed speech type is usually defined as extending from New Jersey on the Atlantic Coast through the Middle West and the entire Pacific Coast. Nor does a Midwestern dialect as such exist. Clearly, such descriptions of dialects in the U. S. A. are vastly oversimplified.

Another interesting fact revealed by the Atlas investigations is that dialect areas do not match up with state lines. Indeed, dialects show practically no respect for man-made boundaries. They are deeper and stronger than such divisions.

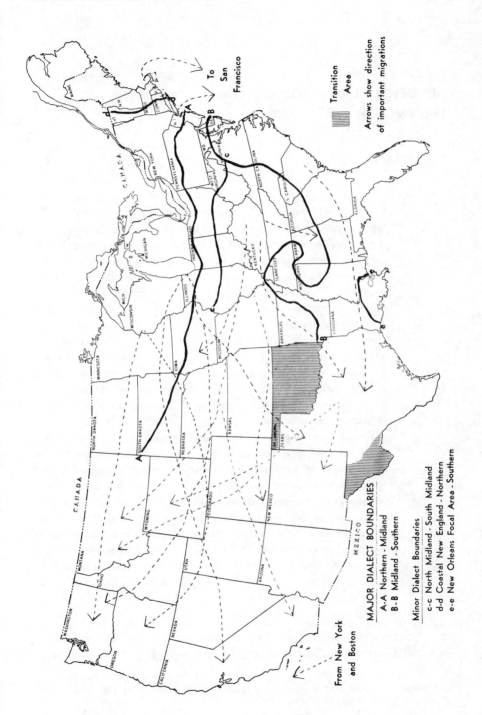

To San Francisco

Transition Area

Arrows show direction of important migrations

From New York and Boston

MAJOR DIALECT BOUNDARIES
A-A Northern - Midland
B-B Midland - Southern

Minor Dialect Boundaries
c-c North Midland - South Midland
d-d Coastal New England - Northern
e-e New Orleans Focal Area - Southern

HISTORICAL BACKGROUNDS OF
THE ENGLISH LANGUAGE

Paul Roberts

An understanding of the history of English is important for the
teacher, not for any specific facts it provides, but for the perspective
it gives on the present state of the language. It helps to see that the
present is but a transitory phase in the ongoing history of the
language, and just as we cannot understand the English of 1,000
years ago, so in another millenium our descendants will not be able
to understand the language we use today. No dialect can therefore
lay claim to any greater purity or correctness, since all are equally
historical products. Any language is a historical accretion of elements
of greatly varying age. In English, a few, such as the possessive suffix,
go back several thousand years; some, such as the third person
singular suffix on the verb, go back only a few hundred years;
while others, such as the suffix -nik in beatnik, originated only a
little over a decade ago.

English is a member of the Indo-European stock of languages,
which number some 300, or only about 10 percent of the total of
3,000 languages spoken in the world. Within Indo-European, English
is most closely allied with German, Dutch, and the Scandinavian
languages as a member of the Germanic family of languages. Despite popular misconceptions to the contrary, English is not de-
scended from Latin or French, which belong to a different branch of
the Indo-European family. In the present essay, Paul Roberts sketches
some of the characteristics of English at various periods since it became separated from its Germanic relatives on the continent.

No understanding of the English language can be very satisfactory
without a notion of the history of the language. But we shall have to

From *Understanding English*, Paul Roberts (New York: Harper & Row, 1958).
Reprinted by permission of Harper & Row.

make do with just a notion. The history of English is long and complicated, and we can only hit the high spots.

It is customary to divide the history of the English language into three periods: Old English, Middle English, and Modern English. Old English runs from the earliest records—i.e., seventh century—to about 1100; Middle English from 1100 to 1450 or 1500; Modern English from 1500 to the present day. Sometimes Modern English is further divided into Early Modern, 1500–1700, and Late Modern, 1700 to the present.

A SPECIMEN OF OLD ENGLISH

We may now have an example of Old English. The favorite illustration is the Lord's Prayer, since it needs no translation. This has come to us in several different versions. Here is one.

> Faeder are þu ðe eart on heofonum si þin nama gehalgod. Tobecume þin rice. Gewurðe þin willa on eorðan swa swa on heofonum. Urne gedaeghwamlican hlaf syle us to daeg. And forgyf us ure gyltas swa swa we forgyfaþ urum gyltendum. And ne gelaed þu us on costnunge ac alys us of yfele. Soðlice.

Some of the differences between this and Modern English are merely differences in orthography. For instance, the sign æ is what Old English writers used for a vowel sound like that in modern *hat* or *and*. The *th* sounds of modern *thin* or *then* are represented in Old English by the þ or ð. But of course there are many differences in sound too. *Ure* is the ancestor of modern *our*, but the first vowel was like that in *too* or *ooze*. *Hlaf* is modern *loaf*; we have dropped the *h* sound and changed the vowel, which in *hlaf* was pronounced something like the vowel in *father*. Old English had some sounds which we do not have. The sound represented by *y* does not occur in Modern English. If you pronounce the vowel in *bit* with your lips rounded, you may approach it.

In grammar, Old English was much more highly inflected than Modern English is. That is, there were more case endings for nouns, more person and number endings for verbs, a more complicated pronoun system, various endings for adjectives, and so on. Old English nouns had four cases—nominative, genitive, dative, accusative. Adjectives had five—all these and an instrumental case besides. Present-day English has only two cases for nouns—common case and possessive case. Adjectives now have no case system at all. On the other hand, we now use a more rigid word order and more structure words (prepositions, auxiliaries, and the like) to express relationships than Old English did.

Some of this grammar we can see in the Lord's Prayer. *Heofonum*, for instance, is a dative plural; the nominative singular was *heofon*. *Urne* is an accusative singular; the nominative is *ure*. In *urum gyltendum* both words are dative plural. *Forgyfaþ* is the third person plural form of the verb. Word order is different: "urne gedaeghwamlican hlaf syle us" in place of "Give us our daily bread." And so on.

In vocabulary Old English is quite different from Modern English. Most of the Old English words are what we may call native English: that is, words which have not been borrowed from other languages but which have been a part of English ever since English was a part of Indo-European.

Sometime between the years 1000 and 1200 various important changes took place in the structure of English, and Old English became Middle English.

Middle English, then, was still a Germanic language, but it differed from Old English in many ways. The sound system and the grammar changed a good deal. Speakers made less use of case systems and other inflectional devices and relied more on word order and structure words to express their meanings. This is often said to be a simplification, but it isn't really. Languages don't become simpler; they merely exchange one kind of complexity for another. Modern English is not a simple language, as any foreign speaker who tries to learn it will hasten to tell you.

For us Middle English is simpler than Old English just because it is closer to Modern English. It takes three or four months at least to learn to read Old English prose and more than that for poetry. But a week of good study should put one in touch with the Middle English poet Chaucer. Indeed, you may be able to make some sense of Chaucer straight off, though you would need instruction in pronunciation to make it sound like poetry. Here is a famous passage from the *General Prologue* to the *Canterbury Tales*, fourteenth century:

> Ther was also a nonne, a Prioresse,
> That of hir smyling was ful symple and coy,
> Hir gretteste oath was by Seinte Loy,
> And she was cleped Madame Eglentyne.
> Ful wel she song the service dyvyne,
> Entuned in hir nose ful semely.
> And Frenshe she spak ful faire and fetisly,
> After the scole of Stratford-atte-Bowe,
> For Frenshe of Parys was to hir unknowe.

EARLY MODERN ENGLISH

Sometime between 1400 and 1600 English underwent a couple of sound changes which made the language of Shakespeare quite different from that of Chaucer. Incidentally, these changes contributed much to the chaos in which the English spelling now finds itself.

One change was the elimination of a vowel sound in certain unstressed positions at the end of words. For instance, the words *name, stone, wine, dance* were pronounced as two syllables by Chaucer but as just one by Shakespeare. The *e* in these words became, as we say, "silent." But it wasn't silent for Chaucer; it represented a vowel sound. So also the words *laughed, seemed, stored* would have been pronounced by Chaucer as two-syllable words. The change was an important one because it affected thousands of words and gave a different aspect to the whole language.

The other change is what is called the Great Vowel Shift. This was a systematic shifting of half a dozen vowels and diphthongs in stressed syllables. For instance, the word *name* had in Middle English a vowel something like that in the modern word *father; wine* had the vowel of modern *mean; he* was pronounced something like modern *hey; mouse* sounded like *moose; moon* had the vowel of *moan.* Again the shift was thoroughgoing and affected all the words in which these vowel sounds occurred. Since we still keep the Middle English system of spelling these words, the differences between Modern English and Middle English are often more real than apparent.

The vowel shift has meant also that we have come to use an entirely different set of symbols for representing vowel sounds than is used by writers of such languages as French, Italian, or Spanish, in which no such vowel shift occurred. If you come across a strange word—say, *bine*—in an English book, you will pronounce it according to the English system, with the vowel of *wine* or *dine.* But if you read *bine* in a French, Italian, or Spanish book, you will pronounce it with the vowel of *mean* or *seen.*

The greatest writer of the Early Modern English period is of course Shakespeare, and the best-known book is the King James Version of the Bible, published in 1611. The Bible (if not Shakespeare) has made many features of Early Modern English perfectly familiar to many people down to present times, even though we do not use these features in present-day speech and writing. For instance, the old pronouns *thou* and *thee* have dropped out of use now, together with their verb forms, but they are still familiar to us in prayer and in Biblical quotation: "Whither thou goest, I will go." Such forms as *hath* and *doth* have been replaced by *has* and *does;* "Goes he hence tonight?" would be "Is he going away tonight?"; Shakespeare's "Fie on't, sirrah" would be "Nuts to that, Mac." Still, all these expressions linger with us because of the power of the works in which they occur.

It is not always realized, however, that considerable sound changes have taken place between Early Modern English and the English of the present day. Shakespearian actors putting on a play speak the words, properly enough, in their modern pronunciation. But it is very doubtful that this pronunciation would be understood at all by Shakespeare. In Shakespeare's time, the word *reason* was pronounced like modern *raisin*; *face* had the sound of modern *glass*; and *l* in *would, should, palm* was pronounced. In these points and a great many others the English language has moved a long way from what it was in 1600.

RECENT DEVELOPMENTS

But probably the most important force on the development of English in the modern period has been the tremendous expansion of English-speaking peoples. In 1500 English was a minor language, spoken by a few people on a small island. Now it is perhaps the greatest language of the world, spoken natively by over a quarter of a billion people and as a second language by many millions more. When we speak of English now, we must specify whether we mean American English, British English, Australian English, Indian English, or what, since the differences are considerable. The American cannot go to England or the Englishman to America confident that he will always understand and be understood. The Alabaman in Iowa or the Iowan in Alabama shows himself a foreigner every time he speaks. It is only because communication has become fast and easy that English in this period of its expansion has not broken into a dozen mutually unintelligible languages.

4

Sociolinguistics

The field of sociolinguistics is a broad one, comprehending the whole subject of how language is used in different social contexts, and the attitudes held toward its use. It has been suggested that a speech community might be defined not only in terms of similarities in grammar, pronunciation, and vocabulary, but in terms of a common set of values, largely unconscious, regarding the uses of language in various situations. These common attitudes may involve feelings toward in-group versus out-group dialects or styles of speaking (including shared conflicts in values), role-identifications, appropriate ways of expressing oneself, proper occasions for the use of particular kinds of language, ways to mediate or manipulate personal relations in encounter situations, the patterns by which people communicate, and stereotypes regarding the use of language by members of the group and others. It is to an important degree the sharing of these attitudes and patterns of interaction which serves to define membership in a group.

Language, then, is very much a reflection of the society which uses it. Although sociolinguistics is a relatively new area of study, and its research techniques and concepts still in the developmental stage, the significance of its findings to education is already enormous, for sociolinguistic conflict in the classroom is one of the most potent sources of problems in cross-cultural communication between teacher and student. Many misunderstandings arise over the intent of messages when these are sent and received in different dialects or languages. And institutional depreciation of students' speech patterns both prevents an adequate evaluation of their verbal ability and helps alienate them from the teacher and from the goals of education. "Spanish detention" and whippings for speak-

ing Navajo still haunt many schools, serving as a reminder of the traditional attitude of the dominant Anglo majority toward the education of
minority groups.

The information arising from sociolinguistic research is therefore of
vital importance to the schools. The teacher in the cross-cultural situation
(remembering that this includes students from a different socioeconomic
background) needs to learn about his students' attitudes toward language,
and use this as an educational base in working with them. He should accept
the dictum that there is no such thing as a non-verbal child, and realize
that the *apparently* "non-verbal" child may actually be employing silence
as a successful defensive tactic in a threatening situation. He should recognize that in American society, females are much more sensitive to social
class variation and are more likely to adopt middle-class speech norms,
while males reject these norms as effeminate and seek their own social
identity in the maintenance of non-standard forms. He should see that the
usual pedagogical approaches to this situation fly in the face of these
values, and he should try new approaches which will avoid alienating his
male students. He should recognize further that the ability to switch
dialects or languages at will, even in the middle of a sentence, is a communicative skill to be valued, and not evidence of a "mixed-up language."
It should always be kept in mind that the student who knows two languages or dialects may know more than the teacher, and should be respected for his ability. Furthermore, as Gumperz demonstrates, switching
between these languages or varieties is rule-governed and an understanding
of this process is of importance to the teacher.

Different cultural groups may differ radically in regard to the meanings they attach to specific communicative behaviors, and serious cross-
cultural failures in communication can occur as a result: Navajo children
are taught to speak softly to show respect, while teachers exhort them to
speak louder so they can be heard; Negro children learn to show respect
by not looking directly into the eyes of a person to whom they are speaking, while this is interpreted by white teachers as implying deviousness;
conversely, when a white teacher speaks in a loud voice to call for order,
Negro children interpret this as an expression of anger, while Indian
children may take even a "normal" tone of voice as indicating anger.
These are the matters treated by the Bauman, Philips, and Abrahams and
Gay articles.

In teaching a standard variety of English to students from a different
language or dialect background, the teacher should be aware that language
involves more than just a fixed set of forms, meanings, or pronunciations.
There is, besides, a cultural "grammar of speaking" which must be learned
as well (including such matters as gesture, intonation, and the uses of
silence). Linguists, such as Martin Joos, have described a number of
"styles" in English, ranging from the most formal for large-scale public

communication to the most informal for intimate in-group exchanges. Part of learning a standard variety of English is learning what style is appropriate for which situation. One of the principal tasks of the teacher should be to help students internalize these unconscious rules in their own sociolinguistic grammars. In this framework there is no room nor reason for stigmatizing one form of speech or another, but different varieties can be seen to be relevant for different contexts of use. The teacher should also remember that in their own cultural group, students have learned another set of rules for speaking which may be quite different from that taught in the schools. By showing respect for the speech patterns and cultural behaviors which his students bring to the classroom and which are so much a badge of their own group identity, the teacher may be helping them learn how to successfully integrate the conflicting values which often beset the bicultural individual.

Finally, it should be remembered that the classroom is the place where most of our cultural attitudes toward language are passed on, either consciously or unconsciously. Not only by what is taught but how, the teacher can have a great influence on public thinking about the subject. The linguistic intolerance in our society, which is a legacy from an elitest past, is largely learned in the schools, and it can be unlearned, given an informed body of teachers. An understanding of the sociolinguistic dimensions of language is therefore important not only for the teacher of minority group children, but for the teacher of the majority as well.

THE STYLES OF THE FIVE CLOCKS

Martin Joos

A great deal of discussion has ensued concerning Basil Bernstein's sociolinguistic distinction between elaborated and restricted codes. Bernstein has demonstrated that the British working class tends to communicate primarily in the non-discursive restricted code and many who have been working in line with the deficit model have leapt upon this as being one frame of reference by which lower-class school performance might be explained. (See Labov, "The Logic of Nonstandard English" in Section 5 for a discussion of this literature.)

Long before the Bernstein controversy, Martin Joos had described with delightful good humor and with greater subtlety, in The Five Clocks, the variety of styles characteristic of Standard English and other national languages. The present article consists of excerpts from that work.

English usage guilt feelings have not yet been noticeably eased by the work of linguistic scientists, parallel to the work done by the psychiatrists. It is still our custom unhesitatingly and unthinkingly to demand that the clocks of language all be set to Central Standard Time. And each normal American is taught thoroughly, if not to keep accurate time, at least to feel ashamed whenever he notices that a clock of his is out of step with the English Department's tower-clock. Naturally he avoids looking aloft when he can. Then his linguistic guilt hides deep in his subconscious mind and there secretly gnaws away at the underpinnings of his public personality.

English, like national languages in general, has five clocks. And the times that they tell are not simply earlier and later; they differ sidewise too, and in several directions. Naturally. A community has a complex structure, with variously differing needs and occasions. How could it scrape along with only one pattern of English Usage?

From *The Five Clocks, Martin Joos* (New York: Harcourt Brace Jovanovich, 1967).
Reprinted by permission of Harcourt Brace Jovanovich.

STYLE: Here are the five clocks to which we shall principally devote our attention. They may be called "higher" and "lower" for convenience in referring to the tabulation; but that doesn't mean anything like relative superiority.

frozen
formal
consultative
casual
intimate

With a single exception, there is no law requiring a speaker to confine himself to a single style for one occasion; in general, he is free to shift to another style, perhaps even within the sentence. But normally only two neighboring styles are used alternately, and it is anti-social to shift two or more steps in a single jump, for instance from casual to formal. When the five styles have been separately and comparatively described, the details of shifting will be obvious.

The two defining features of consultative style are: (1) The speaker supplies background information—he does not assume that he will be understood without it; (2) The addressee participates continuously. Because of these two features, consultative style is our norm for coming to terms with strangers—people who speak our language but whose personal stock of information may be different.

But treating the listener as a stranger is hard work in the long run; therefore we sooner or later try to form a social group with him. Our most powerful device for accomplishing this is the use of casual style. Casual style is for friends, acquaintances, insiders; addressed to a stranger, it serves to make him an insider simply by treating him as an insider. Negatively, there is absence of background information and no reliance on listeners' participation. This is not rudeness; it pays the addressee the compliment of supposing that he will understand without those aids. On the positive side, we have two devices which do the same job directly: (1) ellipsis, and (2) slang, the two defining features of casual style.

The purpose of ellipsis and the purpose of slang are the same; but they are opposite in their description and opposite in their history. Ellipsis is a minus feature and is very stable historically; slang is a plus feature and is absolutely unstable. Yet both signify the same: that the addressee, an insider, will understand what not everybody would be able to decipher.

Ellipsis (omission) makes most of the difference between casual grammar and consultative grammar. "I believe that I can find one" is proper (though not required) in consultative grammar, but casual English requires a shorter form, say "I believe I can find one" if not the still more elliptical "Believe I can find one." "Thank you" from "I thank you" has been promoted all the way to formal style, while "Thanks" from "Many thanks" or "Much thanks" (Shakespeare) has been promoted only to consultative. Aside from such little shifts in the tradition, ellipsis is stable: the elliptical expressions in use today can nearly all be found in Shakespeare, for instance "Thanks."

As an institution, slang is also ancient; but each individual slang expression is, on the contrary, necessarily unstable. The reason is obvious. Because the utility of any slang expression for classing the addressee as an insider (or excluding an unwanted listener as an outsider) depends on the fact—or at least the polite fiction—that only a minority of the population understands this bit of slang, each slang expression is necessarily ephemeral; for when that fiction has become transparent with age, its purpose is foiled, and then the useless slang is abandoned while new slang has to be created to take its place.

Besides these two pattern devices—ellipsis and slang—casual style is marked by an arbitrary list of formulas, all very stable, which are learned individually and used to identify the style for the hearer's convenience. 'Come on!' has been one of these identifiers since before the time of Shakespeare (*The Tempest* I, ii, 308). Each style has its own list of such conventional formulas, which we may call "code-labels" because they serve both to carry part of the message and to identify the style. Consultative code-labels include the standard list of listener's insertions "yes [professorial for *yeah*], yeah, unhunh, that's right, oh, I see, yes I know" and a very few others, plus the "well" that is used to reverse the roles between listener and speaker.

Both colloquial styles—consultative and casual—routinely deal in a public sort of information, though differently: casual style takes it for granted and at most alludes to it, consultative style states it as fast as it is needed. Where there happens to be no public information for a while, a casual conversation (among men) lapses into silences and kidding, a consultative one is broken off or adjourned. These adjustments help to show what sort of role public information plays in the two colloquial styles: it is essential to them both.

Now in intimate style, this role is not merely weakened; rather, it is positively abolished. Intimate speech excludes public information. Definition: An intimate utterance pointedly avoids giving the addressee information from outside of the speaker's skin. Example: "ready" said in quite a variety of situations, some of them allowing other persons to be present; note that this could be equivalent to either a statement or a question.

The systematic features of intimate style are two, just as in the other styles: (1) extraction; (2) jargon. Both are stable, once the intimate group (normally a pair) has been formed. Extraction: the speaker extracts a minimum pattern from some conceivable casual sentence. Extraction is not ellipsis. An elliptical sentence still has wording, grammar, and intonation. Intimate extraction employs only part of this triplet. Our printed "Engh" represents an empty word, one that has no dictionary meaning but serves as a code-label for intimate style. (The parallel word in casual style, spelled "unh," has a different vocal quality.) There is, however, a message-meaning; this is conveyed by the intonation, the melody, with which "Engh" is spoken. The speaker has extracted this intonation from a possible casual sentence, and that is all he uses of the grammatical triplet "wording, grammar, intonation." Once more, this is not rudeness; this pays the addressee the highest compliment possible.

Intimate style tolerates nothing of the system of any other style: no slang, no background information, and so on. Any item of an intimate code that the folklore calls "slang" is not slang but jargon—it is not ephemeral, but part of the permanent code of this group—it has to be, for intimacy does not tolerate the slang imputation that the addressee needs to be told that she is an insider. The imputations of all other styles are similarly corrosive. Accordingly, intimate codes, or jargons, are severely limited in their use of public vocabulary. Each intimate group must invent its own code. Somehow connected with all this is the cozy fact that language itself can never be a topic in intimate style. Any reaction to grammar, for instance, promptly disrupts intimacy.

We return briefly to consultative style. It supplies background information currently, and the listener participates fully. The diction is kept in accurate balance with the requirements: the pronunciation is clear but does not clatter, the grammar is complete but for an occasional anacoluthon, the semantics is adequate without fussiness. All is adjusted by instantaneous homeostasis, and the speaker does not compose text more than two or three seconds in advance. Being thus entirely automatic, it is the most strictly organized type of language. Its grammar is central to all the possibilities of grammar, and the grammars of all other styles are formed by adding archaisms and other complications to the consultative grammar; the pronunciations of all other styles are most simply described as departures from consultative pronunciation; the meanings of any word which occurs at all in consultative style are basically its consultative meanings, to which each other style adds specific meanings as necessitated by its own function.

Describing formal style by departure from consultative style, the crucial difference is that participation drops out. This is forced whenever the group has grown too large. A competent manic is able to convert a tête-à-tête into a formal assembly; but normal persons maintain consultation up to a group-size of approximately six, which sets the limits on the size and composition of a "committee" in the English-speaking sense. Beyond that, parliamentary law is requisite, i.e., a division into active and chair-warming persons.

Non-participating is also forced whenever a speaker is entirely uncertain of the prospective response. Thus conversations between strangers begin in formal style; among urbane strangers in English-speaking cultures, the formal span is only the ceremony of introduction.

Formal style is designed to inform: its dominating character, something which is necessarily ancillary in consultation, incidental in casual discourse, absent in intimacy. The formal code-labels inform each hearer that he is in a formal frame, is not to make insertions but must wait until authorized to speak, and is being given time to plan reactions—as much as half a century. The leading code-label is "may," any message requiring either "might" or "can" in other styles is suppressed or paraphrased, giving "May I help you?" and "We may not see one another for some time," the consultative equivalent of which was cited previously. We may most economically label an introduction as formal by saying "May I present Mr. Smith?"—or petrify a child by saying "No, you may not." Originally, the well-placed "may" was as effective as a hat-pin.

Form becomes its dominant character. It endeavors to employ only logical links, kept entirely within the text, and displays those logical kinks with sedulous care. The pronunciation is explicit to the point of clattering; the grammar tolerates no ellipsis and cultivates elaborateness; the semantics is fussy. Formal text therefore demands advance planning.

The defining features of formal style are two: (1) detachment; (2) cohesion. One feature, of the highest importance, is retained from the basal styles: intonation. Since the audience hears the text just once, any deficiency in the intonation is dangerous, any major defect is disastrous. Lack of intonation, as in print, is simply a blank check; but false intonation will mulct the listener in triple damages.

SOCIAL INFLUENCES ON THE CHOICE
OF A LINGUISTIC VARIANT

John L. Fischer

The following essay has been a classic in the field of dialectology ever since its first appearance, and has served as a model for recent developments in the study of social dialects and stylistic variation in language. In this study, Fischer shows how careful observation of variations in pronunciation in different social situations can provide valuable information regarding the status of particular variants. Equally significantly, he provides evidence that even very young

From Word, vol. 14 (1958), pp. 47–56. Reprinted by permission of Word.

children are aware of and respond to the social relevance of such a distinction as that between -in' and -ing for the present participle ending (e.g., going, working). Interestingly, the findings in this study agree with others conducted with adults which show that female speakers are more socially sensitive (insecure?) and use a higher percentage of "formal" or "careful" forms than do male speakers.

During the year 1954–55 my wife and I were engaged in a study of child-rearing in a semi-rural New England village.[1] In the course of the study I had occasion to record two or more interviews on Audograph discs or tapes, with each of the 24 children of our sample. Previously certain inconsistencies in the children's speech had attracted my attention, especially the variation between *-in* and *-ing* for the present participle ending.[2] Accordingly, in transcribing the discs and tapes, I decided to note the choice of these two variants, and this paper is intended to summarize and discuss this information.

To begin with, all of the 24 children, except three, used both forms to some extent at least. The three exceptions used only the *-ing* form, and since they were less loquacious than most of the other children, it is possible that a larger sample of their speech would have revealed the use of the other variant as well. This may then be regarded as a case of so-called free variation of two linguistic forms within a local speech community, and within the speech of most individual members of our sample community. In general, the choice of one or the other of the variants would not affect the denotation of acts, states, or events by the word.

"Free variation" is of course a label, not an explanation. It does not tell us where the variants came from nor why the speakers use them in differing proportions, but is rather a way of excluding such questions from the scope of immediate inquiry. Historically, I presume that one could investigate the spread of one of these variants into the territory of another through contact and migration, and this would constitute one useful sort of explanation. However, another sort of explanation is possible in terms of current factors which lead a given child in given circumstances to produce one of the variants rather than another, and it is this which I wish to discuss here.

Before discussing the determinants of selection of the variants it will

[1] This study was part of a larger cross-cultural study of socialization financed by the Ford Foundation and under the general direction of John Whiting of the Harvard Graduate School of Education and others.

[2] The variation in this dialect between *-in* and *-ing* in the participle ending does not extend to words with a final *-in* in an unstressed syllable in standard speech. This variation is therefore probably best viewed as a case of free alternation of two allomorphs which happen to differ in respect to one phoneme, rather than as a case of phonological free variation.

be helpful to understand a little of the general background of the data. The 24 children in our sample consisted of an equal number of boys and girls, both divided into two equal age groups, ages 3–6 and 7–10. By the time the recordings were made my wife and I had been observing the children periodically for eight to ten months and most of the children were fairly well acquainted with us. Most of the children were interviewed in an office in our house, which was located in the middle of the village. Most of the children had visited our house before, some a number of times. Four younger children who had not were interviewed in their own homes. Three general types of text were obtained:

(1) Protocols for all children for a verbal thematic apperception test (TAT) in which the children were asked to make up stories starting out from short sentences given by the investigator.

(2) For older children only, answers to a formal questionnaire.

(3) For a few of the older children, informal interviews asking them to recount their recent activities.

I shall present first some counts of variants in the TAT protocols, since this test was administered to all the children. As is shown in Table I, a markedly greater number of girls used *-ing* more frequently, while more boys used more *-in*.

TABLE I • *Number of children -ing and -in variant suffixes in TAT protocols according to sex.*

	-ing > -in	-ing < -in	
Boys	5	7	Chi square: 2.84; 05 < P < .1
Girls	10	2	(by two-tailed test)

This suggests that in this community (and probably others where the choice exists) *-ing* is regarded as symbolizing female speakers and *-in* as symbolizing males.

Within each sex, differences in personality are associated with the proportion of frequency of *-ing* to *-in* as illustrated in Table II.

TABLE II • *Frequency of use of -ing and -in in TAT protocols of two boys.*

	-ing	-in	
Model boy	38	1	Chi square: 19.67; P < .001
Typical boy	10	12	

The first boy was regarded by his teacher and others as a "model" boy. He did his school work well, was popular among his peers, reputed to be thoughtful and considerate. The second boy was generally regarded as a typical boy—physically strong, dominating, full of mischief, but dis-armingly frank about his transgressions. The "model" boy used almost ex-clusively the *-ing* ending here, while the "typical" boy used the *-in* ending more than half the time, as shown above.

In Table III below, one may also note a slight tendency for the *-ing* variant to be associated with higher socio-economic status, although this is not statistically significant with a sample of this size. The community studied is fairly small and does not have strong class lines, which is prob-ably why more marked results did not appear.[3]

TABLE III • *Number of children favoring* **-ing** *and* **-in** *endings according to family status.*

Family status	-ing > -in	-ing < -in	
Above median	8	4	Chi square (corrected):
Below median	7	5	0:P > .9

Besides asking *who* uses which variant and how much, we may also ask whether there are situational differences in *when* a single speaker uses these variants. One variant in the situation may be described as degree of formality: in the children's terms I would think of this as degree of simi-larity to a formal classroom recitation. The best child to examine for this variable is the "model" boy of Table II since he was interviewed in all three situations mentioned above and was obligingly talkative in each. As Table IV shows, the frequency of choice of variants changed from an al-most exclusive use of *-ing* in the TAT situation to a predominance of *-in* in the informal interviews.

TABLE IV • *Frequency of* **-ing** *and* **-in** *in a ten-year-old boy's speech in three situations in order of increasing informality.*

	TAT	Formal Interview	Informal Interview	
-ing	38	33	24	Chi square: 37.07
-in	1	35	41	P < .001

Of course, these three situations should not be regarded as exhaustive of the frequency range of these variants in this boy's speech. In the inter-

---

[3] Most previous studies of sociological factors connected with linguistic variants have been concerned with linguistic indices of class, caste, or occupational groups. Group boundaries have been regarded, implicitly or explicitly, as barriers to com-munication analogous to political boundaries, geographical distance, etc. The emphasis in this paper is rather on variations within a face-to-face community whose members are in frequent free communication: variations between social categories of speakers and between individual speakers, and situational variations in the speech of individual speakers, as noted below.

views I myself used the *-ing* variant consistently and this probably influenced the informant's speech somewhat. Probably in casual conversation with his peers the *-in/-ing* ratio is even higher than in the informal interview.

Another measure similar in implication to the frequency of variants by type of interview would be differences in frequency between the beginning and later parts of a single interview. Especially in that TAT protocols, which are the most formal texts, I noticed for a number of children that the *-ing* frequency was higher in the beginning of the interview and later dropped off, presumably as the child became more relaxed and accustomed to the situation. In only one child was the reverse trend noted, and there are reasons to believe that this particular child may have become more tense during the administration of the test.

In brief, then, the choice between the *-ing* and *-in* variants appears to be related to sex, class, personality (aggressive/cooperative), and mood (tense/relaxed) of the speaker,[4] to the formality of the conversation and to the specific verb spoken. While these are "free variants" in the standard type of description of languages in which only grammatical facts and differences in none but "denotative" meaning are taken into account, if we widen our scope of study to include the meaning of these variants to the conversants we might call them "socially conditioned variants," or "socio-symbolic variants," on the grounds that they serve to symbolize things about the relative status of the conversants and their attitudes toward each other, rather than denoting any difference in the universe of primary discourse (the "outer world").

---

[4] And doubtless of the person spoken to, although this was not investigated.

AN ETHNOGRAPHIC FRAMEWORK
FOR THE INVESTIGATION OF
COMMUNICATIVE BEHAVIORS

Richard Bauman

*The ethnography of communication, pioneered by the anthropo-
logical linguist Dell Hymes, is a special branch of anthropology concerned with observing the variety of speaking behaviors in different
cultures. This means not only taking note of different levels of style
but also the rules for their appropriate usage. It brings together
interest in language codes or varieties with micro-behavioral descriptions of cultures and societies. In this article, greatly revised for this
reader, Dr. Bauman demonstrates the usefuless of the ethnographic
approach for language teachers dealing with culturally different
children.*

Our recent experience in communications failures has compelled us
to realize that we have to come to terms with the cultural heterogeneity of
our society in the face of a massive institutional system which denies the
validity of this heterogeneity if not its very existence. By all rights, the
American myth tells us, the culturally different should have melted into
the mainstream long ago. Some of us, though few I hope, may be sorry
it didn't; most, I gather, are happy it did not. More significant, however,
is that growing numbers of the people who have not melted are happy
they did not, and they want an end to every sort of effort, covert as well as
overt, to force them into the pot as a price for their bowlful of the American dream.

In the face of the needs and demands of these people, the responsibility
of educators and language specialists is to devise ways of giving the culturally different in this country the full benefit of our pedagogical and
clinical expertise in a manner which honors and respects those aspects of
their own cultures which are consistent with the universal right to human
dignity and self-realization and not solely a demeaning adaptation to cultural domination by the selfish and the powerful. This cannot be done, I
am convinced, except on the basis of a free and ready willingness to under-

stand other cultures in their own terms instead of viewing them through the distorting lens of the values and biases imposed on us all—black, white, brown, yellow, or red—by the dominant culture of the American mainstream.

Of all the ways the dominant culture has seen fit to impose itself on others, the one in which we here have the biggest stake is language. When a member of the State Board of Education in my own state of Texas is publicly and adamantly opposed to making a place for Spanish in the education of Mexican-Americans, when an educational psychologist can achieve high national prominence on the basis of a theory which takes Black children to have no language at all, and when federal education programs can be constructed on the premise that minority group children are "linguistically impoverished," we know we have our work cut out for us.

There are two related lines of investigation which must be followed if we are to achieve a productive understanding of the language systems of other cultures, namely, the linguistic and the sociolinguistic. Linguistic analysis has to do with languages in their own right, as analytically isolable codes. For the most part, as far as minority group languages in this country are concerned, their status as autonomous natural languages is not questioned. No one denies that Spanish, Chinese, or Navajo are real languages; it remains only for us to take the structure of these languages into account in our educational, clinical, or social relations with their speakers—a big enough step, to be sure.

When it comes to dialects, however, especially Black dialects, the situation is otherwise. Here we have serious, highly educated, and well-intentioned specialists telling us that Black children are best treated as if they have no language at all, that their speech is distorted, defective, and unsystematic (see discussion and references in Baratz 1969 and Labov 1970a). [Complete references will be found at the end of this selection.—Ed.] Such dangerous and ignorant notions may be controverted in large part through the application of time-honored linguistic methods based on the principle that no people is without language, that all natural languages are equivalent in potential for serving the cognitive and communicative needs of their users, and that all languages are strictly and systematically rule-governed, never random. When approached in these terms, the various forms of Black English have been shown to be as ordered, systematic and rule-governed as any other language. There is much more that needs to be done, but the work is systematically under way, and there is already enough ammunition available to establish the principle at least that Black English is a language and that its speakers are at no *intrinsic* disadvantage by virtue of using it (see discussion and references in Labov 1970b). It is others who put them at a disadvantage by refusing to accept it.

The other line of attack is the one I want to discuss in more detail.

Let me repeat before proceeding further that the distinction between the linguistic and sociolinguistic approaches, especially in this field, is largely artificial. Still, there are differences of perspective and emphasis which may usefully be pointed out and developed upon, not only between the linguistic and the sociolinguistic approaches, but among various kinds of sociolinguistic analysis as well. The kind of approach I will be talking about is a characteristically anthropological one and is of fairly recent development. While recognizing the analytical usefulness of isolating linguistic codes, languages, for study, it focuses rather on the social acquisition and use of language, its overall place within the culture, and its function in the conduct of social life. I would suggest that of all approaches to the social dimensions of language this approach is—or ought to be—the one of greatest concern to those concerned with the understanding and teaching of oral language.

Anthropologists have been late in getting around to this kind of investigation themselves, perhaps because they were in the forefront of the battle against the notion that some languages are intrinsically superior to others, and this battle fostered an emphasis on the universality of the functions which are served by language, such as socialization, the accumulation of culture and tradition, the expression of individuality, and so on (Sapir 1933). Only recently have anthropologists begun working systematically on the idea that the place of language in culture and society is not always and everywhere the same, but cross-culturally variable (Hymes 1966). People of different societies think differently about language, value it differently, evaluate it differently, acquire it through different social mechanisms, use it in different situations, and turn it to different ends. Among the Cuna Indians of San Blas, Panama, for example, both speaking and listening are especially satisfying activities. Men and women are capable of sitting for long periods of time listening to the speeches of others, even if the content of those speeches repeats itself time and time again. Individuals never interrupt others, but wait patiently for them to finish before beginning to speak themselves, no matter how long they have to wait. The Cuna may be contrasted with the Paliyans of South India who communicate very little at all times and become almost silent by the age of forty. Verbal, communicative persons are regarded as abnormal and often as offensive (Sherzer, in press; Gardner, in press). The point is that these differences are not inherent in the formal structure of the languages involved, but you can see how important they are for an understanding of the place of language in the lives of its users.

What is more, we may expect the same kind of variability among the different cultures and subcultures which make up our own heterogeneous society, and I submit that it is this variability which underlies most of the so-called language problems of the culturally different in this country when it is confronted by the built-in ethnocentric assumption of our dominant educational institutions that there is one and only one way to acquire and use language.

There is no need to establish that the minority groups in this country are culturally different from the dominant mainstream. For groups like Indians, Mexican-Americans, Puerto Ricans, or Chinese, no one disputes it. For Afro-Americans, though, the situation is different once again. Listen to this statement, for example, from the introduction to a widely used text on the so-called disadvantaged learner: "The American Negro comprises the largest segment of this country's disadvantaged and ethnic-minority-group populations. While differing languages and identification with cultures different from that dominant in the United States serve to isolate as well as insulate certain of our ethnic minority groups, such is not true of the Negro. While not accorded full social acceptance in American society, the Negro ideationally and culturally is *Anglo-Saxon in his orientation*" (Webster 1966:4–5 emphasis added). The patent ridiculousness of this statement will be clear to anyone who is acquainted with the researches of Herskovits (1958), Hannerz (1969), Abrahams (1970a, b), among many others, all of which establishes that fundamental cultural differences exist between Afro-American and mainstream American culture in areas running the whole gamut from kinship to expressive behavior. (See the bibliography of Whitten and Szwed, 1970, for the important recent studies.) The distribution and intensity of these differences among Black Americans is still under investigation and will be for a long time; the question of whether the differences are best considered within a framework of cultural pluralism, cultural heterogeneity, dominant culture vs. subcultures, etc., is, for our purpose, academic. All we here need to know—and we do know it—is that differences do exist, not least in patterns of communicative behavior.

The way should be open, then, for the investigation of cross-cultural differences in the social use of language in America. And while we are at it, let me add that white speakers of Standard English or any other kind of English should be brought into this circle too; they are just as culturally different from the others as the others are from them, and just as much in need of investigation. An important point will be reached in America when WASPs can consider *themselves* culturally different.

Now, how do we go about conducting such investigations? The approach of anthropologists to the study of speech behavior, as to any form of human social behavior, is an ethnographic one. Ethnography is the process of constructing, through direct personal observation of social behavior, a theory of the workings of a particular culture in terms as close as possible to the way the members of that culture view the universe and organize their behavior within it. That is to say that while culture is man's way of imposing order on the universe, every culture is unique in the organization it imposes; members of different cultures group things in different ways, conceive of cause and effect relationships in different terms, rank things in different hierarchies of preference, develop different operational procedures for getting things done, and segment the flow of behavior and experience in terms of different systems of acts, scenes, situations, and events. In basic terms, the ethnographer seeks to discover what one needs to know and how one needs to behave to function as a member of a particular culture and how one acquires this cultural competence (Goodenough 1957, 1963:257-259; Frake 1964:111-112). Within an overall framework of this kind, anthropologists have been working to develop a method for the ethnographic study of language, or, more appropriately, of speaking, taking as the focal point of their efforts the ways of speaking of particular speech communities and the role of speaking in the social life of those communities (Hymes 1964, 1967; Darnell, Hymes and Sherzer, in press).

It should be emphasized, before proceeding further, that this kind of undertaking is very different from one kind of conventional sociolinguistics, which involves the mapping of linguistic features onto populations. The latter is an essentially correlational operation; the linguistic data and the sociological data are the products of separate investigations and are only subsequently combined by the analyst, with an eye towards such things, say, as the omission of word-final consonant clusters among middle- vs. working-class Blacks (Shuy 1970:342-344). This operation can be extremely valuable in defining internally relevant social matrices for investigation, but the association between speakers and language is not investigated *in situ*, at the very source of the association in the speech event.

The ethnographic approach is also very different from the experimental investigation in the laboratory or by questionnaire of factors involved in and affecting speech behavior through the operationalizing of variables and their experimental manipulation. This too is an important scientific task, but ethnographic investigation is logically prior to it, as a means of determining what the culturally relevant variables are in the first place. As long as the experimenter is the one who selects the variables for manipulation, he does potential violence to the realities of the subjects' own culture. One can obtain very precise data on how lower-class Black mothers teach their children in the laboratory, but if, as ethnographic investigation seems to indicate, lower-class Black children learn the verbal skills of their culture from other figures and in ways other than by direct instruction, one has not only learned nothing of real usefulness but has been misled by the false and ethnocentric assumption that maternal teaching techniques are the most important factor in the acquisition of verbal skills to a distorted picture of the subjects' true situation (Hess, Shipman, Brophy and Bear 1968; cf. Hannerz 1969:118-138, Stewart 1970a:365-368, Labov et al 1968, vol. 2:159-195, Young 1970).

Let me give you an outline of what is involved in an ethnography of speaking (the following discussion draws heavily upon Hymes 1967 and

Darnell, Hymes and Sherzer, in press). The first requirement is the definition of the speech community to be investigated. I follow Hymes in defining a speech community as a community sharing both rules for the
conduct and interpretation of acts of speech, and rules for the interpretation of at least one common linguistic code. Obviously, the first delimita-
tion of a speech community for analysis will be tentative and partly
intuitive, since its precise definition will depend upon the subsequent findings of the ethnographer, but the work of prior anthropologists and sociol-
ogists, as well as the sociolinguistic analyses of the kind mentioned above
can be of great help here.

Once the speech community is defined, the investigation proceeds to
an empirical determination of the components of speaking behavior within
the community. A list of relevant components might include the following:

I. Linguistic varieties in use in the community: The ethnographic
approach points up the crucial fact that the notion of one language per
speech community is an analytical abstraction. The members of every
speech community have recourse to a range of linguistic varieties including
different styles (e.g., formal/informal), different dialects (e.g., Black
English/Standard English), or different languages (e.g., English/Spanish),
the use of which will vary socially and situationally. The old notion of one
homogeneous language per one homogeneous speech community will
simply not hold up in the light of the situation on the ground. Given that
every speech community employs a variety of styles or codes, the rules for
switching from one to another become an important part of any ethnographic description (see Labov 1970a:19–22, Ervin-Tripp 1969:121–139,
Gumperz 1970).

II. Linguistic units of description: What are the local categories of
speech acts, speech events, speech situations and genres in use in the community: In other words, how do people segment their experience and
activity with regard to speaking? Many of the acts, situations, events and
genres will be named, and the terms for these will provide an important
entree into patterns of speaking within the community (Abrahams and
Bauman, in press). Probably the most productive analyses of speaking behaviors in Black communities which have been done thus far are based
upon this kind of analysis. Abrahams (1970a, b), Labov (Labov et al 1968),
Kochman (1970) and Mitchell-Kernan (1969) have provided us with information on a number of key acts and events, including rapping, capping,
playing the dozens, signifying, shucking, rifting, louding, loud talking,
marking, toasting, gaming, and others. How many of the whites among you
know what these are? Yet to many of your Black clients they are the most
important speech activities in which one can engage. Good talking for
them means proficiency in these activities, not talking like an English
teacher.

III. Messages: What are the rules governing what is talked about in each kind of act or event?

IV. Tone or mood or manner: What are the various tones, moods or manners in which speech may be conducted, e.g., serious, mocking, belligerent, playful?—as in "smile when you say that."

V. Settings: Where does the act, event or situation occur and at what times? In other words, what are the locally defined contexts for speaking?

VI. Participants: Who engages in each event and performs each act? The relevant attributes may include age, sex, social class, education, profession, or any other locally defined identity feature. This is tied to the matter of the definition of communicative roles within the community— which roles are defined by attributes having to do with the use of language?

VII. Goals and consequences of the activity: Why do the participants engage in these speaking activities in the first place, and what are the results of their doing so?

VIII. Norms of interaction: What are the rules and proprieties governing the interaction of the participants, e.g., that one must not interrupt, that one must not raise one's voice, etc.?

IX. Norms of interpretation: What are the shared understandings about such things as what to take seriously, what to take literally, what to discount, etc.?

The above list is intended merely as a guide to the kinds of factors which may enter into an ethnographic description of speaking. It should be stressed that these are merely the building blocks for such a description, for it is the structural interrelationships among the components in which the ethnographer is truly interested, the ways in which the components are functionally interrelated in culture-specific ways to constitute the ways of speaking of a particular community. For instance, when Mitchell-Kernan notes among working class Blacks in Oakland that in casual conversation particularly between solidary individuals this solidarity may be signaled by: 1) resorting to a speaking variety which is characterized by stereotyped Black southern usages which are currency for the interlocutors only in such contexts; 2) forms which are invented on the spot and which are a kind of take-off on areas of deviation between Standard English and Black English, but are not the variants which ordinarily obtain; and 3) exaggeration of the Black English phonological component. And when she adds further that it is clear to the interlocutors that these are not the normal usages of the speaker, she is actually formulating a descriptive rule for speaking in that community which relates communicative varieties, participants, norms of interpretation, and goals or consequences of the activity (Mitchell-Kernan 1969:73-73).

In addition to the components enumerated above, the ethnographer is interested in a number of other factors which are not productively considered components of speech events but which are crucial to the place of speaking in culture and society nevertheless. He is, first of all, interested in determining the people's own values and beliefs concerning speech and language: what is good speech, bad speech, appropriate speech, inappropriate speech, defective speech, how are these acquired, how may they be changed, and so on? These factors will be of very great importance to people in the speech, hearing and language professions, and they cannot be taken for granted. To cite a pertinent example, it is one of the ironies of teaching programs which incorporate dialect, as pointed out by Stewart, that the children frequently value them highly but the parents are strongly opposed to them because they have been taught to be ashamed of dialect and to view Standard English as the vehicle to social and economic success (Stewart 1970b:222). On the other hand, as Labov and his associates point out, the school holds up to the lower-class Black youngster sentimental speech models which he considers "weak" and which are presented to him through the medium of the lower-middle-class white female whose values are at a world of remove from his own (Labov et al 1968, vol. 2:346).

Of [as] great interest to the language teacher as to the ethnographer, is the social matrix of language acquisition, in the sense of the acquisition of the linguistic code itself. Studies of language acquisition are conventionally pursued in the laboratory, or under closely controlled observational conditions, and although they frequently display a high degree of methodological and conceptual sophistication they can never reveal some of the most basic kinds of causal and explanatory factors to which true ethnographic investigation would give one access. The point is important enough to warrant an extended example. The following is from an ethnographic study of family and childhood in a Black community in Georgia, by Virginia H. Young: "Babies are taught to be responsive orally. The baby held up before the mother's or father's face is teased about biting for a while, and then is likely to be urged to imitate the parent's sounds. One hears five-month-old babies spontaneously imitating single sounds of their parents, and often babies show precociousness that tends to be lost in later childhood when the stimulus falls off." She goes on to describe how, at around three years of age the "knee baby" is pushed out of that position by a growing sibling and becomes attached to a gang of older children. "The most apparent loss at this time due to the abrupt ending of parental stimulation is not seen in the form of anxiety, but in loss of precociousness of speech development. Often speech becomes an indistinct children's patois in contrast to the clear enunciation used by the knee-baby with his parents. Children speak less to adults and get along adequately with " 'Yes'm' and 'No'm' " (Young 1970:279–282).

Now, no claim is made either by Young or myself for the applicability of her findings to other Negro communities. But how useful it would be if we did have information of this kind, tied to empirically identified, culture-specific patterns of child rearing and kinship, for other communities and other age levels. They would constitute a supplement to the work of the laboratory psycholinguists and an antidote to the foolish speculations or a priori assumptions of the deprivationists. Moreover, they would be of direct help in clinical and instructional practice—look what this example alone tells us about the response patterns of children of a certain age within the community. And once again information of this kind can only be obtained ethnographically.

In addition to the acquisition of language itself, there is another dimension that must be explored ethnographically, namely, the processes, sequences and mechanisms involved in the acquisition of the cultural knowledge which enables members of the society to speak in culturally appropriate ways, that is, the acquisition of what has been called communicative or sociolinguistic competence (the following discussion draws heavily upon Hymes, n.d.). The term competence in its most widely current sense was introduced into linguistic discourse by Noam Chomsky and is a cornerstone of transformational generative linguistics. Linguistic competence, for Chomsky, has a very special meaning; it does not mean the full range of knowledge and ability possessed by the user of a language, but rather, grammatical knowledge, "the underlying system of rules that has been mastered by the speaker-hearer" in a "completely homogeneous speech community" (1965:2–4). Everything else has been relegated to the residual category of performance, and although performance must involve all kinds of knowledge and ability beyond the grammatical that enters into the use of language, Chomsky often employs the term in the sense of "mere" performance, raw external behavior. Here is the crux of the matter. The anthropologist is committed to the notion that all behavior, including speaking, is rule-governed, patterned, and requires the acquisition of competence to achieve cultural appropriateness. No amount of grammatical knowledge will tell the user of a language how to choose between equally possible utterances in a particular social situation—e.g., "What's happ'nin', baby?" vs. "How do you do, Ma'am?"—and it is this kind of competence and its acquisition which is of principal interest to the anthropologists, a competence for the social use of language, involving both knowledge and the ability to use it. There are, of course, instances where to be sociolinguistically competent is to make oneself appear incompetent, as in those situations where members of minority groups have learned to accommodate to the stereotypic expectations of the superordinate and powerful and to appear stupid, childlike and harmless as a means of self-defense (Labov 1970b:158).

For an example of the kind of ethnographic data which bear upon the nature and acquisition of communicative competence in a particular

American community, consider the following observations made by Carol
Talbert among Black families in St. Louis (Talbert 1969):

> Our observations in the homes of the children made it clear that though the
> children may be non-interacting with the adults, they were exposed and listening
> to the exchange of information of the adults. The verbal interchange between the
> children often did not ease while adults were talking but rather it continued along-
> side the adults' own conversation. The children were rarely asked to participate in
> the adults' conversation, though they might be asked for information or to perform
> a task. A child's occasional spontaneous contribution would be met with approval,
> usually, if it were witty or in some other way "adult like." . . . Frequently, the
> child would respond to a command or a request for information with a "no re-
> sponse" or possibly a nod of the head. This "no response" appears to be more
> tolerable to the parent than an assertive erroneous response which would stand
> the chance of eliciting a threat, ridicule, or physical reprimand by the mother.

A little later, Talbert goes on to say, "At first glance this information may
seem to indicate that the child would be in a position of "non-learning"
but the child was privy to the continual exchange of information between
the adults concerning problems, aspirations, and often feelings and comments about the child himself. The child is then learning, not by direct
and elaborate explanations but rather by exposure, listening and peer interaction."

In these short passages, then, Talbert has given us much suggestive
information concerning norms and expectations within this community for
the speech behavior of children in the presence of adults, including when
to speak, what kinds of things to speak about, and even when to remain
silent, which, though widely recognized as an essential communicative skill
—a person has to learn when to keep his mouth shut as well as when to
speak—cannot even enter into the notion of linguistic competence in the
orthodox sense of the term. Talbert's discussion of the "no-response" pattern suggests that when a Black child clams up in the presence of a superordinate adult, like an educational psychologist or a speech clinician,
perhaps, he may be demonstrating a high degree of sociolinguistic competence in his own cultural terms, though his behavior is usually taken for
something considerably less. My argument, then, is that clinicians, educators, and all those who are concerned with the language problems con-
fronting culturally different children must be as aware—perhaps more
aware—of sociolinguistic competence as of linguistic competence in
Chomsky's sense of the term. The complementarity between the linguistic
and the ethnographic approaches is nowhere more apparent than in the
juxtaposition of these two orders of competence, and the language specialist who is sensitive to both will be in a position to benefit all children on a
level of greater understanding than either one alone can afford.

REFERENCES

ABRAHAMS, ROGER.
1970a   *Positively Black.* Englewood Cliffs, N.J.: Prentice-Hall.
1970b   *Deep Down in the Jungle,* Rev. ed. Chicago: Aldine.
────── and RICHARD BAUMAN.
In Press   "Sense and Nonsense in St. Vincent: speech behavior and
          decorum in a Caribbean community." *American Anthropologist.*

BARATZ, JOAN.
1969   "Linguistic and cognitive assessment of Negro children: as-
          sumptions and research needs." *Asha,* vol. 11, pp. 87–91.

CHOMSKY, NOAM.
1965   *Aspects of the Theory of Syntax.* Cambridge, Mass.: MIT.

DARNELL, REGNA, DELL HYMES and JOEL SHERZER.
In press   *Field Guild for the Ethnographic Study of Speech Use.* New
          York: Holt, Rinehart and Winston.

ERVIN-TRIPP, SUSAN.
1969   "Sociolinguistics." In *Advances in Experimental Social Psy-
          chology,* vol. 4, edited by Leonard Berkowitz. New York:
          Academic Press, pp. 91–165.

FRAKE, CHARLES O.
1964   "A Structural description of Subanun religious behavior." In
          *Explorations in Cultural Anthropology: Essays in Honor of
          George Peter Murdock,* edited by Ward H. Goodenough. New
          York: McGraw-Hill, pp. 111–129.

GARDNER, PETER.
In press   "The Paliyans." In Darnell, Hymes and Sherzer, in press.

GOODENOUGH, WARD H.
1957   "Cultural anthropology and linguistics." In *Report of the
          Seventh Annual Round Table Meeting on Linguistics and Lan-
          guage Study* (Monograph Series on Languages and Linguistics,
          No. 9), edited by Paul L. Garvin. Washington, D.C.: George-
          town University, pp. 167–173.

1963   *Cooperation in Change.* New York: Russell Sage.

GRIMSHAW, ALLEN D.
1969   "Language as obstacle and data in sociological research." *Items,*
          vol. 23, pp. 17–21.

GUMPERZ, JOHN.
1970   "Verbal strategies in multilingual communication." Berkeley:
          Working Paper No. 36, Language-Behavior Research Labora-
          tory.

HANNERZ, ULF.
1969   *Soulside.* New York: Columbia University Press.

HERSKOVITS, MELVILLE.
1958   *The Myth of the Negro Past.* 2nd ed. Boston: Beacon.
HESS, ROBERT D., VIRGINIA SHIPMAN, JERE BROPHY and ROBERT BEAR.
1968   *The Cognitive Environments of Urban Preschool Children.* Chicago: The Graduate School of Education.
HYMES, DELL.
1964   "Introduction: toward ethnographies of communication." In *The Ethnography of Communication,* edited by John Gumperz and Dell Hymes. *American Anthropologist,* vol. 66, no. 6, part 2, pp. 1–34.
1966   "Two types of linguistic relativity (with examples from Amerindian ethnography)." In *Sociolinguistics* edited by William Bright. The Hague: Mouton, pp. 114–158.
1967   "Models of the interaction of language and social setting." In *Problems of Bilingualism,* edited by John Macnamara. *Journal of Social Issues,* vol. 22, no. 2, pp. 8–28.
n.d.   "On communicative competence." MS.
KOCHMAN, THOMAS.
1970   "Toward an ethnography of Black American speech behavior." In Whitten and Szwed 1970: pp. 145–162.
LABOV, WILLIAM.
1970a   "The logic of nonstandard English." In Williams 1970: pp. 153–189.
1970b   *The Study of Nonstandard English.* Champaign, Ill.: National Council of Teachers of English.
———, PAUL COHEN, CLARENCE ROBINS and JOHN LEWIS.
1968   *A Study of the Non-Standard English of Negro and Puerto Rican Speakers in New York City.* 2 vols. New York: Dept. of Linguistics, Columbia University, mimeographed.
MITCHELL-KERNAN, CLAUDIA.
1969   *Language Behavior in a Black Urban Community.* Berkeley: Working Paper No. 23, Language-Behavior Research Laboratory.
SAPIR, EDWARD.
1933   "Language." In *Encyclopaedia of the Social Sciences.* New York: Macmillan, vol. 9, pp. 155–169. Reprinted in *Selected Writings of Edward Sapir,* edited by David Mandelbaum. Berkeley and Los Angeles: University of California, 1963, pp. 7–32.
SHERZER, JOEL.
In press   "The San Blas Cuna." In Darnell, Hymes and Sherzer, in press.
SHUY, ROGER.
1970   "The sociolinguists and urban language problems." In Williams 1970: pp. 335–350.
STEWART, WILLIAM.
1970a   "Toward a history of American Negro dialect." In Williams 1970: pp. 351–379.

1970b   "Sociopolitical issues in the linguistic treatment of Negro dialect." In *Linguistics and Language Study* (Monograph Series on Languages and Linguistics, No. 22), edited by James E. Alatis. Washington, D.C.: Georgetown University Press, pp. 215–223.

TALBERT, CAROL.
1969   "Socio-linguistic analysis of teacher and pupils." Paper delivered at the 1969 Annual Meetings of the American Anthropological Association, New Orleans, La.

VALENTINE, CHARLES.
1968   *Culture and Poverty: Critique and Counter-Proposals.* Chicago: University of Chicago.

WEBSTER, STATEN W.
1966   *The Disadvantaged Learner.* San Francisco: Chandler.

WHITTEN, NORMAN and JOHN F. SZWED, EDS.
1970   *Afro-American Anthropology.* New York: Free Press.

WILLIAMS, FREDERICK.
1970   *Language and Poverty: Perspectives on a Theme.* Chicago: Markham.

YOUNG, VIRGINIA H.
1790   "Family and childhood in a southern Negro community." *American Anthropologist,* vol. 72, pp. 269–288.

ACQUISITION OF ROLES FOR
APPROPRIATE SPEECH USAGE

Susan Philips

In this article on an Indian community's speaking behavior (as well
as the two which follow) the ethnography of communication approach
developed by Hymes and described above by Bauman is brought to
bear on educational problems. Philips' argument is especially relevant because of its focus on cultural differences and its wealth of
ethnographic detail. We have long misunderstood Indian attitudes
toward speaking and remaining silent—a situation misread by
teachers of Indians as sullenness, lack of attention, or hostility.
Philips does much to clear this stereotypical response. For another
important ethnographic reporting of silence behavior in an Indian
group, see Keith H. Basso, " 'To Give up on Words': Silence in
Western Apache Culture," Southwestern Journal of Anthropology,
vol. 26 (1970), pp. 213-230.

On the Warm Springs Indian Reservation in central Oregon the
majority of children now enter school having learned English as a first
language from parents who are bilingual speakers of a Sahaptin or Chin-
ookan dialect and English. Comparative observations and tape recordings
in Indian and non-Indian classrooms and observations of family interaction
in Indian households indicate, however, that the Indians' rules for appropriate social usage of English differ distinctively from those of the surrounding non-Indian populations. And in school the children continue to
experience considerable difficulty comprehending and participating in the
structured verbal interaction between teacher and students which provides
the context and mode for classroom learning.

In this paper, discussion will focus on some of the specific ways in
which Indian and non-Indian rules for and/or assumptions about appropriate speech usage differ and the consequences these differences have for

From Monograph Series on Languages and Linguistics, 21st Annual Round Table,
number 23 (1970) (Georgetown University School of Languages and Linguistics,
Georgetown University Press). Reprinted by permission of the Georgetown University
School of Languages and Linguistics.

the Indian children's development of communicative competence. Particular attention will be given to the structure of speech events which are an integral part of classroom interaction, such as question-answer sessions, ordering, and instruction, and to the ways in which the Indian ideas of appropriate roles for the senders and receivers of messages in such speech activities differ from those of non-Indians.

INTRODUCTION

Recent studies of North American Indian education problems have indicated that in many ways Indian children are not culturally oriented to the ways in which classroom learning is conducted. The Wax-Dumont study (Wax, Wax and Dumont 1964) of the Pine Ridge Sioux discusses the lack of interest children show in what goes on in school and Wolcott's (1967) description of a Kwakiutl school describes the Indian children's organized resistance to his ways of organizing classroom learning. [Complete references will be found at the end of this selection.—Ed.] Cazden and John (1968) suggest that the "styles of learning" through which Indian children are enculturated at home differ markedly from those to which they are introduced in the classroom. And Hymes has pointed out that this may lead to sociolinguistic interference when teacher and student do not recognize these differences in their efforts to communicate with one another (Hymes 1967).

On the Warm Springs Indian Reservation, in central Oregon, where I have been carrying out research in patterns of speech usage during this past year, teachers have pointed to similar phenomena, particularly in their repeated statements that Indian children show a great deal of reluctance to talk in class, and that they participate less and less in verbal interaction as they go through school. To help account for the reluctance of the Indian children of Warm Springs (and elsewhere as well) to participate in classroom verbal interactions, I am going to demonstrate how some of the social conditions governing or determining when it is appropriate for a student to speak in the classroom differ from those which govern verbal participation and other types of communicative performances in the Warm Springs Indian community's social interactions.

The end goal of this discussion will be to demonstrate that the social conditions which define when a person uses speech in Indian social situations are present in classroom situations in which Indian students use speech a great deal, and absent in the more prevalent classroom situations in which they fail to participate verbally.

There are several aspects of verbal participation in classroom contexts which should be kept in mind during the discussion of why Indians are reluctant to talk. First of all, a student's use of speech in the classroom during structured lesson sessions is a communicative performance in more than one sense of "performance." It involves demonstration of sociolinguistic competency, itself a complex combination of linguistic competency and social competency involving knowledge of when and in what style one must present one's utterances, among other things. This type of competency, however, is involved in every speech act. But in classrooms there is a second sense in which speaking is a performance that is more special, although not unique, to classroom interactions. In class, speaking is the first and primary mode for communicating competency in all of the areas of skill and knowledge which schools purport to teach. Children communicate what they have learned to the teacher and their fellow students through speaking; only rarely do they demonstrate what they know through physical activity or creation of material objects. While writing eventually becomes a second important channel or mode for communicating knowledge or demonstrating skills, writing as a skill is to a great extent developed through verbal interaction between student and teacher, as is reading.

Consequently, if talk fails to occur, then the channel through which learning sessions are conducted is cut off, and the structure of classroom interaction which depends on dialogue between teacher and student breaks down and no longer functions as it is supposed to. Thus while the question "Why don't Indian kids talk more in class?" is in a sense a very simple one, it is also a very basic one, and the lack of talk a problem which needs to be dealt with if Indian children are to learn what is taught in American schools.

CONDITIONS FOR SPEECH USE IN THE SCHOOL CLASSROOM

When the children first enter school, the most immediate concern of the teachers is to teach them the basic rules for classroom behavior upon which the maintenance of continuous and ordered activity depend. One of the most important of these is the distinction between the roles of teacher and student. In this there is the explicit and implicit assumption that the teacher controls all of the activity taking place in the classroom and the students accept and are obedient to her authority. She determines the sociospatial arrangements of all interactions; she decrees when and where movement takes place within the classroom. And most important for our present concern with communication, she determines who will talk and when they will talk.

While some class activities are designed to create the sense of a class of students as an organized group with class officers or student monitors carrying out various responsibilities contributing to the group, actual spon-taneous organization within the student group which has not been officially designated by the teacher is not encouraged. It interferes with the schedul-ing of activities as the teacher has organized them. The classroom situation is one in which the teacher relates to the students as an undifferentiated mass, much as a performer in front of an audience. Or she relates to each student on a one-to-one basis, often with the rest of the class as the still undifferentiated audience for the performance of the individual child.

In comparing the Indian and non-Indian learning of these basic class-room distinctions which define the conditions in which communication will take place, differences are immediately apparent. Indian first-graders are consistently slower to begin acting in accordance with these basic ar-rangements. They do not remember to raise their hands and wait to be called on before speaking, they wander to parts of the room other than the one in which the teacher is conducting a session, and talk to other students while the teacher is talking much further into the school year than do students in non-Indian classes. And the Indian children continue to fail to conform to classroom procedure much more frequently through the school year.

In contrast to the non-Indian students, the Indian students consist-ently show a great deal more interest in what their fellow students are doing than in what the teacher is doing. While non-Indian students con-stantly make bids for the attention of their teachers, through initiating dia-logue with them as well as through other acts, Indian students do very little of this. Instead they make bids for the attention of their fellow stu-dents through talk. At the first-grade level, and more noticeably at the sixth-grade level, with new teachers, Indian students often act in deliberate organized opposition to the teacher's directions. Thus, at the first-grade level, if one student is told not to put his feet on his chair, another will immediately put his feet on his chair, and he will be imitated by other students who see him do this. In non-Indian classrooms, such behavior was observed only at the sixth-grade level in interaction with a substitute teacher.

In other words, there is, on the part of Indian students, relatively less interest, desire, and/or ability to internalize and act in accordance with some of the basic rules underlying classroom maintenance of orderly in-teraction. Most notably, Indian students are less willing than non-Indian students to accept the teacher as director and controller of all classroom activities. They are less interested in developing the one-to-one communi-cative relationship between teacher and student, and more interested in maintaining and developing relationships with their peers, regardless of what is going on in the classroom.

Within the basic framework of teacher-controlled interaction, there are several possible variations in structural arrangements of interaction, which will be referred to from here on as "participant structures." Teachers use different participant structures, or ways of arranging verbal interaction with students, for communicating different types of educational material, and for providing variation in the presentation of the same material to hold children's interest. Often the notion that different kinds of material are taught better and more efficiently through one sort of participant structuring rather than another is also involved.

In the first type of participant structure the teacher interacts with all of the students. She may address all of them, or a single student in the presence of the rest of the students. The students may respond as a group or chorus in unison, or individually in the presence of their peers. And finally, student verbal participation may be either voluntary, as when the teacher asks who knows the answer to her question, or compulsory, as when the teacher asks a particular student to answer, whether his hand is raised or not. And always it is the teacher who determines whether she talks to one or to all, receives responses individually or in chorus, and voluntarily or without choice.

In a second type of participant structure, the teacher interacts with only some of the students in the class at once, as in reading groups. In such contexts, participation is usually mandatory rather than voluntary, individual rather than chorus, and each student is expected to participate or perform verbally, for the main purpose of such smaller groups is to provide the teacher with the opportunity to assess the knowledge acquired by each individual student. During such sessions, the remaining students who are not interacting with the teacher are usually working alone or independently at their desks on reading or writing assignments.

A third participant structure consists of all students working independently at their desks, but with the teacher explicitly available for student-initiated verbal interaction, in which the child indicates he wants to communicate with the teacher by raising his hand, or by approaching the teacher at her desk. In either case, the interaction between student and teacher is not witnessed by the other students in that they do not hear what is said.

A fourth participant structure, and one which occurs infrequently in the upper primary grades and rarely, if ever, in the lower grades, consists of the students being divided into small groups which they run themselves, though always with the more distant supervision of the teacher, and usually for the purpose of so-called "group projects." As a rule such groups have official "chairmen," who assume what is in other contexts the teacher's authority, in regulating who will talk when.

In observing and comparing Indian and non-Indian participation or communicative performances in these four different structural variations of contexts in which communication takes place, differences between the two groups again emerge very clearly.

In the first two participant structures where students must speak out individually in front of the other students, Indian children show considerable reluctance to participate, particularly when compared to non-Indian students. When the teacher is in front of the whole class, they volunteer to speak relatively rarely, and teachers at the Warm Springs grammar school generally hold that this reluctance to volunteer to speak out in front of other students increases as the children get older.

When the teacher is with a small group, and each individual must give some kind of communicative verbal performance in turn, Indian children much more frequently refuse, or fail to utter a word when called upon, and much less frequently, if ever, urge the teacher to call on them than the non-Indians do. When the Indian children do speak, they speak very softly, often in tones inaudible to a person more than a few feet away, and in utterances which are typically shorter or more brief than those of their non-Indian counterparts.

In situations where the teacher makes herself available for student-initiated communication during sessions in which students are working independently on assignments which do not involve verbal communication, students at the first-grade level in the Indian classes at first rarely initiate contact with the teachers. After a few weeks in a classroom, they do so as frequently as the non-Indian students. At the sixth-grade level, Indian students initiate such relatively private encounters with teachers much more frequently than non-Indian students do.

When students control and direct the interaction in small group projects, as described for the fourth type of participant structure, there is again a marked contrast between the behavior of Indian and non-Indian students. It is in such contexts that Indian students become most fully involved in what they are doing, concentrating completely on their work until it is completed, talking a great deal to one another within the group and competing, with explicit remarks to that effect, with the other groups. Non-Indian students take more time in "getting organized," disagree and argue more regarding how to go about a task, rely more heavily on appointed chairmen for arbitration and decision-making, and show less interest, at least explicitly, in competing with other groups from their class.

Observations of the behavior of both Indian and non-Indian children outside the classroom during recess periods and teacher-organized physical education periods provide further evidence that the difference in readiness to participate in interaction are related to the way in which the interaction is organized and controlled.

When such outside-class activity is organized by the teachers, it is for the purpose of teaching children games through which they develop certain physical and social skills. If the games involve a role distinction between leader and followers in which the leader must tell the others what to do—as in Simon Says, Follow the Leader, Green Light, Red Light, and even Farmer in the Dell, Indian children show a great deal of reluctance to assume the leadership role. This is particularly true when the child is appointed leader by the teacher and must be repeatedly urged to act in telling the others what to do before doing so. Non-Indian children, in contrast, vie eagerly for such positions, calling upon the teacher and/or other students to select them.

If such playground activity is unsupervised, and the children are left to their own devices, Indian children become involved in games of team competition much more frequently than non-Indian children. And they sustain such game activities for longer periods of time and at younger ages than non-Indian children. While non-Indian children tend more to play in groups of two and three, and in the upper primary grades to form "friendships" with one or two persons from their own class in school, Indian children interact with a greater number of children consistently, and maintain friendships and teams with children from classes in schools other than their own.

It is apparent that there are situations arising in the classroom which do allow for the Indian students to verbalize or communicate under or within the participant structures which their behavior indicates they prefer; otherwise it would not have been possible to make the distinctions between their behavior and that of non-Indians in the areas just discussed. However, the frequency of occurrence of such situations in the classroom is very low when compared to the frequency of occurrence of the type of participant structuring in which Indian students fail to participate verbally, particularly in the lower grades.

In other words, most verbal communication which is considered part of students' learning experience does take the structure of individual students speaking in front of other students. About half of this speaking is voluntary insofar as students are invited to volunteer to answer, and half is compulsory in that a specific student is called on and expected to answer. In either case, it is the teacher who establishes when talk will occur and within what kind of participant structure.

There are many reasons why most of the verbal communication takes place under such conditions. Within our particular education system, a teacher needs to know how much her students have learned or absorbed from the material she has presented. Students' verbal responses provide one means—and the primary means, particularly before students learn to write—of measuring their progress, and are thus the teacher's feedback. And, again within our particular educational system, it is not group, but individual progress with which our teachers are expected to be concerned.

In addition, it is assumed that students will learn from each other's performances both what is false or wrong, and what is true or correct. Another aspect of this type of public performance which may increase educators' belief in its efficacy is the students' awareness that these communicative acts *are* performances, in the sense of being demonstrations of competency. The concomitant awareness that success or failure in such acts is a measure of their worth in the eyes of those present increases their motivation to do well. Thus they will remember when they make a mistake and try harder to do well to avoid public failure, in a way which they would not, were their performances in front of a smaller number of people. As I will try to demonstrate further on, however, the educators' assumption of the validity or success of this type of enculturation process, which can briefly be referred to as "learning through public mistakes," is not one which the Indians share, and this has important implications for our understanding of Indian behavior in the classroom.

The consequences of the Indians' reluctance to participate in these speech situations are several. First of all, the teacher loses the primary means she has of receiving feedback on the children's acquisition of knowledge, and is thus less able to establish at what point she must begin again to instruct them, particularly in skills requiring a developmental sequencing, as in reading.

A second consequence of this reluctance to participate in speech situations requiring mandatory individual performances is that the teachers in the Warm Springs grammar school modify their teaching approach whenever possible to accommodate, in a somewhat ad hoc fashion, what they refer to as the Indian students' "shyness." In the first grade it is not easy to make very many modifications because of what teachers perceive as a close relationship between the material being taught and the methods used to teach it. There is some feeling, also, that the teaching methods which can be effective with children at age six are somewhat limited in range. However, as students go up through the grades, there is an increasing tendency for teachers to work with the notion, not always a correct one, that given the same body of material, there are a number of different ways of "presenting" it, or in the terms being used here, a range of different participant structures and modes of communication (e.g. talking versus reading and writing) which can be used.

Even so, at the first grade level there are already some changes made to accommodate the Indian children which are notable. When comparing the Indian first-grade classes with the non-Indian first-grade classes, one finds very few word games involving students giving directions to one another being used. And even more conspicuous in Indian classes is the absence of the ubiquitous Show and Tell or Sharing through which students learn to get up in front of the class, standing where the teacher stands, and presenting, as the teacher might, a monologue relating an experience or describing a treasured object which is supposed to be of interest to the rest of the class. When asked whether this activity was used in the classroom one teacher explained that she had previously used it, but so few children ever volunteered to "share" that she finally discontinued it.

By the time the students reach the sixth grade, the range of modes and settings for communication have increased a great deal, and the opportunity for elimination of some participant structures in preference to others is used by the teachers. As one sixth-grade teacher put it, "I spend as little time in front of the class as possible." In comparison with non-Indian classes, Indian classes have a relatively greater number of group "projects." Thus, while non-Indian students are learning about South American history through reading texts and answering the teacher's questions, Indian students are doing group-planned and executed murals depicting a particular stage in Latin American history; while non-Indian students are reading science texts and answering questions about how electricity is generated, Indian students are doing group-run experiments with batteries and motors.

Similarly, in the Indian classes "reports" given by individual students are almost nonexistent, but are a typical means in non-Indian classes for demonstrating knowledge through verbal performance. And finally, while in non-Indian classes students are given opportunities to ask the teacher questions in front of the class, and do so, Indian students are given fewer opportunities for this because when they do have the opportunity they don't use it. Rather, the teacher of Indians allows more periods in which he is available for individual students to approach him alone and ask their questions quietly where no one else can hear them.

The teachers who make these adjustments, not all do, are sensitive to the inclinations of their students and want to teach them through means to which they most readily adapt. However, by doing so, they are avoiding teaching the Indian children how to communicate in precisely the contexts in which they are least able, and most need to learn how to communicate if they are to do well in school. The teachers handicap themselves by setting up performance situations for the students in which they are least able to arrive at the evaluations of individual competence upon which they rely for feedback to establish at what level they must begin to teach. And it is not at all clear that students do acquire the same information through one form of communication as they do through another. Thus these manipulations of communication settings and participant structures, which are intended to creatively transmit knowledge to the students through the means to which they are most adjusted, may actually be causing the students to completely miss types of information which their later high school teachers will assume they picked up in grammar school.

The consequences of this partial adaption to Indian modes of communication become apparent when the Indian students join the non-Indian students at the junior and senior high school levels. Here, where the

Indian students are outnumbered one to five, there is no manipulation and selection of communication settings to suit the inclinations of the Indians. Here the teachers complain that the Indian students never talk in class, and never ask questions, and everyone wonders why.

CONDITIONS FOR SPEECH USE IN THE
WARM SPRINGS INDIAN COMMUNITY

To understand why the Warm Springs Indian children speak out readily under some social conditions, but fail to do so under others, it is necessary to examine the sociolinguistic assumptions determining the conditions for communicative performances, particularly those involving explicit demonstrations of knowledge or skill, in the Indian community. It will be possible here to deal with only some of the many aspects of communication which are involved. Attention will focus first on the social structuring of learning situations or contexts in which knowledge and skills are communicated to children in Indian homes. Then some consideration will be given to the underlying rules or conditions for participation in the community-wide social events that preschool children, as well as older children, learn through attending such events with their families.

The Indian child's preschool and outside-school enculturation at home differs from that of many non-Indian or white middle-class children in that a good deal of the responsibility for the care and training of children is assumed by persons other than the parents of the children. In many homes the oldest children, particularly if they are girls, assume these responsibilities when the parents are at home, as well as when they are not. Frequently, also, grandparents, uncles and aunts assume the full-time responsibility for care and instruction of children. Children thus become accustomed to interacting with and following the instructions and orders of a greater number of people than is the case with non-Indian children. Equally important is the fact that all of the people with whom Indian children form such reciprocal nurturing and learning relationships are kinsmen. Indian children are rarely, if ever, taken care of by "baby-sitters" from outside the family. Most of their playmates before beginning school are their siblings and cousins, and these peer relationships typically continue to be the strongest bonds of friendship through school and adult life, later providing a basis for reciprocal aid in times of need, and companionship in many social activities.

Indian children are deliberately taught skills around the home (for girls) and in the outdoors (for boys) at an earlier age than many middle-class non-Indian children. Girls, for example, learn to cook some foods before they are eight, and by this age may be fully competent in cleaning a house without any aid or supervision from adults.

There are other areas of competence in which Indian children are expected to be proficient at earlier ages than non-Indian children, for which the means of enculturation or socialization are less visible and clear-cut. While still in grammar school, at the age of 10 or 11, some children are considered capable of spending afternoons and evenings in the company of only other children, without the necessity of accounting for their whereabouts or asking permission to do whatever specific activity is involved. At this same age, many are also considered capable of deciding where they want to live, and for what reasons one residence is preferable to another. They may spend weeks or months at a time living with one relative or another, until it is no longer possible to say that they live in any particular household.

In general, then, Warm Springs Indian children become accustomed to self-determination of action, accompanied by very little disciplinary control from older relatives, at much younger ages than middle-class white children.

In the context of the household, learning takes place through several sorts of somewhat different processes. First of all, children are present at many adult interactions as silent but attentive observers. While it is not yet clear how adult activities in which children are not full participants are distinguished from those in which children may participate fully, and from those for which they are not allowed to be present at all, there are clearly marked differences. What is most remarkable, however, is that there are many adult conversations to which children pay a great deal of silent, patient attention. This contrasts sharply with the behavior of non-Indian children, who show little patience in similar circumstances, desiring either to become a full participant through verbal interaction, or to become completely involved in some other activity.

There is some evidence that this silent listening and watching was, in the Warm Springs culture, traditionally the first step in learning skills of a fairly complex nature. For example, older women reminisce about being required to watch their elder relatives tan hides when they were very young, rather than being allowed to play. And certainly the winter evening events of myth-telling, which provided Indian children with their first explicitly taught moral lessons, involved them as listening participants rather than as speakers.

A second type of learning involves the segmentation of a task by an older relative, and the partial carrying out of the task or one of its segments by the child. In household tasks, for example, a child is given a very simple portion of a job (e.g., in cleaning a room, the child may begin by helping move the furniture) and works in cooperation with and under the supervision of an older relative. Such activities involve a small amount of verbal instruction or direction from the older relative, and allow for questions on the part of the child. Gradually the child comes to learn all of the skills involved in a particular process, consistently under the supervision of an older relative who works along with him.

This mode of instruction is not unique to the Warm Springs Indians, of course; many non-Indian parents use similar methods. However, there are aspects of this type of instruction which differ from its use among non-Indians. First of all, it is likely to be preceded by the long periods of observation just described when it occurs among the Indians. The absence of such observation among non-Indian children is perhaps replaced by elaborate verbal instructions outlining the full scope of a task before the child attempts any part of it.

A second way in which this type of instruction among the Warm Springs Indians differs from that of non-Indians is the absence of "testing" of the child's skill by the instructing kinsman before the child exercises the skill unsupervised. Although it is not yet clear how this works in a diversity of situations, it appears that in many areas of skill, the child takes it upon himself to test the skill unsupervised and alone, without other people around. In this way, if he is unsuccessful, his failure is not seen by others. If he is successful, he can show the result of his success to those by whom he has been taught, whether it be in the form of a deer that has been shot, a hide tanned, a piece of beadwork completed, or a dinner on the table when the adults come home from work.

Again there is some evidence that this type of private individual's testing of competency, followed by public demonstration only when competency is fully developed and certain, has been traditional in the Warm Springs Indian culture. The most dramatic examples of this come from the processes of acquisition of religious and ritual knowledge. In the vision quests through which adolescents, or children of even younger ages, acquired spirit power, individuals spent long periods in isolated mountain areas, from which they were expected to emerge with skills they had not previously demonstrated. While some of these abilities were not fully revealed until later in life, the child was expected to be able to relate some experience of a supernatural nature which would prove that he had, in fact, been visited by a spirit. Along the same lines, individuals until very recently received and learned ritual songs through dreams and visions, which they would sing for the first time in full and completed form in the presence of others.

The contexts described here in which learning takes place can be perceived as a sequence, idealized, of three steps: (1) observation, which of course includes listening; (2) supervised participation; and (3) private, self-initiated self-testing. It is not the case that all acquisitions of skills proceed through such phases, however, but rather only some of those skills which Indian adults consciously and deliberately teach their children, and which the children consciously try to learn. Those which are learned through less deliberate means must to some extent invoke similar structuring, but it is difficult to determine to what extent.

The use of speech in the process is notably minimal. Verbal directions or instructions are few, being confined to corrections and question-answering. Nor does the final demonstration of skill particularly involve verbal performance, since the validation of skill so often involves display of some material evidence or nonverbal physical expression.

This process of Indian acquisition of competence may help to explain, in part, Indian children's reluctance to speak in front of their classmates. In the classroom, the process of "acquisition" of knowledge and "demonstration" of knowledge are collapsed into the single act of answering questions or reciting when called upon to do so by the teacher, particularly in the lower grades. Here the assumption is that one will learn, and learn more effectively, through making mistakes in front of others. The Indian children have no opportunity to observe others performing successfully before they attempt it, except for their fellow classmates who precede them, and are themselves initiated. They have no opportunity to "practice," and decide for themselves when they know enough to demonstrate their knowledge; rather, their performances are determined by the teacher. And finally, their only channel for communicating competency is verbal, rather than nonverbal.

Turning now from learning processes in the home to learning experiences outside the home, in social and ritual activities involving community members other than kinsmen, there is again considerable evidence that Indian children's understanding of when and how one participates and performs individually and thus demonstrates or communicates competence, differs considerably from what is expected of them in the classroom.

Children of all ages are brought to every sort of community-wide social event sponsored by Indians (as distinct from those sponsored by non-Indians). There is rarely, if ever, such a thing as an Indian community event which is attended by adults only. At many events, children participate in only certain roles, but this is true of everyone. Sociospatially and behaviorally, children must always participate minimally as do all others in sitting quietly and attentively alongside their elders.

One of the social features which characterizes social events that are not explicitly kin group affairs, including activities like political General Councils, social dinners, and Worship Dances, is that they are open to participation by all members of the Warm Springs Indian community. While different types of activities are more heavily attended by certain Indians rather than others, and fairly consistently sponsored and arranged by certain individuals, it is always clear that everyone is invited, both by community knowledge of this fact, and by explicit announcements on posters placed in areas where most people pass through at one time or another in their day-to-day activities.

A second feature of such activities is that there is usually no one person directing the activity verbally, or signalling changes from one phase to another. Instead, the structure is determined either by a set procedure or ritual, or there is a group of people who in various complementary ways provide such cueing and direction. Nor are there any participant roles which can be filled or are filled by only one person. In dancing, singing, and drumming there are no soloists, and where there are performers who begin a sequence and are then joined by others, more than one performer takes a turn at such initiations. The speaking roles are handled similarly. In contexts where speeches are appropriate, it is made clear that anyone who wants to may "say a few words." The same holds true for political meetings, where the answerer to a question is not necessarily one who is on a panel or council, but rather the person who feels he is qualified, by his knowledge of a subject, to answer. In all situations thus allowing for anyone who wants to speak, no time limit is set, so that the talking continues until everyone who wants to has had the opportunity to do so.

This does not mean that there are never any "leaders" in Indian social activities, but rather that leadership takes quite a different form than it does in many non-Indian cultural contexts. Among the people of Warm Springs, a person is not a leader by virtue of holding a particular position, even in the case of members of the tribal council and administration. Rather, he is a leader because he has demonstrated ability in some sphere and activity, and many individuals choose to follow his suggestions because they have independently each decided they are good ones. If, for example, an individual plans and announces an activity, but few people offer to help him carry it out or attend it, then that is an indication that the organizer is not a respected leader in the community at the present time. And the likelihood that he will repeat his efforts in the near future is reduced considerably.

This type of "leadership," present today among the people of Warm Springs, is reminiscent of that which was described by Hoebel (1954: 132) for the Comanche chiefs:

> In matters of daily routine, such as camp moving, he merely made the decisions himself, announcing them through a camp crier. Anyone who did not like his decision simply ignored it. If in time a good many people ignored his announcements and preferred to stay behind with some other man of influence, or perhaps to move in another direction with that man, the chief had then lost his following. He was no longer chief, and another had quietly superseded him.

A final feature of Indian social activities, which should be recognized from what has already been said, is that all who do attend an activity may participate in at least some of the various forms participation takes for the given activity, rather than there being a distinction made between participants or performers and audience. At many Indian gatherings, particularly those attended by older people, this aspect of the situation is reflected in its sociospatial arrangement: people are seated in such a way that all present are facing one another, usually in an approximation of a square, and the focus of activity is either along one side of the square, or in its center, or a combination of the two.

And each individual chooses the degree of his participation. No one, other than perhaps those who set up the event, is committed to being present beforehand and all participating roles beyond those of sitting and observing are determined by the individual at the point at which he decides to participate, rather than being pre-scheduled.

In summary, the Indian social activities to which children are early exposed outside the home generally have the following properties: (1) they are community-wide, in the sense that they are open to all Warm Springs Indians; (2) there is no single individual directing and controlling all activity, and to the extent that there are "leaders," their leadership is based on the choice to follow which is made by each person; (3) participation in some form is accessible to everyone who attends. No one need be exclusively an observer or audience, and there is consequently no sharp distinction between audience and performer. And each individual chooses for himself the degree of his participation during the activity.

If one now compares the social conditions for verbal participation in the classroom with the conditions underlying many Indian events in which children participate, a number of differences emerge.

First of all, classroom activities are not community-wide, but, more importantly, the participants in the activity are not drawn just from the Indian community. The teacher, as a non-Indian, is an outsider and a stranger to these events. In addition, by virtue of her role as teacher, she structurally separates herself from the rest of the participants, her students. She places herself outside the interaction and activity of the students. This encourages their cultural perceptions of themselves as the relevant community in opposition to the teacher, perhaps much as they see themselves in opposition to other communities, and on a smaller scale as one team is in opposition to another. In other words, on the basis of the Indians' social experiences, one is either a part of a group or outside it. The notion of a single individual being structurally set apart from all others, in anything other than an observer role, and yet still a part of the group organization, is one which children probably encounter for the first time in school, and continue to experience only in non-Indian derived activities (e.g. in bureaucratic, hierarchically-structured occupations). This helps to explain why Indian students show so little interest in initiating interaction with the teacher in activities involving other students.

Second, in contrast to Indian activities where many people are involved in determining the development and structure of an event, there is only one single authority directing everything in the classroom, namely the teacher. And the teacher is not the controller or leader by virtue of the individual students' choices to follow her, as is the case in Indian social activities, but rather by virtue of her occupation of the role of teacher. This difference helps to account for the Indian children's frequent indifference to the directions, orders, and requests for compliance with classroom social rules which the teacher issues.

Third, it is not the case in the classroom that all students may participate in any given activity, as in Indian community activities. Nor are they given the opportunity to choose the degree of their participation which, on the basis of evidence discussed earlier, would in Indian contexts be based on the individual's having already ascertained in private that he was capable of successful verbal communication of competence. Again these choices belong to the teacher.

CONCLUSION

In summary, Indian children fail to participate verbally in classroom interaction because the social conditions for participation to which they have become accustomed in the Indian community are lacking. The absence of these appropriate social conditions for communicative performances affect the most common and everyday speech acts which occur in the classroom. If the Indian child fails to follow an order or answer a question, it may not be because he doesn't understand the linguistic structure of the imperative and the interrogative, but rather because he does not share the non-Indian's assumption in such contexts that use of these syntactic forms by definition implies an automatic and immediate response from the person to whom they were addressed. For these assumptions are sociolinguistic assumptions which are not shared by the Indians.

Educators cannot assume that because Indian children (or children from other cultural backgrounds than that which is implicit in American classrooms) speak English, or are taught it in school, that they have also assimilated all of the sociolinguistic rules underlying interaction in classrooms and other non-Indian social situations where English is spoken. If the children are to participate in the classroom verbal interaction upon which the learning process depends, they must first be taught the rules for appropriate speech usage in contexts where talking is necessary.

REFERENCES

BERRY, BREWTON. 1969. *The education of American Indians: A survey of the literature.* Prepared for the Special Subcommittee on Indian Education of the Committee on Labor and Public Welfare, United States Senate (Washington, D.C.: Government Printing Office).

CAZDEN, COURTNEY B., and VERA P. JOHN. 1968. "Learning in American Indian children." In *Styles of Learning Among American Indians: An Outline for Research,* 1–19 (Washington, D.C.: Center for Applied Linguistics.)

HOEBEL, E. ADAMSON. 1954. *The Law of Primitive Man* (Cambridge: Harvard University Press).

HYMES, DELL. 1967. "On Communicative Competence." MS due to be published in a volume edited by Renira Huxley and Elizabeth Ingram, tentative title: *Mechanisms of Language Development.* (To be published by Centre for Advanced Study in the Developmental Science and CIBA Foundation, London).

WAX, MURRAY, ROSALIE WAX, and ROBERT DUMONT, JR. 1964. *Formal Education in an American Indian Community.* Social Problems Monograph no. 1 (Kalamazoo, Michigan: Society for the Study of Social Problems).

WOLCOTT, HENRY. 1967. *A Kwakiutl Village and School.* (New York City: Holt, Rinehart, and Winston).

ZENTNER, HENRY. 1960. Volume II: Education (Oregon State College Warm Springs Research Project).

VERBAL STRATEGIES IN MULTILINGUAL COMMUNICATION

John J. Gumperz

> Minority group members live in two social, cultural, and linguistic
> worlds—their own and that of the majority group. It is difficult for
> majority group members, who have never known such a disjuncture
> in their social lives, to appreciate the meaning of this experience, or
> even to perceive the patterns of behavior of the minority group
> except in terms of differences from their own.
>   Both in bilingual and bidialectal circumstances, members of
> minority groups often exhibit code-switching between their own lan-
> guage or dialect and that of the dominant group. This behavior is
> sometimes mistakenly interpreted as indicating that such speakers
> "mix up" their two languages or dialects and "have no grammar."
> The conclusion could not be farther from the truth, and reflects a
> typical misconception of minority group behavior by the majority
> group. Code-switching is in fact a communicative skill, which speakers
> use as a verbal strategy in conveying meanings.
>   Many of the problems of minority group students with reading
> and the appropriate use of school language may be not so much in
> specific linguistic differences as in differing values and associations,
> both on the part of the teacher and the student, regarding styles
> and occasions of language use.

Recent systematic research in the inner city has successfully disproved
the notions of those who characterize the language of low-income populations as degenerate and structurally underdeveloped. There is overwhelming evidence to show that both middle-class and non-middle-class children,
no matter what their native language, dialect, or ethnic background, when
they come to school at the age of five or six, have control of a fully formed
grammatical system. The mere fact that their system is distinct from that

From *Monograph Series on Languages and Linguistics*, 21st Annual Round Table,
number 23 (1970) (Georgetown University School of Languages and Linguistics,
Georgetown University Press). Reprinted by permission of the Georgetown University
School of Languages and Linguistics.

of their teacher does not mean that their speech is not rule governed. Speech features which strike the teacher as different do not indicate failure to adjust to some universally accepted English norm; rather, they are the output of dialect or language-specific syntactic rules which are every bit as complex as those of Standard English (Labov 1969). [Complete references will be found at the end of this selection.—Ed.]

It is clear furthermore that the above linguistic differences also reflect far-reaching and systematic cultural differences. Like the plural societies of Asia and Africa, American urban society is characterized by the coexistence of a variety of distinct cultures. Each major ethnic group has its own heritage, its own body of traditions, values, and views about what is right and proper. These traditions are passed on from generation to generation as part of the informal family or peer group socialization process and are encoded in folk art and literature, oral or written.

To understand this complex system, it is first of all necessary to identify and describe its constituent elements. Grammatical analysis must be, and has to some extent been, supplemented by ethnographic description, ethnohistory, and the study of folk art (Stewart 1968; Hannerz 1969; Abrahams 1964; Kochman 1969). But mere description of component subsystems is not enough if we are to learn how the plurality of cultures operates in everyday interaction and how it affects the quality of individual lives. Minority groups in urbanized societies are never completely isolated from the dominant majority. To study their life ways without reference to surrounding populations is to distort the realities of their everyday lives. All residents of modern industrial cities are subject to the same laws and are exposed to the same system of public education and mass communication. Minority group members, in fact, spend much of their day in settings where dominant norms prevail. Although there are significant individual differences in the degree of assimilation, almost all minority group members, even those whose behavior on the surface may seem quite deviant, have at least a passive knowledge of the dominant culture. What sets them off from others is not simply the fact that they are distinct, but the juxtaposition of their own private language and life-styles with that of the public at large.

This juxtaposition, which is symbolized by constant alternation between in-group and out-group modes of acting and expression has a pervasive effect on everyday behavior. Successful political leaders such as the late Martin Luther King and Bobby Seale rely on it for much of their rhetorical effect. Kernan in her recent ethnographic study of verbal communication in an Afro-American community reports that her informants' everyday conversation reveals an overriding concern—be it positive or negative—with majority culture.

Majority group members who have not experienced a similar disjuncture between private and public behavior frequently fail to appreciate its effect. They tend merely to perceive minority group members as different, without realizing the effect that this difference may have on everyday communication. This ignorance of minority styles of behavior seems to have contributed to the often discussed notion of "linguistic deprivation." No one familiar with the writings of Afro-American novelists of the last decade and with the recent writings on Black folklore can maintain that low-income Blacks are nonverbal. An exceptionally rich and varied terminological system, including such folk concepts as "sounding," "signifying," "rapping," "running it down," "shucking," "jiving," "marking," etc., all referring to verbal strategies, (i.e. different modes of achieving particular communicative ends) testifies to the importance which Afro-American culture assigns to verbal art (Kochman 1969; Kernan 1969). Yet, inner-city Black children are often described as nonverbal, simply because they fail to respond to the school situation. It is true that lower-class children frequently show difficulty in performing adequately in formal interviews and psychological tests. But these tests are frequently administered under conditions which seem unfamiliar and, at times, threatening to minority group children. When elicitation conditions are changed, there is often a radical improvement in response (Labov 1969; Mehan 1970).

The fact that bilingualism and biculturalism have come to be accepted as major goals in inner-city schools is an important advance. But if we are to achieve this goal, we require at least some understanding of the nature of code alternation and its meaning in everyday interaction. Bilingualism is, after all, primarily a linguistic term, referring to the fact that linguists have discovered significant alternations in phonology, morphology, and syntax, in studying the verbal behavior of a particular population. While bilingual phenomena have certain linguistic features in common, these features may have quite different social significance.

Furthermore, to the extent that social conditions affect verbal behavior, findings based on research in one type of bilingual situation may not necessarily be applicable to another socially different one. Much of what we know about second language learning or [about] bilingual interference derives from work with monolingual college students learning a foreign language in a classroom. Other research on bilingualism has dealt with isolated middle-class bilinguals residing in monolingual neighborhoods or with immigrant farmers or their descendants. We know least about the kind of situation where—as in the case of big-city Afro-Americans or Chicanos—bilingualism has persisted over several generations and where strict barriers of caste limit or channel the nature of communication between the groups in question. Most importantly, we only have a minimal amount of information about the ways in which bilingual usage symbolizes the values of speakers and the social conditions in which they live.

The accepted paradigm for the linguistic study of bilingualism is the code-switching paradigm. Having observed that linguistic alternates exist at the level of phonology and syntax, we proceed to ask which alternates are used when and under what social circumstances. The assumption is that the stream of behavior can be divided into distinct social occasions, interaction sequences, or speech events. These events are assumed to be associated with culturally specific behavioral norms which, in turn, determine the speech forms to be used. To some extent this is indeed the case.

In every society there are certain performative occasions, such as ceremonial events, court proceedings, greetings or formal introductions and the like, where the form of the language used is strictly prescribed and where deviations also change the definition of the event (Blom and Gumperz 1970). When asked to report about their language usage, speakers tend to respond in such all-or-none terms. Hence, language censuses of urban neighborhoods in the U.S. usually indicate that the minority languages are used for informal, in-group, family interaction, while the majority language serves for communication with outsiders.

Tape recordings of conversation in natural settings, however, frequently reveal quite a different picture. A recent study of bilingual behavior in Texas, for example, reports many instances of what seems almost random language mixture (Lance 1969: 75–76).

(1) **Te digo que este dedo** (*I tell you that this finger*) has been bothering me so much.

Se me hace que (*it seems that*) I have to respect her porque 'ta (*because she is*)

But this arthritis deal, boy you get to hurting so bad you can't hardly even . . . 'cer masa pa tortillas (*make dough for tortillas*)

In Texas, such language mixture tends to be disparaged and referred to by pejorative terms such as Tex-Mex. It is rarely reported in the literature and frequently dismissed as abnormal. Nevertheless, such apparent language mixture is a common feature of informal conversation in urban bilingual societies.

When asked why they used English in situations where, according to their own reports, the minority language is normal, speakers tend to respond by stating that the English items in question are loan words, words for which there are no equivalents in the home language. But this is not always the case. On a number of occasions, Puerto Rican mothers in Jersey City could be heard calling to their children as follows:

(2) **Ven aquí ven aquí.** [Come here, come here.]

If the child would not come immediately, this would be followed with:

Come here, you.

Clearly, it would be difficult to justify such alternation on the grounds of ease of expression. There is more to this message than can be conveyed by usage surveys. The English is used for stylistic effect to convey meaning. An English-speaking mother under similar conditions might respond to her child's failure to obey with something like:

(3) John Henry Smith, you come here right away.

Both the English and the Puerto Rican mothers indicate annoyance, but they use different verbal strategies for doing so.

Let me illustrate this point with some additional examples from conversations recorded in Chicano and Afro-American groups in California, and analyzed in more detail in Gumperz and Hernandez (1969). Recordings in question were made by participants in group discussion, who also assisted in the analysis. The tapes were transcribed by a linguist, using detailed phonetic transcription wherever necessary, in order to isolate instances of code-switching. The contextual meaning of code-switches was then determined by a procedure which derives from the apparatus for conversational analysis developed by ethno-methodologists (Sacks 1970; Schegloff 1970). When in doubt, our hypothesis as to what was meant was checked with other participants in the conversation.

In the first two examples, the speakers are a faculty member at the University of California (E), and (M), a social worker in a day care center where E is working as a volunteer. Both speakers are native Americans of Mexican ancestry. The conversation ranges over a number of topics from the speakers' personal experience.

(4) E.   What do you dream in?
    M.   I don't think I ever have any conversations in my dreams. I just dream.
         Ha. I don' hear people talking; I jus' see pictures.
    E.   Oh, they're old-fashioned, then. They're not talkies yet, huh?
    M.   They're old-fashioned. No. they're not talkies yet. No, I'm trying' to think.
         Yeah, there too have been talkies. Different. In Spanish and English both.
         An' I wouldn't be too surprised if I even had some in Chinese. (Laughter)
         Yeah, Ed. Deveras (Really). (M. offers E. a cigarette which is refused.)
         Tu no fumas, verdad? Yo tampoco. Dejé de fumar. (You don't smoke,
         do you? I don't either; I stopped smoking) and I'm back to it again.

M breaks into Spanish, just as she is about to offer E a cigarette. The shift is accompanied by lowering of the voice of the type that accompanies confidentiality in monolinguals. She continues to talk about her smoking problem, explaining that she had given up the habit for awhile, but that she had begun again during a period when she was visiting a friend in a local institution. On each visit she would buy a pack of cigarettes; the friend would smoke some and she would take the rest home and smoke them herself. Now notice the passage:

(5) E. That's all you smoked?

M. That's all I smoked.

E. An' how about . . . how about now?

M. Estos . . . melos halle . . . estos Pall Malls me los . . . me los hallaron. (*These . . . I found . . . these Pall Malls I . . . they were found for me.*) No, I mean . . . that's all the cigarettes . . . that's all. They're the ones I buy.

Later on M goes on to analyze her struggle with the smoking habit as follows:

(6) M. Mm-huh. Yeah. An' . . . an' . . . an' they tell me, "How did you quit, Mary?" I di'n' quit. I . . . I just stopped. I mean it wasn't an effort that I made. Que voy a dejar de fumar porque me hace daño (*That I'm going to stop smoking because it's harmful to me*), or this or tha,' uh-uh. It just . . . that . . . eh . . . I used to pull butts out of the . . . the . . . the wastepaper basket. Yeah. (Laughter) I used to go looking in the (unclear) . . . Se me acababan los cigarros en la noche. (*My cigarettes would run out on me at night.*) I'd get desperate, y ahi voy al basurero a buscar, a sacar, you know? (Laughter) (*And there I go to the wastebasket to look for some, to get some, you know?*) Ayer los (unclear) . . . no había que no traia cigarros Camille, no traia Helen, no traia yo, el Sr. de Leon, (*Yesterday the . . . there weren't any. Camille didn't have any, I, Mr. de Leon didn't have any*) and I saw Dixie's bag crumpled up, so I figures she didn't have any, y ahi ando en los ceniceros buscando a ver onde estaba la . . . (*And There I am in the ashtrays looking to see where there was the . . .*) I din' care whose they were.

Here again, what someone studying the passage sentence by sentence might regard as almost random alternation between the two languages, is highly meaningful in terms of the conversational context. M is quite ambivalent about her smoking and she conveys this through her language use. Her choice of speech forms symbolizes her alternation between embarrassment and clinical detachment about her own condition. Spanish sentences reflect personal involvement (at least in this particular conversation), while English marks more general or detached statements.

Our next example derives from a discussion session recording in Richmond, California, by a Black community worker. Participants include his wife and several teenage boys. Here we find alternation between speech features which are quite close to standard English and such typically Black English features as lack of post-vocalic *r*, double negation, and copula deletion.

(7) You can tell me how your mother worked twenty hours a day and I can sit here and cry. I mean I can cry and I can feel for you. But as long as I don't get up and make certain that I and my children don't go through the same, *I ain't did nothin' for you, brother.* That's what I'm talking about.

(8) How Michael is making a point, where that everything that happens in that house affects all the kids. It does. And Michael and *you makin' a point,* too. *Kids suppose to learn how to avoid these things.* But let me tell you. We're all in here. *We talkin' but you see* . . .

Note the underlined phrase in passage seven, with the typically Black English phrases *ain't did nothin'* embedded in what is otherwise a normal standard English sequence. On our tape the shift is not preceded by a pause or marked off by special stress or intonation contours. The speaker is therefore not quoting from another code; his choice of form here lends emphasis to what he is saying. Passage eight begins with a general statement addressed to the group as a whole. The speaker than turns to one person, Michael, and signals this change in focus by dropping the copula *is* and shifting to Black phonology.

It seems clear that in all these cases, what the linguist sees merely as alternation between two systems, serves definite and clearly understandable communicative ends. The speakers do not radically switch from one style to another, but they build on the coexistence of alternate forms to create meanings. To be sure, not all instances of code alternation are meaningful. Our tapes contain several instances where the shift into Black English or the use of a Spanish word in an English sentence can only be interpreted as a slip of the tongue, frequently corrected in the next sentence, or where it must be regarded merely as a sign of the speaker's lack of familiarity with the style he is employing. But, even though such errors do occur, it is nevertheless true that code switching is also a communicative skill, which speakers use as a verbal strategy in much the same way that skillful writers switch styles in a short story.

How and by what devices does the speaker's selection of alternate forms communicate meaning? The process is a metaphoric process somewhat similar to what linguists interested in literary style have called foregrounding (Garvin 1964). Foregrounding in the most general sense of the term relies on the fact that words are more than just names for things. Words also carry a host of culturally specific associations, attitudes, and values. These cultural values derive from the context in which words are usually used and from the activities with which they are associated. When a word is used in other than its normal context, these associations become highlighted or foregrounded. Thus to take an example made famous by Leonard Bloomfield (1936), the word *fox* when it refers to a man, as in *he is a fox,* communicates the notions of slyness and craftiness which our culture associates with the activities of foxes.

We assume that what holds true for individual lexical items also holds true for phonological or syntactic alternates. Whenever a speech variety is associated with a particular social category of speakers or with certain activities, this variety comes to symbolize the cultural values associated with these features of the nonlinguistic environment. In other words, speech varieties, like words, are potentially meaningful and, in both cases, this is brought out by reinterpreting meanings in relation to context. As long as the variety in question is used in its normal environment, only its basic referential sense is communicated. But when it is used in a new context, it becomes socially marked, by virtue of the fact that the values associated with the original context are mapped onto the new message.

In any particular instance of code-switching, speakers deduce what is meant by an information processing procedure which takes account of the speaker, the addressee, the social categories to which they can be assigned in the context, the topic, etc. (Blom and Gumperz 1970). Depending on the nature of the above factors, a wide variety of contextual meanings can be communicated. In the examples cited in this paper, all contextual meanings derive from the basic meaning inclusion (we) versus exclusion (they). This underlying meaning is then reinterpreted in the light of the co-occurring contextual factors to indicate such things as degree of involvement (items 4 and 5), anger (items 2 and 3), emphasis (item 7), change in focus (8). In the following additional example, taken from a graduate student's recording of a Korean-English family conversation, Korean seems to be used simply as a device to direct one's question to one out of several potential addressees.

(9) A. No, the lady used to know us. Ka mirri saram ya, ku wife-uga, mariji, odi University . . . yoginga, odinga . . . (You know that man, his wife, I mean, which university . . . Here, or where . . .)

 U. Tokaebbi katchi saenging saram? (Yeah, the one that looks like a ghost?)

 A. Unn. Dr. Kaeng katchiin saram. (Yeah, the one that is like Dr. Kaeng.)

 L. Do teachers that teach in Japan have to have teaching credentials?

 C. Well, it depends. If you're going to teach in a military installation.

Speakers A and U here are of the older generation of immigrants who are somewhat more imbued with Korean culture. L and C are college students who are probably most at home in English. Thus, A's shift to Korean is interpreted by U as an invitation to respond similarly. L's use of English, along with her topic, mark her message as addressed to C.

On other occasions, switching may simply serve as a sign to indicate that the speaker is quoting someone else:

(10) Because I was speakin' to my baby . . . my ex-baby sitter, and we were talkin' about the kids you know, an' I was tellin' her . . . uh, 'Pero, como,

*you now, . . . uh . . . la Estela y la Sandi . . . relistas en el telefon. (But,
how, you know . . . uh . . . Estela and Sandi are very precocious on the
telephone.)*

We have chosen examples of code-switching from a number of languages to highlight the fact that the meanings conveyed by code-switching
are independent of the phonological shape or historical origin of the
alternates in question. The association between forms and meaning is
quite arbitrary. Any two alternates having the same referential meaning
can become carriers of social meaning.

The ability to interpret a message is a direct function of the listener's
home background, his peer group experiences, and his education. Differences in background can lead to misinterpretation of messages. The sentence *he is a Sikh* has little or no meaning for an American audience. To
anyone familiar with speech behavior in Northern India, however, it conveys a whole host of meanings, since Sikhs are stereotypically known as
bumblers. Similarly the above-cited statement *he is a fox*, which conveys
slyness to middle-class whites, is interpreted as a synonym for *he is hand-
some* in Black culture. The process of communication thus requires both
shared grammar and shared rules of language usage. Two speakers may
speak closely related and, on the surface, mutually intelligible varieties of
the same language, but they may nevertheless misunderstand each other
because of differences in usage rules resulting from differences in background. We must know the speakers' normal usage pattern, i.e. which
styles are associated as unmarked forms with which activities and relationships, as well as what alternates are possible in what context, and what
cultural associations these carry.

We know very little about the distribution of usage rules in particular
populations. For example, there seems to be no simple correlation with
ethnic identity, nor is it always possible to predict usage rules on the basis
of socioeconomic indexes. To go back for a moment to the Puerto Rican
neighborhood referred to above: While the majority of the Puerto Ricans
in our Jersey City block followed usage patterns like those described above,
there are others residing among them whose patterns differ significantly. A
Puerto Rican college student took a tape recorder home and recorded informal family conversation over a period of several days. It is evident from
his recording, and he himself confirms this in interviews, that in his family
English serves as the normal medium of informal conversation, while
Spanish is socially marked and serves to convey special connotations of
intimacy and anger.

Our final example derives from classroom observation of first-grade
reading sessions in a racially integrated California school district. Classes
in the district include about 60% white and 40% Black, Chicano, and
oriental children. College student observers find that most reading classes

have a tracking system such that children are assigned to fast or slow reading groups and these groups are taught by different methods and otherwise receive different treatment.

Even in first-grade reading periods, where presumably all children are beginners, the slow reading groups tend to consist of 90% Blacks and Chicanos. Does this situation reflect real learning difficulties, or is it simply a function of our inability to diagnose reading aptitude in culturally different children? Furthermore, given the need for some kind of ability grouping, how effective and how well adapted to cultural needs are the classroom devices that are actually used to bridge the reading gap?

Recently we observed a reading session with a slow reading group of three children, and seven fast readers. The teacher worked with one group at a time, keeping the others busy with individual assignments. With the slow readers she concentrated on the alphabet, on spelling of individual words, and supposedly basic grammatical concepts such as the distinctions between questions and statements. She addressed the children in what white listeners would identify as pedagogical style. Her enunciation was deliberate and slow. Each word was clearly articulated with even stress and pitch, as if to avoid any verbal sign of emotion, approval, or disapproval. Children were expected to speak only when called upon, and the teacher would insist that each question be answered before responding to further ideas. Unsolicited remarks were ignored even if they referred to the problem at hand. Pronunciation errors were corrected whenever they occurred, even if the reading task had to be interrupted. The children seemed distracted and inattentive. They were guessing at answers, "psyching out" the teacher in the manner described by Holt (1965) rather than following her reasoning process. The following sequence symbolizes the artificiality of the situation:

(11) Teacher: Do you know what a question is? James, ask William a question.
James: William, do you have a coat on?
William: No, I do not have a coat on.

James asks his question and William answers in a style which approaches in artificiality that of the teacher, characterized by citation form pronunciation of ([ey] rather than [ə]) of the indefinite article, lack of contraction of *do not*, stress on the *have*, staccato enunciation as if to symbolize what they perceive to be the artificiality and incomprehensibility of the teacher's behavior.

With the advanced group, on the other hand, reading became much more of a group activity and the atmosphere was more relaxed. Words were treated in context, as part of a story. Children were allowed to volunteer answers. There was no correction of pronunciation, although some deviant forms were also heard. The children actually enjoyed competing with each other in reading, and the teacher responded by dropping her pedagogical monotone in favor of more animated natural speech. The activities around the reading table were not lost on the slow readers who were sitting at their desks with instructions to practice reading on their own. They kept looking at the group, neglecting their own books, obviously wishing they could participate. After a while one boy picked up a spelling game from a nearby table and began to work at it with the other boy, and they began to argue in a style normal for Black children. When their voices were raised the teacher turned and asked them to go back to reading.

In private conversation, the teacher who is very conscientious and seemingly concerned with all her children's progress, justified her ability grouping on the grounds that children in the slow group lacked books in their homes and "did not speak proper English." She stated they needed practice in grammar and abstract thinking and pronunciation, and suggested that given this type of training they would eventually be able to catch up with the advanced group. We wonder how well she will succeed. Although clearly she has the best motives and would probably be appalled if one were to suggest that her ability grouping and her emphasis on the technical aspects of reading and spelling with culturally different children is culturally biased, her efforts are not so understood by the children themselves. Our data indicates that the pedagogical style used with slow readers carries different associations for low-middle-class and low-income groups. While whites identify it as normal teaching behavior, ghetto residents associate it with the questioning style of welfare investigators and automatically react by not cooperating. In any case, attuned as they are to see meaning in stylistic choice, the Black children in the slow reading group cannot fail to notice that they are being treated quite differently and with less understanding than the advanced readers.

What are the implications of this type of situation for our understanding of the role of dialect differences on classroom learning? There is no question that the grammatical features of Black dialects discovered by urban dialectologists in recent years are of considerable importance for the historical study of origin of these dialects and for linguistic theory in general, but this does not necessarily mean that they constitute an impediment to learning. Information on Black dialect is often made known to educators in the form of simple lists of deviant features with the suggestion that these features might interfere with reading. There is little, if any, experimental evidence that the pronunciations characteristic of urban Black English actually interfere with the reading process. Yet the teacher in our classroom, for example, spent considerable time attempting to teach her slow readers the distinction between pin and pen. Lack of a vowel distinction in these two words is widespread among Blacks, but also quite common among whites in northern California. In any case, there is no reason why homophony in this case should present more difficulty than homophony in such words as *sea* and *see,* and *know* and *no.*

It is not enough simply to present the educator with the descriptive linguistic evidence. What we need is properly controlled work on reading as such, work which does not deal with grammar alone. Our data suggests that urban language differences, while they may or may not interfere with reading, do have a significant influence on a teacher's expectation and hence on the learning environment. Since bilinguals and bidialectals rely heavily on code-switching as a verbal strategy, they are especially sensitive to the relationship between language and context. It would seem that they learn best under conditions of maximum contextual reinforcement. Sole concentration on the technical aspects of reading, grammar, and spelling may so adversely affect the learning environment as to outweigh any advantages to be gained.

The problem of contextual relevance is not confined to contact with speakers of Black English. It also applies, for example, to the teaching of both English and Spanish in bilingual schools. When interviewed about their school experiences, Puerto Rican high school students in New York as well as Texas and California Chicano students uniformly complain about their lack of success in Spanish instruction. They resent the fact that their Spanish teachers single out their own native usages as substandard and inadmissable both in classroom speech and in writing.

It seems clear, furthermore, that progress in urban language instruction is not simply a matter of better teaching aids and improved textbooks. Middle-class adults have to learn to appreciate differences in communicative strategies of the type discussed here. Teachers themselves must be given instruction in both the linguistic and ethnographic aspects of speech behavior. They must become acquainted with code selection rules in formal and informal settings, as well as those themes of folk literature and folk art that form the input to these rules, so that they can diagnose their own communication problems and adapt methods to their children's background.

NOTES

Research reported on in this paper has been supported by grants from the Urban Crisis Program and the Institute of International Studies, University of California, Berkeley. I am grateful to Edward Hernandez and Louisa Lewis for assistance in field work and analysis.

REFERENCES

ABRAHAMS, ROGER D. 1964. *Deep Down in the Jungle* (Hatboro, Pennsylvania: Folklore Associates).

BLOM, JAN PETTER, and JOHN J. GUMPERZ. 1970. *Social Meaning in Linguistic Structures.* In John J. Gumperz and Dell Hymes, eds., *Directions in Sociolinguistics* (New York: Holt, Rinehart & Winston, in press).

BLOOMFIELD, LEONARD. 1933. *Language* (New York: Holt, Rinehart & Winston).

GARVIN, PAUL, ed. 1969. *A Prague School Reader* (Washington, D.C.: Georgetown University Press).

GUMPERZ, JOHN J., and EDWARD HERNANDEZ. 1969. *Cognitive Aspects of Bilingual Communication.* Working Paper No. 28, Language Behavior Research Laboratory (University of California, Berkeley, December).

HANNERZ, ULF. 1969. *Soulside.* Stockholm.

HOLT, JOHN CALDWELL. 1964. *How Children Fail.* (New York: Pitman).

KOCHMAN, T. H. 1969. "Rapping in the Black Ghetto," *Trans-action* (February).

LABOV, WILLIAM. 1969. "The Logic of Nonstandard Negro English." In *Linguistics and the Teaching of Standard English.* Monograph Series on Languages and Linguistics No. 22. (Washington, D.C.: Georgetown University Press).

LANCE, DONALD M. 1969. *A Brief Study of Spanish-English Bilingualism.* (Research report, Texas A and M University).

MEHAN, B. 1970. Unpublished lecture delivered to the Kroeber Anthropological Society meetings, April 25.

MITCHELL-KERNAN, CLAUDIA. 1969. *Language Behavior in a Black Urban Community.* Unpublished doctoral dissertation. (University of California, Berkeley).

ROSENTHAL, ROBERT. 1968. *Pygmalion in the Classroom.* (New York: Holt, Rinehart, and Winston).

SACKS, HARVEY. 1970. "On the Analyzability of Stories by Children." In John J. Gumperz and Dell Hymes, eds., *Directions in Sociolinguistics* (New York: Holt, Rinehart, and Winston, in press).

SCHEGLOFF, EMANUEL. 1970. "Sequencing in Conversational Openings." In John J. Gumperz and Dell Hymes, eds., *Directions in Sociolinguistics* (New York: Holt, Rinehart, and Winston, in press).

SHUY, ROGER W. 1964. *Social Dialects and Language Learning.* Proceedings of the Bloomington, Indiana Conference. N. C. Y. E. Co-operative Research Project No. OE5-10-148.

SONG, LINDA M. 1970. "Language Switching in Korean-English Bilinguals."
   Unpublished manuscript (University of California, Berkeley).
STEWART, W. 1968. "Continuity and Change in American Negro Dialects."
   The Florida FL Reporter (Spring).
TROIKE, RUDOLPH C. 1969. "Receptive Competence, Productive Competence
   and Performance." In James E. Alatis, ed., *Linguistics and the Teaching of
   Standard English*. Monograph Series on Languages and Linguistics No.
   22 (Washington, D.C.: Georgetown University Press), pp. 63–75.

A SOCIAL PSYCHOLOGY OF BILINGUALISM

Wallace E. Lambert

*Ethnocentrism, the tendency to evaluate other cultures and
societies in terms of a belief in the superiority of one's own way of
life, is a universal phenomenon, but one more highly developed in
Euro-American culture than in almost any other. Here Lambert suggests that the bilingual-bicultural individual may avoid becoming
ethnocentric because he learns to recognize the relativity of different
cultures and languages. He shows also that many bilinguals suffer
from problems of conflicting allegiances and values, but that there
is an emergent middle way, in which individuals can achieve a
balanced and integrated competence in both languages, and enjoy
the advantages of being able to participate freely in both cultures. In
this, the attitudes inculcated in the schools can have a significant
effect, either for good or ill.*

My argument is that bilinguals, especially those with bicultural experiences, enjoy certain fundamental advantages which, if capitalized on,
can easily offset the annoying social tugs and pulls they are normally
prone to. Let me mention one of these advantages that I feel is a tremendous asset. Recently, Otto Klineberg and I conducted a rather comprehensive international study of the development of stereotyped thinking
in children. . . . We found that rigid and stereotyped thinking about in-
groups and out-groups, or about own groups in contrast to foreigners, starts
during the pre-school period when children are trying to form a conception

From *Journal of Social Issues*, vol. XXIII, no. 2 (1967), pp. 106–8. Reprinted
by permission of the *Journal of Social Issues* and the author.

of themselves and their place in the world. Parents and other socializers attempt to help the child at this stage by highlighting differences and contrasts among groups, thereby making their own group as distinctive as possible. This tendency, incidentally, was noted among parents from various parts of the world. Rather than helping, however, they may actually be setting the stage for ethnocentrism with permanent consequences. The more contrasts are stressed, the more deep-seated the stereotyping process and its impact on ethnocentric thought appear to be. Of relevance here is the notion that the child brought up bilingually and biculturally will be less likely to have good versus bad contrasts impressed on him when he starts wondering about himself, his own group, and others. Instead he will probably be taught something more truthful, although more complex: that differences among national or cultural groups of peoples are actually not clear-cut and that basic similarities among peoples are more prominent than differences. The bilingual child in other words may well start life with the enormous advantage of having a more open, receptive mind about himself and other people. Furthermore, as he matures, the bilingual has many opportunities to learn, from observing changes in other people's reactions to him, how two-faced and ethnocentric *others* can be. That is, he is likely to become especially sensitive to and leery of ethnocentrism.

BILINGUALS AND SOCIAL CONFLICTS

This is not to say that bilinguals have an easy time of it. In fact, the final investigation I want to present demonstrates the social conflicts bilinguals typically face, but, and this is the major point, it also demonstrates one particular type of adjustment that is particularly encouraging.

In 1943, Irving Child investigated a matter that disturbed many second-generation Italians living in New England: what were they, Italian or American? Through early experiences they had learned that their relations with certain other youngsters in their community were strained whenever they displayed signs of their Italian background, that is, whenever they behaved as their parents wanted them to. In contrast, if they rejected their Italian background, they realized they could be deprived of many satisfactions stemming from belonging to an Italian family and an Italian community. Child uncovered three contrasting modes of adjusting to these pressures. One subgroup rebelled against their Italian background, making themselves as American as possible. Another subgroup rebelled the other way, rejecting things American as much as possible while proudly associating themselves with things Italian. The third form of adjustment was an apathetic withdrawal and a refusal to think of themselves in ethnic terms at all. This group tried, unsuccessfully, to escape the conflict by avoiding situations where the matter of cultural background might come up. Stated in other terms, some tried to belong to one of their own groups or the other, and some, because of strong pulls from both sides, were unable to belong to either.

Child's study illustrates nicely the difficulties faced by people with dual allegiances, but there is no evidence presented of second-generation Italians who actually feel themselves as belonging to both groups. When in 1962, Robert Gardner and I studied another ethnic minority group in New England, the French-Americans, we observed the same types of reactions as Child had noted among Italian-Americans. But in our study there was an important difference.

We used a series of attitude scales to assess the allegiances of French-American adolescents to both their French and American heritages. Their relative degree of skill in French and in English were used as an index of their mode of adjustment to the bicultural conflict they faced. In their homes, schools, and community, they all had ample opportunities to learn both languages well, but subgroups turned up who had quite different patterns of linguistic skill, and each pattern was consonant with each subgroup's allegiances. Those who expressed a definite preference for the American over the French culture and who negated the value of knowing French were more proficient in English than French. They also expressed anxiety about how well they actually knew English. This subgroup, characterized by a general rejection of their French background, resembles in many respects the rebel reaction noted by Child. A second subgroup expressed a strong desire to be identified as French, and they showed a greater skill in French than English, especially in comprehension of spoken French. A third group apparently faced a conflict of cultural allegiances since they were ambivalent about their identity, favoring certain features of the French and other features of the American culture. Presumably because they had not resolved the conflict, they were retarded in their command of both languages when compared to the other groups. This relatively unsuccessful mode of adjustment is very similar to the apathetic reaction noted in one subgroup of Italian-Americans.

A fourth subgroup is of special interest. French-American youngsters who have an open-minded, nonethnocentric view of people in general, coupled with a strong aptitude for language learning are the ones who profited fully from their language learning opportunities and became skilled in *both* languages. These young people had apparently circumvented the conflicts and developed means of becoming members of both cultural groups. They had, in other terms, achieved a comfortable bicultural identity.

It is not clear why this type of adjustment did not appear in Child's study. There could, for example, be important differences in the social pressures encountered by second-generation Italians and French in New

England. My guess, however, is that the difference in findings reflects a new social movement that has started in America in the interval between 1943 and 1962, a movement which the American linguist Charles Hockett humorously refers to as a "reduction of the heat under the American melting pot." I believe that bicultural bilinguals will be particularly helpful in perpetuating this movement. They and their children are also the ones most likely to work out a new, nonethnocentric mode of social intercourse which could be of universal significance.

TALKING BLACK IN THE CLASSROOM

Roger D. Abrahams and Geneva Gay

This article parallels the last but focuses more exclusively on the implications of Black English usage in the classroom situation.

Cultural patterns of communication and interaction are probably the most essential and distinctive features of Black culture. They form the core of the culture and permeate all of its aspects. If this characteristic is to be clearly understood and used by middle-class teachers in working with Black pupils, extensive research is needed in three major areas. These include the function or role language plays in the culture, the variety of styles, and the methodical and systematic structure of the language of Black English.

According to the advocates of the cultural deprivation theory, Black children have *poorly* developed verbal skills because their families provide neither opportunity nor encouragement for verbalization during their formative years. The irony of this situation is that middle-class teachers cry out in frustration because their Black students are so loud and talk so much, yet these same teachers claim that students from ghettos cannot verbalize. The contradiction seems to lie in the distinction between "talking" or "making noise" and verbalizing. Undoubtedly, these teachers assume that since a child is not adept in the use of Standard English, he is not adept in the use of any language. This is a myth that must be destroyed if teachers are to ever accept Black students for what they are. They must accept the fact that Black children do not speak Standard English, and they must accept Black English as a systematized, distinct language—not merely a collection of disjointed phrases, slang, profanity, and a simple dialect of substandard English.

Language in the largest sense plays a fundamental role in the process of survival in ghetto neighborhoods, in addition to being the basis of acquiring leadership, status, and success. The popularly held belief that it takes brute physical strength to survive in the ghetto is a myth. It may help one endure temporarily, but fists alone are not the answer to survival. Survival is based on one's versatility and adeptness in the use of words. The man-of-words is the one who becomes the hero to ghetto youth. Consider the current conditions and compile a profile of spokesmen of ghetto action groups. These persons in the spotlight are dynamic speakers whose jobs are frequently dependent on the effective use of words, such as lawyers and ministers. Verbal ability can make the difference between having or not having food to eat, a place to live, clothes to wear, being accepted or rejected by one's peers, and being personally and emotionally secure or risking a complete loss of ego. Therefore, for a member of street culture, language is not only a communicative device but also a mechanism of control and power. It is the medium through which students learn to deal with the demands of middle-class teachers without losing all resemblance of self-respect. The words themselves are not very important unless one understands the context in which they are used, the social setting, and the style of delivery of the speaker. Teachers make their mistakes by looking at individual words or phrases as proof that the children are limited in their verbal abilities. For example, they fail to understand that what they choose to call profanity and coarse four-letter words may be used as tools to indicate importance and emphasis. Street people are not inclined to use words for the mere sake of using them. They are used for their performance qualities.

To understand the relationship that exists between herself and her students, and the students' classroom behavior, the middle-class teacher needs to realize that her older Black students use a variety of verbal techniques, and that they use these techniques to discover her strengths and weaknesses, to find out where she stands on issues ranging from how "hip" she is to her racial attitudes, and to locate her breaking point. Once these are discovered, they help the student to exert some control over the situation.

Because street culture is an oral culture, and is dependent largely upon the spoken word for its perpetuation and transmission, its language is very colorful, creative, and adaptative. It is in a constant state of flux and new words are always being invented. Further, new slang words are constantly created as a way of maintaining an in-group relationship and of excluding outsiders. Thus, there emerges something of a secret code that only in-group members completely understand. It is used by students and others in street culture to convey messages to each other about the "enemy," even in his presence. Of course, some of these terms have been picked up by white "hipsters," but often the meaning is changed because of the different cultural perspective.

"Rapping" * is one of those terms which has been borrowed from Black slang and has achieved wide currency among whites, who use it to describe a fluent, interesting, and engaging conversation. Street culture may also use it in this context, but it is generally used in initial male-female relations as an introductory device. The greatest difference between white and Black uses of "rapping" is in the middle-class context one "raps with" while in the Black usage one "raps to." The ghetto male who "raps to a broad" is interested in "pushing a line." He wants to test the receptiveness of the female and the possibilities for a sexual conquest. If the relationship develops into something other than a conquest, "rapping" is not used to describe subsequent verbal exchange. A "rap" is not usually involved with factual commentary. Instead, it is a sales pitch with the rapper advertising the goods he has to offer. It is given and received not on the authenticity of the factual content but on how convincingly the pitch is delivered.

Black students have an interesting way of asking for information or additions or clarification of a point already made. They ask the speaker to "run it down," "run it down again," "lay it on me," or "run it through again." Here the request is for an explanation or a repetition of the information that has already been given. The request may also be precipitated by disbelief or surprise, or it may be an inverted way of paying a compliment to the speaker. The listener may have been so impressed by the delivery that he wants to *see* it again. If this is the case, the interest is centered not on what was said but *how* it was said. It is not surprising that the teacher is unaware of what the student means when he reacts to her lectures or discussions by saying, "Would you run that through again?" She is likely to think he is being flippant, trying to get laughs, and pass it off as that or ignore him entirely. His purpose may be exactly that, but he may also be quite serious about his confusion and really need to hear the explanation again so that he can better understand it. He may not be able to handle Standard English well enough to express his particular concern in a way that the teacher can understand his confusion, so he asks for the entire message to be repeated. To categorically deny or ignore all such requests may be to ignore a student's appeal for help. If this happens too often, the child will stop asking for any assistance at all and become withdrawn.

"Jiving" is a style of speech used to "put someone on." This label is

* The terms used here are the current ones among some Blacks around the United States. They change constantly, but the verbal strategies they name do not.

frequently applied by the audience, whereas "rapping" receives the label from both speaker and audience. For example, after listening to a description of an event, or when the speaker is putting a member of the audience on, a listener might respond with, "Man, stop that jiving." It suggests a commentary that is hard to believe or the description of a less than favorable feat, and it conveys some distrust that the speaker is being completely honest. "Jive" is equivalent to invalidation. When one is said to be talking "all that jive" or "off-the-wall stuff," he means that the speaker is saying things that both he and his audience recognize as being void of any real meaning, impractical, and impossible to realize. A student may refer to a teacher's idle threats of punishment or her course as "jive." In the one instance he is saying, "I know that you know you can't carry through with your promises or threats;" in the other he is saying there is no way he can believe in the truthfulness and value of what the teacher is trying to teach. It has no value whatever to him, and when the student classifies it as "jive" this means that he has totally rejected it.

"Shucking," as it is used by some Blacks, is a special kind of "jive," a manner of speech used to accommodate "the man"—any person who is a symbol of white oppressive authority such as a policeman, teacher, judge, employer—to create a false impression of cooperativeness. One who "shucks" uses whatever devices in his repertory necessary to produce an acceptable appearance—but does so aggressively, hostilely. According to this description, the "Uncle Toms" and "Aunt Janes" who are quick to do whatever their white employers ask with a smile and a "Yessir, Boss" are likely to be "shucking" or "shucking and jiving."

When Black people "shuck and jive" with "the man," they take the stereotypes he has of them and use them to their advantage. The ghetto Black knows that the white man is convinced that he is afraid of him, will do everything he can to please him, and that he is too stupid to try to outsmart a white person. So, when confronted with a compromising and dangerous situation (whether the danger is physical or emotional), he does exactly what is expected of him. He portrays simple-mindedness, pleading, and submission, and even confession of guilt along with oaths of penance. Mr. Charlie may walk away with a boisterous, "Look how I had that nigger crawling." The Black man simply smiles or grins. Is it gratitude for being given a second chance or is it the taste of vengeance that makes him smile? A clear understanding of how "shucking and jiving" operates would cause one to wonder which one of the two is really on his knees!

The Black student is aware of the effectiveness of "shucking" school personnel, and he is not above using it. He may resort to such techniques as "give me another chance," "Ah, I was just fooling around," hurt indignation, anger and/or total withdrawal. He has heard enough innuendos in school to know how he is supposed to act and he acts accordingly. Even though the student may personally want to face the encounter straight-forwardly, he knows that the odds are heavily stacked against him and his chances of being heard are almost nil, so he resorts to his most familiar defensive strategies. Are Black students devious and cunning? Indeed they are. If they weren't, many would not have survived for as long as they have.

"Copping a plea" is similar to "shucking and jiving." Both are techniques used to get out of a compromising situation, but they differ in approach. One is more direct than the other. When one "cops a plea" he acclaims the superiority of another and makes an appeal for pity, mercy, or some other form of sympathy. Whether this appeal is authentic or merely a play on one's sympathies and ego is virtually impossible to determine by someone who is unfamiliar with the styles of verbal behavior prevalent among American Blacks.

"Sounding" is a verbal exchange designed to insult. Its forms and intensity vary. It may be nothing more than a word game to test the attitude and disposition of another person, a friendly exchange of bickering, or it can be a prelude to physical encounter. It may be as stylized as "playing the dozens" (mother-rapping) or as simple as answering a "put on" (challenge) with a quick, sharp, unexpected response. Its effectiveness depends largely on the listeners who attribute quality to the "sound" by their reactions and encouragements. Another element of the quality of any given "sound" is whether it can be countered with a quick answer. The longer it takes the contender to think of a response, the better is the "sound." "Sounding" also includes "coming down hard," and being "cold" or "foul," both of which indicate the absence of feeling—i.e., being very calculating and using sharp, cutting responses without any of the verbal elaboration or gestures that are usually part of ghetto speech. When the listener attributes the compliment, "that's cold," to a particular sound, the sounder knows he has really scored.

"Playing the dozens" is one of the most popular forms "sounding" takes. It may be stylized to the point of rhyming verses or as simple as answering another person's comments with "Ya mamma." Whatever format the "dozens" take, all are essentially the same—a contest of words involving slurring references to the family, especially the mother. Rhyming is prevalent among young adolescents. By the time the youths reach their teens they have reached the point of "playing the dozens" with finesse and cool. Rhyming is considered kid stuff. The participants are now inclined to "play" by rephrasing the comments of the challenger to make them apply to his own mother.

A verbal maneuver often used by Black students to challenge their teachers is "loud-talking" or "back-talking." This maneuver involves talking about the teacher to another student in a voice loud enough for the teacher to hear what is being said. It is a challenge and the purpose is to push the teacher to the point of "blowing her cool." If the teacher accepts the challenge, becomes unnerved by what she has overheard, and issues a reprimand, the student becomes indignant and responds with, "I wasn't talking to you." To the teacher this is the epitome of rudeness and insolence. The exchange might proceed thus:

Teacher: "What did you say?"
Student: (With impatient anger) "I wasn't talking to you."
Teacher: "But I heard you say something."
Student: "I didn't say anything."
Teacher: "I'm almost sure I heard you saying something about me."
Student: (Does not answer the teacher directly but murmurs—i.e., "loud talks") "If you hadn't been listening you wouldn't have heard."

For the student two things were accomplished in this exchange. First, the teacher becomes unglued and loses her cool. Second, the student has the last word. "Loud-talking" is a play for power, and both of these are essential in the process if the student is to come out on top of the situation. To succeed in unnerving the teacher is one of the most effective power plays a student can execute. It fits perfectly into his cultural perspective of what constitutes status and leadership. If one ever expects to rise to the position of a leader in street culture he must know how to handle himself and this involves, above all else, "keeping his cool." If he cannot respond to a challenge without becoming frustrated and unnerved, he is not likely to have the respect of others or remain a leader for long. "Loud-talking" baits the teacher to see if she can maintain her position. When she fails the test the student is inclined to feel he has no obligation to recognize her as a leader any longer. Not only does he lose respect for her as a teacher, but also as a person, and when this happens it is next to impossible to create a productive working relationship.

Students themselves testify to the effectiveness of their use of language as a means of exerting power and control over the teacher and the classroom situation. Black kids claim that the middle-class teacher is "stupid," "lacks common sense," "dumb," "naïve," and that she will "believe anything." Her vulnerability and ignorance about Black life and how Black students function makes her an easy prey for the students. They are so easy to "run a game on" [her] that the exercise is hardly worth the effort. There is little or no challenge because the student has two advantages. First, he chooses the battlefield, the strategy, and the weapons, all of which involve the use of words. Second, his skill and adeptness at "keeping cool" are so well developed that they are hard to shake or to surpass. One example will serve to illustrate how a student emerges as the winner in

such a contest. The teacher issues a command to a student. He decides
to comply but does it deliberately slow. He therefore shows his antagonism
even while he is in the act of complying with the demand. The teacher is
in a difficult position. She knows, as do the rest of the class, that she is
being "gamed on," and that the student's attitude has nullified the effectiveness of his actions. But, what can she do about it? After all, the student
is doing what he was told to do! She is likely to become shaken and take
some action to try to force the student toward a more rapid compliance.
Whatever she does, the student still comes out the victor. Throughout the
entire exchange he has remained perfectly calm and collected—while the
teacher becomes frustrated and distraught. The following example, related
to us by a high-school junior, helps to clarify exactly how this maneuver
operates:

> On this particular day the students have decided not to do anything in class.
> The teacher enters and instructs the students to begin work. No one says or does
> anything. Then one student begins to sing softly to himself. The teacher asks the
> singer to be quiet and to return to his regularly assigned seat. The student re-
> sponds with, "Right on man, I'm gonna move," and he does. The teacher says
> something else and the student answers, "Right on, brother." The teacher, very
> much irritated, says, "Shut up." The student answers very softly, "Right on,
> brother." The teacher says, "I don't like your attitude today and if you don't
> be quiet I'm gonna put you out." The student, more forceful this time, says, "Right
> on, brother." The teacher answers with, "get out," and the student responds,
> "Right on, brother," as he walks slowly out of the door.

The narrator ended the commentary with the rather astute observation
that the class still refused to do anything, the "leader" had been removed
from the class, but the teacher lost because she ended up "looking like a
fool."

The above examples illustrate just how effectively a Black student can
wield power and control over teachers if he is adept in the use of words.
This is his most reliable tool in coping with the alien—and sometimes
hostile—environment of the school. He knows the value of verbal skills
and he develops them at a very early age. Yet, teachers say that he is
non-verbal, simply because he does not use Standard English. They perceive his language as nothing more than signs of illiteracy which must be
stamped out as soon as possible. Quite the contrary is true.

One of the clearest examples of his verbal ability is how he reverses
the meaning of words. Terms which have negative connotations in Standard English are given positive qualities or vice-versa. For example, "bad"
comes to mean something impressive, beautiful, good, while "tough" can
mean good-looking, attractive, stylishly dressed. On the other hand, a word
like "square," which used to mean honest in standard parlance, was reversed to indicate a number of negative personal traits.

Another technique used in the reversal of meanings is to take words associated with the expression of white prejudicial and stereotypic attitudes, such as "nigger," and use them in intimate relations among in-group members. Whites are completely bewildered by this apparent self-prejudice and self-hatred. They can't understand why a Black student would use these terms and phrases to degrade a fellow Black student. In many cases the intentions are the exact opposite of degradation. The object may be to convey in-group compliments. When a Black youth uses such phrases as, "that's my nigger," "the niggers are gittin' it on," and "hey nigger, what you think you doing," in intergroup relations, the connotations may more closely approximate pride that his is *my* boyfriend or girlfriend or that there is cohesiveness and unity among Blacks in their efforts for equality. It is simply another way of communicating a feeling of identity and brotherhood and is thus a substitute for "Brother," "Sister," "Man," or "Dude." Again, social setting, frame of reference, and context are essential in determining word meanings.

These patterns of Black verbal behavior explain why Black students often find it so difficult to achieve academic success in middle-class schools. This information may also explain why they shy away from even attempting written assignments. The child soon learns that if he writes the way he thinks and talks the teacher is going to consider it all wrong. To protect himself from hurt and criticism he refuses to do anything. Since traditional classroom teachers rely almost exclusively on samples of written work to evaluate the students' academic achievement, there is little wonder that Black students always fall short of their middle-class counterparts. Teachers should begin to think of other, more reliable evaluation criteria for their Black students, ones that bear in mind the discourse system by which they operate.

If a teacher is to communicate with her Black students, she needs to learn to understand their language, if not to speak it. She does not necessarily have to imitate the students, for if she doesn't have a natural flare for such performance the results will be disastrous. Nothing is more effective in destroying the beauty and vitality of Black ghetto speech than to anglicize it! What the teacher must do is understand and recognize the important role it plays in the lives of the students, and be able to distinguish the various forms of Black speech, why they are used, and tell when they are being used. She should learn to be a most careful observer so as to get at least an inkling of the extent and diversity of the students' verbal behavior and what the words connote, even if she cannot speak it. Asking a student to explain what is happening is of no use. Even if he would try to explain, he is too close to the situation, and it is so much a part of him that he sees nothing spectacular or unique about it.

5

Black English

The study of Black English, variously referred to as Non-standard Negro English (NNE) or Negro speech, is of very recent growth, coming in large measure as a by-product of the educational problems brought to light by desegregation in the South and the massive expansion of urban ghettos in the North. In both situations, large numbers of white teachers suddenly found themselves faced with students whose speech they could not understand and whose behavior threatened or bewildered them. The forced recognition of disparities in pupil achievement between Blacks and whites (a fact long kept from public awareness) brought forth large-scale research and remediation efforts funded primarily by the U.S. Office of Education. The failure of most of these efforts to achieve lasting results can be attributed primarily to the failure of educators and researchers to recognize the important cultural and linguistic differences between the Negro and middle-class white communities in this country. Only when this is done can the dimensions of the problem be properly understood, and meaningful solutions developed.

An adequate understanding of the position of Black English could not emerge until the work of Melville Herskovits on the survival of African cultural features among New World Negroes, the studies of Lorenzo Turner on the retention of African linguistic elements in the Gullah dialect, and the investigations of Robert Hall and others of Negro creoles of the Caribbean, had provided a framework showing that Negro speech in the United States was not just an aberrant English dialect, but in fact represented the most acculturated form of an earlier creole still found in the West Indies. Many of the differences between Black English and other dialects can most probably be attributed to the carryover of traits from West African languages and the preservation of features from an earlier creole stage. Many characteristics, however, including some of the most remarked-upon, simply reflect features of the Southern dialects which Negroes learned as they acquired English. (It is a frequent experience for white Southerners looking for housing in Northern cities to be told nothing is available when they inquire over the telephone.) In some instances these involve archaic elements which have subsequently disappeared from most white dialects.

Given the conditions of social isolation imposed upon Negroes in this country for over two centuries, it is not surprising that their dialects should have followed, and continue to follow, their own line of development. (Despite a great deal of uniformity nationally, there are regional differences, as yet little studied, in Negro speech.) As with any other living language or dialect, elements of diverse origin have been merged in a systematic whole, so that it is no longer possible to identify with certainty the source of a particular feature. In addition, new structures, new usages, and new meanings have arisen within the dialect itself, and are uniquely part of Black English.

While linguists such as Labov, Stewart, and Bailey have begun to define some of the structural characteristics of Black English, folklorists such as Abrahams and sociolinguists such as Gumperz have focused on the functional characteristics, and have found equally great differences from white speech in the discourse systems used, the types of settings for speaking, the values and expectations placed on speech acts and speaking ability, and even the purposes to which speech is put. To members of the group, the *way* the dialect is used in various situations may be more important for defining membership in the group than the actual linguistic forms used. And in many ways, survival in the group may literally depend on one's ability to use the dialect.

Educators for many years have assumed that everyone with any intelligence and ability would "naturally" be upwardly mobile in their aspirations, and would therefore welcome the opportunity offered by education to achieve success in our modern industrialized society. Since many Negro students failed, or even refused, to recognize the apparent advantages of education, educators sought to explain this behavior in terms of some supposed deficiency on the part of the students. One of the more pernicious explanations was that Negro students were lacking in intelligence because they spoke a nonstandard dialect. But linguists and anthropologists have repeatedly shown that intelligence is completely independent of any given dialect or language, so that such an ethnocentric judgment is completely without foundation. Since I.Q. tests favor speakers of the language or dialect in which they are constructed, they are of no validity in determining the intelligence of students from other linguistic or cultural backgrounds.

Evidence is forthcoming, in fact, that those Black students who do best in school may not be the most intelligent, while those possessing the greatest intelligence may be among the poorest in terms of grades. This seeming paradox presents a major challenge to education, for it shows that the schools have failed in their efforts to reach such students, and that traditional approaches have actually been counterproductive, for they have alienated the most competent students and left them to focus their energies on achievement within the peer group.

The papers in this section attempt to survey the most significant information available on Black English, and indicate some of its possible educational relevance. Language is at the interface of relations between teacher and student, and is the principal instrument of instruction, both through speaking and through reading. If the educational failures of the past are not to be perpetuated, teachers must learn to communicate with their pupils. It is the purpose of this section to provide some of the essential information to help them do that.

THE RELATIONSHIP OF THE SPEECH
OF AMERICAN NEGROES TO THE
SPEECH OF WHITES

Raven I. McDavid, Jr., and Virginia Glenn McDavid

This pioneer article on the relationship of Negro to White speech in the United States sets forth some of the major considerations which have guided much of subsequent research on the question. The McDavids point out the fallacy of believing that speech differences are caused by racial differences, and show instead that for the historical origins of Negro speech to be properly understood, it must be studied in the broader context of a three-way comparison with West African languages, creole languages elsewhere in the New World, and White dialects of the United States and England. Against such a background, it can be seen that many of the distinctive features of Negro speech derive either from African or from native English dialect sources, or else reflect the process of creolization during the preceding three centuries.

Almost without exception, any scholar studying American Negro speech, whether as an end in itself or as part of a larger project, must dispose of two widely held superstitions: (1) he must indicate that there is no speech form identifiable as of Negro origin solely on the basis of Negro physical characteristics; (2) he must show that it is probable that some speech forms of Negroes—and even of some whites—may be derived from an African cultural background by the normal processes of cultural transmission. Such a necessity of refuting folk beliefs seldom arises when one is studying the English of other American minority groups. For these, it is generally assumed, though not necessarily in the terms anthropologists would use, that all linguistic patterns are culturally transmitted, that where a group with a foreign-language background—such as the Pennsylvania Germans—has been speaking a divergent variety of English for several generations in an overwhelmingly English-speaking area, there is

From *American Speech*, vol. 26 (1951), pp. 3–17. Reprinted by permission of *American Speech*.

nothing in their speech that cannot be explained on the basis of the culture contracts between the speakers of two languages. We are generous in recognizing Scandinavian linguistic survivals in Minnesota and the Dakotas, German in Wisconsin and Pennsylvania, and Dutch in the Hudson Valley. We do not explain this influence on the basis of Scandinavian hair color, German skull configuration, or Dutch mouth shape, but on the grounds that two languages were spoken side by side, so that bilingualism developed in the community.

In forming judgments on the speech of the American Negro, however, the process has been reversed: the cultural transmission of speech forms of African origin has been traditionally denied, and the explanation of Negro dialects given in terms of a "simple, childlike mind," or of physical inability to pronounce the sounds of socially approved English. So widely spread is this superstition that Gunnar Myrdal felt obliged to explain that Negro speech, like all other speech, is culturally transmitted. As late as 1949 the author of a widely syndicated "popular science" newspaper quiz explained that the Negro cannot pronounce a post vocalic /-r/ in such words as *car, beard,* or *bird* because his lips are too thick.

There are reasons for this popular misinterpretation. One of the most obvious is that the Negro, unlike the other groups of foreign-language origin, is readily identifiable by skin pigmentation. Whatever differences the naïve observer notices between his speech and that of the average Negro he encounters, he interprets as a function of the identifiable physical difference. The fact that the contacts between whites and educated Negroes are limited, the normal contact between the two races being in terms of the situation of white master and Negro servant, means that Negro speech is generally judged on the basis of nonstandard speakers, or at best on the basis of speakers from a different dialect area.[1]

Other reasons for such misconceptions can be seen in the history of Negro-white relationships. Most obvious, of course, is the fact that the Negroes constituted the only large group of the American population that came here against their will, and with their cultural heritage overtly overridden in the effort to fit them into the new pattern of the basic unskilled labor for the plantation system. Rationalizing the institution of chattel slavery as a benefit to the Negroes required that the whites deny any con-

---

[1] Allen Walker Read in his study, "The Speech of Negroes in Colonial America," *Journal of Negro History,* vol. XXIV (1939), pp. 247–58, drawing his material from the advertisements for runaway slaves, throws a clear light on the process of the Negroes' learning of English. He concludes, p. 258: "The present study shows that during colonial times there were Negroes in all stages of proficiency in their knowledge of English: a constant stratum of recently arrived ones without any English, those who were learning English during their first years in the new country, and a group who had learned successfully. The Negroes born in this country invariably used, according to these records, good English. The colored race were faced, against their will, with a huge problem in adopting a new language in a strange country, and their success, in the light of their opportunities, was equal to that of any other immigrant body."

sequential African cultural heritage. Then when slavery was abolished as an institution but replaced—both in the South and elsewhere—by a racially determined caste system, supported by discriminatory legislation or extralegal covenants, the need for rationalization continued.[2]

It is therefore difficult for the white scholar to approach dispassionately the problem of African survivals in American Negro culture in general and speech in particular. The scholar who accepts the theory of Negro inferiority tends to explain any apparent differences between Negro and white speech on the basis of the Negro's childlike mind or imperfectly developed speech organs. Or if he tries to be fair, he will probably deny that there are any essential differences. This was the position of the late George Philip Krapp:

> . . . The Negro speaks English of the same kind and, class for class, of the same degree, as the English of the most authentic descendants of the first settlers at Jamestown and Plymouth.
>
> The Negroes, indeed, in acquiring English have done their work so thoroughly that they have retained not a trace of any native African speech. Neither have they transferred anything of importance from their native tongues to the general language. A few words, such as *voodoo*, *hoodoo*, and *buckra*, may have come into English from some original African dialect, but most of the words commonly supposed to be of Negro origin, e.g. *tote*, *jazz*, and *mosey*, are really derived from ancient English or other European sources. The native African dialects have been completely lost.[3]

But neither has the Negro scholar found the task an easy one. For a considerable period, he was as reluctant as the white scholar to admit a consequential African cultural heritage, reckoning Africa "a badge of shame . . . the remainder of a savage past not sufficiently remote, as is that of the European savagery, to have become hallowed." [4] The inevitable overemphasis of possible African survivals, which one sometimes discovers in the works of recent Negro scholars, is perhaps no nearer an objective presentation than the old attitude, but ultimately should be as salutary a corrective of perspective as it is inevitable.

Even where the investigator is seriously interested in gathering new evidence for reinterpreting the old, he is likely to run into difficulties in

[2] The generation after the Civil War was of course also the last period of European colonial expansion at the expense of the nonwhite races, the period in which the Nordic myth was so widely publicized by Gobineau, Chamberlain, Madison Grant in his *The Passing of the Great Race* (New York, 1918), and Homer Lea in his *The Day of the Saxon* (New York, 1912), and in which European imperialism was rationalized by Kipling and others as a benign paternalism—"the white man's burden."

[3] "The English of the Negro," *American Mercury*, vol. II (1924), pp. 190–95, at p. 190. See also Krapp, *The English Language in America* (New York, 1925), vol. I, pp. 161–63; vol. II, p. 226.

[4] Melville J. Herskovits, *The Myth of the Negro Past* (New York, 1941), p. 32.

the field. A Negro community that has been too often pointed out as a Negro community, and exploited as such by political and propaganda groups, is reluctant to accept the outside investigator, no matter how well intentioned. If the speech of the Negro group has a situational dialect variety employed to conceal information or attitudes from the white man, there is reluctance to give away the in-group secret to the investigator.[5] Where the Negro is accustomed to telling the white man what he thinks the white man wants to be told—where, in fact, his survival often depends on his skill in guessing that—the investigator may find informants too co-operative, too ready to offer evidence supporting a stereotype.[6] And in communities where the caste lines are most sharply drawn, even an experienced field worker may inadvertently lose rapport with his Negro informants by transgressing taboos of speech or manner.

In spite of these difficulties, the last half century has seen much information gathered about both white and Negro speech, and the cultures in which they are used, so that we are now able to speak more intelligently, if somewhat more tentatively, than before. Perhaps the most important force in the revision of older attitudes has been the development of the culture concept by anthropologists, with the realization that long-established ways of saying and doing things or thinking about them can persist in the face of almost inconceivable disadvantages, simply because they are what people are used to. More particularly, there has been a great deal of serious study of Negro communities in Africa and various parts of the New World, and a large-scale study of the American Negro under the direction of the Swedish sociologist Gunnar Myrdal and the auspices of the Carnegie Corporation.[7] There have been scientific studies, both descriptive and comparative, of African languages and of pidgin and creolized languages, especially the studies of Melanesian pidgin, Chinese pidgin, Taki-Taki, and Haitian Creole by Hall, of Haitian Creole by Sylvain-Comhaire, of Louisiana Negro-French by Lane, and of Papiamento (the creolized Negro-Dutch-Spanish of Curaçao) by Frederick Agard and C. Cleland Harris. The South Atlantic records for the *Linguistic Atlas of*

[5] Lorenzo D. Turner reports that his earlier Gullah records contained far fewer Africanisms—especially the African-derived personal names—than his later ones. See his *Africanisms in the Gullah Dialect* (Chicago, 1949), p. 12.

[6] I found among Negro informants a somewhat greater willingness than among whites to accept as authentic the responses suggested by the field worker, no matter how deliberately far-fetched some of these suggestions might be. On the other hand, I found at least one Negro informant who conformed to the traditional stereotype of Negro speech during the part of the interview conducted in the presence of his white patron, but who abandoned that role when we were alone. (R.I.M.)

[7] Myrdal was chosen as director of the project because Sweden is a nation without colonies, and therefore without institutionalized attitudes toward the nonwhite races. The Negro problem is summarized in *An American Dilemma*; no person unfamiliar with this book can claim to "know the Negro." Herskovits's *The Myth of the Negro Past* is one of the special studies prepared for the project.

the United States and Canada provide material for comparing white and Negro speech in the same communities, and Turner has made a significant contribution by his seventeen years of research in Gullah.

The study of African languages has served two purposes, in addition to the obvious one of indicating actual or potential etyma for vocabulary items in American Negro speech. By providing a record of the structural features of African languages—phonemics, morphology, and syntax—it has enabled us to see that some features of American Negro speech may not be baby talk or the misinterpretations of ignorant savages, but rather the persistence of something from African speech. Moreover, the comparative work in African languages has revealed a high degree of structural similarity between the languages of the area from which most of the slaves were taken, so as to make for common trends in the speech of American Negroes, regardless of the mutual unintelligibility of their original languages.

The study of pidgins and creolized languages has likewise facilitated the intelligent study of the relationship between white and Negro speech. It has definitely been shown that these languages are not linguistic freaks, with quaint and curious ways of saying things, but that each of them has its own definite structure, and that they are as worthy of serious study as the better-known languages of Western Europe. Consequently, the investigator of Negro speech in this country has precedent for making a scientific description, as one should make of any dialect. More immediately pertinent, the research into Taki-Taki, Brazilian Negro Portuguese, and Haitian Creole enables the student of American Negro speech to assay whether a particular structural feature is of African origin or not. If a certain feature of Gullah syntax, say, is also found in Brazilian Negro Portuguese, in Haitian Creole, and in Papiamento, and resembles a structural feature of several West African languages, it is likely that it is not taken from British peasant speech.

"Gullah" is the creolized variety of English spoken by the descendants of Negro slaves in the area of rice, indigo, and Sea Island cotton plantations along the South Carolina and Georgia coasts. The term *Geechee* is sometimes used, either as a synonym for Gullah or as a designation for the Gullah spoken in Georgia.

Perhaps the greatest single contribution to an intelligent reappraisal of the relationships between white and Negro speech has been the investigation of the speech of the Gullah Negroes by Lorenzo D. Turner. Though embodying only part of his findings, his recent book, *Africanisms in the Gullah Dialect*, dispels effectively the notion that the American Negro lost all his language and his culture under the impact of chattel slavery and the plantation system. Turner's overt statement is impressive enough: that an investigation of Gullah speech discloses several thousand items presumably derived from the languages of the parts of Africa from which the slaves were taken. But the implicit conclusions are yet more impressive: that many structural features of Gullah are also to be found in creolized languages of South America and the Caribbean, in the pidgin-like trade English of West Africa, and in many African languages—this preservation of fundamental structural traits is a more cogent argument for the importance of the African element in the Gullah dialect (and, by inference, in the totality of Gullah culture) than any number of details of vocabulary. Perhaps most significant of all, though hardly hinted at by Turner, is the evidence from phonological structure: like the languages of West Africa described by Westermann and Ward, Gullah has a far less complex system of vowel phonemes than any known variety of English; furthermore, Gullah has a remarkable uniformity, not only in phonemic structure but in the phonetic shape of vowel allophones, along a stretch of nearly four hundred miles of the South Atlantic coast, in the very region where there is a greater variety among the dialects of white speech than one can find elsewhere in English-speaking North America—a uniformity difficult to explain by chance, or by any of the older explanations of Negro speech. Turner's work has already made scholars aware of the importance of the African background in American Negro speech.

As by-products of the field work for the *Linguistic Atlas* and other dialect studies, several bits of evidence have been found that suggest how a comparative study of Negro and white speech may be useful in indicating areas of actual or potential interracial tension. It is not without significance that Chicago-born Negro students at the University of Illinois have preserved many characteristic Southern words that are unknown to white students of the same age and city, or that Michigan-born Negroes in the age group between twenty and thirty have the South Midland diphthongs in *dance* and *law*, although the dialect of older-generation Michigan-born Negroes is indistinguishable from that of their white contemporaries. Nor can one overlook the fact that educated Negroes in such Southern communities as Greenville and Atlanta tend to avoid the forms having prestige in local white speech in favor of their conception of New England speech. Even though this evidence is spotty and unsystematized, it already indicates that future community social analyses should include a study of dialect differences within the community—and especially if the community contains a large Negro group.

In summary, we must evaluate the relationships between Negro and white speech in the same scientific spirit as any anthropologist studies acculturation. We must lay aside ethnocentric prejudices of all kinds—no less the traditional Southern assumption of Negro inferiority than the equally glib statement of career Negroes (perhaps oftener in Africa than in the United States) that no study of Negro culture by whites can be valid because "the white man doesn't understand the Black man's mind." We must remember that conclusions are valid only in so far as they are based on valid data, and that the discovery of new data may call for new conclusions.

As with many other aspects of dialect investigation, the half century of investigations of Negro speech and its affiliations with white speech has left many questions unanswered. But it has provided a framework within which these questions can be both asked and answered more intelligently than heretofore.[8] The linguistic scientist has learned not to look down upon other forms of speech that happen to differ from his own; he can hope that the public will cease to look down upon the speech of those whose skin pigmentation or hair form may be different, or to fancy any necessary correlation between the pigmentation of a speaker's skin and the phonemic system of his dialect.

SOCIOLINGUISTIC FACTORS IN THE HISTORY OF AMERICAN NEGRO DIALECTS

William A. Stewart

In this important paper, Stewart documents some of the historical evidence showing that during the seventeenth and eighteenth centuries, American Negroes used a pidginized form of English which in time became a creole as speakers grew up using it as their native tongue. This creole shows many similarities to the Gullah dialect and to various present-day creoles of the Caribbean. Stewart argues that American Negroes gradually "standardized" their speech by adopting elements, particularly vocabulary, from standard varieties of the language, but that nonstandard Negro dialects today still retain grammatical features which reflect their creole origin.

Although the linguistic history of the Negro in the United States can be reconstructed from the numerous literary attestations of the English of

Abridged from *The Florida FL Reporter*, vol. 5, no. 2 (Spring, 1957), pp. 11, 22, 24, 26, 30; Alfred C. Aarons, ed. Reprinted by permission of *The Florida FL Reporter*.

[8] H. L. Mencken, in *The American Language* (4th ed.; New York, 1936), pp. 112–13, accepted the earlier theory of the paucity of African survivals in American Negro speech. However, in his *Supplement I* (New York, 1945), pp. 198–99, Turner's work had enabled him to revise his judgment.

New World Negroes over the last two and a half centuries, and by comparing these with the English of Negroes in the United States, the Caribbean, and West Africa today, this has never been done for the English
teaching profession. In presenting a historical sketch of this type, I realize
that both the facts presented and my interpretations of them may em-
barrass or even infuriate those who would like to whitewash American
Negro dialects by claiming that they do not exist—that (in spite of all
sorts of observable evidence to the contrary) they are nothing but Southern
white dialects, derived directly from Great Britain. I will simply make no
apologies to those who regard human behavior as legitimate only if observed in the white man, since I feel that this constitutes a negation of
the cultural and ethnic plurality which is one of America's greatest
heritages. On the other hand, I do regret that such a historical survey,
although linguistically interesting, may at times conjure up out of the
past memories of the Negro-as-slave to haunt the aspirations of the Negro-
as-equal.

Of those Africans who fell victim to the Atlantic slave trade and were
brought to the New World, many found it necessary to learn some kind
of English. With very few exceptions, the form of English which they acquired was a pidginized one, and this kind of English became so well
established as the principal medium of communication between Negro
slaves in the British colonies that it was passed on as a creole language
to succeeding generations of the New World Negroes, for whom it was
their native tongue.[1] Some idea of what New World Negro English may

---

[1] In referring to types of languages, linguists use the terms pidgin and creole in a
technical sense which has none of the derogatory or racial connotations of popular uses
of these terms. When a linguist says that a variety of language is pidginized, he merely
means that it has a markedly simplified grammatical structure compared with the
"normal" (i.e., unpidginized) source-language. This simplification may be one way in
which speakers of different languages can make a new language easier to learn and use—
particularly if they have neither the opportunity nor the motivation to learn to speak
it the way its primary users do. In addition, some of the unique characteristics of a
pidgin language may be due, not to simplification, but to influences on it from the
native languages of its users. What is important to realize, however, is that pidginized
languages do have grammatical structure and regularity, even though their specific patterns may be different from those of the related unpidginized source-language of higher
prestige. Thus, the fact that the sentence *Dem no get-am* in present-day West African
Pidgin English is obviously different from its standard English equivalent "They don't
have it" does not necessarily indicate that the Pidgin English speaker "talks without
grammar." In producing such a sentence, he is unconsciously obeying the grammatical
rules of West African Pidgin English, and these determine that *Dem no get-am* is the
"right" construction, as opposed to such ungrammatical or "wrong" combinations as
No dem get-am, No get dem-am, Get-am dem no, etc. If a pidgin finally becomes the
native language of a speech community (and thereby becomes by definition a creole
language), it may expand in grammatical complexity to the level of "normal" or unpidginized languages. Of course, the resulting creole language may still exhibit structural
differences from the original source-language, because the creole has gone through a
pidginized stage. For more details, see Robert A. Hall, Jr., *Pidgin and Creole Languages*,
(Ithaca, N.Y.: Cornell U. Press, 1966).

have been like in its early stages can be obtained from a well-known example of the speech of a fourteen-year-old Negro lad given by Daniel Defoe in *The Family Instructor* (London, 1715). It is significant that the Negro, Toby, speaks a pidginized kind of English to his boy master, even though he states that he was born in the New World.

A sample of his speech is: [2]

Toby: Me be born at Barbadoes.

Boy: Who lives there, Toby?

Toby: There lives white mans, white womans, negree mans, negree womans, just so as live here.

Boy: What and not know God?

Toby: Yes, the white mans say God prayers,—no much know God.

Boy: And what do the black mans do?

Toby: They much work, much work,—no say God prayers, not at all.

Boy: What work do they do, Toby?

Toby: Makee the sugar, makee the ginger,—much great work, weary work, all day, all night.

Even though the boy master's English is slightly non-standard (e.g. *black mans*), it is still quite different from the speech of the Negro.

. . .

Early examples of Negro dialect as spoken in the American colonies show it to be strikingly similar to that given by DeFoe for the West Indies. In John Leacock's play, *The Fall of British Tyranny* (Philadelphia, 1776), part of the conversation between a certain "Kidnapper" and Cudjo, one of a group of Virginia Negroes, goes as follows: [3]

Kidnapper: . . . what part did you come from?

Cudjo: Disse brack man, disse one, disse one, disse one, come from Hamton, disse one, disse one, come from Nawfok, me come from Nawfok too.

Kidnapper: Very well, what was your master's name?

Cudjo: Me massa name Cunney Tomsee.

Kidnapper: Colonel Thompson—eigh?

Cudjo: Eas, massa, Cunney Tomsee.

Kidnapper: Well then I'll make you a major—and what's your name?

Cudjo: Me massa cawra me Cudjo.

Again, the enclitic vowels (e.g., *disse*) and the subject pronoun *me*

---

[2] The same citation is given in a fuller form, along with a number of other attestations of early New World Negro speech, in George Philip Krapp, *The English Language in America* (New York: The Century Co., 1925), vol. I, pp. 255–265. Other attestations are cited in Tremaine McDowell, "Notes on Negro Dialect in the American Novel to 1821" *American Speech*, vol. V (1930), pp. 291–296.

[3] This citation also occurs in Krapp, and with others in Richard Walser, "Negro Dialect in Eighteenth-Century American Drama" *American Speech*, vol. XXX (1955), pp. 269–276.

are prominent features of the Negro dialect. In the sentence *Me Massa name Cunney Tomsee* "My master's name is Colonel Thompson," both the verb "to be" and the standard English possessive suffix *-s* are absent Incidentally, Cudjo's construction is strikingly similar to sentences like *My sister name Mary* which are used by many American Negroes today.

One possible explanation why this kind of pidginized English was so widespread in the New World, with widely separated varieties resembling each other in so many ways, is that it did not originate in the New World as isolated and accidentally similar instances of random pidginization, but rather originated as a *lingua franca* in the trade centers and slave factories on the West African coast.[4] It is likely that at least some Africans already knew this pidgin English when they came to the New World, and that the common colonial policy of mixing slaves of various tribal origins forced its rapid adoption as a plantation *lingua franca*.

In the course of the eighteenth century, some significant changes took place in the New World Negro population, and these had their effect on language behavior. For one thing, the number of Negroes born in the New World came to exceed the number of those brought over from Africa. In the process, pidgin English became the creole mother-tongue of the new generations, and in some areas it has remained so to the present day.[5]

In the British colonies, the creole English of the uneducated Negroes and the English dialects of both the educated and uneducated whites were close enough to each other (at least in vocabulary) to allow the speakers of each to communicate, although they were still different enough so that the whites could consider creole English to be "broken" or "corrupt" English and evidence, so many thought, of the mental limitations of the Negro. But in Surinam, where the European settlers spoke Dutch, creole English was regarded more objectively. In fact, no less than two language courses specifically designed to teach creole English to Dutch immigrants were published before the close of the eighteenth century.[6]

Another change which took place in the New World Negro population primarily during the course of the eighteenth century was the social cleavage of the New World-born generations into underprivileged field-hands (a continuation of the older, almost universal lot of the Negro

[4] See, for example, Basil Davidson, *Black Mother; The Years of the African Slave Trade* (Boston: Little, Brown and Co., 1961), particularly p. 218.

[5] In the West Indies, creole English is usually called *patois*, while in Surinam it is called *Taki-Taki*. In the United States, the only fairly "pure" creole English left today is Gullah, spoken along the coast of South Carolina.

[6] These were Pieter van Dijk, *Nieuwe en nooit bevorens geziende onderwijzinge in het Bastert Engels, of Neeger Engels* (Amsterdam, undated, but probably 1780), and G. C. Weygandt, *Gemeenzame leewijze om het Basterd of Neger-Engelsch op een gemakkelijke wijze te leeren verstaan en spreeken* (Paramaribo, 1798).

slave) and privileged domestic servant. The difference in privilege usually meant, not freedom instead of bondage, but rather freedom from degrading kinds of labor, access to the "big house" with its comforts and "civilization," and proximity to the prestigious "quality" whites, with the opportunity to imitate their behavior (including their speech) and to wear their clothes. In some cases, privilege included the chance to get an education and, in a very few, access to wealth and freedom. In both the British colonies and the United States, Negroes belonging to the privileged group were soon able to acquire a more standard variety of English than the creole of the field hands, and those who managed to get a decent education became speakers of fully standard and often elegant English. This seems to have become the usual situation by the early 1800's, and remained so through the Civil War. In Caroline Gilman's *Recollections of a Southern Matron* (New York, 1838), the difference between field-hand creole (in this case, Gullah) and domestic servant dialect is evident in a comparison of the gardener's "He tief one sheep—he run away las week, cause de overseer gwine for flog him" with Dina's " 'Scuse me, missis, I is gitting hard o' hearing, and yes is more politer dan no" (page 254). A more striking contrast between the speech of educated and uneducated Negroes occurs in a novel written in the 1850's by an American Negro who had traveled extensively through the slave states. In Chapter XVII, part of the exchange between Henry, an educated Negro traveler, and an old "aunty" goes as follows: [7]

> "Who was that old man who ran behind your master's horse?"
>
> "Dat Nathan, my husban'."
>
> "Do they treat him well, aunty?"
>
> "No, chile, wus an' any dog, dat beat 'im foh little an nothin'."
>
> "Is uncle Nathan religious?"
>
> "Yes, chile, ole man an' I's been sahvin' God dis many day, fo yeh baun! Wen any on 'em in de house git sick, den da sen foh 'uncle Nathan' come pray foh dem, 'uncle Nathan' mighty good den!"

After the Civil War, with the abolition of slavery, the breakdown of the plantation system, and the steady increase in education for poor as well as affluent Negroes, the older field-hand creole English began to lose many of its creole characteristics, and take on more and more of the features of the local white dialects and of the written language. Yet, this process has not been just one way. For if it is true that the speech of American Negroes has been strongly influenced by the speech of whites with whom they came into contact, it is probably also true that the speech

[7] Martin R. Delany, *Blake; or the Huts of America*, published serially in *The Anglo-African Magazine* (1859). The quotation is from vol. 1, no. 6 (June 1859), p. 163.

of many whites has been influenced in some ways by the speech of Negroes.[8]

Over the last two centuries, the proportion of American Negroes who speak a perfectly standard variety of English has risen from a small group of privileged house slaves and free Negroes to persons numbering in the hundreds of thousands, and perhaps even millions. Yet there is still a sizeable number of American Negroes—undoubtedly larger than the number of standard-speaking Negroes—whose speech may be radically nonstandard. The nonstandard features in the speech of such persons may be due in part to the influence of the nonstandard dialects of whites with whom they or their ancestors have come in contact, but they also may be due to the survival of creolisms from the older Negro field-hand speech of the plantations. To insure their social mobility in modern American society, these nonstandard speakers must undoubtedly be given a command of standard English. . . . In studying nonstandard Negro dialects and teaching standard English in terms of them, however, both the applied linguist and the language teacher must come to appreciate the fact that even if certain nonstandard Negro dialect patterns do not resemble the dialect usage of American whites, or even those of the speakers of remote British dialects, they may nevertheless be as old as African and European settlement in the New World, and therefore quite widespread and well-established. . . .

Once educators who are concerned with the language problems of the disadvantaged come to realize that nonstandard Negro dialects represent a historical tradition of this type, it is to be hoped that they will become less embarrassed by evidence that these dialects are very much alike throughout the country while different in many ways from the nonstandard dialects of whites, less frustrated by failure to turn nonstandard Negro dialect speakers into Standard English speakers overnight, less impatient with the stubborn survival of Negro dialect features in the speech of even educated persons, and less zealous in proclaiming what is "right" and what is "wrong." . . .

[8] See Raven I. McDavid, Jr. and Virginia Glenn McDavid, "The Relationship of the Speech of American Negroes to the Speech of Whites" [reprinted in this volume].

THE LOGIC OF NONSTANDARD ENGLISH

William Labov

Work in recent years by ill-informed educational psychologists has given rise to the myth that Negro children in urban ghettos are verbally and culturally deprived and that their speech is basically non-logical. This view, which is associated with the work of Bereiter and Engelmann, is the more dangerous because it has been adopted uncritically as the basis for early childhood programs throughout the country, and has been transformed into a modern educational dogma.

Here Labov presents important evidence to refute the deficit model, by showing how investigators' ignorance of language and Negro culture has produced a spurious picture of children's verbal capacity. The deficit theorists have committed the fallacy of identifying features of Negro dialect which differed from their own (such as the omission of the copula be) as reflecting illogical thinking. By interviewing children in unnatural and threatening circumstances, they have obtained low measures of verbality. When the same children are interviewed in pairs by a familiar person, they show very high fluency and verbal skill. Negro culture in fact encourages the development of verbal skills, and Negro children are often much more verbally adept than their white peers, though not in the dialect and types of speech situations rewarded in school. Tests which are based on the performance of middle-class white children will inevitably give a distorted picture of the ability of children from a different cultural and linguistic background.

Labov presents further evidence refuting the claim that speakers of a nonstandard dialect think illogically, and points to the special danger that teachers' low expectations toward their Negro pupils, conditioned by the deficit theory, may in fact contribute to the pupils' failure. If the children fail, it will be taken as evidence of their intellectual inferiority, rather than as evidence of the falseness of the theory. It is vital that the deprivation theory be exposed, and

From *Monograph Series on Languages and Linguistics*, no. 22, James E. Alatis, ed. (Washington, D.C.: Georgetown University Press, 1969). Reprinted by permission.

that teachers be given more information on the nature of language,
culture, and linguistic variation, before irreparable damage has
been done to the children in our schools.

In the past decade, a great deal of federally-sponsored research has been devoted to the educational problems of children in ghetto schools. In order to account for the poor performance of children in these schools, educational psychologists have attempted to discover what kind of disadvantage or defect they are suffering from. The viewpoint which has been widely accepted, and used as the basis for large-scale intervention programs, is that the children show a cultural deficit as a result of an impoverished environment in their early years. Considerable attention has been given to language. In this area, the deficit theory appears as the concept of "verbal deprivation": Negro children from the ghetto area receive little verbal stimulation, are said to hear very little well-formed language, and as a result are impoverished in their means of verbal expression: they cannot speak complete sentences, do not know the names of common objects, cannot form concepts or convey logical thoughts.

Unfortunately, these notions are based upon the work of educational psychologists who know very little about language and even less about Negro children. The concept of verbal deprivation has no basis in social reality: in fact, Negro children in the urban ghettos receive a great deal of verbal stimulation, hear more well-formed sentences than middle-class children, and participate fully in a highly verbal culture; they have the same basic vocabulary, possess the same capacity for conceptual learning, and use the same logic as anyone else who learns to speak and understand English.

The notion of "verbal deprivation" is a part of the modern mythology of educational psychology, typical of the unfounded notions which tend to expand rapidly in our educational system. In past decades linguists have been as guilty as others in promoting such intellectual fashions at the expense of both teachers and children. But the myth of verbal deprivation is particularly dangerous, because it diverts attention from real defects of our educational system to imaginary defects of the child; and as we shall see, it leads its sponsors inevitably to the hypothesis of the genetic inferiority of Negro children which it was originally designed to avoid.

The most useful service which linguists can perform today is to clear away the illusion of "verbal deprivation" and provide a more adequate notion of the relations between standard and nonstandard dialects. In the writings of many prominent educational psychologists, we find a very poor understanding of the nature of language. Children are treated as if they have no language of their own in the preschool programs put forward

by Bereiter and Engelmann (1966).* The linguistic behavior of ghetto
children in test situations is the principal evidence for their genetic inferiority in the view of Arthur Jensen (1969). In this paper, I will examine
critically both of these approaches to the language and intelligence of the
populations labelled "verbally" and "culturally deprived." [1] I will attempt
to explain how the myth of verbal deprivation has arisen, bringing to bear
the methodological findings of sociolinguistic work, and some substantive
facts about language which are known to all linguists. I will be particularly
concerned with the relation between concept formation on the one hand,
and dialect differences on the other, since it is in this area that the most
dangerous misunderstandings are to be found.

1. VERBALITY

The general setting in which the deficit theory has arisen consists
of a number of facts which are known to all of us: that Negro children
in the central urban ghettos do badly on all school subjects, including
arithmetic and reading. In reading, they average more than two years behind the national norm.[2] Furthermore, this lag is cumulative, so that
they do worse comparatively in the fifth grade than in the first grade.
Reports in the literature show that this bad performance is correlated

* [For further information on such references, see the Bibliography at the end of
this selection.—Ed.]

[1] I am indebted to Rosalind Weiner, of the Early Childhood Education group of
Operation Headstart in New York City, and to Joan Baratz, of the Educational Development Corp., Washington D.C., for pointing out to me the scope and seriousness
of the educational issues involved here, and the ways in which the cultural deprivation
theory has affected federal intervention programs in recent years.

[2] A report of average reading comprehension scores in New York City was published in the *New York Times* on December 3, 1968. The schools attended by most of
the peer group members we have studied showed the following scores:

School	Grade	Reading score	National norm
J. H. S. 13	7	5.6	7.7
	9	7.6	9.7
J. H. S. 120	7	5.6	7.7
	9	7.0	9.7
I. S. 88	6	5.3	6.7
	8	7.2	8.7

The average is then more than two full years behind grade in the ninth grade.

most closely with socioeconomic status. Segregated ethnic groups, how-ever, seem to do worse than others: in particular, Indians, Mexican-Americans, and Negro children. Our own work in New York City confirms the fact that most Negro children read very poorly; however, our studies in the speech community show that the situation is even worse than has been reported. If one separates the isolated and peripheral individuals from the members of the central peer groups, the peer group members show even worse reading records, and to all intents and purposes are not learning to read at all during the time they spend in school.[3]

In speaking of children in the urban ghetto areas, the term "lower-class" is frequently used as opposed to "middle-class." In the several sociolinguistic studies we have carried out, and in many parallel studies, it is useful to distinguish a "lower-class" group from "working-class." Lower-class families are typically female-based or "matri-focal," with no father present to provide steady economic support, whereas for the working-class there is typically an intact nuclear family with the father holding a semiskilled or unskilled job. The educational problems of ghetto areas run across this important class distinction; there is no evidence, for example, that the father's presence or absence is closely correlated with educational achievement.[4] The peer groups we have studied in South Central Harlem, representing the basic vernacular culture, include members from both family types. The attack against "cultural deprivation" in the ghetto is overtly directed at family structures typical of lower-class families, but the educational failure we have been discussing is characteristic of both working-class and lower-class children.

In the balance of this paper, I will therefore refer to children from urban ghetto areas, rather than "lower-class" children: the population we are concerned with are those who participate fully in the vernacular culture of the street and who have been alienated from the school system.[5] We are obviously dealing with the effects of the caste system of American society—essentially a "color marking" system. Everyone recognizes this. The question is, by what mechanism does the color bar prevent children from learning to read? One answer is the notion of "cultural deprivation"

[3] See W. Labov and C. Robins, "A Note on the Relation of Reading Failure to Peer-Group Status in Urban Ghettos." (1968).

[4] There are a number of studies reported recently which show no relation between school achievement and presence of a father in the nuclear family. Preliminary findings to this effect are cited from a study by Bernard Mackler of CUE in Thos. S. Langer and Stanley T. Michaels, *Life Stress and Mental Health* (New York: Free Press), Chapter 8. Jensen 1969 cites James Coleman's study *Equality of Educational Opportunity*, p. 506, and others to illustrate the same point.

[5] The concept of "Nonstandard Negro English," and the vernacular culture in which it is embedded, is presented in detail in Labov, Cohen, Robins and Lewis 1968, sections 1.2.3 and 4.1. See volume II, section 4.3, for the linguistic traits which distinguish speakers who participate fully in the NNE culture from marginal and isolated individuals.

THE LOGIC OF NONSTANDARD ENGLISH

put forward by Martin Deutsch and others: the Negro children are said to lack the favorable factors in their home environment which enable middle-class children to do well in school. (Deutsch and assoc. 1967; Deutsch, Katz, and Jensen 1968). These factors involve the development of various cognitive skills through verbal interaction with adults, including the ability to reason abstractly, speak fluently, and focus upon long-range goals. In their publications, these psychologists also recognize broader social factors.[6] However, the deficit theory does not focus upon the interaction of the Negro child with white society so much as on his failure to interact with his mother at home. In the literature we find very little direct observation of verbal interaction in the Negro home; most typically, the investigators ask the child if he has dinner with his parents, and if he engages in dinner-table conversation with them. He is also asked whether his family takes him on trips to museums and other cultural activities. This slender thread of evidence is used to explain and interpret the large body of tests carried out in the laboratory and in the school.

The most extreme view which proceeds from this orientation—and one that is now being widely accepted—is that lower-class Negro children have no language at all. The notion is first drawn from Basil Bernstein's writings that "much of lower-class language consists of a kind of incidental 'emotional' accompaniment to action here and now." (Jensen 1968:118). Bernstein's views are filtered through a strong bias against all forms of working-class behavior, so that middle-class language is seen as superior in every respect—as "more abstract, and necessarily somewhat more flexible, detailed and subtle." One can proceed through a range of such views until one comes to the practical program of Carl Bereiter, Siegfried Engelmann and their associates. (Bereiter et al 1966; Bereiter and Englemann 1966). Bereiter's program for an academically oriented preschool is based upon their premise that Negro children must have a language with which they can learn, and their empirical finding that these children come to school without such a language. In his work with four-year-old Negro children from Urbana, Bereiter reports that their communication was by gestures, "single words," and "a series of badly-connected words or phrases," such as *They mine* and *Me got juice*. He reports that Negro children could not ask questions, that "without exaggerating . . . these four-year-olds could make no statements of any kind." Furthermore, when these children were asked "Where is the book?" they did not know enough to look at the table where the book was lying in order to answer. Thus Bereiter concludes that the children's speech forms are nothing more than a series of emotional cries, and he decides to treat them "as if the children had no language at

---

[6] For example, in Deutsch, Katz and Jensen 1968 there is a section on "Social and Psychological Perspectives" which includes a chapter by Proshansky and Newton on "The Nature and Meaning of Negro Self-Identity" and one by Rosenthal and Jacobson on "Self-Fulfilling Prophecies in the Classroom."

all." He identifies their speech with his interpretation of Bernstein's restricted code: "the language of culturally deprived children . . . is not merely an underdeveloped version of standard English, but is a basically non-logical mode of expressive behavior" (Bereiter et al 1966:113). The basic program of his preschool is to teach them a new language devised by Engelmann, which consists of a limited series of questions and answers such as *Where is the squirrel? The squirrel is in the tree.* The children will not be punished if they use their vernacular speech on the playground, but they will not be allowed to use it in the schoolroom. If they should answer the question *Where is the squirrel?* with the illogical vernacular form *In the tree* they will be reprehended by various means and made to say, *The squirrel is in the tree.*

Linguists and psycholinguists who have worked with Negro children are apt to dismiss this view of their language as utter nonsense. Yet there is no reason to reject Bereiter's observations as spurious: they were certainly not made up: on the contrary, they give us a very clear view of the behavior of student and teacher which can be duplicated in any classroom. In our own work outside the adult-dominated environments of school and home,[7] we do not observe Negro children behaving like this, but on many occasions we have been asked to help analyze the results of research into verbal deprivation in such test situations.

Here, for example, is a complete interview with a Negro boy, one of hundreds carried out in a New York City school. The boy enters a room where there is a large, friendly white interviewer, who puts on the table in front of him a block or a fire engine, and says "Tell me everything you can about this." (The interviewer's further remarks are in parentheses.)

> [12 seconds of silence]
> (What would you say it looks like?)
> [8 seconds of silence]
> A space ship.
> (Hmmmm.)
> [13 seconds of silence]
> Like a je-et.
> [12 seconds of silence]
> Like a plane.
> [20 seconds of silence]
> (What color is it?)
> Orange. [2 seconds]. An' whi-ite. [2 seconds]. An' green.
> [6 seconds of silence]

[7] The research cited here was carried out in South Central Harlem and other ghetto areas in 1965–1968 to describe structural and functional differences between Nonstandard Negro English and Standard English of the classroom. It was supported by the Office of Education as Cooperative Research Projects 3091 and 3288. Detailed reports are given in Labov, Cohen and Robins 1965, Labov 1965, and Labov, Cohen, Robins and Lewis 1968.

(An' what could you use it for?)
   [8 seconds of silence]
A je-et.
   [6 seconds of silence]
(If you had two of them, what would you do with them?)
   [6 seconds of silence]
Give one to some-body.
(Hmmm. Who do you think would like to have it?)
   [10 seconds of silence]
Cla-rence.
(Mm. Where do you think we could get another one of these?)
At the store.
(Oh ka-ay!)

We have here the same kind of defensive, monosyllabic behavior which is reported in Bereiter's work. What is the situation that produces it? The child is in an asymmetrical situation where anything he says can literally be held against him. He has learned a number of devices to *avoid* saying anything in this situation, and he works very hard to achieve this end. One may observe the intonation patterns of

$$^3\,\text{'o'}\,^2\,\text{know}$$
$$^1\,\text{a} \underline{}$$
$$\text{ip}^3$$
$$^2\,\text{a space}\,^2\,\text{shi}\underline{}$$

which Negro children often use when they are asked a question to which the answer is obvious. The answer may be read as "Will this satisfy you?"

If one takes this interview as a measure of the verbal capacity of the child, it must be as his capacity to defend himself in a hostile and threatening situation. But unfortunately, thousands of such interviews are used as evidence of the child's total verbal capacity, or more simply his "verbality"; it is argued that this lack of verbality *explains* his poor performance in school. Operation Headstart and other intervention programs have largely been based upon the "deficit theory"—the notions that such interviews give us a measure of the child's verbal capacity and that the verbal stimulation which he has been missing can be supplied in a preschool environment.

The verbal behavior which is shown by the child in the test situation quoted above is not the result of the ineptness of the interviewer. It is rather the result of regular sociolinguistic factors operating upon adult and child in this asymmetrical situation. In our work in urban ghetto areas, we have often encountered such behavior. Ordinarily we worked with boys 10–17 years old; and whenever we extended our approach downward to 8- or 9-year olds, we began to see the need for different techniques to explore the verbal capacity of the child. At one point we began a series of interviews with younger brothers of the "Thunderbirds" in 1390 5th Avenue. Clarence Robins returned after an interview with 8-year-old Leon L., who showed the following minimal response to topics which arouse intense interest in other interviews with older boys.

CR: What if you saw somebody kickin' somebody else on the ground, or was using a stick, what would you do if you saw that?
Leon: Mmmm.
CR: If it was supposed to be a fair fight—
Leon: I don' know.
CR: You don' know? Would you do anything . . . huh? I can't hear you.
Leon: No.
CR: Did you ever see somebody get beat up real bad?
Leon: Nope ? ? ?
CR: Well—uh—did you ever get into a fight with a guy?
Leon: Nope.
CR: That was bigger than you?
Leon: Nope.
CR: You never been in a fight?
Leon: Nope.
CR: Nobody ever pick on you?
Leon: Nope.
CR: Nobody ever hit you?
Leon: Nope.
CR: How come?
Leon: Ah 'on' know.
CR: Didn't you ever hit somebody?
Leon: Nope.
CR: [incredulous] You never hit nobody?
Leon: Mhm.
CR: Aww, ba-a-a-be, you ain't gonna tell me that.

It may be that Leon is here defending himself against accusations of wrong-doing, since Clarence knows that Leon has been in fights, that he has been taking pencils away from little boys, etc. But if we turn to a more neutral subject, we find the same pattern:

CR: You watch—you like to watch television? . . . Hey, Leon . . . you like to watch television? [Leon nods] What's your favorite program?
Leon: Uhhmmmm . . . I look at cartoons.
CR: Well, what's your favorite one? What's your favorite program?
Leon: Superman . . .
CR: Yeah? Did you see Superman—ah—yesterday, or day before yesterday: when's the last time you saw Superman?
Leon: Sa-aturday . . .

CR: You rem—you saw it Saturday? What was the story all about? You remember the
        story?
Leon: M-m.
CR: You don't remember the story of what—that you saw of Superman?
Leon: Nope.
CR: You don't remember what happened, huh?
Leon: Hm-m.
CR: I see—ah—what other stories do you like to watch on T.V.?
Leon: Mmmm ? ? ? ? . . . umm . . . [glottalization]
CR: Hmm? [4 seconds]
Leon: Hh?
CR: What's th'other stories that you like to watch?
Leon: ^{2} Mi-ighty ^{2}Mouse^2 . .
CR: And what else?
Leon: Ummm . . . ahm . . .

This nonverbal behavior occurs in a relatively *favorable* context for adult-
child interaction; since the adult is a Negro man raised in Harlem, who
knows this particular neighborhood and these boys very well. He is a
skilled interviewer who has obtained a very high level of verbal response
with techniques developed for a different age level, and he has an extraordinary advantage over most teachers or experimenters in these respects.
But even his skills and personality are ineffective in breaking down the
social constraints that prevail here.

When we reviewed the record of this interview with Leon, we decided to use it as a test of our own knowledge of the sociolinguistic factors
which control speech. We made the following changes in the social situation: in the next interview with Leon, Clarence

    (1) brought along a supply of potato chips, changing the "interview" into some-
        thing more in the nature of a party;
    (2) brought along Leon's best friend, 8-year-old Gregory;
    (3) reduced the height imbalance (when Clarence got down on the floor of Leon's
        room, he dropped from 6 ft. 2 in. to 3 ft. 6 in);
    (4) introduced taboo words and taboo topics, and proved to Leon's surprise that
        one can say anything into our microphone without any fear of retaliation.

The result of these changes is a striking difference in the volume and style
of speech.

CR: Is there anybody who says *your momma drink pee*?
Leon: [rapidly and breathlessly] Yee-ah!
Greg: Yup!
Leon: And your father eat doo-doo for breakfas'!
CR: Ohhh!! [laughs]

Leon: And they say your father—your father eat doo-doo for dinner!
Greg: When they sound on me, I say C. B. S.
CR: What that mean?
⌈ Leon: Congo booger-snatch! [laughs]
⌊ Greg: Congo booger-snatcher! [laughs]
Greg: And sometimes I'll curse with B. B.
CR: What that?
Greg: Black boy! [Leon—crunching on potato chips] Oh that's a M. B. B.
CR: M. B. B. What's that?
Greg: 'Merican Black Boy!
CR: Ohh . . .
Greg: Anyway, 'Mericans is same like white people, right?
Leon: And they talk about Allah.
CR: Oh yeah?
Greg: Yeah.
CR: What they say about Allah?
⌈ Leon: Allah—Allah is God.
⌊ Greg: Allah—
CR: And what else?
Leon: I don' know the res'.
Greg: Allah i—Allah is God, Allah is the only God, Allah—
Leon: Allah is the son of God.
Greg: But can he make magic?
Leon: Nope.
Greg: I know who can make magic.
CR: Who can?
Leon: The God, the real one.
CR: Who can make magic?
Greg: The son of po'—[CR: Hm?] I'm sayin' the po'k chop God! He only a po'k chop God! [8] [Leon chuckles].

The "nonverbal" Leon is now competing actively for the floor; Gregory and Leon talk to each other as much as they do to the interviewer.

One can make a more direct comparison of the two interviews by examining the section on fighting. Leon persists in denying that he fights, but he can no longer use monosyllabic answers, and Gregory cuts through his façade in a way that Clarence Robins alone was unable to do.

CR: Now, you said you had this fight, now, but I wanted you to tell me about the fight that you had.
Leon: I ain't had no fight.

[8] The reference to the *pork chop* God condenses several concepts of Black nationalism current in the Harlem community. A *pork chop* is a Negro who has not lost traditional subservient ideology of the South, who has no knowledge of himself in Muslim terms, and the *pork chop* God would be the traditional God of Southern Baptists. He and his followers may be pork chops, but he still holds the power in Leon and Gregory's world.

```
┌Greg:   Yes you did!                      He said Barry,
└CR:     You said you had one! you had a fight with Butchie,
┌Greg:                     An he say Garland . . . an' Michael.
└CR:     an' Barry . . .
┌Leon:   I di'n'; you said that, Gregory!
└Greg:         You did.
┌Leon:   You know you said that!
└Greg:                   You said Garland, remember that?
┌Greg:   You said Garland!           Yes you did!
└CR:                           You said Garland, that's right.
 Greg:   He said Mich—an' I say Michael.
┌CR:     Did you have a fight with Garland?
└Leon:                                   Uh-uh.
 CR:     You had one, and he beat you up, too!
 Greg:   Yes he did!
 Leon:   No, I di—I never had a fight with Butch! . . .
```

The same pattern can be seen on other local topics, where the interviewer brings neighborhood gossip to bear on Leon and Gregory acts as a witness.

```
 CR:       . . . Hey Gregory! I heard that around here . . . and I'm 'on' tell you who
           said it, too . . .
 Leon:                                          Who?
┌CR:      about you . . .
┌Leon:                   Who?
└Greg:                             I'd say it!
 CR:      They said that—they say that the only person you play with is David Gilbert.
┌Leon:    Yee-ah! yee-ah! yee-ah! . . .
└Greg:        That's who you play with!
┌Leon:    I 'on' play with him no more!
└Greg:                   Yes you do!
 Leon:    I 'on' play with him no more!
 Greg:    But remember, about me and Robbie?
 Leon:    So that's not—
 Greg:        and you went to Petey and Gilbert's house, 'member? Ah haaah!!
 Leon:    So that's—so—but I would—I had came back out, an' I ain't go to his house
          no more . . .
```

The observer must now draw a very different conclusion about the verbal capacity of Leon. The monosyllabic speaker who had nothing to say about anything and cannot remember what he did yesterday has disappeared. Instead, we have two boys who have so much to say they keep interrupting each other, who seem to have no difficulty in using the English language to express themselves. And we in turn obtain the volume of speech and the rich array of grammatical devices which we need for analyzing the structure of Nonstandard Negro English (NNE): negative concord [*I 'on' play with him no more*], the pluperfect [*had came back out*], negative perfect [*I ain't had*], the negative preterite [*I ain't go*], and so on.

One can now transfer this demonstration of the sociolinguistic control of speech to other test situations—including I. Q. and reading tests in school. It should be immediately apparent that none of the standard tests will come anywhere near measuring Leon's verbal capacity. On these tests he will show up as very much the monosyllabic, inept, ignorant, bumbling child of our first interview. The teacher has far less ability than Clarence Robins to elicit speech from this child; Clarence knows the community, the things that Leon has been doing, and the things that Leon would like to talk about. But the power relationships in a one-to-one confrontation between adult and child are too asymmetrical. This does not mean that some Negro children will not talk a great deal when alone with an adult, or that an adult cannot get close to any child. It means that the social situation is the most powerful determinant of verbal behavior and that an adult must enter into the right social relation with a child if he wants to find out what a child can do: this is just what many teachers cannot do.

The view of the Negro speech community which we obtain from our work in the ghetto areas is precisely the opposite from that reported by Deutsch, Englemann and Bereiter. We see a child bathed in verbal stimulation from morning to night. We see many speech events which depend upon the competitive exhibition of verbal skills: sounding, singing, toasts, rifting, louding—a whole range of activities in which the individual gains status through his use of language.[9] We see the younger child trying to acquire these skills from older children—hanging around on the outskirts of the older peer groups, and imitating this behavior to the best of his ability. We see no connection between verbal skill at the speech events characteristic of the street culture and success in the schoolroom.

2. VERBOSITY

There are undoubtedly many verbal skills which children from ghetto areas must learn in order to do well in the school situation, and some of these are indeed characteristic of middle-class verbal behavior. Precision in spelling, practice in handling abstract symbols, the ability to state explicitly the meaning of words, and a richer knowledge of the Latinate vocabulary, may all be useful acquisitions. But is it true that *all* of the

[9] For detailed accounts of these speech events, see Labov, Cohen, Robins and Lewis 1968, section 4.2.

middle-class verbal habits are functional and desirable in the school situation? Before we impose middle-class verbal style upon children from other cultural groups, we should find out how much of this is useful for the main work of analyzing and generalizing, and how much is merely stylistic —or even dysfunctional. In high school and college middle-class children spontaneously complicate their syntax to the point that instructors despair of getting them to make their language simpler and clearer. In every learned journal one can find examples of jargon and empty elaboration— and complaints about it. Is the "elaborated code" of Bernstein really so "flexible, detailed and subtle" as some psychologists believe? (Jensen 1968:119). Isn't it also turgid, redundant, and empty? Is it not simply an elaborated *style*, rather than a superior code or system? [10]

Our work in the speech community makes it painfully obvious that in many ways working-class speakers are more effective narrators, reasoners and debaters than many middle-class speakers who temporize, qualify, and lose their argument in a mass of irrelevant detail. Many academic writers try to rid themselves of that part of middle-class style that is empty pretension, and keep that part that is needed for precision. But the average middle-class speaker that we encounter makes no such effort; he is enmeshed in verbiage, the victim of sociolinguistic factors beyond his control.

I will not attempt to support this argument here with systematic quantitative evidence, although it is possible to develop measures which show how far middle-class speakers can wander from the point. I would like to contrast two speakers dealing with roughly the same topic—matters of belief. The first is Larry H., a 15-year-old core member of the Jets, being interviewed by John Lewis. Larry is one of the loudest and roughest members of the Jets, one who gives the least recognition to the conventional rules of politeness.[11] For most readers of this paper, first contact with Larry would produce some fairly negative reactions on both sides: it is probable that you would not *like* him any more than his teachers do. Larry causes trouble in and out of school; he was put back from the eleventh grade to the ninth and has been threatened with further action by the school authorities.

[10] The term *code* is central in Bernstein's description of the differences between working-class and middle-class styles of speech. (1966) The restrictions and elaborations of speech observed are labelled as "codes" to indicate the principles governing selection from the range of possible English sentences. No rules or detailed description of the operation of such codes are provided as yet, so that this central concept remains to be specified.

[11] A direct view of Larry's verbal style in a hostile encounter is given in Labov, Cohen, Robins and Lewis 1968, vol. II, pp. 39–43. Gray's Oral Reading Test was being given to a group of Jets on the steps of a brownstone house in Harlem, and the landlord tried unsuccessfully to make the Jets move. Larry's verbal style in this encounter matches the reports he gives of himself in a number of narratives cited in section 4.8.

JL: What happens to you after you die? Do you know?
Larry: Yeah, I know.
JL: What?
Larry: After they put you in the ground, your body turns into—ah—bones, an' shit.
JL: What happens to your spirit?
Larry: Your spirit—soon as you die, your spirit leaves you.
JL: And where does the spirit go?
Larry: Well, it all depends . . .
JL: On what?
Larry: You know, like some people say if you're good an' shit, your spirit goin' t'heaven
         . . . 'n' if you bad, your spirit goin' to hell. Well, bullshit! Your spirit goin' to
         hell anyway; good or bad.
JL: Why?
Larry: Why? I'll tell you why. 'Cause, you see, doesn' nobody really know that it's a
         God, y'know, 'cause I mean I have seen black gods, pink gods, white gods, all
         color gods, and don't nobody know it's really a God. An' when they be sayin'
         if you good, you goin' t'heaven, tha's bullshit, 'cause you ain't goin' to no
         heaven, 'cause it ain't no heaven for you to go to.

Larry is a paradigmatic speaker of Nonstandard Negro English (NNE) as
opposed to Standard English (SE). His grammar shows a high concentra-
tration of such characteristic NNE forms as negative inversion [*don't
nobody know* . . .], negative concord [*you ain't goin' to no heaven* . . .],
invariant *be* [*when they be saying* . . .], dummy *it* for SE *there* [*it ain't no
heaven* . . .], optional copula deletion [*if you're good* . . . *if you bad* . . .],
and full forms of auxiliaries [*I have seen* . . .]. The only SE influence in
this passage is the one case of *doesn't* instead of the invariant *don't* of
NNE. Larry also provides a paradigmatic example of the rhetorical style of
NNE: he can sum up a complex argument in a few words, and the full
force of his opinions comes through without qualification or reservation. He
is eminently quotable, and his interviews give us many concise statements
of the NNE point of view. One can almost say that Larry *speaks* the NNE
culture.[12]

It is the logical form of this passage which is of particular interest
here. Larry presents a complex set of interdependent propositions which
can be explicated by setting out the SE equivalents in linear order. The
basic argument is to deny the twin propositions

(A)   If you are good,   (B) then your spirit will go to heaven.
(-A) If you are bad,   (C) then your spirit will to to hell.

Larry denies (B), and asserts that *if* (A) *or* (=A), *then* (C). His argument
may be outlined as follows:

[12] See Labov, Cohen, Robins and Lewis 1968, vol. II, pp. 38, 71–73, 291–292.

(1)   Everyone has a different idea of what God is like.
(2)   Therefore nobody really knows that God exists.
(3)   If there is a heaven, it was made by God.
(4)   If God doesn't exist, he couldn't have made heaven.
(5)   Therefore heaven does not exist.
(6)   You can't go somewhere that doesn't exist.
(=B) Therefore you can't go to heaven.
(C)   Therefore you are going to hell.

The argument is presented in the order: (C), because (2) because (1), therefore (2), therefore (=B) because (5) and (6). Part of the argument is implicit: the connection (2) therefore (=B) leaves unstated the connecting links 3 and (4), and in this interval Larry strengthens the propositions from the form (2) *Nobody knows if there is . . .* to (5) *There is no . . .* Otherwise, the case is presented explicitly as well as economically. The complex argument is summed up in Larry's last sentence, which shows formally the dependence of (=B) on (5) and (6):

> An' when they be sayin' if you good, you goin' t'heaven,
> [The proposition, if A, then B]
> Tha's bullshit,
> [is absurd]
> 'cause you ain't goin' to no heaven
> [because =B]
> 'cause it ain't no heaven for you to go to.
> [because (5) and (6)].

This hypothetical argument is not carried on at a high level of seriousness. It is a game played with ideas as counters, in which opponents use a wide variety of verbal devices to win. There is no personal commitment to any of these propositions, and no reluctance to strengthen one's argument by bending the rules of logic as in the (2-5) sequence. But if the opponent invokes the rules of logic, they hold. In John Lewis' interviews, he often makes this move, and the force of his argument is always acknowledged and countered within the rules of logic. In this case, he pointed out the fallacy that the argument (2-3-4-5-6) leads to (=C) as well as (=B), so it cannot be used to support Larry's assertion (C):

JL: Well, if there's no heaven, how could there be a hell?
Larry: I mean—ye-eah. Well, let me tell you, it ain't no hell, 'cause this is hell right here, y'know!
JL: This is hell?
Larry: Yeah, this is hell right here!

Larry's answer is quick, ingenious and decisive. The application of the (3-4-5) argument to hell is denied, since hell is here, and therefore conclusion (C) stands. These are not ready-made or preconceived opinions, but new propositions devised to win the logical argument in the game being played. The reader will note the speed and precision of Larry's mental operations. He does not wander, or insert meaningless verbiage. The only repetition is (2), placed before and after (1) in his original statement. It is often said that the nonstandard vernacular is not suited for dealing with abstract or hypothetical questions, but in fact speakers from the NNE community take great delight in exercising their wit and logic on the most improbable and problematical matters. Despite the fact that Larry H. does not believe in God, and has just denied all knowledge of him, John Lewis advances the following hypothetical question:

JL: . . . But, just say that there is a God, what color is he? White or black?
Larry: Well, if it is a God . . . I wouldn' know what color, I couldn' say,—couldn'
         nobody say what color he is or *really* would be.
JL: But now, jus' suppose there was a God—
Larry: Unless'n they say . . .
JL: No, I was jus' sayin' jus' suppose there is a God, would he be white or black?
Larry: . . . He'd be white, man.
JL: Why?
Larry: Why? I'll tell you why. 'Cause the average whitey out here got everything, you
         dig? And the nigger ain't got shit, y'know? Y'understan'? So—um—for—in order
         for *that* to happen, you know it ain't no black God that's doin' that bullshit.

No one can hear Larry's answer to this question without being convinced that they are in the presence of a skilled speaker with great "verbal presence of mind," who can use the English language expertly for many purposes. Larry's answer to John Lewis is again a complex argument. The formulation is not SE, but it is clear and effective even for those not familiar with the vernacular. The nearest SE equivalent might be: "So you know that God isn't black, because if he was, he wouldn't have arranged things like that."

The reader will have noted that this analysis is being carried out in Standard English, and the inevitable challenge is: why not write in NNE, then, or in your own nonstandard dialect? The fundamental reason is, of course, one of firmly fixed social conventions. All communities agree that SE is the "proper" medium for formal writing and public communication. Furthermore, it seems likely that SE has an advantage over NNE in explicit analysis of surface forms, which is what we are doing here. We will return to this opposition between explicitness and logical statement in sections 3 and 4. First, however, it will be helpful to examine SE in its primary natural setting, as the medium for informal spoken communication of middle-class speakers.

Let us now turn to the second speaker, an upper-middle-class, college

educated Negro man being interviewed by Clarence Robins in our survey
of adults in Central Harlem.

CR: Do you know of anything that someone can do, to have someone who has
            passed on visit him in a dream?

Chas. M.:   Well, I even heard my parents say that there is such a thing as something
            in dreams some things like that, and sometimes dreams do come true. I have
            personally never had a dream come true. I've never dreamt that somebody
            was dying and they actually died, (Mhm) or that I was going to have ten
            dollars the next day and somehow I got ten dollars in my pocket. (Mhm). I
            don't particularly believe in that, I don't think it's true. I do feel, though,
            that there is such a thing as—ah—witchcraft. I do feel that in certain cultures
            there is such a thing as witchcraft, or some sort of *science* of witchcraft; I
            don't think that it's just a matter of believing hard enough that there is
            such a thing as witchcraft. I do believe that there is such a thing that a
            person can put himself in a state of *mind* (Mhm), or that—er—something
            could be given them to intoxicate them in a certain—to a certain frame of
            mind—that—that could actually be considered witchcraft.

Charles M. is obviously a "good speaker" who strikes the listener as well-
educated, intelligent, and sincere. He is a likeable and attractive person—
the kind of person that middle-class listeners rate very high on a scale of
"job suitability" and equally high as a potential friend.[13] His language is
more moderate and tempered than Larry's; he makes every effort to qualify
his opinions, and seems anxious to avoid any misstatements or over-state-
ments. From these qualities emerge the primary characteristic of this
passage—its *verbosity*. Words multiply, some modifying and qualifying,
others repeating or padding the main argument. The first half of this
extract is a response to the initial question on dreams, basically:

(1) Some people say that dreams sometimes come true.
(2) I have never had a dream come true.
(3) Therefore I don't believe (1).

Some characteristic filler phrases appear here: *such a thing as, some things
like that, particularly*. Two examples of dreams given after (2) are after-
thoughts that might have been given after (1). Proposition (3) is stated
twice for no obvious reason. Nevertheless, this much of Charles M.'s
response is well-directed to the point of the question. He then volunteers a
statement of his beliefs about witchcraft which shows the difficulty of
middle-class speakers who (a) want to express a belief in something but

---

[13] See Labov, Cohen, Robins and Lewis 1968, section 4.6, for a description of
subjective reaction tests which utilize these evaluative dimensions.

(b) want to show themselves as judicious, rational and free from superstitions. The basic proposition can be stated simply in five words:

But I believe in witchcraft.

However, the idea is enlarged to exactly 100 words, and it is difficult to see
what else is being said. In the following quotations, padding which can be
removed without change in meaning is shown in brackets.

(1) "I [do] feel, though, that there is [such a thing as] witchcraft."
Feel seems to be a euphemism for "believe."

(2) "[I do feel that] in certain cultures [there is such a thing as
witchcraft.]" This repetition seems designed only to introduce the word
culture, which lets us know that the speaker knows about anthropology.
Does *certain cultures* mean "not in ours" or "not in all"?

(3) "[or some sort of *science* of witchcraft.]" This addition seems to
have no clear meaning at all. What is a "science" of witchcraft as opposed
to just plain witchcraft? [14] The main function is to introduce the word
"science," though it seems to have no connection to what follows.

(4) "I don't think that it's just [a matter of] believing hard enough
that [there is such a thing as] witchcraft." The speaker argues that witchcraft is not merely a belief; there is more to it.

(5) "I [do] believe that [there is such a thing that] a person can put
himself in a state of *mind* . . . that [could actually be considered] witchcraft." Is witchcraft as a state of mind different from the state of belief
denied in (4)?

(6) "or that something could be given them to intoxicate them [to a
certain frame of mind] . . ." The third learnèd word, *intoxicate*, is introduced by this addition. The vacuity of this passage becomes more
evident if we remove repetitions, fashionable words and stylistic decora-
tions:

But I believe in witchcraft.
I don't think witchcraft is just a belief.
A person can put himself or be put in a state of mind that is witchcraft.

Without the extra verbiage and the O.K. words like *science, culture,* and
intoxicate, Charles M. appears as something less than a first-rate thinker.
The initial impression of him as a good speaker is simply our long-con-
ditioned reaction to middle-class verbosity: we know that people who use

---

[14] Several middle-class readers of this passage have suggested that *science* here
refers to some form of control as opposed to belief; the "science of witchcraft" would
then be a kind of engineering of mental states; other interpretations can of course be
provided. The fact remains that no such subtleties of interpretation are needed to
understand Larry's remarks.

these stylistic devices are educated people, and we are inclined to credit them with saying something intelligent. Our reactions are accurate in one sense: Charles M. is more educated than Larry. But is he more rational, more logical, or more intelligent? Is he any better at thinking out a problem to its solution? Does he deal more easily with abstractions? There is no reason to think so. Charles M. succeeds in letting us know that he is educated, but in the end we do not know what he is trying to say, and neither does he.

In the previous section I have attempted to explain the origin of the myth that lower-class Negro children are nonverbal. The examples just given may help to account for the corresponding myth that middle-class language is in itself better suited for dealing with abstract, logically complex and hypothetical questions. These examples are intended to have a certain negative force. They are not controlled experiments: on the contrary, this and the preceding section are designed to convince the reader that the controlled experiments that have been offered in evidence are misleading. The only thing that is "controlled" is the superficial form of the stimulus: all children are asked "What do you think of capital punishment?" or "Tell me everything you can about this." But the speaker's interpretation of these requests, and the notion he believes is appropriate in response is completely uncontrolled. One can view these test stimuli as requests for information, commands for action, as threats of punishment, or as meaningless sequences of words. They are probably intended as something altogether different: as requests for display; [15] but in any case the experimenter is normally unaware of the problem of interpretation. The methods of educational psychologists like Deutsch, Jensen and Bereiter follow the pattern designed for animal experiments where motivation is controlled by such simple methods as withholding food until a certain weight reduction is reached. With human subjects, it is absurd to believe that an identical "stimulus" is obtained by asking everyone the "same question." Since the crucial intervening variables of interpretation and motivation are uncontrolled, most of the literature on verbal deprivation tells us nothing about the capacities of children. They are only the trappings of science: an approach which substitutes the formal procedures of the scientific method for the activity itself. With our present limited grasp of these problems, the best we can do to understand the verbal capacities of children is to study them within the cultural context in which they were developed.

It is not only the NNE vernacular which should be studied in this way, but also the language of middle-class children. The explicitness and precision which we hope to gain from copying middle-class forms are often

---

[15] The concept of a "request for verbal display" is here drawn from Alan Blum's treatment of the therapeutic interview in *The Sociology of Mental Illness*, mimeographed (to appear in *For Thomas Szasz*).

the product of the test situation, and limited to it. For example, it was stated in the first part of this paper that working-class children hear more well-formed sentences than middle-class children. This statement may seem extraordinary in the light of current belief of many linguists that most people do not speak in well-formed sentences, and that their actual speech production or "performance" is ungrammatical.[16] But those who have worked with any body of natural speech know that this is not the case. Our own studies of the "Grammaticality of Every-day Speech" show that the great majority of utterances in all contexts are complete sentences, and most of the rest can be reduced to grammatical form by a small set of "editing rules." [17] The proportions of grammatical sentences vary with class backgrounds and styles. The highest percentage of well-formed sentences are found in casual speech, and working-class speakers use more well-formed sentences than middle-class speakers. The widespread myth that most speech is ungrammatical is no doubt based upon tapes made at learnèd conferences, where we obtain the maximum number of irreducibly ungrammatical sequences.

It is true that technical and scientific books are written in a style which is markedly "middle-class." But unfortunately, we often fail to achieve the explicitness and precision which we look for in such writing; and the speech of many middle-class people departs maximally from this target. All too often, "Standard English" is represented by a style that is simultaneously over-particular and vague. The accumulating flow of words buries rather than strikes the target. It is this verbosity which is most easily taught and most easily learned, so that words take the place of thought, and nothing can be found behind them.

When Bernstein describes his "elaborated code" in general terms, it emerges as a subtle and sophisticated mode of planning utterances, achieving structural variety, taking the other person's knowledge into account, and so on. But when it comes to describing the actual difference between middle-class and working-class speakers, we are presented with a proliferation of "I think," of the passive, of modals and auxiliaries, of the first person pronoun, of uncommon words; these are the bench marks of hemming and hawing, backing and filling, that are used by Charles M., devices which often obscure whatever positive contribution education can

[16] In a number of presentations, Chomsky has asserted that the great majority of the sentences which a child hears are ungrammatical ("95 percent"). In Chomsky 1965:58, this notion is presented as one of the arguments in his general statement of the "nativist" position: "A consideration of the character of the grammar that is acquired, *the degenerate quality and narrowly limited extent of the available data,* [my emphasis] the striking uniformity of the resulting grammars, and their independence of intelligence, motivation, and emotional state, over wide ranges of variation, leave little hope that much of the structure of the language can be learned . . ."

[17] The editing rules are presented in W. Labov, "On the Grammaticality of Every-day Speech," paper given at the annual meeting of the Linguistic Society of America, New York City, December 1966.

make to our use of language. When we have discovered how much middle-class style is a matter of fashion and how much actually helps us express our ideas clearly, we will have done ourselves a great service; we will then be in a position to say what standard grammatical rules must be taught to nonstandard speakers in the early grades.

3. GRAMMATICALITY

Let us now examine Bereiter's own data on the verbal behavior of the children he dealt with. The expressions *They mine* and *Me got juice* are cited as examples of a language which lacks the means for expressing logical relations—in this case characterized as "a series of badly connected words." (Bereiter 1966:113 ff.) In the case of *They mine*, it is apparent that Bereiter confuses the notions of logic and explicitness. We know that there are many languages of the world which do not have a present copula, and which conjoin subject and predicate complement without a verb. Russian, Hungarian, and Arabic may be foreign; but they are not by that same token illogical. In the case of Nonstandard Negro English we are not dealing with even this superficial grammatical difference, but rather with a low-level rule which carries contraction one step farther to delete single consonants representing the verbs *is, have,* or *will.* (Labov, Cohen, Robins & Lewis 1968:sect. 3.4). We have yet to find any children who do not sometimes use the full forms of *is* and *will,* even though they may frequently delete it. Our recent studies with Negro children four to seven years old indicate that they use the full form of the copula *is* more often than preadolescents 10 to 12 years old, or the adolescents 14 to 17 years old.[18]

Furthermore, the deletion of the *is* or *are* in Nonstandard Negro English is not the result of erratic or illogical behavior: it follows the same regular rules as standard English contraction. Wherever standard English can contract, Negro children use either the contracted form or (more commonly) the deleted zero form. Thus *They mine* corresponds to standard *They're mine,* not to the full form *They are mine.* On the other hand, no such deletion is possible in positions where standard English cannot contract: just as one cannot say *That's what they're* in standard English, *That's what they* is equally impossible in the vernacular we are considering. The internal constraints upon both of these rules show that we are dealing with a phonological process like contraction, sensitive to such phonetic conditions as whether or not the next word begins with a

---

[18] From work on the grammars and comprehension of Negro children four to eight years old being carried out by Professor Jane Torrey of Connecticut College in extension of the research cited above in Labov, Cohen, Robins and Lewis 1968.

vowel or a consonant. The appropriate use of the deletion rule, like the contraction rule, requires a deep and intimate knowledge of English grammar and phonology. Such knowledge is not available for conscious inspection by native speakers: the rules we have recently worked out for standard contraction (Labov, Cohen, Robins & Lewis 1968:3.4) have never appeared in any grammar, and are certainly not a part of the conscious knowledge of any standard English speakers. Nevertheless, the adult or child who uses these rules must have formed at some level of psychological organization clear concepts of "tense marker," "verb phrase," "rule ordering," "sentence embedding," "pronoun," and many other grammatical categories which are essential parts of any logical system.

Bereiter's reaction to the sentence *Me got juice* is even more puzzling. If Bereiter believes that *Me got juice* is not a logical expression, it can only be that he interprets the use of the objective pronoun *me* as representing a difference in logical relationship to the verb: that the child is in fact saying that *the juice got him* rather than *he got the juice!* If on the other hand the child means "I got juice," then this sentence form shows only that he has not learned the formal rules for the use of the subjective form *I* and oblique form *me*. We have in fact encountered many children who do not have these formal rules in order at the ages of four, five, six, or even eight.[19] It is extremely difficult to construct a minimal pair to show that the difference between *he* and *him*, or *she* and *her*, carries cognitive meaning. In almost every case, it is the context which tells us who is the agent and who is acted upon. We must then ask: what differences in cognitive, structural orientation are signalled by the fact that the child has not learned this formal rule? In the tests carried out by Jane Torrey it is evident that the children concerned do understand the difference in meaning between *she* and *her* when another person uses the forms; all that remains is that the children themselves do not use the two forms. Our knowledge of the cognitive correlates of grammatical differences is certainly in its infancy; for this is one of very many questions which we simply cannot answer. At the moment we do not know how to construct any kind of experiment which would lead to an answer; we do not even know what type of cognitive correlate we would be looking for.

Bereiter shows even more profound ignorance of the rules of discourse and of syntax when he rejects *In the tree* as an illogical, or badly-formed answer to *Where is the squirrel?* Such elliptical answers are of course used by everyone; they show the appropriate deletion of subject and main verb, leaving the locative which is questioned by *wh + there*. The reply *In the tree* demonstrates that the listener has been attentive to and apprehended the syntax of the speaker.[20] Whatever formal structure we wish to write

---

[19] From the research of Jane Torrey cited in footnote 18.

[20] The attention to the speaker's syntax required of the listener is analyzed in detail by Harvey Sacks in his unpublished 1968 lectures.

for expressions such as *Yes* or *Home* or *In the tree*, it is obvious that they cannot be interpreted without knowing the structure of the question which preceded them, and that they presuppose an understanding of the syntax of the question. Thus if you ask me "Where is the squirrel?" it is necessary for me to understand the processes of *wh*-attachment, *wh*-attraction to the front of the sentence, and flip-flop of auxiliary and subject to produce this sentence from an underlying form which would otherwise have produced *The squirrel is there*. If the child had answered *The tree*, or *Squirrel the tree*, or *The in tree*, we would then assume that he did not understand the syntax of the full form, *The squirrel is in the tree*. Given the data that Bereiter presents, we cannot conclude that the child has no grammar, but only that the investigator does not understand the rules of grammar. It does not necessarily do any harm to use the full form *The squirrel is in the tree*, if one wants to make fully explicit the rules of grammar which the child has internalized. Much of logical analysis consists of making explicit just that kind of internalized rule. But it is hard to believe that any good can come from a program which begins with so many misconceptions about the input data. Bereiter and Engelmann believe that in teaching the child to say *The squirrel is in the tree* or *This is a box* and *This is not a box* they are teaching him an entirely new language, whereas in fact they are only teaching him to produce slightly different forms of the language he already has.

4. LOGIC

For many generations, American school teachers have devoted themselves to correcting a small number of nonstandard English rules to their standard equivalents, under the impression that they were teaching logic. This view has been reinforced and given theoretical justification by the claim that Nonstandard Negro English lacks the means for the expression of logical thought.

Let us consider for a moment the possibility that Negro children do not operate with the same logic that middle-class adults display. This would inevitably mean that sentences of a certain grammatical form would have different truth values for the two types of speakers. One of the most obvious places to look for such a difference is in the handling of the negative; and here we encounter one of the nonstandard items which has been stigmatized as illogical by school teachers: the double negative, or as we term it, negative concord. A child who says *He don't know nothing* is often said to be making an illogical statement without knowing it. According to the teacher, the child wants to say *He knows nothing* but puts in an extra negative without realizing it, and so conveys the opposite meaning "he does not know nothing" which reduces to "he knows something." I need not emphasize that this is an absurd interpretation: if a nonstandard speaker wishes to say that "he does *not* know *nothing*," he does so by simply placing contrastive stress on both negatives as I have done here (He *don't* know *nothing*) indicating that they are derived from two underlying negatives in the deep structure. But note that the middle-class speaker does exactly the same thing when he wants to signal the existence of two underlying negatives: "He doesn't know *nothing*." In the standard form *He doesn't know anything*, the indefinite *anything* contains the same superficial reference to a preceding negative in the surface structure as the nonstandard *nothing* does. In the corresponding positive sentences, the indefinite *something* is used. The dialect difference, like most of the differences between the standard and nonstandard forms, is one of surface form, and has nothing to do with the underlying logic of the sentence.

The Anglo-Saxon authors of the Peterborough Chronicle were surely not illogical when they wrote *For ne waeren nan martyrs swa pined alse he waeron*, literally "For never weren't no martyrs so tortured as these were." The "logical" forms of current standard English are simply the accepted conventions of our present-day formal style.

We can summarize the ways in which the two dialects differ in the following table:

	SE	NNE
Positive	He knows something.	He know something.
Negative	He doesn't know anything.	He don't know nothing.
Double negative	He *doesn't* know *nothing*.	He *don't* know *nothing*.

This array makes it plain that the only difference between the two dialects is in superficial form. When a single negative is found in the deep structure, SE converts *something* to the indefinite *anything*, NNE converts it to *nothing*. When speakers want to signal the presence of two negatives, they do it in the same way. No one would have any difficulty constructing the same table of truth values for both dialects.

English is a rare language in its insistence that the negative particle be incorporated in the first indefinite only. Russian, Spanish, French and Hungarian show the same negative concord as nonstandard English, and they are surely not illogical in this. What is termed "logical" in Standard English is of course the conventions which are habitual. The distribution of negative concord in English dialects can be summarized in this way: [21]

---

[21] For the detailed analysis of negative concord in NNE, see Labov, Cohen, Robins and Lewis 1968, section 3.6, and W. Labov, "Negative Attraction and Negative Concord in Four English Dialects," paper given at the 1968 annual meeting of the Linguistic Society of America, New York, December 1968.

(1) In all dialects of English, the negative is attracted to a lone indefinite before the verb: *Nobody knows anything,* not: *Anybody doesn't know anything.*

(2) In some nonstandard white dialects, the negative also combines optionally with all other indefinites: *Nobody knows nothing, He never took none of them.*

(3) In other white nonstandard dialects, the negative may also appear in preverbal position in the same clause: *Nobody doesn't know nothing.*

(4) In nonstandard Negro English, negative concord is obligatory to all indefinites within the clause, and it may even be added to preverbal position in following clauses: *Nobody didn't know he didn't* meaning "Nobody knew he did."

Thus all dialects of English share a categorical rule which attracts the negative to an indefinite subject, and they merely differ in the extent to which the negative particle is also distributed to other indefinites in preverbal position. It would have been impossible for us to arrive at this analysis if we did not know that Negro speakers are using the same underlying logic as everyone else.

Negative concord is more firmly established in Nonstandard Negro English than in other nonstandard dialects. The white nonstandard speaker shows variation in this rule, saying one time *Nobody ever goes there* and the next *Nobody never goes there:* core speakers of the NNE vernacular consistently use the latter form. In the repetition tests which we conducted with adolescent Negro boys,[22] standard forms were regularly repeated back instantly with negative concord. Here, for example, are three trials by two 13-year-old members of the "Thunderbirds."

Model:	Nobody ever sat at any of those desks, anyhow.
Boot-1:	Nobody never sa—No [whitey] never sat at any o' tho' dess, anyhow.
-2:	Nobody never sat at any o' tho' dess, anyhow.
-3:	Nobody [es'] ever sat at no desses, anyhow.

David-1:	Nobody ever sat in-in-in-in- none o'—say it again?
-2:	Nobody never sat in none o' tho' desses anyhow.
-3:	Nobody—aww! Nobody never ex— Dawg!

It can certainly be said that Boot and David fail the test; they have not repeated the sentence back "correctly"—that is, word for word. But have they failed because they could not grasp the meaning of the sentence? The situation is in fact just the opposite: they failed because they perceived only the meaning and not the superficial form. Boot and David are typical of many speakers who do not perceive the surface details of the utterance

---

[22] More complete data on these Memory Tests is given in Labov, Cohen, Robins and Lewis 1968, section 3.9.

so much as the underlying semantic structure, which they unhesitatingly translate into the vernacular form. Thus they have an asymmetrical system:

Perception:	Standard	Nonstandard
Production:	Nonstandard	

This tendency to process the semantic components directly can be seen even more dramatically in responses to sentences with embedded questions:

Model:	I asked Alvin if he knows how to play basketball.
Boot:	I ax Alvin do he know how to play basketball.
Money:	I ax Alvin if—do he know how to play basketball.

Model:	I asked Alvin whether he knows how to play basketball.
Larry F.-1:	I axt Alvin does he know how to play basketball.
-2:	I axt Alvin does he know how to play basketball.

Here the difference between the words used in the model sentence and in the repetition is striking. Again, there is a failure to pass the test. But it is also true that these boys understand the standard sentence, and translate it with extraordinary speed into the NNE form—which is here the regular Southern colloquial form. This form retains the inverted order to signal the underlying meaning of the question, instead of the complementizer *if* or *whether* which standard English uses for this purpose. Thus Boot, Money, and Larry perceive the deep structure of the model sentence:

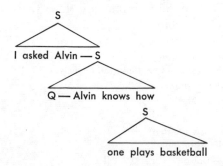

The complementizers *if* or *whether* are not required to express this underlying meaning; they are merely two of the formal options which one dialect selects to signal the embedded question. The colloquial Southern form utilizes a different device—preserving the order of the direct question. To say that this dialect lacks the means for logical expression is to confuse logic with surface detail.

To pass the repetition test, Boot and the others have to learn to listen to surface detail. They do not need a new logic; they need practice in paying attention to the explicit form of an utterance rather than its meaning. Careful attention to surface features is a temporary skill needed for language learning—and neglected thereafter by competent speakers. Nothing more than this is involved in the language training in the Bereiter and Engelman program, or in most methods of "teaching English." There is of course nothing wrong with learning to be explicit—as we have seen, that is one of the main advantages of Standard English at its best—but it is important that we recognize what is actually taking place, and what teachers are in fact trying to do.

I doubt if we can teach people to be logical, though we can teach them to recognize the logic that they use. Piaget has shown us that in middle-class children logic develops much more slowly than grammar, and that we cannot expect four-years-olds to have mastered the conservation of quantity, let alone syllogistic reasoning. Whatever problems working-class children may have in handling logical operations are not to be blamed on the structure of their language. There is nothing in the vernacular which will interfere with the development of logical thought, for the logic of Standard English cannot be distinguished from the logic of any other dialect of English by any test that we can find.

5. WHAT'S WRONG WITH BEING WRONG?

If there is a failure of logic involved here, it is surely in the approach of the verbal deprivation theorists, rather than in the mental abilities of the children concerned. We can isolate six distinct steps in the reasoning which has led to programs such as those of Deutsch, Bereiter and Engelmann:

(1) The lower-class child's verbal response to a formal and threatening situation is used to demonstrate his lack of verbal capacity, or verbal deficit.

(2) This verbal deficit is declared to be a major cause of the lower-class child's poor performance in school.

(3) Since middle-class children do better in school, middle-class speech habits are seen to be necessary for learning.

(4) Class and ethnic differences in grammatical form are equated with differences in the capacity for logical analysis.

(5) Teaching the child to mimic certain formal speech patterns used by middle-class teachers is seen as teaching him to think logically.

(6) Children who learn these formal speech patterns are then said to be thinking logically and it is predicted that they will do much better in reading and arithmetic in the years to follow.

In sections 1–4 of this paper, I have tried to show that these propositions are wrong, concentrating on (1), (4), and (5). Proposition (3) is the primary logical fallacy which illicitly identifies a form of speech as the *cause* of middle-class achievement in school. Proposition (6) is the one which is most easily shown to be wrong in fact, as we will note below.

However, it is not too naïve to ask, "What is wrong with being wrong?" There is no competing educational theory which is being dismantled by this program; and there does not seem to be any great harm in having children repeat *This is not a box* for twenty minutes a day. We have already conceded that NNE children need help in analyzing language into its surface components, and in being more explicit. But there are serious and damaging consequences of the verbal deprivation theory which may be considered under two headings: (1) the theoretical bias, and (2) the consequences of failure.

(1) It is widely recognized that the teacher's attitude towards the child is an important factor in his success or failure. The work of Rosenthal on "self-fulfilling prophecies" shows that the progress of children in the early grades can be dramatically affected by a single random labelling of certain children as "intellectual bloomers." (Rosenthal & Jacobson 1968). When the everyday language of Negro children is stigmatized as "not a language at all" and "not possessing the means for logical thought," the effect of such a labelling is repeated many times during each day of the school year. Every time that a child uses a form of NNE without the copula or with negative concord, he will be labelling himself for the teacher's benefit as "illogical," as a "nonconceptual thinker." Bereiter and Engelmann, Deutsch and Jensen are giving teachers a ready-made, theoretical basis for the prejudice they already feel against the lower-class Negro child and his language. When they hear him say *I don't want none* or *They mine,* they will be hearing through the bias provided by the verbal deprivation theory: not an English dialect different from theirs, but the primitive mentality of the savage mind.

But what if the teacher succeeds in training the child to use the new language consistently? The verbal deprivation theory holds that this will lead to a whole chain of successes in school, and that the child will be drawn away from the vernacular culture into the middle-class world. Undoubtedly this will happen with a few isolated individuals, just as it happens in every school system today, for a few children. But we are concerned not with the few but the many, and for the majority of Negro children the distance between them and the school is bound to widen under this approach.

Proponents of the deficit theory have a strange view of social organization outside of the classroom: they see the attraction of the peer group as a "substitute" for success and gratification normally provided by the school. For example, Whiteman and Deutsch introduce their account of the deprivation hypothesis with an eye-witness account of a child who accidentally dropped his school notebook into a puddle of water and walked away without picking it up.

> A policeman who had been standing nearby walked over to the puddle and stared at the notebook with some degree of disbelief. (Whitman and Deutsch 1968:86-7)

The child's alienation from school is explained as the result of his coming to school without the "verbal, conceptual, attentional and learning skills requisite to school success." The authors see the child as "suffering from feelings of inferiority because he is failing; . . . he withdraws or becomes hostile, finding gratification elsewhere, such as in his peer group."

To view the peer group as a mere substitute for school shows an extraordinary lack of knowledge of adolescent culture. In our studies in South Central Harlem we have seen the reverse situation: the children who are rejected by the peer group are quite likely to succeed in school. In middle-class suburban areas, many children do fail in school because of their personal deficiencies; in ghetto areas, it is the healthy, vigorous popular child with normal intelligence who cannot read and fails all along the line. It is not necessary to document here the influence of the peer group upon the behavior of youth in our society; but we may note that somewhere between the time that children first learn to talk and puberty, their language is restructured to fit the rules used by their peer group. From a linguistic viewpoint, the peer group is certainly a more powerful influence than the family.[23] Less directly, the pressures of peer group activity are also felt within the school. Many children, particularly those who are not doing well in school, show a sudden sharp down turn in the fourth and fifth grades, and children in the ghetto schools are no exception. It is at the same age, at nine or ten years old, that the influence of the vernacular peer group becomes predominant.[24] Instead of dealing with isolated individuals, the school is then dealing with children who are integrated into groups of their own, with rewards and value systems which oppose those of the school. Those who know the sociolinguistic situation cannot doubt that reaction against the Bereiter-Engelmann approach in later years will be even more violent on the part of the students involved, and that the rejection of the school system will be even more categorical.

The essential fallacy of the verbal deprivation theory lies in tracing

---

[23] See for example, Herbert Gans on "The Peer Group Society," *The Urban Villagers* (N.Y.: Free Press, 1962).

[24] For the relationship between age and membership in peer groups, see Peter Wilmott, *Adolescent Boys of East London* (London: Routledge and Kegan Paul, 1966).

the educational failure of the child to his personal deficiencies. At present, these deficiencies are said to be caused by his home environment. It is traditional to explain a child's failure in school by his inadequacy; but when failure reaches such massive proportions, it seems to us necessary to look at the social and cultural obstacles to learning, and the inability of the school to adjust to the social situation. Operation Headstart is designed to repair the child, rather than the school; to the extent that it is based upon this inverted logic, it is bound to fail.

(2) The second area in which the verbal deprivation theory is doing serious harm to our educational system is in the consequences of this failure, and the reaction to it. If Operation Headstart fails, the interpretations which we receive will be from the same educational psychologists who designed this program. The fault will be found not in the data, the theory, nor in the methods used, but rather in the children who have failed to respond to the opportunities offered to them. When Negro children fail to show the significant advance which the deprivation theory predicts, it will be further proof of the profound gulf which separates their mental processes from those of civilized, middle-class mankind.

A sense of the "failure" of Operation Headstart is already in the air. Some prominent figures in the program are reacting to this situation by saying that intervention did not take place early enough. Bettye M. Caldwell notes that:

> . . . the research literature of the last decade dealing with social-class differences has made abundantly clear that all parents are not qualified to provide even the basic essentials of physical and psychological care to their children. (Caldwell 1967:16)

The deficit theory now begins to focus on the "long-standing patterns of parental deficit" which fill the literature. "There is, perhaps unfortunately," writes Caldwell, "no literacy test for motherhood." Failing such eugenic measures, she has proposed "educationally oriented day care for culturally deprived children between six months and three years of age." The children are returned home each evening to "maintain primary emotional relationships with their own families," but during the day they are removed to "hopefully prevent the deceleration in rate of development which seems to occur in many deprived children around the age of two to three years." (Caldwell 1967:17)

There are others who feel that even the best of the intervention programs, such as those of Bereiter and Engelmann, will not help the Negro child no matter when they are applied—that we are faced once again with the "inevitable hypothesis" of the genetic inferiority of the Negro people. Many readers of this paper are undoubtedly familiar with the paper of

Arthur Jensen in the *Harvard Educational Review* (1969) which received early and widespread publicity. Jensen begins with the following quotation from the United States Commission on Civil Rights as evidence of the failure of compensatory education.

> The fact remains, however, that none of the programs appear to have raised significantly the achievement of participating pupils, as a group, within the period evaluated by the Commission. (p. 138)

Jensen believes that the verbal deprivation theorists with whom he had been associated—Deutsch, Whiteman, Katz, Bereiter—have been given every opportunity to prove their case—and have failed. This opinion is part of the argument which leads him to the overall conclusion that "the preponderance of the evidence is . . . less consistent with a strictly environmental hypothesis than with the genetic hypothesis"; that racism, or the belief in the genetic inferiority of Negroes, is a correct view in the light of the present evidence.

Jensen argues that the middle-class white population is differentiated from the working-class white and Negro population in the ability for "cognitive or conceptual learning," which Jensen calls Level II intelligence as against mere "associative learning" or Level I intelligence:

> certain neural structures must also be available for Level II abilities to develop, and these are conceived of as being different from the neural structures underlying Level I. The genetic factors involved in each of these types of ability are presumed to have become differentially distributed in the population as a function of social class, since Level II has been most important for scholastic performance under the traditional methods of instruction.

Thus Jensen found that one group of middle-class children were helped by their concept-forming ability to recall twenty familiar objects that could be classified into four categories: animals, furniture, clothing, or foods. Lower-class Negro children did just as well as middle-class children with a miscellaneous set, but showed no improvement with objects that could be so categorized.

The research of the educational psychologists cited here is presented in formal and objective style, and is widely received as impartial scientific evidence. Jensen's paper has already been reported by Joseph Alsop and William F. Buckley Jr. as "massive, apparently authoritative . . ." (N.Y. Post 3/20/69) It is not my intention to examine these materials in detail; but it is important to realize that we are dealing with special pleading by those who have a strong personal commitment. Jensen is concerned with class differences in cognitive style and verbal learning. His earlier papers incorporated the cultural deprivation theory which he now rejects as a

basic explanation.[25] He classifies the Negro children who fail in school
as "slow-learners" and "mentally-retarded," and urged that we find out
how much their retardation is due to environmental factors and how much
is due to "more basic biological factors." (Jensen 1968:167) His conviction that the problem must be located in the child leads him to accept
and reprint some truly extraordinary data. To support the genetic hypothesis he cites the following table of Heber for the racial distribution of
mental retardation.

Estimated prevalence of children with IQs below 75.

SES	White	Negro
1	0.5	3.1
2	0.8	14.5
3	2.1	22.3
4	3.1	37.8
5	7.8	42.9

This report, that almost half of lower-class Negro children are mentally
retarded, could be accepted only by someone who has no knowledge of
the children or the community. If he had wished to, Jensen could easily
have checked this against the records of any school in any urban ghetto
area. Taking IQ tests at their face value, there is no correspondence between these figures and the communities we know. For example, among
75 boys we worked with in Central Harlem who would fall into Heber's
SES 4 or 5 there were only three with IQs below 75: one spoke very little
English, one could barely see, and the third was emotionally disturbed.
When the second was retested, he scored 91, and the third retested at
87.[26] There are of course hundreds of realistic reports available to Jensen:
he simply selected one which would strengthen his case for the genetic
inferiority of Negro children, and deliberately deleted the information that

[25] In Deutsch, Katz and Jensen 1968, Jensen expounds the verbal deprivation
theory in considerable detail. For example: "During this 'labeling' period . . . some very
important social-class differences may exert their effects on verbal learning. Lower-class
parents engage in relatively little of this naming or 'labeling' play with their children . . .
That words are discrete labels for things seems to be better known by the middle-class
child entering first grade than by the lower-class child. Much of this knowledge is gained
in the parent-child interaction, as when the parent looks at a picture book with the
child . . ." (p. 119).

[26] Heber's studies of 88 Negro mothers in Milwaukee are cited frequently throughout Jensen 1969. The estimates in this table are not given in relation to a particular
Milwaukee sample, but for the general population. Heber's study was specifically designed to cover an area of Milwaukee which was known to contain a large concentration
of retarded children, Negro and white, and he has stated that his findings were "grossly
misinterpreted" by Jensen. (*Milwaukee Sentinel*, June 11, 1969).

this was a study of an area selected in advance because of its high incidence of mental retardation.[27]

In so doing, Jensen was following a standing tradition among the psychologists who developed the deficit hypothesis. The core of Martin Deutsch's environmental explanation of low school performance is the Deprivation Index—a numerical scale based on six dichotomized variables. One variable is "The educational aspirational level of the parent for the child." Most people would agree that a parent who did not care if a child finished high school would be a disadvantageous factor in the child's educational career. In dichotomizing this variable Deutsch was faced with the embarrassing fact that the educational aspiration of Negro parents is in fact very high—higher than for the white population, as he shows in other papers.[28] In order to make the Deprivation Index work, he therefore set the cutting point for the deprived group as "college or less." (Whiteman and Deutsch 1968:100) Thus if a Negro child's father says that he wants his son to go all the way through college, the child will fall into the "deprived" class on this variable. In order to receive the two points given to the "less deprived" on the index, it would be necessary for the child's parent to insist on graduate school or medical school! This decision is never discussed by the author: it simply stands as a *fait accompli* in the tables. This is the type of data manipulation carried on by those who are strongly committed to a particular hypothesis; the selection and presentation of the data are heavily determined by the desire of the writers to make things come out right.

No one can doubt that the inadequacy of Operation Headstart and of the verbal deprivation hypothesis has now become a crucial issue in our society.[29] The controversy which is beginning over Jensen's article will undoubtedly take as given that programs such as Bereiter and Englemann's have tested and measured the verbal capacity of the ghetto child. The cultural sociolinguistic obstacles to this intervention program are not con-

[27] The IQ scores given here are from group rather than individual tests and must therefore not be weighted heavily: the scores are from the Pintner-Cunningham test, usually given in the first grade in New York City schools in the 1950's.

[28] Table 15-1 in Deutsch and associates 1967:312, section C, shows that some degree of college training was desired by 96, 97 and 100 percent of Negro parents in Class Levels I, II and III respectively. The corresponding figures for whites were 79, 95, and 97 percent.

[29] The negative report of the Westinghouse Learning Corporation and Ohio University on Operation Headstart was published in the *New York Times* (on April 13, 1969). This evidence for the failure of the program is widely publicized, and it seems likely that the report's discouraging "conclusions will be used by conservative Congressmen as a weapon against any kind of expenditure for disadvantaged" children, especially Negroes. The two hypotheses mentioned to account for this failure are that the impact of Headstart is lost through poor teaching later on, and more recently, that poor children have been so badly damaged in infancy by their lower-class environment that Headstart cannot make much difference. The third "inevitable" hypothesis of Jensen is not reported here.

sidered; and the argument proceeds upon the data provided by the large, friendly interviewers that we have seen at work in the extracts given above.

6. THE LINGUISTIC VIEW

Linguists are in an excellent position to demonstrate the fallacies of the verbal deprivation theory. All linguists agree that nonstandard dialects are highly structured systems; they do not see these dialects as accumulations of errors caused by the failure of their speakers to master standard English. When linguists hear Negro children saying *He crazy* or *Her my friend* they do not hear a "primitive language." Nor do they believe that the speech of working-class people is merely a form of emotional expression, incapable of expressing logical thought.

All linguists who work with Nonstandard Negro English recognize that it is a separate system, closely related to Standard English, but set apart from the surrounding white dialects by a number of persistent and systematic differences. Differences in analysis by various linguists in recent years are the inevitable products of differing theoretical approaches and perspectives as we explore these dialect patterns by different routes—differences which are rapidly diminishing as we exchange our findings. For example, Stewart differs with me on how deeply the invariant *be* of *She be always messin' around* is integrated into the semantics of the copula system with *am, is, are*, etc. The position and meaning of *have . . . -ed* in NNE is very unclear, and there are a variety of positions on this point. But the grammatical features involved are not the fundamental predicators of the logical system. They are optional ways of contrasting, foregrounding, emphasizing, or deleting elements of the underlying sentence. There are a few semantic features of NNE grammar which may be unique to this system. But the semantic features we are talking about here are items such as "habitual," "general," "intensive." These linguistic markers are essentially *points of view*—different ways of looking at the same events, and they do not determine the truth values of propositions upon which all speakers of English agree.

The great majority of the differences between NNE and SE do not even represent such subtle semantic features as these, but rather extensions and restrictions of certain formal rules, and different choices of redundant elements. For example, SE uses two signals to express the progressive: *be* and *-ing*, while NNE often drops the former. SE signals the third person in the present by the subject noun phrase and by a third singular *-s*; NNE does not have this second redundant feature. On the other hand, NNE uses redundant negative elements in negative concord, uses possessives like *mines*, uses *or either* when SE uses a simple *or*, and so on.

When linguists say that NNE is "system," we mean that it differs from other dialects in regular and rule-governed ways, so that it has equivalent ways of expressing the same logical content. When we say that it is a "separate" sub-system, we mean that there are compensating sets of rules which combine in different ways to preserve the distinctions found in other dialects. Thus as noted above NNE does not use the *if* or *whether* complementizer in embedded questions, but the meaning is preserved by the formal device of reversing the order of subject and auxiliary.

Linguists therefore speak with a single voice in condemning Bereiter's view that the vernacular can be disregarded. I have exchanged views on this matter with all of the participants in the Round Table, and their response shows complete agreement in rejecting the verbal deprivation theory and its misapprehension of the nature of language. The other papers in this series will testify to the strength of the linguistic view in this area. It was William Stewart who first pointed out that Negro English should be studied as a coherent system; and in this all of us follow his lead. Dialectologists like Raven McDavid, Albert Marckwardt, and Roger Shuy have been working for years against the notion that vernacular dialects are inferior and illogical means of communication; and their views are well represented here. As the overwhelming testimony of this conference shows, linguists agree that teachers must know as much as possible about Nonstandard Negro English as a communicative system.

The exact nature and relative importance of the structural differences between NNE and SE are not in question here. It is agreed that the teacher must approach the teaching of the standard through a knowledge of the child's own system. The methods used in "teaching English as a foreign language" are invoked, not to declare that NNE is a foreign language, but to underline the importance of studying the native dialect as a coherent system for communication. This is, in fact, the method that should be applied in any English class.

Linguists are also in an excellent position to assess Jensen's claim that the middle-class white population is superior to the working-class and Negro populations in the distribution of "Level II" or "conceptual" intelligence. The notion that large numbers of children have no capacity for conceptual thinking would inevitably mean that they speak a primitive language, for even the simplest linguistic rules we discussed above involve conceptual operations more complex than those used in the experiment cited by Jensen. Let us consider what is involved in the use of the general English rule that incorporates the negative with the first indefinite. To learn and use this rule, one must first identify the class of indefinites involved: *any, one, ever*, which are formally quite diverse. How is this done? These indefinites share a number of common properties which can be expressed as the concepts "indefinite," "hypothetical," and "nonpartitive."

One might argue that these indefinites are learned as a simple list by "association" learning. But this is only one of the many syntactic rules involving indefinites—rules known to every speaker of English, which could not be learned except by an understanding of their common, abstract properties. For example, everyone "knows" unconsciously that *anyone* cannot be used with preterite verbs or progressives. One does not say, *Anyone went to the party* or *Anyone is going to the party.* The rule which operates here is sensitive to the property [+hypothetical] of the indefinites. Whenever the proposition is not inconsistent with this feature, *anyone* can be used. Everyone "knows" therefore that one can say *Anyone who was anyone went to the party,* or *If anyone went to the party . . .* or *Before anyone went to the party . . .* There is another property of *anyone* which is grasped unconsciously by all native speakers of English: it is [+distributive]. Thus if we need one more man for a game of bridge or basketball, and there is a crowd outside, we ask, *Do any of you want to play?* not *Do some of you want to play?* In both cases, we are considering a plurality, but with *any* we consider them one at a time, or distributively.

What are we then to make of Jensen's contention that Level I thinkers cannot make use of the concept "animal" to group together a miscellaneous set of toy animals? It is one thing to say that someone is not in the habit of using a certain skill. But to say that his failure to use it is genetically determined implies dramatic consequences for other forms of behavior, which are not found in experience; the knowledge of what people must do in order to learn language makes Jensen's theories seem more and more distant from the realities of human behavior. Like Bereiter and Englemann, Jensen is handicapped by his ignorance of the most basic facts about human language and the people who speak it.

There is no reason to believe that any nonstandard vernacular is in itself an obstacle to learning. The chief problem is ignorance of language on the part of all concerned. Our job as linguists is to remedy this ignorance: Bereiter and Englemann want to reinforce it and justify it. Teachers are now being told to ignore the language of Negro children as unworthy of attention and useless for learning. They are being taught to hear every natural utterance of the child as evidence of his mental inferiority. As linguists we are unanimous in condemning this view as bad observation, bad theory, and bad practice.

That educational psychology should be strongly influenced by a theory so false to the facts of language is unfortunate; but that children should be the victims of this ignorance is intolerable. It may seem that the fallacies of the verbal deprivation theory are so obvious that they are hardly worth exposing; I have tried to show that it is an important job for us to undertake. If linguists can contribute some of their available knowledge and energy towards this end, we will have done a great deal to justify the support that society has given to basic research in our field.

REFERENCES

BEREITER, CARL et al. 1966. "An Academically Oriented Pre-School for Culturally Deprived Children." In Fred M. Hechinger (ed.) *Pre-School Education Today* (New York: Doubleday), pp. 105–37.

——— and SIEGFRIED ENGELMANN. 1966. *Teaching Disadvantaged Children in the Preschool* (Englewood Cliffs, N.J.: Prentice-Hall).

CALDWELL, BETTYE M. 1967. "What is the Optimal Learning Environment for the Young Child?" *American Journal of Orthopsychiatry*, vol. XXXVII, no. 1, pp. 8–21.

CHOMSKY, NOAM. 1965. *Aspects of the Theory of Syntax* (Cambridge, Mass.: M.I.T. Press).

DEUTSCH, MARTIN and Associates. 1967. *The Disadvantaged Child* (New York, Basic Books).

———, IRWIN KATZ and ARTHUR R. JENSEN (eds.). 1968. *Social Class, Race, and Psychological Development* (New York: Holt).

JENSEN, ARTHUR. 1968. "Social Class and Verbal Learning." In Deutsch, Katz, and Jensen 1968.

———. 1969. "How Much Can We Boost IQ and Scholastic Achievement?" *Harvard Educational Review*, vol. 39, no. 1.

LABOV, WILLIAM. 1967. "Some Sources of Reading Problems for Negro Speakers of Non-Standard English." In A. Frazier (ed.), *New Directions in Elementary English* (Champaign, Ill.: National Council of Teachers of English), pp. 140–67. Reprinted in Joan C. Baratz and Roger W. Shuy, 1969. *Teaching Black Children to Read* (Washington, D.C.: Center for Applied Linguistics), pp. 29–67.

———, PAUL COHEN and CLARENCE ROBINS. 1965. "A Preliminary Study of the Structure of English Used by Negro and Puerto Rican Speakers in New York City." Final Report, Cooperative Research Project No. 3091 (Office of Education, Washington, D.C.).

———, PAUL COHEN, CLARENCE ROBINS and JOHN LEWIS. 1968. "A Study of the Nonstandard English of Negro and Puerto Rican Speakers in New York City." Final Report, Cooperative Research Project No. 3288 (Office of Education, Washington, D.C.), vol. I and vol. II.

———, and CLARENCE ROBINS. 1969. "A Note on the Relation of Reading Failure to Peer-Group Status in Urban Ghettos." *The Teachers College Record*, volume 70, number 5.

ROSENTHAL, ROBERT and LENORE JACOBSON. 1968. "Self-Fulfilling Prophecies in the Classroom: Teachers' Expectations as Unintended Determinants of Pupils' Intellectual Competence." In Deutsch, Katz and Jensen 1968.

WHITEMAN, MARTIN and MARTIN DEUTSCH. "Social Disadvantage as Related to Intellective and Language Development." In Deutsch, Katz and Jensen 1968.

ON THE USE OF NEGRO DIALECT IN
THE TEACHING OF READING

William A. Stewart

Bilingual education programs in the United States and elsewhere have shown that students of a non-English background often make more rapid progress in reading English if they are taught to read their native language first. Citing a Swedish precedent, as well as his own experience, Stewart here proposes that the same approach may prove effective with students whose native dialect differs markedly from that usually taught in school. He rejects respelling words to approximate the pronunciation of the student (this would require different spellings for each dialect and would increase the difficulties of word-recognition), but proposes a graduated set of reading materials which would slowly, and with coordinated oral practice, move the child from the nonstandard form of his own dialect to the standard forms of the school dialect. Perhaps the best way to develop such materials, and to make them maximally motivational, would be to use the "experience chart" approach of writing out accounts dictated by students, and editing these through controlled steps gradually approximating standard forms.

In at least one area—that of language—there has been a growing awareness of the historical and functional legitimacy of Negro deviations from white behavioral norms. Long regarded by the public in general and educators in particular as the result of carelessness, laziness, ignorance, or stupidity, the nonstandard speech patterns of American Negroes are now coming to be recognized as perfectly normal dialect forms which are just as much the product of systematic (though formally unspecified) linguistic rules as are the speech patterns of whites. That the Negro speech of a given region and social class may differ from the white speech of even the same region and a comparable social class is now understood to be the

From *Teaching Black Children to Read*, Joan C. Baratz and Roger Shuy, eds. (Washington, D.C.: Center for Applied Linguistics, 1969). Reprinted by permission of the Center for Applied Linguistics.

result, not of physiological or mental differences between Negroes and whites, but rather the interrelationship between language history and American social structure. For, if early written samples of North American slave speech are at all reliable, it would seem that the unique characteristics of present-day Negro dialects derive, at least in part, from former pidgin and creole stages. And this would also explain why the most nonstandard varieties of Negro dialect are structurally much more deviant from Standard English than are the most nonstandard dialects of native American whites.

Once this is understood, it should become apparent that language differences, as opposed to language deficits, may well account for most of the chronic difficulty which so many lower-class Negro children have with Standard English in the classroom and, later, on the job. For, wherever the structure of Standard English differs from that of their own nonstandard dialect, the "interference" of the familiar pattern in the production of the unfamiliar pattern may occur. This is, in fact, exactly what happens when a Spanish-speaking child produces a Spanish-like English utterance. Thus, the language-learning problems of a Negro-dialect speaker who is trying to acquire Standard English are, in many ways, more like those of, say, a Spanish speaker who is trying to acquire English than they are like those of a middle-class, English-speaking child. For the first two, the task is one of learning structurally different functional equivalents of patterns which they already know; for the third, the task is merely one of learning additional and compatible patterns to the ones already known. In other words, the learning of Standard English by speakers of Negro dialect is more like foreign-language learning than it is like first-language learning. For this reason, techniques which have been developed in foreign-language teaching to deal with structural conflicts between different language systems are being found to be much more appropriate for teaching Standard English patterns to Negro-dialect speakers than are the pathology-oriented methods of traditional speech therapy and remedial English. And even though the overall structural difference between Negro dialect of the most nonstandard kind and Standard English of the most formal kind is obviously not as great as between any kind of English and a foreign language like Spanish, this does not necessarily make it easier for the Negro-dialect speaker to acquire an acceptably standard variety of English than for the speaker of Spanish to do so. On the contrary, the subtlety of the structural differences between the two forms of English, masked as they are by the many similarities, may make it almost impossible for the speaker of Negro dialect to tell which patterns are characteristic of nonstandard dialect, and which ones are not. Indeed, this may explain why it is that many immigrant populations have been able to make a more rapid and successful transition from their original foreign language to Standard English than migrant Negroes have from their own nonstandard dialect to Standard English.

Although no adequate study of the role of dialect differences in the reading proficiency of American Negro children has yet been undertaken, a suggestion of what is likely to be the case is available from a somewhat comparable European situation. In a Swedish-dialect context, Tore Öster-berg found that the teaching of basic reading skills in the nonstandard dialect of the school children in a particular district (Piteå) increased proficiency, not only in beginning reading in the nonstandard dialect, but also in later reading of the standard language. In fact, one of Österberg's most dramatic findings was that the experimental group (which began with nonstandard dialect materials and then changed to standard Swedish materials) overtook the control group (which used standard Swedish materials from the very beginning) in reading proficiency in standard Swedish—I repeat, standard Swedish—even though the additional steps of the bidialectal approach meant that the students in the experimental group spent less total time with the standard language.

But even before I became aware of the Österberg study, with its obvious implications for American education, the suitability of the bidialectal approach to the reading problems of inner-city Negro children was suggested to me by a fortuitous experience. In the latter part of 1965, I had decided to do a Negro dialect translation of Clement Clarke Moore's famous Christmas poem "A Visit from St. Nicholas" (more widely known as "The Night Before Christmas") for Christmas greetings from the Urban Language Study of the Center for Applied Linguistics. In order to highlight the grammatical differences between nonstandard Negro dialect and Standard English, I decided to retain Standard-English word spellings in the nonstandard version wherever possible. Thus, I wrote *it's, the, night, before,* and *Christmas,* even though a child might be apt to pronounce /is/, /də/, /nay/, /bifów/, and /kismis/. One modification I made in this rule was that, when the nonstandard pronunciation of a particular Negro-dialect word was better represented by the spelling of some Standard-English word other than its direct functional equivalent, that spelling was used. Thus the Negro-dialect verb /fuw/, though equivalent to *fill* in Standard English, was spelled *full* in the poem. In addition, the form and sequencing of the events in Moore's original version were recast to make the nonstandard version more in keeping with Negro discourse style and inner-city cultural reality. Some idea of what the result of this translation process looked like can be gotten from the first few lines, which went:

> It's the night before Christmas, and here in our house,
> It ain't nothing moving, not even no mouse.
> There go we-all stockings, hanging high up off the floor,
> So Santa Claus can full them up, if he walk in through our door.

For those who are not entirely familiar with this kind of dialect, I should probably point out that the Negro-dialect phrase *There go we-all stockings* does not mean "There go our stockings" in Standard English. As often used by Negro children, the idioms *here go* and *there go* serve to point out something (not necessarily in motion) to the listener, and are thus equivalent to Standard English *here is/are* and *there is/are*, or to French *voici* and *voilà*.

One evening, while I was working at home on the translation of the poem (a draft of which was in my typewriter, with the original version at the side), two inner-city children dropped by for a visit. While I was busy getting some refreshments for them from the refrigerator, Lenora (then about 12 years old) went over to play with the typewriter and found the draft of the nonstandard version of the poem in it. Lenora was one of the "problem readers" of the public schools; she read school texts haltingly, with many mistakes, and with little ability to grasp the meaning of what she read. Yet, when she began to read the nonstandard version of the poem, her voice was steady, her word reading accurate, and her sentence intonation was natural (for her dialect, of course). This unexpected success in reading so surprised Lenora that she began to discuss the experience with her little brother. They decided that there was something different about the text, but were unable to tell exactly what it was. To compare, I then had Lenora read the Standard English version of the poem, which was sitting beside the typewriter. When she did, all the "problem reader" behaviors returned.

Now, it must be remembered that both the nonstandard and standard versions of the poem were written with the same spellings for similar words, e.g., *Christmas* in both. Therefore, it was clear that Lenora was reacting primarily to the difference between a familiar and an unfamiliar type of grammar. For, if she could read Standard-English words without difficulty when they were presented in a nonstandard grammatical framework, then this meant that word-reading or sound-spelling-meaning correspondences were not the problem that they seemed to be when she attempted to read Standard English. It struck me that this unplanned "experiment" (later duplicated with other inner-city children) suggested an entirely different dimension of possible reading problems for inner-city Negro children than those focused on by such methods as i.t.a. and phonics. This other dimension is that of structural interference between the grammatical patterns of the nonstandard dialect which many Negro children speak and the grammatical patterns of the Standard English in which reading materials are invariably written. And, if it has been considered pedagogically useful to adapt beginning reading materials to the word pronunciations of middle-class white children (as has been done in i.t.a. and phonics), then might it not also be useful to adapt beginning reading materials to the sentence patterns of lower-class Negro children?

One argument which might be advanced against the incorporation of nonstandard-dialect patterns into beginning reading materials is that the process ought to be unnecessary; children from whatever language or dialect background ought to be instructed in oral standard English as part of their pre-reading training, and reading materials ought to be written in Standard English from the very start. Neat though this approach may seem, it is simply impossible to carry out in most rural and inner-city schools. For the fact is that these schools are full of functionally illiterate, nonstandard-dialect-speaking children of all grades and ages—many of whom are simply too far along in the curriculum to be told to stop trying to read, go back, and take remedial oral English with the kindergarten children and first-graders. Even if most predominantly Negro schools were to have effective programs for teaching oral standard English to pre-readers (and most still do not), the migratory and working patterns of rural children and the high geographic mobility of inner-city children would make it difficult for such schools to insure that the children going into beginning reading would all have already had instruction in oral Standard English. Consequently, the recognition of nonstandard dialect in reading instruction will probably be necessary for at least some pupils at all grade levels in such schools. And this is as it should be. Special oral-language programs for Negro-dialect speakers and special reading instruction for Negro-dialect speakers ought, after all, to be complementary activities, not rival ones.

Another argument which is very likely to be advanced against the idea of incorporating Negro-dialect grammatical patterns into beginning reading materials is that the features of Negro dialect which seem to interfere the most with the effective oral reading of Standard English do not seem to be grammatical ones; rather, they seem to be phonological ones (i.e. differences in pronunciation). This is certainly the impression of many reading specialists, and it agrees substantially with the view which most speech therapists and many English teachers have of Negro dialect as more a matter of deviant "speech" (i.e. pronunciation) than of different "language" (i.e. grammar).

It is perhaps inevitable that those who take this view will see the special reading problems of lower-class Negro school children primarily as a difficulty in word or sentence recognition caused by the frequent lack of correspondence between Negro-dialect pronunciations and Standard-English spellings (which, of course, represent Standard-English pronunciations much more closely). That is, the Negro child is seen as having to cope primarily with such problems as learning that there is a correspondence between the spelling and meaning of *pen* and *pin* in written standard English, even though the word for the thing one writes with and the word for the thing one sticks with are both pronounced [pɪn] (or, alternatively, [pɛn] in Negro dialect. And the reading teacher is seen as having to cope primarily with such problems as deciding, when a Negro child reads aloud /ges/ for *guest*, whether he has understood the meaning of the written word and merely given it its Negro-dialect pronunciation, or whether he has misread the word as *guess*.

Now, it is undoubtedly true that sound-spelling-meaning correspondences between spoken Negro dialect and written Standard English are less regular (or, at least, less obviously regular) than between spoken Standard English and written Standard English. Still, they are by no means neat in even the latter case. For example, speakers of Standard English must learn to deal with the correlation to different meanings of the written distinction between homophonic *son* and *sun*, just as speakers of Negro dialect (or, indeed, of southern varieties of Standard English) must learn to deal with what for them are homophonic *pen* and *pin*. And, of course, spellings like *of* and *island* are not representative of the pronunciation either of Negro dialect or Standard English. Yet, most speakers of Standard English do not seem to be hindered very much by such sound-spelling-meaning irregularities when they are learning to read—a fact which would suggest that absolute parallelism between phonology and orthography is not really a prerequisite to literacy in English. Indeed, even relatively inexperienced readers seem to be able to cope with a fair amount of sound-spelling irregularity, provided that they are familiar with the spoken forms of the words and are able to get sufficient cues for associating the written and spoken forms from the lexical and syntactic context.

If, as the foregoing observations seem to indicate, the adverse effects of purely phonological differences between Negro dialect and Standard English on reading comprehension are but slight, then the case for structural interference in a Negro-dialect speaker's attempts to read Standard English will have to be made on other linguistic grounds. A substantial number of lexical differences between the two kinds of English would serve this purpose, but one of the striking features of the relationship between urban Negro dialect and Standard English is that it involves very little lexical divergence. Consequently, if there really is significant dialect interference in the reading process, it can be expected to derive from grammatical differences between Negro dialect and Standard English, and particularly from ones which are more or less independent of non-significant (for reading) phonological differences.

There are actually many grammatical differences between Negro dialect and Standard English which, whether caused by different transformations or by different grammatical processes of a "deeper" type, are nevertheless clearly independent of regular phonological differences between the two kinds of English. Examples of transformationally derived grammatical differences are encountered in the use of question type inversion in Negro-dialect verb phrases where Standard English uses *if* (meaning "whether") with no inversion, e.g. *See can he go* for *See if he can go*, uninverted verb phrases after certain question words in Negro dialect where Standard English requires inversion, e.g. *What it is?* for *What is it?*, and multiple negation in Negro dialect where Standard English has single negation, e.g. *He ain't never bought none* for *He hasn't ever bought any* or *He has never bought any*. As with many of the regular phonological differences between Negro dialect and Standard English, the Negro-dialect speaker is usually able to establish correspondences between grammatical differences of this type—provided, of course, that the context is clear and that such constructions do not pile up in rapid succession. But even so, misinterpretation is quite possible when a Standard-English construction happens to resemble in form some Negro-dialect construction other than the one to which it is functionally equivalent. For example, a seemingly unambiguous Standard-English sentence like *His eye's open* may be misinterpreted by a Negro-dialect speaker as meaning "His eyes are open," simply because it resembles in form the Negro dialect sentence *His eyes open* (with that meaning) more than it does *His eye open* (the Negro-dialect equivalent of the original Standard-English sentence). And this, incidentally, is yet another example of a case in which *viva-voce* performance would be of no help to the reading teacher in deciding whether there was a misinterpretation or not, since the pupil's pronunciation of Standard English *His eye's open* and Negro dialect *His eyes open* would be identical.

Intelligibility problems of a different order—at once more subtle and more ingrained—are posed by grammatical differences between Negro dialect and Standard English which originate deeper in the respective grammars than do differences of the preceding type. Because they are not likely to involve simple one-to-one correlations, and because they may not even use the same perceptual information about the real world, these deeper grammatical differences are apt to lie beyond the scope of the intuitive methods by which speakers of one dialect normally determine structural equivalences between their own and some other dialects. It is this type of grammatical difference which underlies the dissimilar use of *be* in Negro dialect and Standard English. In Negro dialect, *be* is used with adjectives and the *-in'* (= *-ing*) form of verbs to indicate an extended or repeated state or action, e.g. *He be busy, He be workin'*. On the other hand, the absence of this *be* usually indicates that the state or action is immediate or momentary, e.g. *He busy, He workin'*. The auxiliary or tag for *be* in Negro dialect is *do*, e.g. *Do he be busy?* as a question form of *He be busy*, while the explicit form used in the non-*be* construction is usually *is*, e.g. *Is he busy?* as a question form of *He busy*. This means, of course, that *be* and *is* are entirely different morphemes in Negro dialect. But in Standard English, there is no such grammatical distinction, and *be* and *is* are merely inflectional variants of one and the same verb. Thus, for the two grammatical constructions of Negro dialect, Standard English has but one grammatical equivalent, e.g. *He is busy, He is working*, in which the immediacy or duration of the state or action is left entirely unspecified.

Thus far, this difference between Negro dialect and Standard English in the grammatical recognition or not of a contrast between extended or repeated states and actions and immediate or momentary ones may seem to have little significance for reading comprehension, since the Negro-dialect speaker is obviously not going to encounter his own *He busy* and

He be busy constructions (which mark the distinction) in a Standard-English text. In form, the closest Standard-English constructions to these will be the *He is busy* type, which is functionally equivalent to both of the Negro-dialect constructions, and the *He will be busy* type, which represents a future state or action only. Now, if this were indeed the extent of the matter, it would certainly be reasonable to assume that the differences in form between the Standard-English and Negro-dialect constructions would alert the average Negro-dialect speaker to a possible difference in meaning between them. But one more bit of information is necessary to a full understanding of just how much such a seemingly minor grammatical difference can affect intelligibility. This is that exposure to the Standard-English use of present-tense forms of the copula (i.e. *am, is, are*) has made many speakers of nonstandard Negro dialect—even very young ones—aware that their own *He busy* and *He be busy* types of construction are not "proper" in form. Consequently, they often attempt to "correct" these on their own by adding one or another of the Standard-English auxilaries to their *He busy* type of construction, and by changing the *be* of their *He be busy* type of construction into *bees* (on analogy with correcting *he work* to *he works*) and, when they realize that even this is nonstandard, into *will be*. Now, even assuming that those who do this will always end up with forms like *He is busy* (with appropriate person accord of the auxiliary throughout) for *He busy*, and *He will be busy* for *He be busy*, it is nevertheless the case that these phonologically and morphologically "standard" forms are still nonstandard Negro dialect in their grammar and meaning. This means that Negro-dialect speakers—even ones who appear to know "correct" grammar—are apt to misread Standard English *He is busy* constructions as necessarily immediacy (which they do not), and *He will be busy* constructions as possibly indicating repetition or long duration (which they do not) as well as futurity.

Taken altogether, the grammatical differences between Negro dialect and Standard English are probably extensive enough to cause reading-comprehension problems. Even in cases where the differences do not actually obscure the meaning of a sentence or passage, they can be distracting to a young Negro-dialect speaker who is trying to learn to read, and who can find but few familiar syntactic patterns to aid him in word identification. It is true that this child must eventually be taught to read Standard-English sentence patterns, but it is open to question whether he should be made to cope with the task of deciphering unfamiliar syntactic structures at the very same time that he is expected to develop effective word-reading skills. One simple way to avoid placing a double learning load on the lower-class Negro child who is learning to read would be to start with sentence patterns which are familiar to him—ones from his own dialect—and then move to unfamiliar ones from Standard English once he has mastered the necessary word-reading skills. In that way, reading ability could actually become an aid to the learning of Standard English.

A third objection which might well be raised to the use of Negro dialect in beginning reading materials is that it would reinforce the use by lower-class Negro children of their nonstandard dialect, and thereby serve as a barrier to their eventual acquisition of Standard English. But such a claim would be predicated on two false assumptions about language learning and language use. The first false assumption is that the use of language patterns always constitutes reinforcement of those patterns in the user. Although this is a popular belief among educators, it is obviously untrue for native speakers of a language (or a particular variety of a language) who are using familiar patterns of it. If a Standard-English speaker is asked to repeat (or read) a sentence like *Charles and Michael are out playing,* he will not know either the sentence pattern or the individual words any better when he is through than before he started. The reason is, of course, that he already knows these aspects of his language as well as he could possibly learn them. If this is so, then why is it assumed that, if a Negro-dialect speaker is allowed to say (or asked to read) a sentence like *Charles an' Michael, dey out playin,* he will thereby become more addicted to Negro dialect? And what sort of magic is a classroom supposed to have, that the occasional use of nonstandard pronunciations or sentence patterns within its confines is regarded as pregnant with potential effect, while the almost exclusive use of those same pronunciations and sentence patterns outside the classroom is regarded as of little consequence? The second false assumption underlying this particular argument is that the knowledge and use of one language or dialect precludes the learning and use of another language or dialect—or, put more simply, that people's capacity for learning and using different linguistic systems is severely limited. This is a particularly common belief in America, where very few educators have had any exposure to multilingualism or bidialectalism. But Europeans would be likely to be astonished or amused by such an assertion, since most of them accept it as a matter of course that one will use a nonstandard dialect in the village home and a standardized variety of the same language (or even a different language) in the city office. The fact is that, in America too, there is no linguistic reason why an individual ought not to be able to produce sentences like *Charles an' Michael, dey out playin'* in one situation, and *Charles and Michael are out playing* in another. Poor language teaching, rather than the prior knowledge of another language or dialect, is the principal cause of unsuccessful bilingualism or bidialectalism.

Instead of being ignored or made the target of an eradication program, Negro dialect should actually be used as a basis for teaching oral and written Standard English. If Negro dialect is used to teach initial word-reading skills to Negro-dialect speakers, then those word-reading skills can be made the constant in terms of which Standard-English grammatical patterns can be taught through reading and writing. One form which this type of language teaching could take would be to make the transition from Negro dialect to Standard English in a series of stages, each of which would concentrate on a limited set of linguistic differences. An exciting aspect of this approach is that oral language teaching could be combined with the reading program to any degree felt useful. Take, for example, the Negro-dialect sentence just cited, and its Standard-English counterpart. The former would become the initial stage in such a program, and the latter would be the ultimate goal. In this illustration, I will write the Negro-dialect sentence in Standard-English spelling in order to simplify the transition process.

Stage 1

Charles and Michael, they out playing.

Grammatically, sentences at this stage will be pure nonstandard Negro dialect. The vocabulary, also, will be controlled so that no words which are unfamiliar to a Negro-dialect-speaking child will appear. Thus, all linguistic aspects of text will be familiar to the beginning reader, and his full attention can be focused on learning to read the vocabulary. At this stage, no attempt should be made to teach Standard-English pronunciations of the words, since the sentence in which they appear is not Standard English.

Stage 2

Charles and Michael, they are out playing.

At this stage, the most important grammatical features of Standard English are introduced. In the example, there is one such feature—the copula. Apart from that, the vocabulary is held constant. Oral-language drills could profitably be used to teach person accord of the copula (*am, is, are*), and some Standard-English pronunciations of the basic vocabulary might be taught.

Stage 3

Charles and Michael are out playing.

Grammatically, the sentences at this stage are brought into full conformity with Standard English by making the remaining grammatical stylistic adjustments. In the example, the "double subject" of the nonstandard form is eliminated. Oral-language drills could be used to teach this, and additional Standard-English pronunciations of the basic vocabulary could be taught.

Although the complete transition from Negro-dialect grammar to Standard-English grammar was effected in three stages in the foregoing example, more stages would probably be required in a real program of this type. The actual programming of these stages would have to be carried out by competent linguists, but, once done, the resulting materials ought to be usable in regular remedial-reading classes.

These materials will be accepted by the children if they are authentic —that is, if the written language of the materials represents accurately their own spoken language. For the linguist, this authenticity will only come about through careful attention to details of grammar, style, and vocabulary. And the materials will be accepted by Negro parents and other adults when they see that Negro children learn to read Standard English by means of them, where they did not by means of traditional reading materials. For the linguist, the ability of the materials to do this will require meticulous planning of the structural changes which are to be dealt with in each of the successive stages from "pure" nonstandard dialect to "pure" Standard English. Finally, if it can be argued, as it has been in this paper, that beginning reading materials in Standard English are not suitable for children who only speak nonstandard Negro dialect, then it should be equally apparent that beginning reading materials in nonstandard Negro dialect will not be suitable for children who only speak Standard English. In particular, one should guard against the danger of assuming that Negro-dialect materials will be appropriate for *all* Negro school children. Earlier, it was pointed out that most middle-class Negroes do not (and, indeed, many cannot) speak nonstandard Negro dialect. Although this fact cannot serve as an argument that Negro dialect is rare or non-existent, it certainly is an indication that not *all* Negroes speak Negro dialect. Even among lower-class Negroes, some individuals (particularly females) will be found who, either due to a special life history or because of strong upward mobility, have acquired and use Standard English. And, of course, there will be individuals who speak something between Standard English and the type of nonstandard dialect I have characterized as "pure" Negro dialect. This does not make Negro-dialect materials any the less useful for children who actually speak Negro dialect; it merely means that any Negro-dialect reading program will have to have an instrument for determining exactly who does, and who doesn't, speak Negro dialect in the first place. And if such an instrument could actually measure a child's initial language on a Negro-dialect-to-Standard-English continuum, then it would also be useful for measuring that child's program in Standard English as a result of the staging process of the materials. Although still in an embryonic state, the bidialectal oral-language proficiency test designed by Joan C. Baratz and myself is potentially ideal for this purpose. Even children whose initial language is shown by such a test to be somewhere in between "pure" Negro dialect and Standard English can be worked into such a program if, as ought to be the case, the language of its intermediate stages is made to resemble the intermediate dialects in a Negro speech community. Thus, a particular child might be started with, say, Stage Two materials rather than Stage One materials.

What I have had to say about Negro dialect in the course of this paper should make it obvious that it is a highly complex yet well-formed and systematic code—just like any other language. To speak it well, or to use it effectively in pedagogical materials, requires a profound knowledge of its many phonological and grammatical rules, of subtle lexical differences (e.g., that *bright* means "light-skinned" in Negro dialect, while it means "clever" in Standard English), and of countless stylistic and idiomatic details (e.g., that *sisters and brothers* is the "pure" Negro-dialect form, while *brothers and sisters* is an importation from Standard English). This means that attempts to use or to write Negro dialect should not be made by unqualified persons, Black or white, any more than attempts to use or write, say, French should be. For one thing, the inner-city slang or "hip talk" of teenagers and young adults should not be confused with Negro dialect in the linguistic sense, no matter how ethnically-correlated many of the slang terms may be. They are simply deliberate vocabulary substitutions, and have nothing directly to do with dialect grammar or phonology. Nor is the "stage dialect" of Negro bit-players on radio, television, or the screen necessarily close to real Negro dialect. Often, in order to insure its being understood by a wide audience, a stage Negro dialect may be created which is little more than Standard English with a slightly ethnicized or Southernized pronunciation, reinforced by the insertion of such general nonstandardisms as *ain't* and the double negative, and perhaps a sprinkling of Southern or inner-city Negro lexical usages like *honey child* or *man*. And, although literary renditions of plantation Negro dialect (such as appears in Joel Chandler Harris' *Uncle Remus, His Songs and His Sayings*) may represent an older form of Negro dialect rather accurately, and thus share many structural characteristics with present-day Negro dialect, there are still too many intervening variables (nineteenth-century usage vs. twentieth-century usage, adult speech vs. child speech, rural forms vs. urban forms, story-telling style vs. colloquial style, etc.) for that kind of Negro dialect to be directly useful for the purposes I have been suggesting. If used well by educators, living Negro dialect can serve as a bridge between the personal experiences of the Negro child and his acquisition of mainstream language skills. If used poorly, however, it will

only add to the confusion of pupil and teacher alike. The language of the
Negro child can be made an effective educational tool, but it must be
treated with respect and understanding.

SOME SOURCES OF READING PROBLEMS
FOR NEGRO SPEAKERS OF NONSTANDARD
ENGLISH

William Labov

*The failure of the schools, after 12 years of instruction, to teach
speakers of nonstandard dialects to use Standard English forms is
attributed by Labov to ignorance on the part of most teachers of
the grammatical and phonological rules governing the speech of
their students. In this article, he discusses some of the major phonological characteristics of Negro speakers in New York City, and
indicates how these characteristics affect the use and perception of
certain grammatical suffixes.*

*In common with Southern dialects, Negro speech usually "drops"
r and l after vowels (in most instances actually lengthening the
vowel or replacing the consonant with an uh-like or w-like glide),
though perhaps to a greater extent than in most white Southern
speech. In addition, there is a pervasive tendency to simplify final
consonant clusters and to reduce unstressed syllables. Taken together, these rules produce such homonyms as sore-saw; hold-hole-
hoe; Paris-pass; road-row; and in extreme cases, bit-bid-big. Thus in
learning to read and spell, the Negro child may face a much larger
number of homonyms whose spelling he must memorize (as everyone must memorize see and sea, or right and write). The teacher
must recognize this and be prepared to take it into account in her
teaching.*

*These phonological rules profoundly affect various grammatical
suffixes and contractions, perhaps accounting for the frequent omis-*

From *New Directions in Elementary English*, Alexander Frazier, ed. (Champaign,
Illinois: National Council of Teachers of English, 1967). Reprinted by permission of the
National Council of Teachers of English.

sion of the contracted future 'll, the contracted is in he's, the pos-
sessive -s, the third person singular -s, and the past tense suffix.
However, tests show that students omit these much more often than
consonants which belong to a word, indicating that the omission is
in part owing to real grammatical differences between this and other
English dialects (perhaps, as Stewart has suggested, reflecting the
creole origin of Negro speech). Labov concludes with some recom-
mendations for the teacher in dealing with these problems.

It seems natural to look at any educational problem in terms of the particular type of ignorance which is to be overcome. In this discussion, we will be concerned with two opposing and complementary types:

> ignorance of Standard English rules on the part of speakers of Nonstandard English
>
> ignorance of Nonstandard English rules on the part of teachers and text writers

In other words, the fundamental situation that we face is one of reciprocal ignorance, where teacher and student are ignorant of each other's system, and therefore of the rules needed to translate from one system to another.

The consequences of this situation may be outlined in the following way. When the teacher attempts to overcome the first kind of ignorance by precept and example in the classroom, she discovers that the student shows a strong and inexplicable resistance to learning the few simple rules that he needs to know. He is told over and over again, from the early grades to the twelfth, that *-ed* is required for the past participle ending, but he continues to write.

> I have live here twelve years.

and he continues to mix up past and present tense forms in his reading. In our present series of interviews with Harlem youngsters from ten to sixteen years old, we ask them to correct to classroom English such sentences as the following:

> He pick me.
> He don't know nobody.
> He never play no more, man.
> The man from U.N.C.L.E. hate the guys from Thrush.

Words such as *man* and *guys* are frequently corrected, and *ain't* receives a certain amount of attention. But the double negative is seldom noticed, and the absence of the grammatical signals *-s* and *-ed* is rarely detected by children in the fifth, sixth, or seventh grades. There can be little doubt that their ignorance of these few fundamental points of English inflection is connected with the fact that most of them have difficulty in reading sentences at the second-grade level.

There are many reasons for the persistence of this ignorance. Here I will be concerned with the role played by the second type of ignorance: the fact that the child's teacher has no systematic knowledge of the nonstandard forms which oppose and contradict Standard English. Some teachers are reluctant to believe that there are systematic principles in Nonstandard English which differ from those of Standard English. They look upon every deviation from schoolroom English as inherently evil, and they attribute these mistakes to laziness, sloppiness, or the child's natural disposition to be wrong. For these teachers, there is no substantial difference in the teaching of reading and the teaching of geography. The child is simply ignorant of geography; he does not have a well-formed system of nonstandard geography to be analyzed and corrected. From this point of view, teaching English is a question of imposing rules upon chaotic and shapeless speech, filling a vacuum by supplying rules where no rules existed before.

Other teachers are sincerely interested in understanding the language of the children, but their knowledge is fragmentary and ineffective. They feel that the great difficulties in teaching Negro and Puerto Rican children to read are due in part to the systematic contradiction between the rules of language used by the child and the rules used by the teacher. The contribution which I hope to make here is to supply a systematic basis for the study of Nonstandard English of Negro and Puerto Rican children, and some factual information, so that educators and text writers can design their teaching efforts with these other systems in mind.

STRUCTURAL VS. FUNCTIONAL CONFLICTS

We have dealt so far with a series of abilities. Obviously the desire to learn is in some way prior to the act of learning. Our own current research for the Office of Education is concerned with two aspects of the problem:

(a) structural conflicts of Standard and Nonstandard English: interference with learning ability stemming from a mismatch of linguistic structures.

(b) functional conflicts of Standard and Nonstandard English: interference with the desire to learn Standard English stemming from a mismatch in the functions which Standard and Nonstandard English perform in a given culture.

In the discussion that follows, we will be concerned only with the first type of conflict.

Is there a Negro speech pattern? This question has provoked a great deal of discussion in the last few years, much more than it deserves. At many meetings on educational problems of ghetto areas, time which could have been spent in constructive discussion has been devoted to arguing the question as to whether Negro dialect exists. The debates have not been conducted with any large body of factual information in view, but rather in terms of what the speakers wish to be so, or what they fear might follow in the political arena.

For those who have not participated in such debates, it may be difficult to imagine how great are the pressures against the recognition, description, or even mention of Negro speech patterns. For various reasons, many teachers, principals, and civil rights leaders wish to deny that the existence of patterns of Negro speech is a linguistic and social reality in the United States today. The most careful statement of the situation as it actually exists might read as follows: *Many features of pronunciation, grammar, and lexicon are closely associated with Negro speakers—so closely as to identify the great majority of Negro people in the Northern cities by their speech alone.*

The match between this speech pattern and membership in the Negro ethnic group is of course far from complete. Many Negro speakers have none—or almost none—of these features. Many Northern whites, living in close proximity to Negroes, have these features in their own speech. But this overlap does not prevent the features from being identified with Negro speech by most listeners: we are dealing with a stereotype which provides correct identification in the great majority of cases, and therefore with a firm base in social reality. Such stereotypes are the social basis of language perception; this is merely one of many cases where listeners generalize from the variable data to categorical perception in absolute terms. Someone who uses a stigmatized form 20 to 30 percent of the time will be heard as using this form all of the time. It may be socially useful to correct these stereotypes in a certain number of individual cases, so that people learn to limit their generalizations to the precise degree that their experience warrants: but the overall tendency is based upon very regular principles of human behavior, and people will continue to identify as Negro speech the pattern which they hear from the great majority of the Negro people that they meet.

In the South, the overlap is much greater. There is good reason to think that the positive features of the Negro speech pattern all have their origin in dialects spoken by both Negroes and whites in some parts of the South. Historically speaking, the Negro speech pattern that we are dealing with in Northern cities is a regional speech pattern. We might stop speaking of Negro speech, and begin using the term "Southern regional speech," if that would make the political and social situation more manageable. But if we do so, we must not deceive ourselves and come to believe that this is an accurate description of the correct situation.

The existence of a Negro speech pattern must not be confused of course with the myth of a biologically, racially, exclusively Negro speech. The idea that dialect differences are due to some form of laziness or carelessness must be rejected with equal firmness. Anyone who continues to endorse such myths can be refuted easily by such subjective reaction tests as the Family Background test which we are using in our current research in Harlem. Sizable extracts from the speech of fourteen individuals are played in sequence for listeners who are asked to identify the family backgrounds of each. So far, we find no one who can even come close to a correct identification of Negro and white speakers. This result does not contradict the statement that there exists a socially based Negro speech pattern: it supports everything that I have said above on this point. The voices heard on the test are the exceptional cases: Negroes raised without any Negro friends in solidly white areas; whites raised in areas dominated by Negro cultural values; white Southerners in Gullah-speaking territory; Negroes from small Northern communities untouched by recent migrations; college-educated Negroes who reject the Northern ghetto and the South alike. The speech of these individuals does not identify them as Negro or white because they do not use the speech patterns which are characteristically Negro or white for Northern listeners. The identifications made by these listeners, often in violation of actual ethnic membership categories, show that they respond to Negro speech patterns as a social reality.

RELEVANT PATTERNS OF NEGRO SPEECH

One approach to the study of Nonstandard Negro speech is to attempt a complete description of this form of language without direct reference to Standard English. This approach can be quite revealing, and can save us from many pitfalls in the easy identification of forms that are only apparently similar. But as an overall plan, it is not realistic. We are far from achieving a complete description of Standard English, to begin with; the differences between nonstandard Negro speech and Standard English are slight compared to their similarities; and finally, some of these differences are far more relevant to reading problems than others. Let us therefore consider some of the most relevant patterns of Negro speech from the point of view of reading problems.

The simplest way to organize this information seems to be under the headings of the important rules of the sound system which are affected. By using lists of homonyms as examples, it will be possible to avoid a great deal of phonetic notation, and to stay with the essential linguistic facts. In many cases, the actual phonetic form is irrelevant: it is the presence or absence of a distinction which is relevant.

. . . The most important are those in which large-scale phonological differences coincide with important grammatical differences. The result of this coincidence is the existence of a large number of homonyms in the speech of Negro children which are different from the set of homonyms in the speech system used by the teacher. If the teacher knows about this different set of homonyms, no serious problems in the teaching of reading need occur; but if the teacher does not know, there are bound to be difficulties. . . . A linguistic orientation will not supply teachers with a battery of phonetic symbols, but rather encourage them to observe what words can or cannot be distinguished by the children they are teaching.

SOME PHONOLOGICAL VARIABLES AND THEIR GRAMMATICAL CONSEQUENCES

1. *r-lessness.* There are three major dialect areas in the Eastern United States where the *r* of spelling is not pronounced as a consonant before other consonants or at the ends of words: Eastern New England, New York City, and the South (Upper and Lower). Thus speakers from Boston, New York, Richmond, Charleston, or Atlanta will show only a lengthened vowel in *car, guard, for,* etc., and usually an obscure centering glide [schwa] in place of *r* in *fear, feared, care, cared, moor, moored, bore, bored,* etc. This is what we mean by *r*-less pronunciation. Most of these areas have been strongly influenced in recent years by the *r*-pronouncing pattern which is predominant in broadcasting, so that educated speakers, especially young people, will show a mixed pattern in their careful speech. When the original *r*-less pattern is preserved, we can obtain such homonyms as the following:

guard	= god		par	= pa
nor	= gnaw		fort	= fought
sore	= saw		court	= caught

and we find that *yeah* can rhyme with *fair, idea* with *fear.*

Negro speakers show an even higher degree of *r*-lessness than New Yorkers or Bostonians. The *r* of spelling becomes a schwa or disappears before vowels as well as before consonants or pauses. Thus in the speech of most white New Yorkers, *r* is pronounced when a vowel follows in *four o'clock;* even though the *r* is found at the end of a word, if the next word begins with a vowel, it is pronounced as a consonantal [r]. For most Negro speakers, *r* is still not pronounced in this position, and so never heard at the end of the word *four*. The white speaker is helped in his reading or spelling by the existence of the alternation: [fɔːfiːt, fɔrəklak], but the Negro speaker has no such clue to the underlying (spelling) form of the word *four*. Furthermore, the same Negro speaker will often not pronounce intervocalic *r* in the middle of a word as indicated in the dialect spelling *inte'ested, Ca'ol*. He has no clue, in his own speech, to the correct spelling form of such words, and may have another set of homonyms besides those listed above:

Carol = Cal
Paris = pass
terrace = test

2. *l-lessness.* The consonant *l* is a liquid very similar to *r* in its phonetic nature. The chief difference is that with *l* the center of the tongue is up, and the sides are down, while with *r* the sides are up but the center does not touch the roof of the mouth. The pattern of *l*-dropping is very similar to that of *r*, except that it has never affected entire dialect areas in the same sweeping style. When *l* disappears, it is often replaced by a back unrounded glide, sometimes symbolized [ɤ], instead of the center glide that replaces *r*; in many cases, *l* disappears entirely, especially after the back rounded vowels. The loss of *l* is much more marked among the Negro speakers we have interviewed than among whites in Northern cities, and we therefore have much greater tendencies towards such homonyms as:

toll = toe   all = awe
help = hep   Saul = saw
tool = too   fault = fought

3. *Simplification of consonant clusters.* One of the most complex variables appearing in Negro speech is the general tendency towards the simplification of consonant clusters at the ends of words. A great many clusters are involved, primarily those which end in /t/ or /d/, /s/ or /z/. We are actually dealing with two distinct tendencies: (1) a general tendency to reduce clusters of consonants at the ends of words to single consonants, and (2) a more general process of reducing the amount of information provided after stressed vowels, so that individual final consonants are affected as well. The first process is the most regular and requires the most intensive study in order to understand the conditioning factors involved.

The chief /t,d/ clusters that are affected are (roughly in order of frequency) /-st, -ft, -nt, -nd, -ld, -zd, -md/. Here they are given in phonemic notation; in conventional spelling we have words such as *past, passed, lift, laughed, bent, bend, fined, hold, poled, old, called, raised, aimed.* In all these cases, if the cluster is simplified, it is the last element that is dropped. Thus we have homonyms such as:

past	= pass	mend	=	men
rift	= riff	wind	=	wine
meant	= men	hold	=	hole

If we combine the effect of -*ld* simplification, loss of -*l*, and monophthongization of /ay/ and /aw/, we obtain

[ʃi waːɤ]   She wow!   =   She wild!

and this equivalence has in fact been found in our data. It is important to bear in mind that the combined effect of several rules will add to the total number of homonyms, and even more, to the unexpected character of the final result:

told   =   toll   =   toe

The first impression that we draw, from casual listening, is that Negro speakers show much more consonant cluster simplification than white speakers. But this conclusion is far from obvious when we examine the data carefully. It is true that the social distribution of this feature is wider for Negroes than for whites, but the sharpest differences are not in this particular phonetic process. As we shall see below, it is in the nature of the grammatical conditioning that restricts the deletion of the final consonant.

The other set of clusters which are simplified are those ending in /-s/ or /-z/, words like *axe* /æks/, *six* /siks/, *box* /baks/, *parts* /parts/, *aims* /eymz/, *rolls* /rowlz/, *leads* /liydz/, *besides* /bisaydz/, *John's* /dʒanz/, *that's* /ðæts/, *it's* /its/, *its* /its/. The situation here is more complex than with the /t,d/ clusters, since in some cases the first element of the cluster is lost, and in other cases the second element.

In one sense, there are a great many homonyms produced by this form of consonant cluster simplification, as we shall see when we consider grammatical consequences. But many of these can also be considered to be grammatical differences rather than changes in the shapes of words. The /t,d/ simplification gives us a great many irreducible homonyms, where a child has no clue to the standard spelling differences from his own speech pattern. Though this is less common in the case of /s,z/ clusters, we have

six	= sick	Max	= Mack
box	= bock	mix	= Mick

as possible homonyms in the speech of many Negro children.

4. *Weakening of final consonants.* It was noted above that the simplification of final consonant clusters was part of a more general tendency to produce less information after stressed vowels, so that final consonants, unstressed final vowels, and weak syllables show fewer distinctions and more reduced phonetic forms than initial consonants and stressed vowels. This is a perfectly natural process in terms of the amount of information required for effective communication, since the number of possible words which must be distinguished declines sharply after we select the first consonant and vowel. German and Russian, for example, do not distinguish voiced and voiceless consonants at the ends of words. However, when this tendency is carried to extremes (and a nonstandard dialect differs radically from the standard language in this respect), it may produce serious problems in learning to read and spell.

This weakening of final consonants is by no means as regular as the other phonological variables described above. Some individuals appear to have generalized the process to the point where most of their syllables are of the CV type, and those we have interviewed in this category seem to have the most serious reading problems of all. In general, final /t/ and /d/ are the most affected by the process. Final /d/ may be devoiced to a [t]-like form, or disappear entirely. Final /t/ is often realized as glottal stop, as in many English dialects, but more often disppears entirely. Less often, final /g/ and /k/ follow the same route as /d/ and /t/: /g/ is devoiced or disappears, and /k/ is replaced by glottal stop or disappears. Final /m/ and /n/ usually remain in the form of various degrees of nasalization of the preceding vowel. Rarely, sibilants /s/ and /z/ are weakened after vowels to the point where no consonant is heard at all. As a result of these processes, one may have such homonyms as:

Boot = Boo	seat = seed = see
road = row	poor = poke = pope
feed = feet	bit = bid = big

It is evident that the loss of final /l/ and /r/, discussed above, is another aspect of this general weakening of final consonants, though of a much more regular nature than the cases considered in this section.

5. *Other phonological variables.* In addition to the types of homonymy singled out in the preceding discussion, there are a great many others which may be mentioned. They are of less importance for reading problems in general, since they have little impact upon inflectional rules, but they do affect the shapes of words in the speech of Negro children. There is no distinction between /i/ and /e/ before nasals in the great majority of cases. In the parallel case before /r/, and sometimes /l/, we frequently find no distinction between the vowels /ih/ and /eh/. The corresponding

pair of back vowels before /r/ are seldom distinguished: that is, /uh/ and /oh/ fall together. The diphthongs /ay/ and /aw/ are often monoph-thongized, so that they are not distinguished from /ah/. The diphthong /oy/ is often a monophthong, especially before /l/, and cannot be dis-tinguished from /ɔh/.

Among other consonant variables, we find the final fricative /θ/ is frequently merged with /f/, and similarly final /ð/ with /v/. Less fre-quently, /θ/ and /ð/ become /f/ and /v/ in intervocalic position. Initial consonant clusters which involve /r/ show considerable variation: /str/ is often heard as /skr/; /ʃr/ as [sw, sr sɸ]. In a more complex series of shifts, /r/ is frequently lost as the final element of an initial cluster.

As a result of these various phonological processes, we find that the following series of homonyms are characteristics of the speech of many Negro children:

pin = pen	beer = bear	poor = pour
tin = ten	cheer = chair	sure = shore
since = cents	steer = stair	moor = more
	peel = pail	

Ruth = roof	stream = scream	boil = ball
death = deaf	strap = scrap	oil = all

find = found = fond		
time	= Tom	
pound = pond		

CHANGES IN THE SHAPES OF WORDS

The series of potential homonyms given in the preceding sections indicate that Negro children may have difficulty in recognizing many words in their standard spellings. They may look up words under the wrong spellings in dictionaries, and be unable to distinguish words which are plainly different for the teacher. If the teacher is aware of these sources of confusion, he may be able to anticipate a great many of the children's difficulties. But if neither the teacher nor the children are aware of the great differences in their sets of homonyms, it is obvious that confusion will occur in every reading assignment.

However, the existence of homonyms on the level of a phonetic output does not prove that the speakers have the same sets of mergers on the more abstract level which corresponds to the spelling system. For instance, many New Yorkers merge *guard* and *god* in casual speech, but in reading style, they have no difficulty in pronouncing the /r/ where it belongs. Since the /r/ in *car* reappears before a following vowel, it is evident that an abstract //r// occurs in their lexical system: //kar//. Thus the standard spelling system finds support in the learned patterns of careful speech, and in the alternations which exist within any given style of speech.

The phonetic processes discussed above are often considered to be "low level" rules—that is, they do not affect the underlying or abstract representations of words. One piece of evidence for this view is that the deletable final /r, l, s, z, t, d/ tend to be retained when a vowel follows at the beginning of the next word. This effect of a following vowel would seem to be a phonetic factor, restricting the operation of a phonetic rule; in any case, it is plain that the final consonant must "be there" in some abstract sense, if it appears in this prevocalic position. If this were not the case, we would find a variety of odd final consonants appearing, with no fixed relation to the standard form.

We can explore this situation more carefully when we consider grammatical conditioning. But we can point to one situation which proves the existence of nonstandard underlying forms quite clearly. In the most casual and spontaneous speech of the young Negro people whose language we have been examining, the plural //-s// inflection is seldom deleted. It follows the same phonetic rules as in Standard English: (1) after sibilants /s, z, ʃ, ʒ/, the regular plural is [ɨz]; (2) after other voiceless consonants, [s]; and (3) elsewhere, [z]. The regular form of the plural after a word like *test, desk,* is [s], as in [tests]. If the rules were so ordered that we began with the abstract form //test//, added the //-s//, and then deleted the /t/ in the consonant cluster simplification process, we would find the final phonetic form [tɛs:]. We do in fact sometimes find this form, in a context which implies the plural. But more often, we find [tɛsɨz], [gosɨz], [tosɨz], as the plurals of *test, ghost,* and *toast.*

A form such as [tɛsɨz] implies an order of the rules which begins with //tes//, or reduces //test// immediately to /tes/. Then the plural //-s// is added, and the phonetic rules give us [tɛsɨz]. It should be emphasized that those speakers who use this form do so consistently, frequently, and in the most careful speech; it is not a mere slip of the tongue. Furthermore, there is little reason in this case to presuppose a //test// form at all. The phonetic rules for //-s// are fairly "high level" rules, which affect all //-s// suffixes, and precede many other rules. For example, we find as noted above that /-ts/ is frequently simplified to /-s/ in the speech of Negroes and whites. When this /-s/ represents the plural, as in *lots of trouble,* it does not shift to [z]: we do not get the form [lazə], but rather [lasə]. In other words, the phonetic rules for the //-s// form apply first, then the /-t-/ is deleted, and the //-s// rules do not apply again.

We can conclude from this and other data that those children who use forms such as [tɛsɨz] have underlying lexical forms which are different from the spelling forms, and they would have no reason to expect to find *test* spelled T-E-S-T.

GRAMMATICAL CORRELATES OF THE
PHONOLOGICAL VARIABLES

As we examine the various final consonants affected by the phonological processes, we find that these are the same consonants which represent the principal English inflections. The shifts in the sound system therefore often coincide with grammatical differences between Nonstandard and Standard English, and it is usually difficult to decide whether we are dealing with a grammatical or a phonological rule. In any case, we can add a great number of homonyms to the lists given above when we consider the consequences of deleting final /r/, /l/, /s/, /z/, /t/, and /d/.

1. *The possessive.* In many cases, the absence of the possessive //-s// can be interpreted as a reduction of consonant clusters, although this is not the most likely interpretation. The //-s// is absent just as frequently after vowels as after consonants for many speakers. Nevertheless, we can say that the overall simplification pattern is favored by the absence of the //-s// inflection. In the case of //-r//, we find more direct phonological influence: two possessive pronouns which end in /r/ have become identical to the personal pronoun:

    [ðeɪ] book   not [ðɛːə] book

In rapid speech, one can not distinguish *you* from *your* from *you-all.* This seems to be a shift in grammatical forms, but the relation to the phonological variables is plain when we consider that *my, his, her,* and *our* remain as possessive pronouns. No one says *I book, he book, she book* or *we book,* for there is no phonological process which would bring the possessives into near-identity with the personal pronouns.

2. *The future.* The loss of final /l/ has a serious effect on the realization of future forms:

        you'll = you   he'll = he
        they'll = they   she'll = she

In many cases, therefore, the colloquial future is identical with the colloquial present. The form *will* is still used in its emphatic or full form, and the *going to* is frequent, so there is no question about the grammatical category of the future. One form of the future with very slight phonetic substance is preserved, the first person *I'm a shoot you:* there is no general process for the deletion of this *m*.

3. *The copula.* The verb forms of *be* are frequently not realized in sentences such as *you tired* or *he in the way.* If we examine the paradigm, we find that it is seriously affected by phonological processes:

I'm	$\neq$ I	we're	= we
you're	$\cong$ you	you're	$\cong$ you
he's	? he	they're	= they

The loss of final /z/ after vowels is not so frequent as to explain the frequency of the absence of *-s* in *he's*, and it is reasonable to conclude that grammatical rules have been generalized throughout the paradigm—still not affecting *I'm* in the same way as the others, as we would expect, since phonological rules are not operating to reduce /m/.

4. *The past.* Again, there is no doubt that phonological processes are active in reducing the frequency of occurrence of the /t,d/ inflection.

pass	= past	= passed	pick	= picked
miss	= mist	= missed	loan	= loaned
fine	= find	= fined	raise	= raised

At the same time, there is no question about the existence of a past-tense category. The irregular past-tense forms, which are very frequent in ordinary conversation, are plainly marked as past no matter what final simplification takes place.

I told him	[atoɪm]	he kept mine	[hikɛpmaɪn]

The problem which confronts us concerns the form of the regular suffix //-ed//. Is there such an abstract form in the structure of the Nonstandard English spoken by Negro children? The answer will make a considerable difference both to teaching strategy and our understanding of the reading problems which children face.

The -ed reading test. The most effective way of determining the grammatical significance of *-ed* for the groups we have been working with is through a series of sentences in the reading texts used in our interviews. The relevant sentences are as follows:

(a) Last month I read five books.
(b) Tom read all the time.
(c) Now I read and write better than Alfred does.
(d) When I passed by, I read the posters.
(e) When I liked a story, I read every word.
(f) I looked for trouble when I read the news.

These sentences depend upon the unique homograph *read* to indicate whether the reader is interpreting the *-ed* suffix as a past tense signal. The first three sentences show whether the reader can use the time indicators *last month, now,* and the absence of *-s* to distinguish correctly between [riːd] and [rɛd]. In sentences (d), (e), and (f) the reader first encounters the *-ed* suffix, which he may or may not pronounce. If he interprets this visual signal as a sign of the past tense, he will pronounce *read* as [rɛd]; if not, he is apt to say [riːd]. The distance between the *-ed* suffix and the word *read* is kept as short as possible in sentence (d), so that here at least there is no problem of understanding *-ed* and then forgetting it.

The overall results of this test show that *-ed* is interpreted correctly less than half the time by the Thunderbirds [a group of Negro boys 10 to 12 years old]—less often than the *-ed* suffix is pronounced. The Cobras [another group of boys, 14 to 16 years old] show no material improvement in this respect. . . . The degree of uncertainty . . . indicates that the *-ed* cannot function as an effective marker of the past tense for many children. Though the Cobras are four years older than the Thunderbirds, they show little change in their use of *-ed*. It is also true that some children—a minority in this case—can recognize *-ed* as a past tense marker, and use it effectively in reading, even though they usually do not pronounce it.

GRAMMATICAL STATUS OF THE //-S// SUFFIXES

The same quantitative method which was effective in interpreting the status of *-ed* can be used to analyze the various *-s* suffixes used by Negro children.

Z_{MM}	monomorphemic *-s* in root clusters: *axe, box*
Z_{PL}	the plural *-s*
Z_V	the 3rd person singular marker of the verb
Z_{POS}	the possessive *-'s*

For each category, we can compare the extent of simplification before consonants and before vowels. . . .

We can infer that this is no longer effectively described as consonant cluster simplification, but rather as a grammatical fact. The third-person singular marker //-s// docs not exist in the particular grammar being used here. The same argument holds for the possessive //-s// marker, though as noted above, we cannot extend this argument to infer a loss of the possessive in general.

CONSEQUENCES FOR THE TEACHING OF READING

Let us consider the problem of teaching a youngster to read who has the general phonological and grammatical characteristics just described. The most immediate way of analyzing his difficulties is through the interpretation of his oral reading. As we have seen, there are many phonological rules which affect his pronunciation, but not necessarily his understanding of the grammatical signals or his grasp of the underlying lexical forms. The two questions are distinct: the relations between grammar and pronunciation are complex, and require careful interpretation.

If a student is given a certain sentence to read, say *He passed by both of them,* he may say [hi pæs baɪ bof ə dɛm]. The teacher may wish to correct this bad reading, perhaps by saying, "No, it isn't [hi pæs baɪ bof ə dɛm], it's [hi pæst baɪ boθ əv ðɛm]." One difficulty is that these two utterances may sound the same to many children—both the reader and those listening—and they may be utterly confused by the correction. Others may be able to hear the difference, but have no idea of the significance of the extra [t] and the interdental forms of *th-*. The most embarrassing fact is that the boy who first read the sentence may have performed his reading task correctly, and understood the *-ed* suffix just as it was intended. In that case, the teacher's correction is completely beside the point.

We have two distinct cases to consider. In one case, the deviation in reading may be only a difference in pronunciation on the part of a child who has a different set of homonyms from the teacher. Here, correction might be quite unnecessary. In the second case, we may be dealing with a boy who has no concept of *-ed* as a past-tense marker, who considers the *-ed* a meaningless set of silent letters. Obviously the correct teaching strategy would involve distinguishing these two cases, and treating them quite differently.

How such a strategy might be put into practice is a problem that educators may be able to solve by using information provided by linguists. As a linguist, I can suggest several basic principles derived from our work which may be helpful in further curriculum research and application.

1. In the analysis and correction of oral reading, teachers must begin to make the basic distinction between differences in pronunciation and mistakes in reading. Information on the dialect patterns of Negro children should be helpful toward this end.

2. In the early stages of teaching reading and spelling, it may be necessary to spend much more time on the grammatical function of certain inflections, which may have no function in the dialect of some of the children. In the same way, it may be necessary to treat the final elements of certain clusters with the special attention given to silent letters such as *b* in *lamb*.

3. A certain amount of attention given to perception training in the first few years of school may be extremely helpful in teaching children to hear and make Standard English distinctions. But perception training need not be complete in order to teach children to read. On the contrary, most of the differences between Standard and Nonstandard English described here can be taken as differences in the sets of homonyms which must be accepted in reading patterns. On the face of it, there is no reason why a person cannot learn to read Standard English texts quite well in a nonstandard pronunciation. Eventually, the school may wish to teach the child an alternative system of pronunciation. But the key to the situation in the early grades is for the teacher to know the system of homonyms of Nonstandard English, and to know the grammatical differences that separate her own speech from that of the child. The teacher must be prepared to accept the system of homonyms for the moment, if this will advance the basic process of learning to read, but not the grammatical differences. Thus the task of teaching the child to read *-ed* is clearly that of getting him to recognize the graphic symbols as a marker of the past tense, quite distinct from the task of getting him to say [pæst] for *passed*.

If the teacher has no understanding of the child's grammar and set of homonyms, she may be arguing with him at cross purposes. Over and over again, the teacher may insist that *cold* and *coal* are different, without realizing that the child perceives this as only a difference in meaning, not in sound. She will not be able to understand why he makes so many odd mistakes in reading, and he will experience only a vague confusion, somehow connected with the ends of words. Eventually, he may stop trying to analyze the shapes of letters that follow the vowel, and guess wildly at each word after he deciphers the first few letters. Or he may lose confidence in the alphabetic principle as a whole, and try to recognize each word as a whole. This loss of confidence seems to occur frequently in the third and fourth grades, and it is characteristic of many children who are effectively nonreaders.

The sources of reading problems discussed in this paper are only a few of the causes of poor reading in the ghetto schools. But they are quite specific and easily isolated. The information provided here may have immediate application in the overall program of improving the teaching of reading to children in these urban areas.

INTERRELATEDNESS OF CERTAIN DEVIANT GRAMMATICAL STRUCTURES IN NEGRO NONSTANDARD DIALECTS

Riley B. Smith

William Stewart, in several of the essays included in this volume, has emphasized the importance of syntactic (grammatical) differences between Negro and white dialects, and has stressed the possibility of confusion in cross-dialectal communication because of misinterpretation of seemingly identical structures. Here Smith presents an excellent example of a structure which has a different interpretation in the two dialects: I saw the man did it *in standard varieties of English is understood as meaning* I saw that the man did it, *but in Nonstandard Negro speech it usually has the interpretation* I saw the man who did it, *though it may less often have the other interpretation as well. Smith shows how the so-called pleonastic subject ("My brother, he . . ."), often regarded as redundant and hence a flaw in standard dialects, serves an important function of preventing confusion between potentially ambiguous structures in the Negro dialect investigated. A teacher's failure to recognize such cross-dialectal differences can lead to misunderstanding and ineffective treatment of these structures in teaching.*

Research in highly divergent dialects of American English, especially in what has been termed Negro Nonstandard English (NNE), has lately been thriving, and quite a number of hitherto unnoticed divergences have been disclosed and published.

The two deviant grammatical structures of a dialect of NNE to be discussed in this paper are 1) the pleonastic subject pronoun, and 2) the

From the *Journal of English Linguistics*, vol. 3 (March, 1969), pp. 82–88. Reprinted by permission of the *Journal of English Linguistics* and the author.

deletion of the subject relative pronoun. A relationship between the two structures within the dialect will be shown, and some conjecture about interference phenomena attributable to the relationship will be made. And it is hoped that this discussion will have more general ramifications for future research and analysis in dialectology.

Among Negro informants of East Texas,[1] the frequency of the pleonastic subject pronoun is extremely high among speakers of all age-groups, and its occurrence is quite widespread.[2]

> So the older peoples *they* got herbs and stuff and help made medicine theirself. (67, Atlanta, #122) [3]
>
> My mother *she* used to wash and iron and cook. (46, Marshall, #101)
>
> And then my daughter *she* is a secretary for a store manager. (46, Marshall, #101)
>
> My brother from Lubbock *he* visit to get his wife and baby. (17, Tyler, #085)
>
> Some of them *they* put the needle in the fire. (9 Tyler, #041)
>
> Teenager(s) *they* don't much like his rock. (14, Nacogdoches, #065)

Among this same group of informants, the frequency of the deletion of the subject relative pronoun (usually *what* in this dialect of NNE), not optionally deletable in SE as it is in this dialect, is extremely high and its occurrence is widespread.

> He look like a little man have on a hat with a round circle on it. (8, Marshall, #021)
>
> This here is one family eat anything. (53, Nacogdoches, #121)
>
> I have a brother work at Ralston Purina here in town. (13, Nacogdoches, #061)
>
> She be the kind like to go. (17, Tyler, #085)
>
> It's a bush grow up like that, and it's good for fever. (67, Atlanta, #122)

[1] The fieldwork and analysis were one phase of a project to reevaluate English instructional material and curricula in the wake of integration in five independent school districts of East Texas: Atlanta, Clarksville, Marshall, Nacogdoches, and Tyler. The project was sponsored by the school districts under grants from ESEA and NDEA, and by the Texas Education Agency. All the interviews were conducted between August and December, 1967.

The 253 informants, of whom 170 were Negro, were selected to include a wide range of ages, and of ethnic and educational backgrounds. Because grammatical as well as phonological data were of interest to the project, the interviews were in general topical and did not follow a standard worksheet. With modifications, the interviews followed techniques suggested in Roger W. Shuy, Walter A. Wolfram, and William K. Riley, *Linguistic Correlates of Social Stratification in Detroit Speech* (East Lansing, Mich., 1967), and in William Labov, *The Social Stratification of English in New York City* (Washington, D.C., 1966).

[2] I do not wish to suggest that all Negro informants used particular deviant grammatical structures with the same frequency in all cases. The data have in some measure been selected to reflect what I consider to be "basilect" structures.

[3] The age of the informant, city of domicile, and my informant number follow the responses cited, in that order.

Further, in strings where both of these structures occur in this dialect, the pleonasm is highly stable even where the relative pronoun is present.

> The one stay here in Clarksville *she* don't do anything at all. (44, Clarksville, #101)
>> The one who lives here in Clarksville doesn't do anything at all. (SE translation)
>
> The man *what* own(ed) the land *he* come over. (18, Clarksville, #084)
>> The man who owned the land came over. (SE translation)
>
> The boy won *he* did a three. (15, Tyler, #069)
>> The boy who won did a three. (SE translation)
>
> My other sister *she* fourteen go to Dogan. (10, Tyler, #047).
>> My other sister is fourteen who goes to Dogan. (SE translation)
>> *Not:* My other sister who is fourteen goes to Dogan.

These strings, which consist of *one* sentence, not two, suggest that there is an interrelatedness between the two structures such that the high frequency of the deletion of the relative pronoun exerts an influence in some way on the stability of the pleonastic subject pronoun, or that the pleonasm is in some sense itself a disambiguating formative.

The string *I saw the man did it* is ambiguous in NNE in a way that it cannot be in SE. In the shorthand derivations below, the second sentences of both A and B are embedded, but in A they are relativized, in B they are nominalized. (The dotted line indicates a possible but infrequent deletion transformation.)

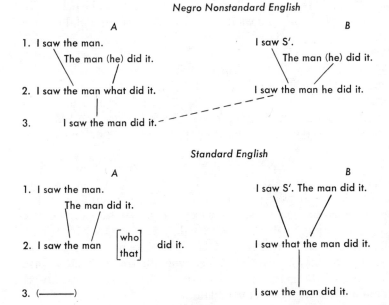

It will be noted that though the *what* in NNE above (A2) could be retained—i.e., the deletion transformation could be blocked—to disambiguate, the relative *what* is a rare formative in any terminal string, and the pleonasm usually takes over this function, i.e., its deletion is usually blocked. The relatives *who* and *that* in SE (A2 above) are not deletable and therefore the string never ambiguates with B3. It will be further noted that there is cross-code ambiguity between the terminals (3) of NNE and SE, such that the speakers of the two dialects may decode different underlying phrase-markers for the terminal string *I saw the man did it.*

To the speaker of NNE, the SE string *My sister plays the piano* may reflect not a sentence, but a noun-phrase with an embedded relative clause, i.e., *My sister who plays the piano.* The pleonastic pronoun is usually present in NNE, as in *My sister she play the piano,* to disambiguate the two structures. Thus both intracode and cross-code ambiguation militate against the NNE speaker's learning to leave out the subject pronoun pleonasm, which seems to have more a grammatical than a strictly stylistic function in his dialect.

There is at present no clear way to describe what appear to be synchronic influences of transformational rules upon each other, rules apparently unrelated except that they have the potential of generating ambiguous terminal strings within a dialect. Optionally deletable markers occasionally, though rarely, perform such a disambiguating function in Standard English. *I see the men do it* is ambiguous in SE, reflecting phrase-markers which are clearly different when we pronominalize *the men:* 1) *I see they do it,* and 2) *I see them do it.* But the SE speaker normally disambiguates with the clause marker *that* when he wants to reflect the structure of 1): *I see that the men do it.*

Analogously, the NNE string *The man did it* is ambiguous; *The man he did it* disambiguates with the pleonasm. Whatever the generative provenience of the pleonastic subject pronoun (it appears to be neither a clause marker nor a relative pronoun in the SE sense), it is a marker in the sense that it marks nonrelativization of the following verb phrase, a function stabilized by the regular deletion of the relative pronoun in this dialect of NNE.

. . . The failure of the NNE speaker to recognize the complexity of certain ambiguations between divergent dialects is certainly no more serious than this same failure on the part of the SE speaker. The dialectologist should look for relationships within a dialect which may be indispensable to a proper description of it. And the English teacher, in her struggle against "ungrammatical" forms, should begin to recognize that some of her students' failures may be identical to her own, resulting from a blockage of understanding of the grammatical structures of the unfamiliar dialect because of ambiguity across dialect boundaries.

6

Applications

It seemed appropriate in this, our final section, to demonstrate how some of these ideas and procedures have been put into practice success-fully. A number of articles in earlier sections have made comments in this area but have devoted themselves to the theoretical dimension of the study. The essays in this section will focus directly on application.

The first of these is a description of the dialect project and in-service course out of which this reader arose. It shows how important the col-lection and analysis of language and culture data can be on the local level, and how it can be keyed into programs developed for specific school sys-tems. The second essay, by Troike, explores some basic but usually ignored considerations in developing strategies for the teaching of standard English to nonstandard-speaking groups. It focuses on how important the recogni-tion of language differences can be in an understanding of the impediments of communication, learning, and evaluation. This recognition becomes absolutely crucial in the bilingual situation, as Saville demonstrates in the third article here; this article provides vital information which should form the basis for instructional materials and methods for teaching English to students from non-English speaking backgrounds. Virginia Allen's article, which follows, describes the differences between bidialectalism and bi-lingualism, especially as concerns language teaching strategies. Finally, in another study by Muriel Saville, we present her conception of how an education program for bilingual Spanish-speakers would be established, and what weaknesses in current programs should be avoided.

THE EAST TEXAS DIALECT PROJECT: A PATTERN FOR EDUCATION

Mary M. Galvan and Rudolph C. Troike

The following essay describes a project in dialect research and teacher training carried out in Texas under the auspices of the state department of education, which can serve as a model for other states or even local school districts. White and Negro students and adults in several communities were interviewed, and the tape recordings of the interviews were analyzed to determine features of pronunciation or grammar which might have educational relevance. An intensive three-week workshop was held to give teachers the necessary background to interpret the information provided by the linguistic analysis and to translate it into classroom application. This training was paralleled with sensitization to the nature and presence of deep-seated cultural differences between the white and Negro communities, many of which receive their expression through language. Teachers came to realize that cultural as well as linguistic relativity was necessary if they were to succeed in creating a classroom environment more conducive to effective learning.

There can be little argument that a state department of education has a moral, if not a legal, responsibility for involving itself in the more critical educational issues of the day. Such involvement is hardly the most comfortable situation possible, but it is necessary if an educational system is to exert leadership in anticipating needs rather than creating crash programs to deal with crises only after they arise. The Texas Education Agency is increasingly aware of the needs of members of the 26 cultural groups which make up the school population of the state, and began in 1967, before pressures from some of these groups began to be felt, to develop action programs for dealing with problems involving language

From *The Florida FL Reporter* special anthology issue entitled *Linguistic-Cultural Difference and American Education*, vol. 7, no. 1 (Spring/Summer 1969), pp. 29–31, 152; Alfred C. Aarons, Barbara Y. Gordon, and William A. Stewart, eds. Reprinted by permission of *The Florida FL Reporter*.

variety. The present article is a report on one such project which the writers feel offers a pattern which might be effective in other states and areas affected by similar problems.

Problems and proposed solutions coming from local school districts relative to the education of members of minority groups are often naive. Requests are periodically received by the TEA to help "improve" the speech of Negro teachers. Schools making such a request would typically give English consultants about four weeks to accomplish this miracle. Again, teachers claim they can not understand the speech of children of another race, yet some of the same teachers are irritated when consultants *are* able to comprehend these children. Schools report that the standards of excellence in their school would stigmatize any child who erred in the speaking of "Standard English"; one school's answer to this problem was to not require children of minority groups to speak in class, in order to prevent their being embarrassed. Another school instituted an entire second dialect program (utilizing consultant personnel from a nearby college) which had as its aim conditioning Negro teachers (!) to place a retroflex *r* in terminal position. Such examples illustrate the distressing lack of knowledge concerning language, language learning, and dialect variation to be found at the local school level.

Feeling that better answers could surely be found at the state level, English consultants at the Texas Education Agency cooperated during 1967–1968 with staff members from the University of Texas at Austin in a pilot project, funded under ESEA Title I, involving five school districts in Northeast Texas.[1] The study was made of white and Negro speech in contact in this primarily rural area of the state. The project had three major goals: 1) To study the language patterns which exist in Texas, particularly the phonology and syntax which have most bearing on learning, 2) To develop an in-service course for teachers which would affect their attitudes toward linguistic variety and which could be replicated in several parts of the state, 3) To produce teaching materials which could be used in schools to provide for language variety and add additional language patterns to pupils' speech.

Two fieldworkers interviewed some 250 informants in the five communities, representing both races and several socio-economic levels. The informants came from all age groups—preschool, grades 2, 4, 8, 11, and adult. The half-hour interviews were essentially free conversation, though questions were structured to elicit specific phonological and syntactic features as well as lexical items. New techniques were developed for interviewing small children which allowed the field workers to get fairly con-

---

[1] Communities were chosen partly on the basis of regional location and partly on the basis of type, in order to give a representative cross-section of the area. Two of the communities were small rural towns, two were large rapidly-growing towns and one was a small city.

sistent information from these often unpredictable informants. The interviews usually involved two children at a time, a situation which produced some interesting peer-group dialogue. Analysis of the material for the most part demonstrated what features were likely to show up in the dialect of the area. The tapes are now being re-examined for the frequency of a feature in terms of the number of times it could have appeared. The report must be written so that it is useful not only to the linguists working with the project but is comprehensible to public school officials and staffs without much training in linguistics. In essence the project has been an exercise in translating scientifically valid data into terms public schools can use and finding out how much training is needed for teachers to utilize this information in the classroom.

During the interviews the fieldworkers became aware of extralinguistic information and behaviors which were relevant in a variety of ways, but whose significance could not be adequately interpreted. They elicited a large number of rope-skipping rhymes, game songs, and narrative accounts which seemed to hold promise if their full implication could be understood. The cultural pattern of eye-aversion on the part of many Negro children provided some problems in interviews before it was understood. The verbal contests of some Negroes and small children of both races were being badly handled in the interviews. About this point the project was fortunate in acquiring the consultative services of another University of Texas staff member, a folklorist with a specialty in Negro culture, whose role was to explain many cultural patterns of behavior to staff members. His contribution became larger as time passed and is at present equally important as the linguists'.

During the period of analysis, the staff became increasingly impressed with its information about languages in contact. The target area of the state is heavily populated with Negroes who have lived closely with their white neighbors for decades. Contact between groups is frequent and often close. The influence of both cultures has been felt one on the other. Sociolinguistic isoglosses can be drawn—there are enough differences to make it possible—but few would completely exclude a member of another race. The sharing of features, then, is a necessary observation. It logically became a valuable basis for talking to teachers about respect for language variety.

The data in the analysis are presented in terms of the *system* of which each feature is a part. Not only is this necessary for the description of any language or cultural pattern, it is vital for teachers to see the systematic nature of a given dialect and to structure educational experiences to build on the knowledge regarding similarities and differences between the systems.

The first-year pilot project included a two-phase teacher-training component. The first phase brought together large numbers of teachers for short-term instruction in a bare minimum of linguistic and educational information which would, hopefully, alert them to the implications of dialect differences in the classroom. The results were discouraging. Teachers long inured to lecture-type in-service courses proved highly resistant to the attempt to develop in them a greater awareness and understanding of language variation. It is now apparent that effective in-service training can be done, but only with a limited number of teachers who have time to be intensely involved with the issues.

During June the staff directed a three-week workshop for 48 teachers from all grade levels from the five pilot schools. These teachers received some 105 clock hours of rigorous instruction in which they assimilated large amounts of sometimes quite technical information, acquired new skills, achieved breakthroughs in the formation of new attitudes, and prepared instructional materials. For seven hours each day the participants were given instruction in linguistics, folklore, second-language instruction methods and curriculum development, all related to dialect and language development.

The linguistics component took up such matters as interview and inventory techniques, general dialectology, elementary phonological transcription (one principal, while wrestling manfully with the new code, said he had developed new tolerance for the six-year old just learning to write), and syntax. Features mentioned in the fieldworker's report were studied in depth in terms of the possible interference each might provide in education and what curriculum devices could provide for it.

The folklore component led teachers to some understanding of the potential of folklore collections in the classroom, methods of examining expressive dimensions of cultural groups, stereotyping and information which would affect stereotyping, and rhetorical devices typical of cultural groups. Each class was, in effect, a sensitivity session; it was based on sound information and was conducted by a man who combined unusual skills in both group dynamics and cultural insight.

Second-language teaching took up the skills usually associated with that field and adapted the material to second-dialect learning. Teachers oriented to teaching only one type of student and only by "right-or-wrong," "fill-in-the-blank" methods found these new skills and insights a revelation. It should be said here that the essential goal at the beginning of the project was the creation of a cadre of teachers trained to develop bidialectal competence in their students. By the time of the workshop, it was still a goal but not nearly so important. One reason for the shift was that second-dialect teaching devices are still not readily available to teachers, particularly ones which were consistent with the philosophy of this project. Another reason is that staff members had formulated somewhat more modest goals which seemed much more possible of realization, such as enabling teachers to understand and accept the variety of language patterns of the children in a given classroom, showing them how to build in a positive way upon the strengths of these patterns, and helping them to create a different kind of educational climate in their schools and in their communities.

In workshop sessions teachers were asked to describe a classroom climate which would provide for the variety of language and cultural patterns which exist side by side in our schools. They were asked to prepare lesson plans in which they would collect and utilize childlore, including the preparation of readers in several dialects. They analyzed and made provision for adaptation of textbooks currently used in the classroom.[2] Teachers investigated new literature anthologies with which minority cultures could identify. The teachers themselves asked not so much for "culture-fair" as for "culture-positive" materials. Each teacher contributed to a growing stock of instructional materials which are being field-tested in classrooms at the present time.

The workshop was evaluated by several independent evaluators, and each one indicated that the project should not only be continued but accelerated. Participants were virtually unanimous in describing it as the most traumatic and attitude-changing experience of their professional lives. Staff members, most of them from universities, found that the project opened for them a new and exciting involvement in public education.

A follow-up program during the past year in the five pilot schools has indicated markedly different reactions on the part of the local communities involved. One small school district associated the project's efforts with violent social upheaval as well as abandonment of linguistic standards and asked that "dialect" not be mentioned for a year. The other four schools have made extensive use of their participants as resource persons in the school. Their activities range from teaching special classes for students whose dialect background creates special educational problems, to organizing the rest of the faculty into groups for study. One team of participants has met regularly every week since June to study and help each other. They have invited other faculty members to attend as interest is indicated. Administrators in all five districts concede that the workshop has had tremendous influence on staff members.

As a result of requests from other school districts for a similar project, the program in the state for the current school year is considerably expanded. Methods of conducting fieldwork and the format for in-service

2 It should be of some general interest to learn that the Texas Education Agency is now instructing book publishers to change portions of textbooks which do not recognize dialect variety and which take an uninformed traditional view of language "correctness" and uniformity. Authors are asked to acknowledge, for example, homonyms in other than their own dialect, even to the suggestion that for most educated Texans horse and hoarse are not homonyms, while pin and pen most emphatically are.

courses have now been refined so that the project can serve a wider area, more schools, and more complex social situations. Two urban areas, Dallas and Houston, are participating in the project this year. The analysis considers three large language groups in contact—Anglo, Negro, and Mexican-American—as well as the regional variations which appear in mobile urban groups. Cultural patterns associated with the urban situation are getting particular attention.

In trying to meet the needs of so many school districts for in-service education in the field of dialect and language development, the project staff suggested that if teachers could be given two non-consecutive weeks in the school year of released time, the staff could conduct one week of instruction, ask teachers to read and try out materials during a two-week interval, and then present a second week of instruction. However, this pattern proved to be inadequate, since much of the continuity and intensity of the group experience is lost, and not enough content can be presented or assimilated. It is now clear that only the three-week intensive workshop "package," given during a time when school is not in session, can achieve the intended effect.

The fieldwork last year indicated that there were significant differences between the dialects of the five communities studied. Two communities represented some elements of Interior Southern speech, two represented South Midland, and the small city held the variety to be expected of urban growth. Age differences and trends were also noted. The project staff had hypothesized that information gathered from East Texas would also describe the language of Dallas, less than 100 miles away from one of the original pilot schools. If this theory proved correct then the time-consuming and expensive fieldwork could be reduced to spot checking. The hypothesis was not correct; the speech of Dallas is different enough that extensive field work is necessary. The Texas Education Agency, if it is to work with sound information, is facing the mapping of the entire state.

In addition to the two urban areas, fieldwork will be done in five school districts in Southeast Texas and five more schools in Central Texas. This will give the project information about the speech of a little more than one-third of the state and more than half of the school children in the state.

In the conviction that the pattern developed in the project would apply in any situation involving cultural and language differences, during the current school year the project was also extended to the Lower Rio Grande Valley of Texas to study speech and culture patterns of Mexican-Americans in that part of the state. A bilingual fieldworker is collecting data on both English and Spanish dialects in five communities in that area. A trained folklorist, he is able to collect valuable cultural data along with the linguistic information. A University of Texas faculty member who is a specialist in Mexican-American folklore and a native Mexican-

American himself, has been added to the staff as consultant and will participate with linguists and curriculum specialists in a workshop for teachers of Mexican-American children in the Valley this summer. It now appears that the project is sufficiently flexible to study language and culture patterns of any of our 26 cultural groups and to provide educational resources to meet their special needs.

Though many projects of a similar type are being conducted in and for public schools around the nation, this is the only one being operated through a state department of education. Certainly the findings of the project and the materials developed from it will be the foundation for educational policy in the State of Texas in the near future. Several implications are clear: 1) A state agency needs to look outside its doors for expertise and assistance. The teamwork of university scholars and representatives of public education produces insights and results neither could achieve without the other. 2) A state agency can organize resources to gather and utilize scientifically valid information which is a prerequisite to the mounting of innovative educational programs. 3) Procedures such as textbook adoption and curriculum building should consider specific information about language variety and dialect interference in learning. 4) Educational programs can be adapted by influencing the insights and attitudes of classroom teachers, as well as their methodological competencies. 5) The project points the way to fundamental concepts in any education program involving intercultural understanding. Information from this project is being utilized in programs involving dialect, English as a second language, bilingual education, urban education, and vocational education. As a direct result of the project a committee of advisors from the fields of anthropology, sociology, linguistics, history, and education has been appointed to consult with the Texas Educational Agency on programs of intercultural education. The assumption is that education should depend upon more than just good intentions; sound information and broad insights from a variety of fields must be brought to bear on educational problems.

The authors indicated earlier that a shift of emphasis took place during the first year of the project. Training teachers to help children become bidialectal is still an important goal, but it must be taken together with several other goals which seem to be fundamental to any attempt on the part of schools to add language patterns to any child's repertory. In a multi-ethnic, multi-cultural society, teachers are called upon daily to recognize the *fact of variety* in the classroom and to regard it as a rich educational resource. Teachers, then, should be trained to know what to listen for in children's language. What features are significant? What features might cause some interference in the learning process? Teachers must understand that language is one of several cultural patterns which make up a child's behavior. To look at language in isolation is to be blind to factors that work with language in the learning process. Teachers must be trained to take a *sociolinguistic* view, recognizing systematic social and cultural differences, and the correlated linguistic modes for their expression. Teachers must learn to accept, intellectually as well as emotionally, the validity of various patterns of behavior, realizing that they fill significant adaptive and emotional needs of those who possess them. Cultural, as well as linguistic, relativity must be part of the teacher's basic approach if he is to effectively reach those who differ in language or culture. Teachers must accept that once a pattern of language is internalized, there is no eradication of it but only addition to it. Brain surgery, the only effective way of getting rid of a pattern, is simply not an acceptable classroom procedure in our society. Education for alternatives must be the goal of instruction.

Having accepted the above foundations, teachers are then ready to consider means for adding new language or cultural patterns to equip a child to participate in some new group or activity. The single most important consideration in the treatment of dialect addition is that the child sees some sound reason or has practical motivation for adding a new feature. This would suggest that the teacher needs better information and a more realistic attitude than most now have about what language is appropriate in the world-as-it-really-is. In adding new features the child should be given the security of feeling comfortable in his native dialect as he explores new formal and social areas of language use. Further, the child must feel that any addition to his language is *his* choice and that the school is equipping him to make wise choices which will expand the range of possibility for his linguistic participation with other groups for the rest of his life.

RECEPTIVE BIDIALECTALISM: IMPLICATIONS FOR SECOND-DIALECT TEACHING

Rudolph C. Troike

Research work on the language of children and adolescents has shown that speakers of nonstandard dialects are often readily able to understand "standard" speech, and in repetition testing, unconsciously translate from the standard stimulus into their own normal nonstandard forms. Repetition testing provides a valuable means of assessing receptive knowledge of other dialects. A program for teaching productive competence in a second dialect can and should build upon this receptive competence. Despite cultural beliefs to the contrary, even very young children are often quite aware of the social relevance of stylistic and dialect differences, so that second-dialect instruction should not be delayed. The optimum years for learning a second language or dialect are ages five to eight.

It has long been a matter of common knowledge that a person's receptive competence in his language far exceeds his productive competence: one's "passive" or "recognition" vocabulary is always larger than one's "active" vocabulary. Even from the time he is first learning to talk, a child understands more than he can say, and this state of affairs continues throughout his lifetime. Most people, for example, can understand a speaker from another area even though they might be quite unable to sound like him. It is this capacity, then, and its relevance for education, that we will be concerned with in the present discussion.

The usual assumption of the teacher, and the assumption on which most language testing is based, is that a student's production will adequately reveal his linguistic competence. That is, if a student consistently uses such forms as *He don't, We done ate,* or *She come home at five,* it is usually assumed that he *does not know* the forms *He doesn't, We have eaten* (or *finished eating*) and *She comes* (or *came*). While this may sometimes be true, such an assumption, by ignoring the receptive aspect of linguistic competence, can often lead to serious mistakes in evaluation and teaching strategy.

A considerable amount of recent work has shown convincingly that students from the first grade on (and often earlier) have a well-developed receptive knowledge of dialects other than the one which they normally speak. (Here it should be noted that we are using the term *dialect* in the sense employed by most linguists as referring to any distinguishable variety of a language, either regional or social, of which the so-called "standard" is but one.) The clearest evidence has come from testing in which children and adolescents of various ages have been asked to repeat sentences which they hear recorded on tape, or spoken by an investigator. The following examples represent the responses of some preschool and first-grade children from Texas and West Virginia to such a taped oral-repetition test ("N" indicates Negro, "A" indicates Appalachian white):

Model	Response
Mother helps Gloria.	Mother help Gloria. (N)
Gloria has a toothbrush.	Gloria have a toothbrush. (N)
She cleans her teeth with her brush.	Her clean her teeth with her brush. (N)
David has a brush for his hair.	David have a brush for he hair. (N)
She has soap on her head.	She has soap(t) on hers head. (A)
David and Gloria are clean.	David and Gloria is clean. (A)
They are on their knees.	They are on theirs knees. (A)
The socks are on Gloria's feet.	The socks is on Gloria's feet .(A)
The children go to bed.	The children goes to bed. (A)

William Labov has obtained similar results with Negro teenagers in New York. Some examples follow:

Model:	Nobody ever sat at any of those desks, anyhow.
Response:	Nobody never sat in none of those desks anyhow.
Model:	I asked Alvin if he knows how to play basketball.
Response:	I ask Alvin do he know how to play basketball.

In order to explain why the repetitions differ from the model, we must assume that the child does not merely attempt to mimic the sentence as the model says it, but rather he first *decodes* the sentence for its meaning, and then *re-encodes* it in the form he might have used in framing the sentence as an original utterance. Essentially, then, he is *translating* from the dialect of the model into his native dialect. So consistent is this behavior that oral-repetition testing provides both a rapid diagnostic instrument for determining native dialect characteristics and an excellent device for evaluating receptive knowledge of a second dialect.

A necessary conclusion which must be drawn from the preceding examples is that the students certainly understood the sentences which they heard, or else they would not have been able to translate them into their native dialect.[1] In short, we must recognize that in most instances, children are already receptively bidialectal by the time they come to school.

The effects of this phenomenon are not limited to oral repetition, but extend to reading as well. An early but very revealing example is given by Daniel Defoe in 1724 (in a chapter on Somerset in his book *A Tour Through the Whole Island of Great Britain*):

> It cannot pass my Observation here, that, when we are come this Length from London, the Dialect of the English Tongue, or the Country-way of expressing them-selves, is not easily understood. . . . It is not possible to explain this fully by Writing, because the Difference is not so much in the Orthography, as in the Tone and Accent; their abridging the Speech, *Cham*, for *I am*; *Chil*, for *I will*; *Don*, for *do on*, and *Doff*, for *do off*, or *put off*; and the like.
>
> I cannot omit a short Story here on this Subject: Coming to a Relation's House, who was a Schoolmaster at Murtock in Somersetshire, I went into his School to beg the Boys, or rather the Master, a Play-day, as is usual in such Cases. I ob-served one of the lowest Scholars was reading his Lesson to the Usher in a Chapter in the Bible. I sat down by the Master, till the Boy had read it out, and observed the Boy read a little oddly in the Tone of the Country, which made me the more attentive; because, on Inquiry, I found that the Words were the same, and the Orthography the same, as in all our Bibles. I observed also the Boy read it out with his Eyes still on the Book, and his Head, like a mere Boy, moving from Side to Side, as the Lines reached cross the Columns of the Book: His Lesson was in the *Canticles of Solomon*; the Words these:
>
> "I have put off my Coat; how shall I put it on? I have washed my Feet; how shall I defile them?" The Boy read thus, with his Eyes, as I say, full on the Text: "Chav a doffed my Coot; how shall I don't? Chav a washed my Feet; how shall I moil 'em?"
>
> How the dexterous Dunce could form his Mouth to express so readily the Words (which stood right printed in the Book) in his Country Jargon, I could not but admire.

It is interesting to note that in this instance the boy's translation into his native dialect included not just changes in pronunciation and grammar, but in vocabulary as well. The rapidity and unconsciousness with which the translation was carried out leave no doubt that the boy under-stood the passage he was reading.

Conversely, if a vocabulary item or grammatical construction is not in a child's receptive competence, he will experience great difficulty in attempting to repeat a model sentence, often producing only incoherent fragments. Labov has found that though Negro teenagers will readily

---

[1] In fact, this is the best sort of evidence for the correctness of their understanding, since if they simply repeated the sentences as given by the model, there would be no way of assuring that they actually understood them.

convert a question such as *I don't know if he can come* into *I don't know can he come*, they are frequently unable to repeat otherwise identical sentences containing *whether* instead of *if*. Similarly, most first-graders tested cannot repeat a sentence such as *John and Bill both have their shoes on*, seemingly because of the *both* in the sentence. Apparently if the brain does not possess the necessary information to process a sentence as it is heard, the speaker will be unable to re-encode it or even to simply imitate it as said. Thus, repetition testing can also be a useful means of discovering what grammatical or lexical features *are not* in the receptive repertory of speakers at various age levels.

These observations indicate that a teacher engaged in teaching a standard variety of English as a second dialect should not make the mistake of assuming that because students do not use the standard form they do not know it. Rather, their already existing receptive competence in the second dialect should be recognized, and the task of the teacher should be seen as one of building on this knowledge to enable the students to make use of it in their own production (in the appropriate situations, of course). The speaker who says *It is a book on the table*, but understands and recognizes its equivalence to *There is a book on the table*, clearly does not have to be taught the second structure from scratch, but only needs practice and training in using it in his own production.

However, since not all students are bidialectal to the same degree, it is equally important to assess what grammatical structures are not present in a student's receptive competence. It is patently absurd as well as frustrating to the learner to base reading lessons or classroom questions on structures which are absent from his native dialect and which he does not yet understand in the second dialect. Testing for receptive competence should therefore be an integral part of any second-dialect program (or, for that matter, any language arts program).

It has sometimes been suggested that the first-grade child is too innocent of the social world around him to realize the significance of dialect differences, or to be adequately motivated to acquire command of a second dialect. But five- and six-year-olds are far more socially perceptive than most adults give them credit for, and it is only a cultural myth which prevents the recognition of this fact. Several anecdotes will serve to illustrate the point. As is well known, there are two ways in American English of pronouncing the word *creek*: in northern dialects it is pronounced to rhyme with *pick* (even by educated speakers), while elsewhere it rhymes with *peek*. An acquaintance of the writer happens to be a "crick" speaker, while his wife is a "creek" speaker. Several years ago his son, who was then five, said something to his father about the "creek" behind their home, and was promptly reproved by his four-year-old sister with "Don't you know that you're supposed to say 'crick' to Daddy and 'creek' to Mommy?" In another instance, when a father scolded his five-year-old son for saying *crawdad* instead of *crayfish* when playing with a friend, Jimmy, the boy replied, "All right, I'll say *crayfish* when I'm talking to you, but I'll say *crawdad* when I'm playing with Jimmy, because that's what he calls it."

In still another example, a first-grade girl who was being interviewed was asked to make up a story about a picture in a magazine. The girl drew herself up, began "Once upon a time, . . ." , and launched into a very formal narrative which was notable for containing no contractions. At the end of the story, she visibly relaxed, and from there on freely used contractions for the remainder of the interview. The whole subject of the range of styles and dialects in the productive and receptive repertory of children is only just beginning to receive attention, and a great deal yet remains to be learned. Nevertheless, it is clear that even pre-first-graders are far from linguistically naïve and have already learned a great deal about the adaptive significance of linguistic behavior within their own very real social world.[2]

We do not need to wait until the student is a teenager to begin second-dialect instruction, on the grounds that he is insufficiently aware before then of social significance of a standard dialect. Indeed, this would be a grave mistake, for the optimum age for language learning is before eight, after which it declines, dropping radically after puberty. To be most effective, second-dialect teaching should begin as early as possible. Given sufficient opportunity to practice the patterns of the second dialect, children will readily develop unconscious, automatic control over their use. The longer such instruction is delayed, the less effective it will be, and the lower will be the students' chances of developing complete and unconscious control over the forms of the second dialect.

A satisfactory program should recognize and build upon students' existing linguistic strengths, and where their receptive knowledge already encompasses standard forms, students should be given adequate practice in bringing these to the productive level. Recognizing further that receptive ability always exceeds productive ability, greater efficiency and effectiveness in teaching may be attained by the use of materials and techniques specifically designed to expand receptive competence, which in turn can form the basis for expanding productive ability. There is ample evidence available to show that, given the proper materials and teaching techniques (including the use of tape-recorded materials for repetition practice), even students in the first grade can develop control over the forms of the standard dialect.

All of the discussion to this point has seemed to assume that second-dialect teaching and learning is a one-way process. But it need not be, and indeed probably should not. One of the most common complaints heard

[2] For further evidence on this point, see "Social Influences on the Choice of a Linguistic Variant," by John L. Fischer, elsewhere in this volume.

from teachers working in integrated schools is that they cannot understand the speech of their Negro pupils. From this it is apparent that the teachers simply lack any receptive competence in their students' dialect (though inasmuch as the students can understand their teacher, *their* receptive competence clearly exceeds that of the teacher). Since a teacher can achieve greater rapport (not to speak of communication) with her students if she can understand them, it might well be desirable to devise materials to help teachers acquire an adequate receptive, if not productive, competence in the dialect of their students. Such an experience might, if nothing else, impart a greater respect for the students' achievement, and an appreciation of the difficulties involved in learning to speak a second dialect.

LANGUAGE AND THE DISADVANTAGED

Muriel R. Saville

This excerpt from a longer essay presents some of the differences in phonology, grammar, and semantics between English and Spanish, Louisiana French, and Navajo which are relevant to the work of any teacher dealing with speakers from these language backgrounds. Applying the techniques of contrastive linguistics, Saville indicates some of the problems students from each group will have in learning English, and shows how a knowledge of the system of each language permits one to predict what these problems will be. (The same considerations apply to predicting the problems of English speakers learning other languages.)

Most linguistically different children in the United States come from homes where a nonstandard dialect of English is spoken or where the primary language is Spanish, French, or one of the many American Indian languages. The particular problems that children with these language backgrounds have with English are considered below as are the reasons such problems can be predicted from linguistic analysis.

From *Reading for the Disadvantaged: Problems of Linguistically Different Learners,* Thomas D. Horn, ed. (New York: Harcourt Brace Jovanovich, 1970). Reprinted by permission of Harcourt Brace Jovanovich.

Spanish

Disadvantaged children with Spanish-language backgrounds present a major educational challenge to many schools, particularly in New York and the Southwest. The degree of language handicap exhibited by these children in an English-language classroom setting is sufficiently great to explain much of their academic underachievement and their high dropout rate. Contrasts between English and Spanish have been well described by linguists, and Spanish-speaking children have so far received most of the attention in elementary-school programs for teaching English as a second language. More reading and oral language materials for them will be published soon.

Not all Spanish-speaking children have the same language system any more than all English-speaking children do. Some of their families have come to the United States from Puerto Rico, Cuba, and various parts of Mexico. Others have lived for generations in parts of the United States where various dialects of Spanish have developed. When one considers that there are social dialects within the regional ones, the language problem seems very complex. There has been sufficient research to show that these dialectal differences in Spanish influence the children's use of English, but no comprehensive analysis is yet available.

In general the Spanish sound system does not contrast /š/ and /č/, and substitution or interchange of these English phonemes is the most obvious error Spanish-speaking children make in pronouncing English words. They may often say /čuw/ for *shoe* or /šer/ for *chair*. Spanish has one phoneme that covers the range of both English /b/ and /v/, and it often sounds as if the children say /beriy/ for *very* and /kəvərd/ for *cupboard*. Other common substitutions are /s/, /f/, or /t/ for /θ/; and /z/, /v/, or /d/ for /ð/. Consonant clusters cause many problems, particularly when they contain a sibilant, such as /s/.

Spanish uses only five vowel phonemes; children learning English must distinguish several more. The range of Spanish /i/ includes the vowel sounds of *mit* and *meat*; /e/ those of *met* and *mate*; /u/, those of *pull* and *pool*; /o/, those of *coat* and *caught*; and /a/ covers a range that includes the vowel sounds of *cut* and *cot*.

There are several basic differences in the grammatical structures of Spanish and English that cause interference for a pupil learning English as a second language.[1] The verb-noun pattern of *es un hombre* must be equated with the noun-verb-noun pattern of *this is a man*. Similarly, the interrogative-verb pattern of *¿qué es?* is patterned in English as interrogative-verb-noun, *what is that?* A difference in word order is seen in the

[1] Fred Brengelman, "Contrasted Grammatical Structures in English and Spanish" (Unpublished paper, Fresno State College, 1964).

following examples: *la mano derecha* (D-N-Adj): *the right hand* (D-Adj-N); *le da el sombrero* (IO-V-DO): *he gives him the hat* (S-V-IO-DO); *¿está abierta una ventana?* (V-Adj-N): *is a window open?* (V-N-Adj). A relationship that has been indicated by word order in *la cabeza de un perro* must be indicated by inflection in *a dog's head;* the situation is reversed in the case of *dará,* which is expressed in English as *he will give.* Many Spanish-speaking children transfer the use of double negatives from Spanish to English. It is good Spanish to say *no hay nada en la mesa,* but the sentence literally translated is *there's not nothing on the table.*

The semantic structure of English also presents a number of problems for speakers of Spanish. There are many cognates in the two languages. The most difficult new words to learn are the "false friends," words that sound the same but have different meanings. An example is the Spanish verb *asistir,* which means in English *to attend* and not *to assist.*

Teachers often comment that their Spanish-speaking pupils read without expression. To understand and correct the real problem they should first know that the Spanish intonational system has one less degree of stress than the English system, different rhythm and stress patterns, and different intonational contours. A Spanish-speaker will pronounce every syllable for about the same length of time, shorten English stressed syllables, put the stress on the wrong syllable, and not reduce vowels in unstressed syllables. He will use a rising pitch for a confirmation response and a low-mid-low pitch pattern for statements instead of the mid-high-low contour usual in English.

Improper intonation in reading English questions and exclamations may be partly a problem with symbols. If the pupil has learned to read in Spanish, he is used to the signals ¿ and ¡ at the beginning of questions and exclamations, respectively. Because the initial signals are missing in English he may get close to the end of these constructions before he realizes that they are questions or exclamations.

Most of the problems Spanish-speaking children have in learning to read and spell English words are due to the different correspondences between sounds and symbols. Vowels cause the greatest difficulty; pupils could conceivably write *cat* for *cot, mit* for *meat,* and *met* for *mate.* They might read *fine* as /fine/ instead of /fayn/ and *but* as /buwt/ instead of /bət/. These reading and spelling errors cannot be corrected unless the pupils can first consistently hear and use the vowel phonemes of English. The symbols can then be related to these sounds.

A similar problem may be noted in arithmetic if pupils have learned to write numerals in Mexico or one of several other countries. They will write 1 as *1* and 7 as *7*. Consequently, teachers and pupils may confuse 1's and 7's in problems and answers.

Acadian French

Many families in the United States speak some variety of French as a native language. The largest concentration of French-speakers is found in Louisiana; they are primarily the descendents of Acadians who were forced to leave Nova Scotia in 1755. These groups of Louisiana French, or Cajuns as they are frequently called, have been very persistent in preserving their linguistic identity. Other French-speakers came directly to Louisiana from Europe, and a sizable Black population in the region developed still another variety of French. The complex of French dialects in Louisiana transcends race, social status, and geographical boundaries.

In 1960, according to the United States Bureau of the Census. Louisiana had the highest rate of illiteracy in the United States, and the illiteracy rate within this state was highest in its twenty-six predominantly French-speaking parishes. A variety of factors contributes to this educational problem, and one of the most serious is the inability of pupils to cope with Standard English in the classroom. A correlation between linguistic and economic factors was found by Bertrand and Beale.[2] They report that of the families they interviewed in the region who used predominantly French at home, 69 percent of the whites and 88 percent of the Blacks had annual incomes under $1500, and 19 percent of the whites and 12 percent of the blacks had annual incomes between $1500 and $2999.

Cajuns typically have difficulties with standard English phonology, syntax, and vocabulary.[3] The phoneme /d/ is substituted for /o/, resulting in /diy/ for *the*, /diyz/ for *these*, /doz/ for *those*, and /dæt/ for *that*. English phonemes /š/ and /č/, and /ž/ and /j/ are not contrastive pairs in Cajun speech. The /č/ and /j/ variants may be substituted for /š/ and /ž/ under emphatic stress. Final /-s/ is omitted in some words.

English consonant clusters are often simplified by Cajuns. The phonemes /l/ and /r/ are often dropped before a consonant, and *like to* may be pronounced without the /k/. Final /-nd/ may be reduced to /n/ in *mind*, /-bl/ to /b/ in *noble* or *terrible*, /-br/ to /b/ in *September*, /-kl/ to k in *miracle*, and /-pl/ to /p/ in *simple*.[4] Variant pronunciations are not uncommon; in one interview a single informant pronounced *asks* as

---

[2] Alvin L. Bertrand and Calvin L. Beale, *The French and Non-French in Rural Louisiana: Study of the Relevance of Ethnic Factors to Rural Development* (Baton Rouge: Louisiana Agricultural Experiment Station Bulletin No. 606, 1965).

[3] The description of Acadian French presented here draws on data collected by the author from speakers of the Lafayette region and on data collected by Marilyn Conwell in the same parish.

[4] Marilyn J. Conwell and Alphonse Juilland, *Louisiana French Grammar I* (The Hague: Mouton & Co., 1963).

/æks/, /æst/, and /æs/. Initial clusters may also be simplified: /pl/ to /p/, /pt/ to /t/, and /str/ to /st/. Whenever /r/ or /l/ forms part of a cluster, that phoneme is the first element deleted.

Vowels present additional problems, for variant pronunciation is allowed within Louisiana French phonemes that cross phoneme boundaries in English, making an unwanted difference in meaning in English words. The phoneme /ə/ may alternate with /e/ in emphatic speech or be deleted after a single consonant or at the ends of words. An /o/ may alternate with /u/ in unstressed syllables or with /ɔ/ in some environments. An /e/ may alternate with either /a/ or /æ/ before /r/, /l/, or /m/.

The syntactical errors made by Cajun informants include the plural inflection of mass nouns (*hairs*), the deletion of *to* in infinitive constructions (*I'm going get it*), and the omission of modals and auxiliaries in questions (*What I do?*). Other common expressions are *talking at you, listening at you,* and *I have you an idea.*

Some French words are used by these speakers in otherwise English sentences. The most frequent seem to be the interjection /me/, *well* and /æ/ *what?* In many sentences the words are all English, but the sequence is nonstandard. At mealtime you may hear, *Put me some potatoes, please,* or *Save the sugar,* meaning "store" it. Instead of being "delivered," *the mail passes,* and a Cajun may ask, *is the mail passed?* The same verb is used for *visit: you make a pass on town.*

In some parts of Louisiana a child may go through elementary school without hearing Standard English spoken because his teachers come from the same region and speak the same dialect. The language system of the textbooks is therefore kept separate from the language system he speaks and hears. This barrier to learning is hurdled by some, but it is part of the educational and economic barricade surrounding thousands of French-speaking citizens.

Navajo

A number of unrelated languages are spoken by the more than half a million Indians who live on reservations in the United States. Many groups have adopted some form of English as a primary language, and some continue to use the languages of their ancestors. On the Navajo reservation, forty-thousand pupils are now attending schools and the number increases each year. The teaching of English is recognized there as one of the most serious problems in education and one that must be solved as part of the assault on generally low wages, high unemployment rates, and poor living conditions.

The specific problems Navajo children have with English are considered here because the Navajos are the largest tribe in the United States. Their problems, as well as those of speakers of Spanish and French, depend on the points of contrast between their language and English, and thus cannot be generalized to include all Indian languages. These points should serve to indicate, however, the types of problems that may be encountered by speakers of languages completely unrelated to English.

There are many differences between English and Navajo both in the articulation of sounds that have similar positions in the phonemic systems of the two languages and in the articulation of sounds that occur in one language but have no correspondents in the other.

Navajo-speakers do not distinguish between English /p/ and /b/ and usually substitute their own slightly different /b/ for both. This sound never occurs in syllable final position in Navajo, however, so they often substitute /ʔ/ (a glottal stop) for final /-p/ or /-b/ or reduce all final stops to the Navajo /-d/. This /d/, which sounds like the /t/ in /stap/, is also typically substituted for English /t/ or /d/ in initial position. The /ʔ/ is frequently substituted for stopped consonants and added before initial vowels, making Navajo speech sound choppy to speakers of English. In Navajo there are no correspondents to /f/, /v/, /θ/, /ð/, and /ŋ/.

The primary differences between the vowel systems are the use of vowel length and nasalization to distinguish meaning in Navajo and the greater variety of vowel sounds in English. The vowels /æ/ and /ə/ do not occur in Navajo and are the hardest for pupils to learn. Navajo-speakers must also learn to distinguish among English /o/, /u/, and /uw/.

English consonant clusters present a major problem for Navajo-speakers, who often substitute similar affricates for them. Much of the Navajos' difficulty with noun and verb inflections may be traced to their failure to hear or produce final consonant clusters.[5]

Tonal pitch in Navajo serves as the only distinctive feature to differentiate meaning in such words as /nílí/ *you are,* /nilí/ *he is,* /átʔí/ *he does,* /atʔí/ *he is rich,* /azéé ʔ/ *mouth,* and /azeeʔ/ *medicine.* Whereas Navajo uses fixed tones with relation to vowels and syllabic nasals to distinguish meaning, English uses a variety of sentence pitch patterns, or intonational contours. Navajo-speakers must learn to disregard the pitch of individual phonemes. On the other hand, English makes use of stress to distinguish meaning in some words, whereas stress is never distinctive in Navajo.

The use of a rising sentence inflection to indicate interrogation or the use of other types of pitch to convey, for example, the connotation of surprise is not possible in a tone language, is not used as a mechanism for this purpose, or is used in a different way. Particles in Navajo convey meanings expressed by intonation in English. For instance, /daʔ-iš/ and /-ša/ added to Navajo words signal questions, /-gaʔ/ gives emphasis, and /-ʔas/ in-

[5] Mary Jane Cook and Margaret Sharp, "Problems of Navajo Speakers in Learning English," in *Language Learning,* XVI, Nos. 1 and 2 (1966), 21–30.

dicates disbelief. Navajos may speak and read English without the appropriate modulations and inflections because they are unaccustomed to the use of intonation to express meaning in these situations.[6]

Other very general phonological problems that teachers of Navajo children should concentrate on are the voicing of stops, the production of most consonants in final position, and the production of glides.

Many features of English syntax are difficult for Navajo-speakers. Articles and adjectives are very troublesome because, with a few exceptions, they do not exist in Navajo. The idea of prettiness would be expressed by a verb and conjugated "I am pretty, you are pretty," and so forth. English adjectives present problems in both their word order and comparative patterns. Few Navajo nouns are inflected for plural; thus a common type of error in English is *four dog*. Possessive *-s* is also a problem, since the Navajo pattern for *the boy's book* would be *the boy his book*. English third-person pronouns are commonly confused. Navajo /bí/translates as any of the following: *he, she, it, they, him, her, them, his, her, its, their*. This means that gender, number, and case distinctions must all be learned. Navajo makes other distinctions among third-person pronouns not found in English, however, such as distance from the subject. There are also numerous and complicated differences in the verb structure.

Even if a Navajo child has mastered the phonological and syntactic components of the English language, he is faced with a semantic system that categorizes experience in a very different way. English often uses several unrelated words to describe something that is seen as different aspects of the same action in Navajo; or one word to describe an action seen as unrelated events. For example, if the object of each action is the same, the English verbs *give, take, put,* and several others are translated by one Navajo verb stem that means roughly "to handle." Different Navajo verb stems will be used for *to handle* depending on the shape of the object.

There has been no interference from written Navajo because the language has been recorded only by linguists and missionaries. Programs are now under way to teach reading and writing to Navajos in their native language. A standardized orthography has been developed. Questions concerning its possible interference with learning the English writing system have been raised, but some leading educators agree that basing the orthography on the Navajo language itself is a far more important consideration than any interference with English that may result.[7]

[6] Robert W. Young, "A Sketch of the Navaho Language," in *The Navaho Yearbook* (Window Rock, Ariz.: Navaho Agency, 1961).

[7] Sirarpi Ohannessian, *Conference on Navajo Orthography* (Washington, D.C.: Center for Applied Linguistics, 1969).

QUESTIONS OF METHOD

Linguistic principles may be applied in language teaching to challenge traditional methods as well as to offer alternatives, to note weaknesses in existing instructional materials as well as to develop new ones, and to point out the vast complexities of second-language acquisition as well as to help teachers understand the process. While linguists are generally in agreement on the benefits of initial contrastive language analyses, the presentation of all elements of language in graded sequence, and the importance of drill methods to instill language habits, they voice some differences of opinion on other language-teaching issues that concern teachers and administrators.

First, it has not been decided whether homogeneous groups are preferable to mixed classes, which may present the teacher with a wide variety of instructional problems at one time. Segregation of the disadvantaged pupils from the more "typical" children in a school district is almost completely achieved whenever there is a pre-first or similar "special" class. The children thus set apart may at best have the advantages of a teacher specifically trained to meet their unique learning problems and a curriculum designed to meet their interests and needs. At worst, such administrative divisions continue in effect on the playground and in the community and deprive the children of the motivation to learn and practice English in order to communicate with friends.

Mixing children with different instructional needs in the same classrooms is quite common. It does not mean they will get uniform instruction. Children learning Standard English as a second language certainly do need different lessons in language usage than those learning more about their native language. Even so, they have many learning needs in common. All prereading pupils, for instance, need training in auditory discrimination, and exercises on the contrastive phonology of English would be of value to the whole class. In a heterogeneous class children can be grouped for separate drill on vocabulary and syntax in the same way as for any other type of instruction.

If the classroom teacher cannot teach English effectively for some reason, a special language teacher can take groups from each class for a short time each day. This is unlikely to prove as satisfactory because such language instruction has fewer possibilities for integration into the total curriculum. A special language teacher could better serve as consultant, resource teacher, and assistant in preparing drill material for the classroom teachers to use.

Another controversial question concerns when to begin teaching the second language or dialect. Although linguists agree that oral command of the language, whether native or second, should precede the introduction of reading in it, there is disagreement on which language should be taught first in school. Many believe it is easier to introduce the new language system in kindergarten, or earlier if possible, and use it as a vehicle of reading instruction. Others maintain that reading should be taught in the vernacular of the child and that no attempt should be made to modify the spoken language until basic reading skills have been acquired. There has been some research on the stages of grammatical development during which exposure to instruction is most effective and efficient,[8] but further study on this issue is required before many conclusions are reached.

Finally, there are still some individuals who believe that the purpose of language instruction is to eradicate nonstandard English. This attitude has contributed to the resistance of many children to the speech model prescribed in school. There are those who do not wish to adopt the middle-class pattern as their language system but prefer to retain that of their friends and family. They can communicate more effectively in their neighborhoods if they use their nonstandard dialect or native language. Teachers have the best chance for success in teaching English to these children if they try to *add to* rather than replace the dialect or language of the home.

The children should be made aware of other levels of language and of the difference their use can make in occupational opportunities, but their own patterns of speech should not be rejected as "sloppy" or inferior. The goal of language instruction for disadvantaged children should be to enable them to achieve sufficient flexibility to communicate easily on more than one level and in diverse situations.

[8] William Labov, "Contraction, Deletion, and Inherent Variability of the English Copula" (Paper presented to the Linguistic Society of America, Chicago, December, 1967).

A SECOND DIALECT IS NOT A FOREIGN LANGUAGE

Virginia F. Allen

Because the average person understands so little about the nature of language, there is constant danger that statements about language made by specialists will be misinterpreted, sometimes with damaging consequences. The observation that second-language teaching methods are applicable to second-dialect teaching has unfortunately sometimes been misinterpreted to mean that Standard English is a foreign language to many Negro speakers in the United States. Here Allen points out the similarities between teaching a second language and teaching a second dialect, but warns that the differences are even greater than the similarities, and must be recognized if an effective program is to be developed. In particular it is important to recognize that the learner of English as a second language does not know English, and accepts this fact, while the speaker of a nonstandard dialect does speak English, and realizes this. The psychological difference must be taken into account, and drill activities must be made relevant.

ENGLISH A FOREIGN LANGUAGE TO NEGROES, a recent newspaper headline declares. Below the headline there is a description of a second-dialect program which, according to the report, centers around the use of tape recorders in a laboratory. There the students hear and repeat material originally intended for foreigners because, says the article, English to Negroes is "virtually a foreign language."

News stories like this one are turning up all too frequently in the public press. It is disturbing to wonder how the students involved (and other members of their ethnic group) feel about such articles. Surely few can feel elated over finding themselves treated not even as second-class citizens, but as foreigners in their own native land.

From *Monograph Series on Languages and Linguistics*, Number 22 (1969), James E. Alatis, ed. (Georgetown University School of Languages and Linguistics; Georgetown University Press). Reprinted by permission of Georgetown University School of Languages and Linguistics.

Of course most writers of such reports mean no harm. They simply have done what journalists have done since time immemorial—failed to get all the facts quite right. It is up to us in the language teaching profession to try to set the record straight.

Misinterpretations of present trends in second-dialect teaching are of particular concern to me, because I am partly responsible for setting the trends, having initiated correspondence with the Office of Education which led to the funding, in 1961, of San-su Lin's Claflin Project of South Carolina. It was through working with Claflin students and their teachers that important differences between second-dialect teaching and foreign-language teaching began to be clarified for me. Since then, the distinctions and the parallels have become clearer, thanks to the work of many colleagues, and to my own experience with Harlem teachers, gang leaders in North Philadelphia, and speakers of Pidgin in Hawaii. There is still a great deal more to be learned than any of us will ever learn. But before misunderstandings become compounded, it would be well to review some of the observations we have made so far with regard to second-dialect learning vis-à-vis the learning of a foreign language.

What do people mean when they say that present-day approaches to the teaching of Standard English to speakers of other dialects have much in common with modern approaches to foreign language teaching, especially the teaching of English as a foreign language? Five points of similarity stand out:

(1) Both foreign-language programs and second-dialect programs are based on a contrastive analysis of the target language (or dialect) and the students' home language (or dialect). And the "target" chosen for analysis is not the literary form of the language, nor the idealized language prescribed by the older grammar textbooks, but rather the "language of educated ease."

(2) Both foreign-language programs and second-dialect programs view the target language and the students' home language as equally valid systems of communication in their own respective orbits. The target language is not considered "better"; the students' vernacular is not considered "faulty."

(3) Both programs tend to be structure-centered. That is, major attention is given to the grammatical structure of the target language or dialect, not to the vocabulary.

(4) In both second-dialect classes and foreign-language classes, the linguistic system of the target is presented to the student in a series of small steps, each step rising out of the one before.

(5) Both programs emphasize habit-formation. Success is measured in terms of the students' oral fluency in handling the language patterns that are habitual among native speakers of the target language or dialect.

Achievement is *not* measured by the students' ability to recite rules or definitions, or to diagram sentences, or to label parts of speech.

In these five ways, among others, second-dialect programs have more in common with foreign-language programs than with "English," as that subject is traditionally conceived. There are also similarities apart from general principles and policies—similarities in classroom techniques. In both second-dialect and foreign-language teaching, standard procedures include mimicry, repetition, and substitution. That is, the students first hear, then say, a number of utterances which repeatedly exemplify the linguistic point featured in the day's lesson. The students then construct similar sentences which "fit the pattern," but they replace some or all of the words in the "model" with words of their own choosing.

It can readily be seen, then, that current programs for teaching Standard English to speakers of other dialects do significantly resemble modern programs for teaching foreign languages, or for teaching English to speakers of other languages.

The fact remains, however, that a second dialect is not a foreign language. To the inner city American, to the Hawaiian child who speaks Pidgin English with his playmates, to the boy on a Navajo reservation who uses Boarding School English with his peers, to anyone who uses English of any sort for everyday communication, English is not a foreign language. Teachers in second-dialect programs had better remember that.

Because second-dialect learners are not foreign-language learners, procedures that have proved generally acceptable in teaching English as a foreign language cannot be carried over into a second-dialect situation without modification.

Take for example the mimicry-repetition-substitution sequence previously mentioned. Since English is not a foreign language for second-dialect students, and since most second-dialect students have already achieved passive bidialectalism (they can respond appropriately to grammatical signals employed by standard dialect speakers, even though they do not consistently use those signals themselves), many members of a second-dialect class may need to be convinced of the *need* for mimicry-repetition-substitution exercises on a given grammatical feature. Until the student has recognized that he individually is not yet ready to control a specific linguistic feature on the level of oral production, many teachers find that mimicry, repetition, and substitution accomplish practically nothing. The student has to know that a problem exists, *for him,* before he can give due attention to an exercise designed to solve that problem.

There is value in an old pedagogical precept: never start a drill until the need for that drill has been demonstrated. As far as second-dialect teaching is concerned, it is not enough for the need to be perceived by the teacher: it must be perceived by the individual student himself.

Suppose the teacher has decided that most members of a class need practice on the preterit ending *-ed*, as in *waited, wanted, needed, landed,* etc., because those students seem to be saying things like *We wait a long time yesterday* and *He need a doctor last night*. Before the class is asked to hear and repeat a string of sentences in which the *-ed* inflection occurs, two or three minutes ought to be invested in finding out just which students need that sort of drill, through an exercise that makes each of those students aware of his need. A simple means is the following:

The teacher writes on the chalkboard: *Every day we wait around.* Next the teacher announces: "I'm going to keep changing *Every day* to some other time expression, like *Yesterday,* or *Last week,* or *Every morning,* or *Three days ago.* Depending on which time expression I say, you'll finish the sentence by saying either *wait around* or *waited around.* We're going to work fast. I'll call on you one by one, and I want you to finish the sentence immediately. There won't be time to stop and think. Are you ready? All right, *Every morning we . . . , Last Wednesday we . . . , A week ago we . . . , Every Tuesday we . . . , The summer before last we . . .*" (etc., etc., until each student's control over the *-ed* inflection in such phonetic environments has been gauged).

Quick oral quizzes of this sort, which Robert L. Allen had long used in his own teaching, worked well with the Claflin second-dialect students, who dubbed them "pop tests." The essence of a "pop test" is speed. The teacher must keep one mental foot in the present while the other is in the future; he must be thinking ahead to the next "trigger" while noting the student's response to the preceding one. The students must be required to respond *instantly*: a faltering response should be interpreted as a sign the student needs further practice along mim-mem-substitution lines (known as "fluency drills" in some programs). Naturally the responses should be individual, though half a minute of choral work may come first, to set the pace. And of course the students should be called on in random order, so that no one will know whose turn will come next.

A device like the "pop test" also has its uses in advanced classes in English as a Foreign Language, where an individual student may require proof of the gap between his receptive and productive skills. But it is even more useful in second-dialect teaching. It helps supply the kind of short-range motivation that is essential there. Once a student has been made to notice that he has yet to achieve oral control over a linguistic feature he thought he had mastered, he feels challenged to prove that he *can* produce sentences of that kind after all.

In EFL programs inspired by the Michigan prototype, everything possible has been done to protect the student from the risk of making wrong choices. At the beginning of each lesson, the class is given a model to hear and imitate. The substitutions that are later called for involve relatively "safe" areas of the sentence. "Teaching before testing" is the slogan;

accuracy before fluency is the aim. But a second-dialect student is already fluent in his own brand of English; and sometimes he has to be tested before he can really be taught.

Of course the "pop test" device is only a small piece of a big puzzle, a small answer to this big question: how can we enlist the student's interest in the language-learning enterprise? Here is where one finds the most crucial difference between second-language and second-dialect learning.

Teaching Burmese to a platoon of American paratroopers during World War II was not child's play, but at least it had some advantages: the paratroopers knew their survival might depend on their mastery of Burmese, and the Burmese language had what Jespersen has called "the charm of the unknown." These two advantages have also characterized many classes in English as a Foreign Language, classes for adults in particular. Generally, however, neither of these advantages can be enjoyed by a teacher of Standard English as a Second Dialect. One can expect to find inertia and even hostility when Standard English is being offered to young Americans, each of whom is understandably attached to some other dialect.

Some resourceful teachers have taken this into account, and have done something about it. They have decided that practice materials for the second-dialect student need to do more than merely put him through certain linguistic paces. They have observed that many students get little out of repeating a series of sentences like *Susan lives in Memphis, My aunt gives piano lessons, Our school needs a new gym.* Being human, students expect language to communicate something either edifying or entertaining. When all the words in a sentence sound familiar, yet add up to nothing worth saying, the exercise seems pointless to many in a second-dialect class. Moral: add another dimension to the pattern practice, a dimension calculated to make the exercise seem worthwhile from the students' point of view.

If, for instance, the students need practice on -s endings, some teachers engineer the repetition of third-singular verb forms within the context of a song or a game (for younger students) or (for older students) as a series of answers to vocabulary questions. Sample: "Who can say what each of the following does? An undertaker; a pawn broker; a blood donor; a night watchman." After it has been decided what each of these functionaries does, some of the resulting sentences with -s are repeated aloud. Chances are, they will arouse more interest than the ones about piano lessons and the new school gym.

If no one in the class knows what an undertaker does, the class can learn. However, many second-dialect students know far more words than they are credited with knowing. Hence this sort of exercise is better adapted to second-dialect learning than to foreign-language learning, where one cannot count on nearly the same familiarity with lexical items.

Practice materials that do something more than exemplify a linguistic point are being improvised by teachers in many parts of the country. Several other varieties could be mentioned, but for present purposes the message has already been spelled out: since second-dialect speakers have grown to expect English to *say* something, they lack patience with sentences that merely illustrate a point—especially if nothing has been done to make the student realize he, personally, needs to work on that point.

A second dialect is not a foreign language. We have been reviewing a few of the many implications of that fact. Mainly they have been implications related to classroom techniques. But there is something more important than any instructional device. That is the attitude of the teacher toward the students, toward the total learning situation in which teacher and students interact.

Obviously the teacher of Standard English as a second dialect stands in a very delicate relationship to the students in the class. The students need acceptance and approval; yet there comes a time when the teacher must let them know their English usage is not acceptable under all circumstances, must help them face certain disagreeable facts—the fact that they have yet to master the kind of English required for success in school, the fact that there are new speech habits to be acquired, the fact that important decisions may go against them if they do not learn another way to talk.

The student of English as a Foreign Language has already faced these facts. Though he may not like them, at least they are not in much danger of undermining his self-respect. Somehow the second-dialect student has to be kept secure in his own identity and self-esteem while learning to talk like somebody else. How is this to be done? Evidently it *can* be done; good teachers have always found ways of making changes in students without damaging them. The following trivial anecdote may suggest how.

Not long ago, two young college students were overheard discussing their courses. "How are you doing in Creative Writing?" one of them asked.

"Just great!" was the enthusiastic reply. "Today I got back a paper, and guess what he had written across the top of it. '*This* story is worth revising.'!"

More than the foreign-language student, more than the native speaker of Standard English, the second-dialect student needs to know his teacher considers him truly "worth revising."

REFERENCES

ALLEN, VIRGINIA F. 1967. "Teaching Standard English as a Second Dialect." *Teachers College Record*, vol. 68, no. 5, pp. 355–370.

DACANAY, FE R. 1963. *Techniques and Procedures in Second Language Teaching.* (Dobbs Ferry, New York: Oceana).

FINOCCHIARO, MARY. 1969. *Teaching English as a Second Language* (New York: Harper).

JESPARSEN, OTTO. 1904. *How to Teach a Foreign Language* (London: Allen and Unwin).

LIN, SAN-SU C. 1965. *Pattern Practice in the Teaching of Standard English to Students With a Nonstandard Dialect* (New York: Teachers College Press).

MARCKWARDT, ALBERT H. 1968. "Teaching English as a Foreign Language." *Language Development: Selected Papers from a Ford Foundation Conference on the State of the Art,* pp. 15–31 (New York: Ford Foundation).

DISCUSSION

IRWIN FEIGENBAUM, Center for Applied Linguistics: I agree with you that there are many similarities; however, one point where English as a second language and Standard English as a second dialect would be different is in the use of contrastive analysis. In an EFL program, we don't usually contrast the two language systems in class activities. In teaching Standard English, one of our problems is that the two dialects may appear to be very, very similar. I would suggest many activities in which there is contrasting of standard and nonstandard pronunciation and grammar.

Another point: in discussing mimicry, repetition, and substitution, you said that several or many of the students would have to be convinced of the need for going through these three steps. I, too, must be convinced of the need for mimicry and repetition, since many of the differences—and I would guess the important differences—between the two dialects involved are in grammar. Repetition and mimicry wouldn't serve the purpose as well as some type of grammatical manipulation. There is another problem: my work in the D.C. schools has shown that the students don't like mimicry and repetition. They are hard to do because the students won't put up with them. Substitution, other types of grammatical work, and response activities would be more to the point.

V. F. ALLEN: Thank you. You've raised a very interesting point. First of all, you mentioned the use of contrastive analysis. I work with teachers; I try to make the point that what linguists have for us is a body of knowledge, some of which we apply directly in the classroom and the rest of which is good to know because it guides us in what we do, even though we may not use the data directly. I would say that contrastive analyses are certainly useful to the teacher in showing where the areas of special difficulty will be, and in suggesting reasons why the students have the difficulties that teachers observe. As for the student consciously contrasting the two dialects, it seems to me that the age of the student is rather crucial here. For older students, it may be best simply to come right to the heart of the matter and say: "Here are two dialects we are working with; let us notice when we are using one and when we are using the other, and let's decide which situation requires which dialect." For the younger children, I suppose one can get at it through role-playing and through game-style activities. We can use narrative and dramatic material involving prestige persons in which the children act out the roles of the queen, the princess, the prince, and so on, using the standard dialect.

Now, about the mimicry, repetition, and substitutions. All of those are helpful, and so is code-learning. It seems to me that both are really necessary, especially with older students. They do need "cognitive code-learning." They need to notice the mechanics of the standard dialect. It is helpful for them to discuss it and for the teacher to identify the components of the system. However, I would not discount the need for repetition or mimicry in mastering grammar patterns, because there is so much muscular coordination required here. The youngsters can have an intellectual grasp of the fact that they are supposed to put /-s/ or /-z/ or /-iz/ at the end of a certain word; but unless they have plenty of chances to do it themselves, through repeated oral practice, they are not likely to use it in communication situations. So I'd say that in second-dialect learning there is a need for what could be called "fluency practice," though it needs to be put in the right perspective, and it cannot monopolize the programs.

PROVIDING FOR MOBILE POPULATIONS IN BILINGUAL AND MIGRANT EDUCATIONAL PROGRAMS

Muriel R. Saville

Our final article is concerned with the practical applications of a number of the ideas presented here concerning language and culture, with a special focus on bilingual programs especially for migratory populations. It seems appropriate to end this reader with a series of suggestions for practical steps that can be taken in the classroom and the larger school environment to implement the perspectives arising on the recognition of linguistic and cultural diversity.

One of the major problems in special educational programs for students who learn English as a second language in the United States is the lack of continuity across regional boundaries—or even between schools in the same district, or grade levels within the same school. I consider myself an optimistic person by nature, but I would like to begin by citing a few disheartening personal experiences.

I began teaching in a rural district in California where children of migrant laborers enrolled during the fall grape and cotton harvests and returned in the spring to pick fruit. There was no "special" program for these children, and no teachers or supervisors trained in ESL methodology in my district. My own training in early childhood education was obviously inappropriate for a kindergarten class in which over half the children spoke no English at all. I asked for help from my county school consultant and was given a 700 word vocabulary list and two directives: 1) teach these words and then the children will be ready for first grade, and 2) don't let them speak any Spanish. The teachers and principal were genuinely concerned about the academic retardation of our Spanish-speaking students, but our landowning, taxpaying trustees would not approve a desk or textbooks for each child because "they'll be leaving anyway."

A paper presented to the TESOL Conference, New Orleans, La., March, 1971. Reprinted by permission of the author.

Considering their existing tax burden, the view was partly one of self-preservation.

With state aid, many districts maintained pre-firsts,[1] supposedly a year for concentrated language learning and reading readiness before enrollment in a regular first-grade class. These classes usually had a tape recorder and an overhead projector because of the state funding, but the teachers were generally the least experienced in the school—those who had too little seniority to rate a "better" assignment. Even when there was a good teacher, the children were of course retarded a year in school, did not have English-speaking models in their peer group to learn from, and there was no motivation for the children to learn a new language to communicate with each other. This homogeneous grouping often extended upward through the grades, and observing children in the cafeterias and on the playgrounds convinced me that the social grouping established by classroom assignment was usually maintained. Some states, including Texas, have separate migrant schools so that even the limited playground contact is eliminated.

It is ironic that the same federal government which has taken such strides in integrating Black and white school populations is paying millions to initiate and maintain such segregation of the Mexican-American. Many of the segregated programs continue even if student progress is far below reasonable expectations. But the state of Texas alone is spending 15 million dollars this year on special migrant classes, and that is high motivation to keep any program going.

One of the most theoretically heartening developments in recent years has been the widespread implementation of bilingual education. In practice, however, I have observed even more segregated classes. Even when a few Anglo children are administratively included in such programs, I see them separated for most instructional purposes. And I see children who have mastered basic reading skills in Spanish repeat first grade when they must change schools, because they have not been taught to read in English.

I have promised to make some constructive suggestions for dealing with such problems of articulation, but I must admit my answers are far more tentative than when I first agreed to speak on this topic. When I began to define the problems faced in the programs I contact, I found they are operating without testable hypotheses, and seemingly adhering to a brand of logic that did not make such testing necessary. "It makes sense to do what we have done previously because, in spite of its inadequacy, it works most of the time." And an extension of that, "What we've been doing is better than what we did before."

---

[1] Special classes for students who have reached the normal age for first grade, but are not considered "ready." These students then enter first grade at least a year late. The "beginner class" maintained by Bureau of Indian Affairs schools is a comparable extra year of instruction.

We have more of a choice than that! Not providing needed instruction for migrant children is not the only alternative to segregated schools. Having children of different linguistic and cultural backgrounds together does not imply teaching them all the same thing, or all in the same way. Great strides are being taken in providing for individual differences in the classroom, but we in TESOL are only mincing along in that very promising direction, if not actually dragging our heels.

May I first suggest that we take a more serious look at the potential contribution of educational methods courses to our field. Certainly a knowledge of language learning processes, contrastive structures, and other linguistic content is indispensable to teaching English as a second language. But there have been far-reaching developments in individualized instruction, team-teaching techniques, and other innovative procedures in recent years which may be valuable adjuncts to current language pedagogy. We should invite experts in these areas to participate in our conferences, to consult in our programs, and to offer courses for our teacher candidates. I am not saying that they have pat answers to our problems. I am saying that answers are more likely to come from a broader perspective on teaching and diversified experiences and philosophies in education.

Next, we need financial assistance to meet the special instructional needs of non-English speaking children without the funding priorities and restrictions which make heterogeneous classes more of a burden to local taxpayers than segregated programs. In our part of the country, at least, if projects are funded on the basis of the average socioeconomic status of the students' families, grants go to programs which exclude most Anglos on a *de facto* basis. The state supported kindergartens in Texas are a case in point. Because the initial priority for enrollment is given the Mexican-American or Black child who does not speak Standard English, we are embarking on another level of segregated education. Middle-class Anglo children must go to private kindergartens. The dual system is realized even earlier in Head Start vs. private nursery schools.

Individualized instruction ideally involves accepting each child where he is when he enters a school, providing instructional material and techniques to meet his unique educational needs, and allowing him to progress as fast as he can without pressure or frustration. Such a flexible program would not find the migrant child a problem because he may not arrive at school on time, attend regularly, or fit into one of the three reading groups. The child from a bilingual program who has begun reading in Spanish could continue developing those skills while a flexible reading program in English is added. This ideal is not unapproachable, particularly in the light of monetary resources already available (though in need of some re-channeling).

We need a variety of hardware and software, and teachers trained to use them. We need learning centers with tape recorders, and projectors, and closed-circuit TV. A multi-media project is now field-testing movies, tapes, and film strips for teaching English and Spanish with accompanying programmed work sheets.[2] An individual or small group of children can begin a sequence at any time and continue at different learning rates if such equipment is used properly. The cartridge tape-TV developed for the Gloria and David language materials [3] is designed for individual or small group listening and repetition, and other teaching machinery would prove equally adaptable to meeting individual needs within a group and adjusting to partially migratory attendance patterns. We are talking about a lot of money, of course, and I would like to suggest ways to spend even more.

We need smaller classes if we expect teachers to individualize instruction, and we need adequate consultants or resource teachers available to offer help, guidance and direction for the varied learning problems, needs and interests children have.

Better communication is essential among school districts that share the same migrant students. There is, for instance, a sizeable group that winters in the Rio Grande Valley of Texas, spends the spring in the San Joaquin Valley of California (although often moving within the valley two or three times), travels up the coast to Oregon, Washington, or into Idaho for the summer, back through California in the fall, and "home" to Texas by Thanksgiving or soon after. Cooperative textbook adoptions among these districts would help, particularly in reading, and providing cumulative records that would tell the next teacher what material has been completed is an obvious need. I do not know of any computer which stores profile data on migrant students, but this might be a reasonable way to let teachers know where and what to begin teaching with minimal time loss. On the child's exit from that school, a revised card could be sent back to the centralized location and the current information retrieved by the next teacher. Computerized materials resource centers are already a reality, and we need those, too.

I am still very optimistic about bilingual education. Its primary problem in articulation comes more from an insufficient number of bilingual programs than any other single cause. It is very difficult for any student to transfer between bilingual and monolingual programs, at least until reading is well established in both languages. The only solution I see is to make bilingual education available in *all* school districts where there are students who learn English as a second language.

For both social and academic reasons, these programs should also include native English-speaking students learning a second language, such as Spanish. Since reading should be introduced in the dominant language,

[2] A Title VII project of the Bilingual Development and Demonstration Center, San Antonio, Texas.

[3] Language Arts Associates, Austin, Texas.

grouping for that subject will be necessary (unless we are attaining our ideal of individualized instruction), and also for a brief period a day for direct second-language instruction, including pattern drills, etc.

There is no need in the early grades to separate children according to language dominance for science, social studies, or any other subjects. I would suggest teaching math in English and social studies and science in the other language. The Spanish vocabulary needed for these subjects, for instance, can be presented to English-dominant children in their Spanish-as-a-second-language period. If extensive visual aids and varied examples are used, even I can follow and learn from lessons conducted in Spanish or Navajo. There are at least two reasons for not presenting the same lessons in the native language and in translation—it is a waste of time, and much of the motivation for learning the second language is lost. The availability of instructional material in each language will of course influence the linguistic division.

Computational skills should be developed in English because students continue to perform basic mathematical processes in the language in which they first learned them, and more advanced courses in mathematics will probably require the use of English. For the same reasons, school districts should have math texts available in other languages for students who transfer in with basic skills already established.

Articulation between grade levels in bilingual programs is raising questions as some Title VII projects are now preparing for grade three or beyond. These are largely questions of attitude and philosophy. If the purpose of a bilingual program in a district is to expedite the rapid acculturation of minority groups,[4] then the native language can be dropped as soon as students can be converted from one linguistic medium to another.

If the purpose of a bilingual program is to make children bilingual, then the native language is never replaced, but continues as a viable channel for both learning and self-expression.

I began this paper by citing negative experiences which lend caution to my perception of our special programs for linguistically different learners, and which strongly influence the suggestions I have made for attacking our problems of articulation.

My most positive experience has been the widespread realization among educators that the academic failure of children is not necessarily the failure of children to learn, but may be the failure of the school to teach. We who walk the bridge between linguistics and curriculum development accept this as both a challenge and a mandate to continue our search for answers.

[4] A. Bruce Gaarder, "Organization of the Bilingual School," *The Journal of Social Issues*, vol. 23 (April, 1967), pp. 110–20.

Index

Reed, David, 126
Regional Vocabulary of Texas, The, 133
"Right on, brother," 206
r-lessness, 279–80
road-row, 274, 283
Roberts, Paul, 105–7, 136–40
Robins, Clarence, 236, 241
Rosenthal, Robert, 252
Rote learning, by Navajos, 42
r pronunciation, 133–34
"run it down," 202

Sacks, Harvey, 188
San Antonio, Texas:
  report on educating Mexican-American children, 11
  study of Spanish-speaking homes, 60
Sapir, Edward, 156
Saville, Muriel R., 295, 310–18, 327–31
Scandinavian Minnesota, 214
Schegloff, Emanuel, 188
Schreiber, Daniel, 63
SE (*see* Standard English)
Seale, Bobby, 185
Second-dialect teaching, 319–24
Seeley, John, 54
Shakespeare, 138–39, 140, 146–47
Sharp, John M., 57, 60–61, 63
Sherzer, Joel, 156, 158–59
Shipman, Virginia, 158
"shucking," 203–4
Shuy, Roger, 11, 158, 259
sick to, at, from, with, in, one's stomach, 128, 131
Slang, 146–48
Smith, Donald, 9
Smith, Riley B., 291–94
snap beans, string beans, green beans, 133–134
Social classes:
  behavior of, 47
  differences between, 48
  lower, 2, 49–51, 68–72
  middle, 2–6, 49–51
  movement between, 51
  professional upper-middle, 51
  stereotyping, 20–29
  working, 48–55
Social Order of the Slum, The, 70
Sociolinguistics:
  conflict, 141
    cultural, 142–43
    male/female, 142
  five speaking clocks, 145–49
  "grammer of speaking," 142
"Some Social Differences in Pronunciation," 126
sore-saw, 274–80
Soul Movements, 2
Soulside, 67
"Sounding," 204

South Central Harlem, 228
Southern (U. S.) speech, 122, 133–34, 302
South Midland (U. S.) speech, 130, 132, 302
Southwest, Mexican-Americans in, 56–66
  (*see also* Mexican-Americans)
Southwestern (U. S.) dialect area, 133
Southwestern Journal of Anthropology, 167
"Spanish detention," 141
Spanish-speaking children, and Standard English, 60, 263, 310–12
Spanish-Speaking Children of the Southwest: Their Education and The Public Welfare, 58–60
speaking, 67–68
Speaking:
  cultural differences, 154–63
  ethnographic description, 159
  sociolinguistics, 141–49
Speech habits:
  English, 45
  Navajo, 45
  Spanish, 45
Stability and Change in Human Characteristics, 17
Standard English, 238, 240, 248, 251, 258–59 (*see also* Black English, Language):
  analysis, 122–24
  vs. Black English, 69, 200–207
  five standard styles, 145–49
  flourishing growth, 120
  myth of "correctness," 117–24
  and Negro dialect, 266–74
  rules, 274–91
  as a second dialect, 319–26
  spoken, 122
  as status, 161
  teaching, as second language, 297–331
  as written by Americans, 122–24
Standard school programs, need to reform, 17
Stereotyping:
  in aboriginal tribes, 24–26
  of Blacks by Whites, 26–28
  deep traits, cross-cultural, 24–29
  exaggerated, as prejudice, 22–24
  rationality of, 20
  as social structure, 20–22
  to subordinate stigmatized group, 26
  of Whites by Blacks, 28–29
Stewart, William A., 158, 161, 185, 210, 219–24, 259, 262–274, 291
Street culture (*see* Black culture)
string beans, green beans, snap beans, 133–134
Style, standard varieties, 145–49
Subject relative pronoun, 292–94
Suffixes, in Black English, 288–89
Suttles, Gerald, 71–72

Swedish dialects, and Standard Swedish, 264
Szwed, John F., 157

Taki-Taki, 216–17
Talbert, Carol, 163
talking, 67–68
TAT protocols, 151–53
Teachers:
  as cross-cultural interpreters, 35, 37, 43, 44, 45
    as Anglo-American interpreters, 44
  communicating with the non-English speaking child, summary, 14–15
Texas Education Agency, 1, 297–98, 302
Texas State Board of Education, opposition to Spanish in schools, 155
Texas Western College, 57, 63
Tex-Mex, language mixture, 187
that, which, 118
The Disadvantaged, 16
The Family Instructor, 221
The Five Clocks, 145
"The Night Before Christmas," 264–65
The Tempest, 147
The Urban Villagers, 48
The Way It Spozed To Be, 7
Thirty-Six Children, 7
Thomas, Owen, 108–11, 112
Title VII projects, 330–31
"To Give Up on Words: Silence In Western Apache Culture," 167
to speak, to talk, 67
Troike, Rudolph C., 295, 297–310
Tucson-NEA Survey Committee, 64
  recommended programs for the Spanish-speaking, 66
Turner, Lorenzo D., 209, 217–18

Uncle Remus, His Songs & His Sayings, 273
uninterested, disinterested, 118–19
University of Arizona, 61
University of Chicago, 17
University of New Mexico, 42
University of Texas, 66
Upper-middle-class subculture
  managerial, 50
  professional, 50
Upward Bound, 17
Urban Crisis Program, 195

U. S. Commissioner of Education, 10
U. S. Office of Education, 8, 10, 209, 276, 320:
  bilingual training programs, 13–14
  extensive study of 645,000 pupils, 17
  teacher training programs, 10

Verbal strategies:
  in Black English, 200–207
  in multilingual communication, 184–95
Verb forms, in Navajo, 102–4
Verb Forms of the Eastern United States, 126
Vocabulary:
  in Midland dialect, 133
  in Northern dialect, 131
  in Southern dialect, 134

w, wh pronunciation, 126–27
walk, 101–2
Warm Springs Indian Reservation, 167–168, 172, 176–82
WASPs, 157
Wax, Murray, 168, 183
Wax, Rosalie, 168
Webster's *Third* Dictionary, 129
Weinstein, Gerald, 16
West Enders, 48–53
which, that, 118
Whiteman, Martin, 253, 255
Whites, stereotyping of, by Blacks, 28–29
Whitten, Norman, 157
whom, 118
Williams, Robin M., 27
Wolcott, Harry, 168
Working-class (*see also* West Enders):
  advantages of, 54–55
  educational goals, 48
  fatalism of, 51
  role of family circle, 48
  segregation of the sexes, partial, 49
World Geography of the Eastern United States, 126
Writing, as clever invention, 115–16
Written English, by Americans, 122–24

Yale University, 123
Young, Robert W., 35–47, 101–4
Young, Virginia Heyer, 72–73, 158, 161

Zintz, Dr. Miles V., 42